PRIVATE HIRE
204060
nola

LA MERE ROYAUME
BRASSERIE

Carlson Wagonlit

Images on the previous pages
0.1 Taxingeplan, Tensta, LLP – Front Design, 2006
0.2 Kalvebod Bølge, Copenhagen, JDS Architects – Urban Agency, 2013
0.3 New Road, Brighton, Landscape Projects – Gehl, 2007
0.4 Place Simon-Goulart, Geneva, Atelier Descombes Rampini, 2013
0.5 Theaterplein, Antwerp, Studio Associato Secchi-Viganò, 2008

Public space design of the early 21st century

UNIVERSAL SINGULAR

Sonia Curnier

Birkhäuser
Basel

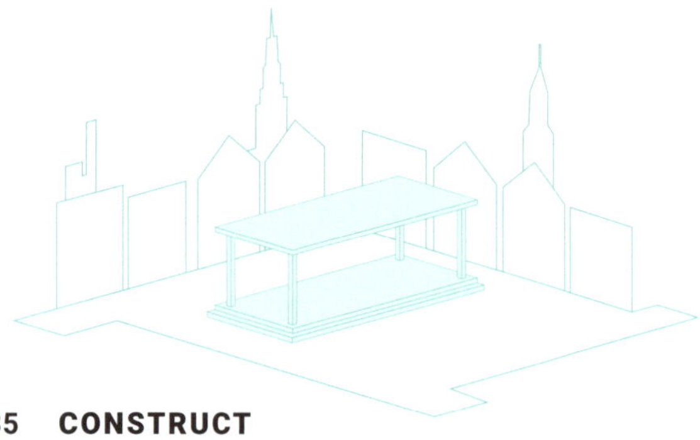

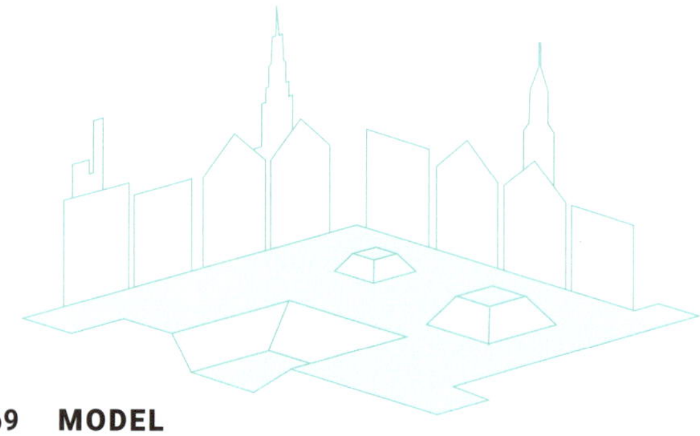

PREFACE

What is public space? Interviewed by a specialized magazine, Sonia Curnier explained: *"There are countless definitions of the term, but in my view, it is an open space, freely accessible to all, and designed to accommodate all activities whether necessary or just for leisure. It is part of the urban fabric with which it can interact. I insist on this precisely because my doctoral thesis reveals a tendency to consider it as autonomous: yet, in principle, urban public space is connected to a network of other spaces and always relates to its built-up environment."*

The scene is set. The term certainly has multiple meanings, with variations in time and according to disciplines. However, in its material sense and in an urban context, it implies a constant relationship between empty and built-up spaces as well as their surroundings. It also implies that public space is part of a network. Nevertheless, at the turn of the 21st century, evolution in the development of public spaces tends rather toward their autonomy. Are we facing a paradigm change, or a conceptual break with canonical practice?

To understand what is emerging, we need a change of focus: while much attention has been paid to the use of public spaces, very little effort has been given to their material reality, and even less to their design. The originality of Sonia Curnier's approach is certainly that she has tackled this question from a new viewpoint, distinguishing her conclusions from those of the past, and which could lead to a renewal in future research on the subject.

Her analysis starts with a critical portrait of the recent evolution of European public spaces. This portrait is founded on a rigorous, well-supported investigation, incorporating research into numerous architectural and landscaping journals, printed as well as online, and books of references. This first step allowed Sonia Curnier to draw up a panorama of the evolution of the practice over the last four decades and to identify a turning point in the history of public-space design, on which she has based her approach. This turning point appeared in the 1980s, when artists and landscape architects got involved, leading to a blurring of the boundaries between disciplines and to multidisciplinary approaches to projects.

The author follows on with an analysis of a limited corpus of ten case studies, which is aimed at explaining this turning point. To acquire in-depth knowledge of these projects, she mobilizes four tools: investigation of the critiques of these public space designs through publications, extended visits of the projects *in situ,* archival study of the genesis of the projects, and finally interviews with the designers. The result is a sharp, novel view of the subject, one likely to inspire other works in the field.

But let us return to the paradigm shift mentioned above. The traditional designs of streets, places, and squares (those "open-air rooms" as Louis I. Kahn called them) are gradually being replaced by new ones. We are far removed from the time when the spatiality and character of public space were defined by the facades of the buildings that bordered it, as in the Middle Ages or the Renaissance, or even more recently in Barcelona or Lyon.

Sonia Curnier demonstrates that public space at the beginning of the 21st century is apprehended as an object *per se*, whose autonomy, obtained through new forms, materialities, and references, is becoming clear. This increase in autonomy – on a theoretical level – will obviously have consequences on their design: it relegates the traditional relationship between architecture and urbanism to the background to create the conditions for an emergence of other design forces, echoing the evolution of society, mores, and lifestyles. The author emphasizes *the aesthetics of experience*, saying: *"The will of designers is clearly to create urban experiences, corresponding to our entry into a* society of experiences, *in which unique and memorable moments must be consumed daily. Designers have found several ways to create such experiences: they focus on sensory and bodily perception, promote the social interactions of living and meeting places, or seek to project users into distant universes."*

"Distant universes": the very notion of context is thus renewed. The context is neither a "pre-existing" one, linked to a vision of *historical continuity*, nor a local *physical entity*, with which the project dialogues: it is now intertwined with new fields of reference and narratives – often stemming from the designer's own imagination, inspired by nature, art, technology, or even games – which invest these places, creating ambiences that are both ambiguous and evocative.

From this perspective, it can be seen that the design of public spaces is the result of a paradoxical movement reflecting the present-day oscillation between the local and the global: the author concludes that it tends to become both singularized and universalized. This paradox results in proposals that are similar even though they are situated in very different places and contexts – it is striking and intriguing to note that a square can take a somewhat similar form in Geneva and in Copenhagen.

Sonia Curnier's work is an original and essential contribution that takes a critical look at a nascent field, reaching out beyond the sole field of architecture. Although her perspective remains that of an architect-urbanist, she has succeeded in addressing design issues that are of course related to the urban sciences, but which are even more relevant to the city and its inhabitants, through the social and public character of our urban spaces.

This last point is fundamental to me: indeed, throughout my career as a teacher and professional, I have seen the importance of the quality of public spaces in the affirmation of a convivial and inclusive urbanity. In this, the adaptation of Sonia Curnier's thesis as a book that is accessible to a wide readership – including practitioners, researchers, public authorities, students – is a valuable contribution to a subject that is certainly topical, but oddly still a very lacunar one.

Bruno Marchand, Professor EPFL
Lausanne, October 5, 2021

FOREWORD

The purpose of this book is to render the fruit of reflections conducted in the context of my doctoral thesis accessible to a wider and international readership. Defended in 2018, the thesis, entitled “Espace public comme objet *per se*? Une analyse critique de la conception contemporaine,” was developed within the Laboratory of Theory and History of Architecture at the Swiss Federal Institute of Technology in Lausanne. The content presented here is both a synthesis and an adaptation of the original doctoral manuscript. It is addressed to practitioners, public authorities, students, researchers, and, more broadly, to those who are curious about the question of public spaces at the turn of the 21st century.

This book aims to provide a critical look at the design of European public spaces during a period of great experimentation that began in the late 1990s. More specifically, the aim is to study the *formal, material,* and *referential* explorations that may have led to the *autonomy* of public spaces in relation to the surrounding built environment and network of public spaces. As a result, there seems to be emerging, simultaneously, a tendency to *singularize* the designs and, in an almost contradictory way, to *universalize* them. The development of this theoretical statement will consist of three stages.

All well-founded critical analysis must be placed in context, be it historical or contemporary. The elaboration of this essential background constitutes the first part of this book, entitled *Genesis*. In concrete terms, it involves explaining the origins of the renewal of public spaces from the 1980s to the present day. This is done by identifying the emblematic projects that have marked these recent decades and by exposing the postulates of the principal actors – practitioners and theorists – who participated in this renaissance.

The central part, *Portraits*, presents critiques of ten European case studies considered representative of the production from the turn of the 21st century. The question of design intentions and choices is explored through an innovative method of critical analysis. This is based on four complementary approaches: literature review, on-site visits, genetic analysis based on archives, and interviews with the designers.

To conclude the book, a *Cross-Examination* of the selected examples invites us to move from the specific to the general, in order to identify a certain number of recurrent and representative practices, and thus reveal trends. The ambition of this third and final part is to draw lessons likely both to encourage designers to question themselves and to allow the decision makers to better orient their future public space projects. More generally, highlighting the most striking project dynamics should serve to fuel professional and scientific debates on the issue of public spaces.

Adaptation of the doctoral manuscript required some necessary cuts to make the text more easily readable and accessible to the largest number of people. The reader who wishes to obtain the more detailed scientific background of the elements presented in this concise version is invited to refer to the thesis, available on request in paper or digital format at the EPFL library. It contains a rich bibliography, and those readers particularly interested in a project presented in the central part will find additional archival documents, a specific bibliography on the project in question, as well as the complete transcript of the interview conducted with its designers. Finally, the reader who would like to learn more about the innovative method developed to analyze the case studies will find a more detailed explanation in the doctoral manuscript.

It should also be noted that the original research was conducted in a Francophone environment. The book's dissemination of theoretical approaches, essentially written in French, represents added value for an international reader. As for the foreign language sources, unless otherwise stated, the translations are by the author.

ACKNOWLEDGEMENTS

This book would not have been possible without the support of a number of people. Their encouragement, advice, and criticism have been essential to its publication. First of all, I would like to sincerely thank Bruno Marchand, my thesis supervisor, for his invaluable contributions and support, from the beginning of this work to its present form. I also warmly thank Lisa Diedrich, Véronique Mauron Layaz, and Marcus Zepf for discussing my work with as much rigor as enthusiasm during my thesis jury, and for their valuable suggestion to adapt the manuscript for publication.

I am particularly indebted to the authors of the ten analyzed projects who have shown their confidence in me, generously donating their time and making their archives available to me: Atelier Descombes Rampini, TVK and JML Water Feature Design, 2b architectes, BIG and Topotek 1, Raderschallpartner, Studio Paola Viganò, OAB, ADEPT, SLA, Valentien + Valentien. Their positive reception testifies to the interest of the designers to expose themselves to critical theoretical reviews in order to evolve practice. I would also like to thank the other design firms and photographers who agreed to have their work published in this book, as well as the archivists who assisted me in my iconographic research.

In many ways, this work owes much to the exciting meetings and discussions with my colleagues at the Institute of Architecture and the Library at the Ecole Polytechnique Fédérale de Lausanne, the Department of Architecture at Kungliga Tekniska Högskolan in Stockholm, and the Department of Landscape at the Swedish University of Agricultural Sciences in Alnarp.

This book was financially supported by the Swiss National Science Foundation, the Office de l'urbanisme – Département du territoire – Canton de Genève and Jean-Claude Girard Architecte. I am extremely grateful for their generous support that made this book possible.

I would like to thank Birkhäuser, in particular Alexander Felix, for believing in this project and encouraging me to see it through, as well as the editorial team carefully coordinated by Nora Kempkens. I am much obliged to Jenna Gesse for the brilliant graphic layout.

Finally, my warmest thanks go to my family and friends, for their unconditional support. A special thought for Thibaud who accompanied me throughout this journey and supported me in the moments when I no longer believed in it. Ella and Tilda, my public space explorers, I wish you a bright urban future!

INTRO DUCTION

1.1 1980–2000. An urban language

PUBLIC SPACE DESIGN, A CRITICALLY UNDEREXAMINED ACTIVITY

Since the reappraisal of functionalism in urban design in the 1960s, public spaces have returned to the center of attention of urban professionals, as fundamental elements of action in the construction of cities. This evolution has created opportunities to rethink the design of public space, as demonstrated by the advent of new designer profiles, the development of unusual types of places, and the consideration of more recreational urban practices over recent decades.

More surprisingly, since the turn of the 21st century, there has been an intriguing diversification of formal and material particularities in the design of public spaces. These particularities depart from a certain tradition of public space design, and are especially surprising because of their original approach and their way of breaking away from the built context and surrounding public spaces, by conferring a particular autonomy to public spaces. Moreover, the designers seem to draw inspiration increasingly from new fields of reference, endowing each design with a singular character conveyed by strong images.

In only 20 years, the field of public space design has literally metamorphosed, without the resulting mutations of the urban landscape being really questioned. Indeed, unlike the Barcelona and Lyon laboratories of the eighties and nineties, which were the subject of considerable theoretical and critical emulation at the time, the profound changes in the design of public spaces that we have recently witnessed remain little debated. More specifically, the significant absence of critical studies of design processes is regrettable. This gap remains despite the fact that in recent years there has been significant interest in the subject, confirmed by the publication of abundant research, books, and specialized journals dealing with public spaces. This book is intended to complement the existing literature and has three main objectives.

RESTORING THE FOCUS ON MATERIALITY

This book is about *public space* in a very precise sense of the term, which should be explained at the outset. This neologism – which appeared in the French language at the end of the seventies and only came into common use in the nineties[1] – was transformed in less than 40 years into a complex notion, which today has a plurality of meanings. In the semantic vagueness that characterizes the concept of public space, the main ambiguity lies in the double understanding of the term *space*, which can be understood as both material, and intangible.[2]

The numerous social, geographical, philosophical, political, and economic studies that have contributed to the recognition of public space as an object of research since the seventies have focused on the uses, functions, and complex development processes of these new levers of urban transformation.[3] In effect, this growing interest has revolved around a critique of the modern movement, which was accused of being too concerned with forms and not enough with people. As a reaction, urban professionals initially focused mainly on the intangible aspects of public space. Consequently, the material component was obscured from critical debate.[4]

While rejection of "formal" concerns still seems firmly anchored in the current mentality, it is necessary to rediscover this tangible dimension of the public space. Neglecting it entails risks, as Jean-Pierre Cohen had affirmed in 1998: "a stated indifference to form is all too often a gesture of renunciation and delegation of decisions to technicians."[5] Practitioners now understand this issue well and fully embrace this field of design that has, in reality, been recognized since the eighties. It is now up to theorists and critics to evaluate these developments in practice, and their repercussions, in order to contribute to an informed debate on public space design.

Bearing these issues in mind, this book aims to reassess the issue of public space in its tangible reality. This does not mean supplanting the theoretical questions of use and function, but rather insisting on a field of investigation that has been neglected until now, that of *materiality*, and understood as follows: *Materiality refers to the tangible dimension of a public space, defined by its composition, shape, and size, but also by the materials and their texture, the equipment, the furniture, the plants that constitute it, the colors, and the light that characterize it.*[6]

In this context, the focus will be on developed public spaces, that is, spaces that have been the subject of design reflection with a view to their future appropriation by users.[7] Hence, in this work, *the term* public space *will be understood as an urban public space, which is an open space, freely accessible to all, designed to accommodate uses of necessity and of relaxation. It is embedded in an urban fabric with which it can interact and is, in principle, connected to a larger network of open spaces.*

This definition is an opportunity to specify that this work focuses on projects designed and delivered by urban professionals – architects, landscape architects, urban designers – and resulting from traditional commissions.[8] The design of public spaces is approached here from a European perspective, occupying as it does an important place in large and medium-sized cities in Western Europe. Indeed, the ideological and project-related innovations of the early 21st century have been principally illustrated in these territories. Finally, it should be noted that the designs concentrate on public spaces in an urban environment, that is, those likely to be more reliant on a relationship with the surrounding built and natural fabric.

BACKTRACKING TO DESIGN

The starting point of this book is that the analysis of the design of a public space can only be complete if it questions the three fundamental phases of the project: *design, materialization,* and *subsequent use*. However, these three stages are usually treated in isolation.

Materialization

The *materialization* phase is the one that has undoubtedly focused the most attention over the past two decades. Leading the way in 2001, Jan Gehl and Lars Gemzøe published *New City Spaces*, presenting a selection of designs produced between 1975 and 2000.[9] A valuable source of documentation of late 20th-century production, this book is distinguished by in-depth project descriptions and a design analysis of each public space that allows for comparison.

Since the mid-2000s, descriptive publications presenting public space projects from around the world have become widespread to meet the expectations of a readership eager for references.[10] However, a lack of critical analysis seems to be the common feature of many of these publications, which all too often present a highly controlled version of the projects, characterized by glowing descriptions, recurring texts presumably provided by the project authors, embellished promotional drawings, or the widespread publication of retouched photographs of newly inaugurated spaces.

Around the same time, public spaces began to appear on the covers of numerous architectural, urban design, and landscape magazines. And similarly, as for the abovementioned publications, both the texts and the iconography seemed to come from the design studios, which disseminated a very stylized image of their production. Thus, similar portraits of projects are repeated indiscriminately from one magazine to another.[11]

From the turn of the century onward, a series of awards also brought public space design to the forefront. The publication of the *European Prize for Urban Public Space*, awarded by the Centre de Cultura Contemporània de Barcelona (CCCB)[12] and the triennial albums[13] produced by the Landscape Architecture Europe (LAE) foundation, are examples of this. Their critical nature, based on selection by jury and an in-depth analysis of each example, makes them real exceptions in the sphere of specialized publications. Nevertheless, the notion of public space is accepted in a broad sense, making it difficult to compare the diversity of projects presented.

It is clear that the theme of public spaces is experiencing a real boom in descriptive publications intended mainly for practitioners. However, in most cases, this type of contribution examines public space designs only in their finished state, that of *materialization*.

Use

The *use* of public spaces is a second strand that has received particular attention during exploration of the subject. One thinks of the research field recently named *Public Life Studies*,[14] which emerged in the sixties. Among the precursors of this movement, Kevin Lynch and Gordon Cullen published, at the beginning of the 1960s, two fundamental texts of urban theory, placing the user at the center of their concerns by focusing their discourse on the visual perception of urban landscapes.[15] In 1961, their contemporary, Jane Jacobs, wrote *The Death and Life of Great American Cities*,[16] a work that marked an essential stage in the recent history of urban planning. In the wake of these three works, a series of researchers and practitioners, mainly based in the United States, explored the issues raised by these authors by examining human behavior in urban space. Among the most significant contributions are the following publications: *The Social Life of Small Urban Spaces*,[17] by William H. Whyte, and *How to Turn a Place Around*,[18] by his successors in the Project for Public Space group (2000), *Life Between Buildings*,[19] and *Cities for People*,[20] by Jan Gehl, and *People Places*, by Clare Cooper Marcus and Carolyn Francis.[21]

Each of these authors approaches the question of public space from a different angle, drawing lessons from their observations of the uses of formal designs and from a measure of public space in its relationship to the body.[22] By encouraging the observation of everyday life, *Public Life Studies* contributes to better identifying our needs and the diversity of human behaviors in the public space. However, having as a starting point that of the user, these studies embrace public spaces in a holistic way, not distinguishing between what is existing and difficult to alter (building, cultural context, activities, designation ...), and what is related to the design. Also, the research mentioned focuses on a finished object, the urban reality, and not on the design choices that led to its realization. These two observations allow us to introduce a crucial distinction between the

1.2 Beginning of the 21st century. New forms, materials, and fields of reference

"analysis of public spaces" that constitutes the subject of *Public Life Studies* and the "analysis of public space design" that we are dealing with here.

Design

Finally, the *design* phase, that is, the project's intellectual development, has clearly received the least attention to date. The challenge of examining this initial stage, a "product of the human mind,"[23] seems fundamental to understanding the foundations that led to the most original achievements in development of public space at the beginning of the 21st century.

A few researchers and critics have begun to open the way to the study of public space design, introducing systematic methods of analysis as well as different keys to reading completed developments. In 2005–2006, for example, the Spanish journal *a+t* devoted four issues to the question of *collective spaces*, which led to the publication of the book *The Public Chance: New Urban Landscapes*[24] in 2008. The systematic analyses of public spaces presented in the book are based on elements of development and organization of uses (*water, vegetation, buildings, roads, rooms, activities*), allowing a form of comparison between projects. In 2011, the same editorial team launched a series of three issues on the theme of "strategy," integrating urban design, landscape, and public space projects.[25] The object of study is broad and not of immediate concern to us. On the other hand, the interest here lies in the way in which the authors seek to distance themselves from the final result in order to focus on the concepts and the project processes, that is, the design phase.

Let us also mention, for its exceptional character, the analysis of more than fifty proposals produced for the competition of the Parc de la Villette in Paris, launched in 1982, that Lodewijk Baljon published in 1992. To our knowledge, this researcher is the first and only one to have systematically and comparatively questioned design intentions for public spaces.[26] While this focus seems interesting, the method used nevertheless has the disadvantage of being based solely on the analysis of competition submissions, and therefore involves an important interpretive dimension. An in-depth study of the design would need to address all phases of the project realization, examining the intentions and decisions that guided each evolution. It would also need to extend beyond the moment of submission of the competition documents.

Therefore, while design does seem to be starting to interest journalists, critics, and researchers, it remains a subject that is still insufficiently considered. In particular, one regrets the absence of all the iconography produced during the design process, the vast majority of projects presenting publication drawings reworked for the occasion. Analyses based on archived design documents remain isolated cases. A look at the intentions, decisions, and operating procedures that guide the project's development processes is imperative to complement the knowledge acquired to date. This is why the second ambition of this book is to place the emphasis firmly on design. In addition to this change of focus, it is necessary to take a critical look at the recent creation of public spaces.

TAKING A CRITICAL LOOK

From the mid-nineties onward, a number of professionals began to state their views of the many innovations in this field that were arousing increasing interest. A number of French voices spoke out against a tendency to consider each public space design as a general solution to urban problems. They questioned the inability to create quality urban environments in the first place, and the overemphasis on public spaces as a way of dealing with this shortcoming.[27] The emphasis given to these public spaces arose in other European level discussions that questioned the proliferation of spectacular developments. The terms "gesturing" or "overkill" were used to denounce public space projects that strove to be yet more unusual and original.[28] In the same vein, others protested against an aestheticization and staging of public spaces that often leads to detachment from their context.[29]

Faced with the question of a decrease in the local anchorage of designs of that time, some researchers and journalists went as far as to denounce a "formal homogenization" of public spaces from the end of the nineties.[30] This concern seems surprising, given the great diversity and innovation in the types of spaces, and the uses, design strategies, and idioms that the last decade seems to have experienced. Nevertheless, French theorist Jacques Lucan formulated an answer to explain this widespread denunciation. He argued that homogenization is more global than local, noting that "public spaces, which tend not to resemble each other in the same city, appear paradoxically to resemble each other from one city to another."[31] However, he did not go into this hypothesis in depth.

Despite the relevance of the questions they raised, these few emerging critical voices cannot be construed as true theories of public space design. Indeed, the arguments put forward by the various researchers, critics, and journalists often remained at the level of summaries and general statements. In the absence of more elaborate demonstrations supported by project analyses, the statements made could not be verified. Conversely, some of the more in-depth critiques focused on examples or contexts so specific that they could not be generalized to the entire production of the turn of the 21st century. Nevertheless, all of these isolated and specific reflections together form the premises of a general critical discourse on the state of public space design over the period. As such, they have largely inspired this work.

These endeavors must be continued and extended, as the appreciation of recent developments in public space design seems essential to the evolution and reform of a rapidly expanding field. Criticism is aimed at two groups in particular: on the one hand, the creators whose work needs to be guided, and on the other, public opinion, which needs to be provided with tools to enable it to make a value judgment on current practice.[32] The former need an external appreciation of their production in order to surpass themselves and respond as closely as possible to the expectations of the greatest number. The latter, on the other hand, expect to be provided with the keys to understanding and the criteria for assessment, which will help to fuel the debate. In this sense, criticism must remain an instructive and operational tool, rather than a mere appreciation.[33]

Criticism also plays a role of interconnection between practice and theory, as the Catalan architect Josep Maria Montaner explained in 1993: "Criticism exists only if theory exists. Any critical activity must be based on a theory from which we can deduce the judgments that support interpretations. In the same way, any theory requires the experience of being tested and exercised on criticism."[34] This has a crucial consequence for the rest of this book; a critique of the production of public space design at the turn of the 21st century cannot be conducted without first formulating a general theory of it. This exploratory theory will then have to be "put to the test" by a series of critical analyses of actual projects, enabling it to be proven.

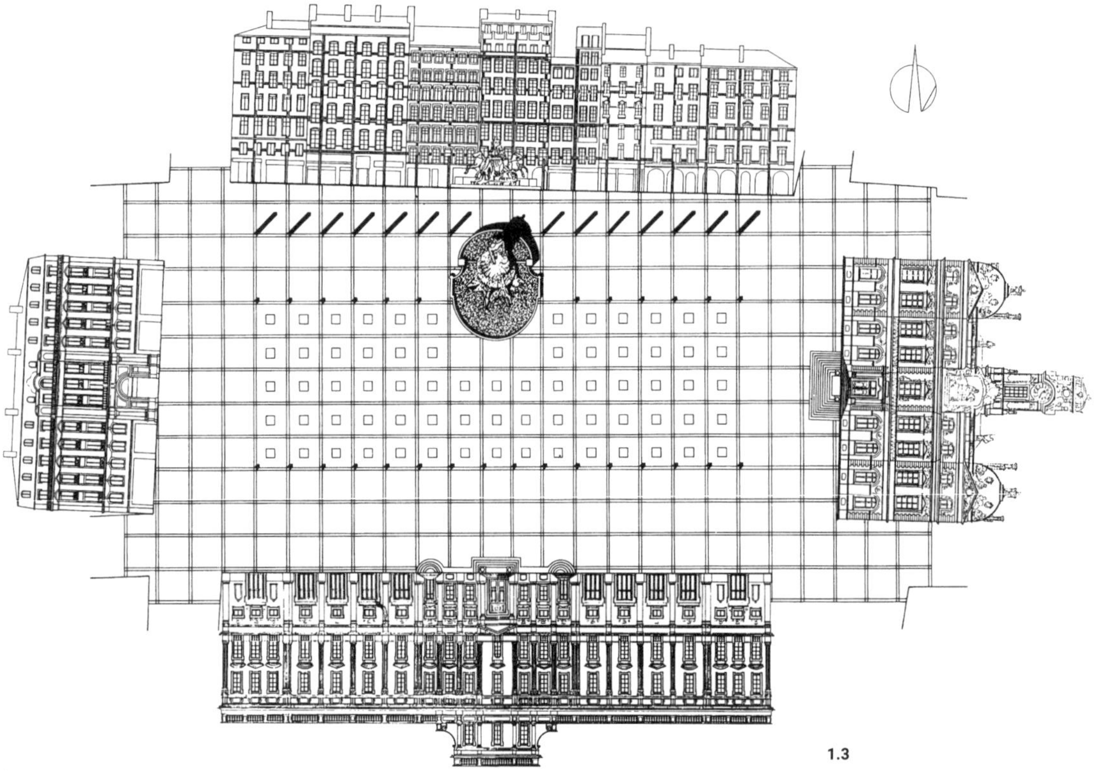

1.3

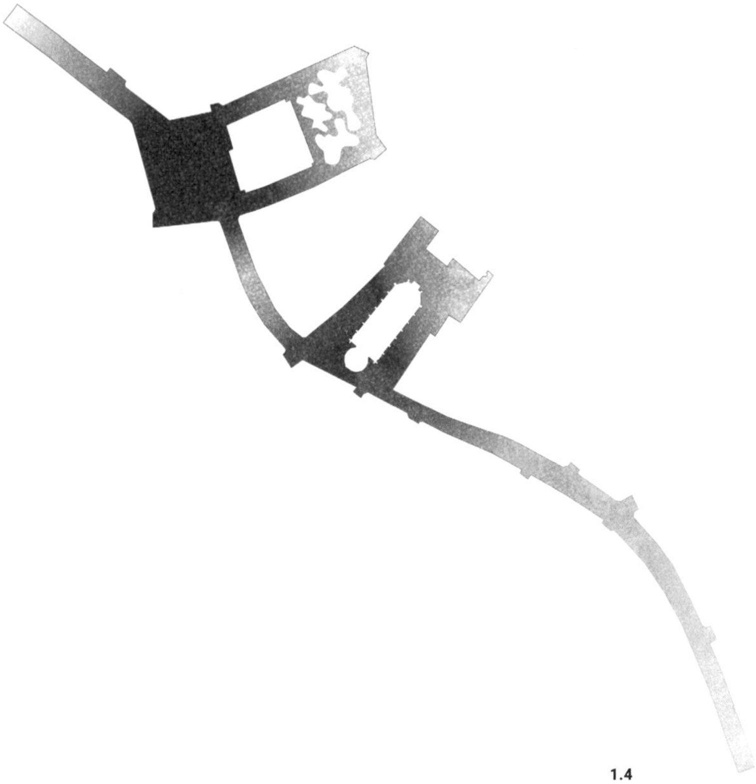

1.4

1.3 Public space composition resulting from the design of the major building fronts. *Place des Terreaux, Lyon, Daniel Buren – Christian Drevet, 1991–1994*
1.4 Representing public space as a figure. *Købmagergade, Copenhagen, KBP. EU (Karres en Brands – Werk Arkitekter – Sangberg Architects), 2008–2013*

THE PUBLIC SPACE, OBJECT PER SE?

This book aims to reach an understanding of what could be described as a profound reform – even a "paradigm" shift – in the design of public spaces, one that has been taking place since the turn of the 21st century. Until then, a typically urban idiom seemed to prevail in their design. This idiom can be defined by the use of mineral surfacing, furniture, and equipment made of wood, stone, or metal, and urban plant species (plane trees, chestnut trees, lime trees, elms, hornbeams, maples, etc.), by a spectrum of colors reduced to mineral tones (gray and beige), and finally, in terms of composition, by a mixture of sobriety and rationality typical of urban fabrics and buildings (simple forms, horizontality, orthogonality, regularity, recurrence, etc.).

Until the end of the 1990s, these design principles, described here in a somewhat caricatural way, dominated the production of public spaces, even the most innovative ones (Fig. 1.1, p. 30). However, the next two decades saw experimentation with new forms of design, exploring all manner of daring avenues: assertive three-dimensionality, sculpted or organic forms, random composition, atypical bright colors, elaborate and figurative ornamental motifs, domestic and collective furniture, wild or artificial landscaping and so on (Fig. 1.2, p. 33). These new expressions tend toward a formal, material, and semantic autonomy, according to the advanced theoretical concept of a public space as an object *per se*.

FORMAL AND MATERIAL AUTONOMY

The first element that leads us to state such a hypothesis lies in the way in which designers tend to singularize each space by conceiving it as a distinct and independent entity. This new value, *per se*, attributed to them, is presented as a rupture, given that urban spaces had traditionally been perceived in connection with the buildings and public areas that surrounded them. Often they were even conceived as backdrops to enhance the surrounding architecture, thereby assimilating as many contextual elements as possible (Fig. 1.3).

However, the role of public spaces as a lever for urban development, from the sixties onward, reversed this established hierarchical relationship. Public spaces were gradually considered as entities in their own right. From the end of the nineties, this reversal was also illustrated in the way in which they were designed: a distinctive ground covering was applied – often including a materialized border, sometimes with a change in ground level – allowing the spaces to be clearly delimited; their composition was no longer necessarily based on elements of the existing urban fabric; the materials used contrasted with the surrounding context; in some cases, the public space even took on a three-dimensional value that competed with the adjacent buildings. All these elements contribute to the questioning of a dichotomous relationship solid/void or built/non-built and lead us to wonder: are public spaces becoming unique figures of our urban landscapes?[35] (Fig. 1.4).

This initial reflection echoes the notions of figure and background borrowed from Gestalt theories by many architects and urban designers and planners from the 1970s onward to illustrate certain changes in urban thinking.[36] One of the current dominant ideas lies in the fact that our perceptive field would be made of solids, "figures," and of voids between these objects, the "background," and that there would be a certain subjective preconception in our perception of the latter.[37] In other words, we perceive or represent as a figure that which we value. Assimilating public spaces to figures would therefore consist in attributing to them a pre-eminent role in relation to the surrounding urban fabric.

However, the notion of figure does not seem sufficient to understand the singularization to which public spaces are subject at the turn of the 21st century. Beyond the intention of formal and material rupture that certain designs unquestionably assume, one observes a quest for contrast that is illustrated on a more symbolic level. This aspect, detailed below, encourages us to prefer the expression "object per se" to that of "figure," nonetheless commonly accepted in urban discourse for several decades.

SEMANTIC AUTONOMY

By their organization and complex forms, their original materials, their atypical plant species, and finally their bright and original colors, the arrangements of public spaces of the turn of the 21st century produce very specific atmospheres contrasting with the urban environment in which they are located. The autonomy they display goes beyond a simple question of Gestalt. These developments reflect a desire to break with the past, in the sense that each space has its own character.[38]

The notion of character used here emerged in the classical age in the field of architecture to describe the adequacy between the form and the function of a building. Little by little, the term integrates the idea of impressions or sensations that a building would be likely to provoke through forms, materials, colors, or textures. "Let's look at an object! The first feeling that we get then comes obviously from the way the object affects us. And I call character the effect which results from this object and causes some impression in us," wrote the architect Etienne-Louis Boullée in his Essai sur l'art, clearly expressing this emotional dimension associated with a built work.[39]

Public spaces that assume a character of their own would therefore seek to evoke emotions other than those usually aroused by urban contexts. A more scenographic dimension of their design seems to be emerging, one that puts the user and their impressions at the heart of the matter.

But in architectural theory, the notion of character also includes a distinctive and significant dimension.[40] Distinctive in the sense that a building – or a public space – is given its own character in order to be noticed, which gives it a certain autonomy, even pre-eminence, in relation to its context. The significant dimension is expressed in the character of the conceived object, which would not only provoke emotions but would also convey a particular symbolism.

Echoing the discourse on urban semiology of the sixties,[41] this interpretation of the notion of character confirms the relevance of considering the design of public spaces from the perspective of their meanings. By resonating with collective mental images, public spaces, which tend to become more and more figurative, are bearers of discourse and testify to the societal concerns of their time. One observes indeed a propensity among the designers to refer to new universes, often leading them to thematize the public spaces that they shape. Fields of reference such as nature, ports, railways, industrial sites, art, domesticity, villages, playful and child universes, affirm themselves as influences of urban fabric at the beginning of the 21st century. By evoking new and sometimes distant references, the designs tend to detach public spaces from their surrounding urban contexts and thus convey meanings of their own.

The expression "object per se," in the sense of a distinct entity that possesses its own integrity and its own references, seems appropriate to describe the double phenomenon of autonomy – formal/material and semantic – to which certain public spaces of the beginning of the 21st century are subject. The rest of the book aims to verify this hypothesis of autonomy of public spaces through the analysis of ten case studies. But before moving on to this theoretical demonstration, let us return to the general context that surrounded the production of these projects.

1 Paquot, Thierry, "Editorial. Espace(s) public(s)," *Urbanisme*, n° 346, January–February 2006, p. 42. The term *public space* in English will experience a similar growing recognition from the 1960s.

2 Lussault, Michel, and Jacques Lévy, "Espace public I," and Michel Lussault, "Espace public II," in Jacques Lévy and Michel Lussault (eds), *Dictionnaire de la géographie et de l'espace des sociétés*, Paris, Belin, 2003, pp. 333–339 and pp. 339–340.

3 For the French-speaking context, one can cite the following examples: Plan Urbain, *Espaces publics*, Paris, Ministère de l'Equipement et du Logement-DAU-DRI, 1988; Michel Bassand et al., *Vivre et créer l'espace public*, Lausanne, Presses polytechniques et universitaires romandes, 2001; Jean-Yves Toussaint and Monique Zimmermann, *User, observer, programmer et fabriquer l'espace public*, Lausanne, Presses polytechniques et universitaires romandes, 2001; "L'espace public," *Géocarrefour*, vol. 76, n° 1, 2001; Thierry Paquot, *L'espace public*, Paris, La Découverte, coll. Repères, 2009.

4 Blanc, Jean-Noël, "Voir l'espace dans l'espace public," *Géocarrefour*, vol. 76, n° 1, 2001, pp. 59–67.

5 Cohen, Jean-Louis, "Learning from Barcelona: Twenty Years of Urban Projects and their Reception," in Pep Subirós (ed.), *Ciutat real, ciutat ideal (Real City, Ideal City)*, Barcelona, Centre de Cultura Contemporània, 1998. Available online: https://www.publicspace.org/multimedia/-/post/learning-from-barcelona-twenty-years-of-urban-projects-and-their-reception [accessed February 23, 2022].

6 The definitions of the basic terms used in this book are listed in a glossary, ref. p. 268.

7 Whether for necessary functional uses (moving, waiting, etc.) or for optional recreational uses (walking, playing, socializing, etc.) as defined by Jan Gehl. This fundamental distinction lies above all in the fact that the second category of uses requires the addition of good quality facilities. Jan Gehl, *Life Between Buildings: Using Public Space*, New York, Van Nostrand Reinhold, 1987, reprinted by Island Press, 2011, pp. 9–14. [Orig. ed. *Livet mellem husene – udeaktiviteter og udemiljøer*, Arkitektens Forlag, 1971]. Jan Gehl and Birgitte Svarre, *How To Study Public Life*, Washington D.C., Island Press, 2013, p. 16.

8 Spontaneous appropriation by citizens, subversive urban artistic actions, and institutionalized ephemeral operations are very current topics in the development of public spaces, in which we recognize the interest and relevance. However, to ensure clarity of the field of investigation, this type of approach has been deliberately left out of this book.

9 Gehl, Jan, and Lars Gemzøe, *New City Spaces, Strategies and Projects*, Copenhagen, The Danish Architectural Press, 2001.

10 To name but a few: Sarah Gaventa, *New Public Spaces*, London, Mitchell Beazley, 2006; Aldo Aymonino, Valerio Paolo Mosco, *Contemporary Public Space – Un-volumetric Architecture*, Milan, Skira, 2006; Jacobo Krauel, *New Urban Spaces*, Barcelona, Links International, 2006; Dimitris Kottas, *Urban Spaces: Squares and Plazas*, Barcelona, Links International, 2007; Arthur Gao, *Public Square Landscapes*, Hong Kong, Design Media Publishing Ltd, 2011; Robert Klanten et al. (eds), *Going Public: Public Architecture, Urbanism and Interventions. The Creative Revival of Public Space*, Berlin, Gestalten Verlag, 2012; Chris van Uffelen, *Urban Spaces: Plazas, Squares & Streetscapes*, Salenstein, Braun, 2012; Jacobo Krauel, *Urban Spaces. Design and Innovation*, Barcelona, Links International, 2013.

11 By way of exception, German and French journals such as *Deutsche Bauzeitung, Topos, Archithese (CH), Criticat*, and *D'architectures*, periodically publish critical analyses personally documented by the journalists.

12 Anglès, Magda (ed.), *In Favour of Public Space. Ten Years of the European Prize for Urban Public Space*, Barcelona, Centre de Cultura Contemporània de Barcelona, Actar, 2010.

13 Diedrich, Lisa, et al. (eds), *Fieldwork*, Basel/Boston/Berlin, Birkhäuser Verlag, Series, Landscape Architecture Europe, 2006; Lisa Diedrich et al. (eds), *On Site*, Basel/Boston/Berlin, Birkhäuser Verlag, Series, Landscape Architecture Europe, 2009; Lisa Diedrich et al. (eds), *In Touch*, Basel/Boston/Berlin, Birkhäuser Verlag, Series, Landscape Architecture Europe, 2012; Lisa Diedrich et al. (eds), *On the Move*, Wageningen, Blauwdruk, Series, Landscape Architecture Europe, 2015.

14 Gehl and Svarre, *op. cit.*, 2013, p. 41

15 Lynch, Kevin, *L'image de la cité*, Paris, Dunod, 1971. [Orig. ed. *The Image of the City*, Cambridge, MIT Press, 1960]; Gordon Cullen, *Townscape*, London, The Architectural Press, 1961.

16 Jacobs, Jane, *Déclin et survie des grandes villes américaines*, Marseille, Parenthèses, 2012. [Orig. ed. *The Death and Life of Great American Cities*, New York, Random House, 1961].

17 Whyte, William H., *The Social Life of Small Urban Spaces*, Washington D.C., The Conservation Foundation, 1980.

18 Madden, Kathy, and Andy Wiley-Schwartz, *How to Turn a Place Around: A Handbook for Creating Successful Public Spaces*, New York, Project for Public Spaces Inc., 2000.

19 Gehl, *op. cit.*, 2011 [1971].

20 Gehl, Jan, *Cities for People*, Washington D.C., Island Press, 2010.

21 Marcus, Clare Cooper, and Carolyn Francis (eds), *People Places*, New York, Van Nostrand Reinhold, 1990.

22 Some venture to propose spatial recommendations for design, observation tools, and evaluation criteria for public spaces. Gehl Institute, "Twelve Quality Criteria," n.d., available at https://gehlinstitute.org/tool/quality-criteria/ [accessed January 11, 2017]. Projects for Public Spaces Inc., *How to Turn a Place Around: A Handbook for Creating Successful Public Spaces*, New York, Project for Public Spaces Inc., 2000, p. 17.

23 Etienne-Louis Boullée clearly distinguishes between design and execution: "You have to design to build. Our forefathers did not build their huts until they had conceived the image of them. It is this thought process, this creation that constitutes architecture, which we can, consequently, define as the art of producing and bringing to perfection any building. The art of building is therefore only a secondary art, which we think it appropriate to call the scientific part of architecture." Etienne-Louis Boullée, *Architecture. Essai sur l'art*, 1799, Jean-Marie Pérouse de Montclos (ed.), Paris, Hermann, 1968, f. 70, p. 49.

24 "In Common, Collective Spaces," *a+t*, n° 25–27, 2005–2006; Aurora Fernández Per, Javier Arpa, *The Public Chance: New Urban Landscapes*, Vitoria-Gasteiz, *a+t* architecture publishers, In Common Series, 2008.

25 "Strategy Public, Landscape Urbanism Strategies," *a+t*, n° 35–36, 2011; "Strategy Space, Landscape Urbanism Strategies," *a+t*, n° 37, 2011; "Strategy and Tactics in Public Space," *a+t*, n° 30, 2011.

26 Baljon, Lodewijk, *Designing Parks*, Amsterdam, Architectura & Natura Press, 1992.

27 During a colloquium on public spaces, organized jointly by the Pavillon de l'Arsenal and the Ecole de Paris Tolbiac in December 1994, Bernard Huet asked the following rhetorical question: "I find it rather suspect that we will turn to public spaces as a panacea, as a means of solving a certain number of problems that cannot be solved where they arise. Intervening in public spaces thus becomes a reflection of our inability to produce public space?" His colleague Bruno Fortier supported his words: "Not knowing how to create urban space, we overvalue public spaces while waiting for the magic and wonders of their workings." Remarks reported in Martine Allaman, "Espaces publics: liberté, identité, continuité," *Diagonal*, n° 112, April 1995, p. 12.

28 *Ibid*, p. 13; Plan Urbain, *Espaces publics*, *op. cit.*, 1988, p. 80; Manuel de Solà-Morales, "The Impossible Project of Public Space," in Magda Anglès (ed.), *In Favour of Public Space. Ten Years of the European Prize for Urban Public Space*, Barcelona, Centre de Cultura Contemporània de Barcelona, Actar, 2010, p. 27.

29 Hajer, Maarten, and Arnold Reijndorp, *In Search of New Public Domain*, Rotterdam, NAi Publishers, 2002, in particular pp. 100–101; Steen Høyer, "Scenografisk landskab/Scenographic Landscape," *Architektur DK*, n° 1, 2002, pp. 4–11.

30 Genestier, Philippe, "Ville culturelle et espace touristique: sur quelques logiques et réification à l'œuvre dans l'économie post-industrielle," in Luc Doumenc et al., *L'espace public dans la ville méditerranéenne. Actes du colloque de Montpellier, 14–15–16 mars 1996*, Montpellier, Editions de l'Esperou, 1997, p. 43; Sven-Ingvar Andersson, "Globale oder regionale Landschaftsarchitektur/Global or Regional Landscape Architecture," *Topos*, n° 50, March 2005, p. 28; Sarah Gaventa, *New Public Spaces*, London, Mitchell Beazley, 2006, pp. 14–15.

31 Lucan, Jacques, *Où va la ville aujourd'hui? Formes urbaines et mixités*, Paris, Editions de la Villette, 2012, p. 182.

32 These two groups of recipients are notably evoked by Pierre Vago, "La critique architecturale – entre carcan et utilité," in Agnès Deboulet, Rainer Hoddé, André Sauvage, *La critique architecturale. Questions-frontières-desseins*, Paris, Editions de la Villette, 2008, p. 30. [Orig. ed. *L'Architecture d'aujourd'hui*, n° 117, 1964–1965].

33 On this subject, see the words of Rem Koolhaas reported in "Rem, Do You Know What This Is?," *Hunch, the Berlage Institute Report*, n° 3, 2001, p. 33, or again Bernard Huet, "Les enjeux de la critique," in Deboulet et al., *op. cit.*, 2008, p. 78. [Orig. ed., *Le visiteur*, n° 1, fall 1995].

34 Montaner, Josep Maria, "Matière et technique de la critique," in Deboulet et al., *op. cit.*, 2008, pp. 123–124. [Orig. ed. *Arquitectura y crítica*, Barcelona, Editorial Gustavo Gili, 1999].

35 As far as we know, Stephanie Bender is the first to raise the question of public space as a figure, in relation to the Schouwburgplein on West 8 in Rotterdam (1990–1997). Stephanie Bender, *Le vide: nouvelles stratégies urbaines*, doctoral thesis n° 4841, Lausanne, Ecole Polytechnique Fédérale de Lausanne, 2011, p. 216.

36 This borrowing was probably initiated by Colin Rowe and Fred Koetter, who appeal to antinomic notions in 1978, in their book *Collage City*, making, according to the passages of the text, mention of the terms *solid* and *void*, or of *object* and *texture*. Colin Rowe, Fred Koetter, *Collage City*, Gollion, InFolio, 2002. [Orig. ed. *Collage City*, Cambridge, MIT Press, 1978].

37 Guillaume, Paul, *La psychologie de la forme*, Paris, Flammarion, 1937, p. 59; Maurice Merleau-Ponty, *Phénoménologie de la perception*, Paris, Gallimard, 1945, p. 39.

38 The terms atmosphere and character are often used interchangeably. Here we prefer to use the term character, which is based on conscious and intentional principles, whereas the creation of an atmosphere is more intuitive. Character also has a symbolic value, and in fact is significant. This distinction is notably based on the reflections of Gernot Böhme and Jean-Paul Thibaud, *The Aesthetics of Atmospheres*, London/New York, Routledge, 2017, pp. 1, 144–145. See also the glossary, p. 268.

39 Boullée, Etienne-Louis, *Architecture. Essai sur l'art*, 1799, Jean-Marie Pérouse de Montclos (ed.), Paris, Hermann, 1968, f. 84, p. 73.

40 On the subject of character, "The use of ordinary language, and particularly that of all theories, teaches us that the word and the idea of character are only applied to a certain type or to a certain number of distinctive signs, that is to say, to those which have the eminent property of designating and making an object stand out among many of its counterparts. [...] Having to limit ourselves here to these arts, and even more particularly to one of them (architecture), we will say that the use of the word character, such as the use of the theory authorizes it, indicates the work of art, not, in a vague and general sense, any distinction whatever the measure or the quality, but rather a predominant distinction that makes it stand out in the first place." Antoine Chrysostome Quatremère de Quincy, "Caractère," in *Dictionnaire historique d'architecture: comprenant dans son plan les notions historiques, descriptives, archéologiques ... de cet art*, Paris, A. Le Clère et Cie, 1832, vol. 1, pp. 302–308. Available online: http://gallica.bnf.fr/ark:/12148/bpt6k1045594m/f316.item.zoom [accessed October 18, 2017].

41 Lynch, *op. cit.*, 1971 [1960], having inspired Roland Barthes, "Sémiologie et urbanisme," *L'Architecture d'aujourd'hui*, n° 153, 1970–71, pp. 11–13; Françoise Choay, "Sémiologie et urbanisme," in Françoise Choay et al., *Le sens de la ville*, Paris, Editions du Seuil, 1972, pp. 8–10. [Text developed from an article published in *L'Architecture d'aujourd'hui*, n° 132, 1967].

GENESIS

PRELUDE (1980–1990): THE LABORATORIES

From the sixties onward, public spaces were restored to the center of urban attention as fundamental elements in the development of cities, breaking with modernist ideologies. This "conceptual turnaround"[1] elevated them to the status of agents of economic and social transformation, as well as symbols of urban culture and identity.[2] Initially revealed in urban debates, this revival took on a much more tangible dimension in the eighties, when the first emblematic projects began to appear. This became a reality in a few large European cities, which were transformed into real urban laboratories, the best known being Barcelona and Lyon. These two models marked a renewal in the design of public spaces that would spread across the European continent over the following decades.

THE BARCELONA MODEL

Spain emerged from nearly forty years of Franco's regime to experience its first free elections in 1977. The newly elected (1979) municipality of the Catalan capital wished to mark this return to democracy with immediate and tangible changes. In December 1980, the architect Oriol Bohigas was appointed deputy city councilor to the Barcelona Urban Planning Commission. He quickly put in place an ambitious urban renewal policy that included the redevelopment of several hundred public spaces.[3] Obviously, squares, streets, parks, boulevards, and promenades were seen as powerful symbols of the reborn democracy. It was hoped that the citizens would regain possession of these places, perceived as real instruments of urban and social reconstruction.

Immediate and specific actions

Initially, public space redesign was undertaken within the existing fabric of the center and of the suburbs, according to the principle of "building the city on the city,"[4] which was starting to assert itself at the time in reaction to the *tabula rasa* attitudes characteristic of the modern movement. The aim was to clean up these historic districts (Fig. 2.1–2.4). To this end, public spaces were used as vectors of urban revitalization, capable of driving the renovation and reconstruction of the surrounding buildings. But attention was also paid to the peripheral sectors where neighborhood squares were to be developed (Fig. 2.5–2.7). Finally, reclamation of the waterfront and the development of parks – exhibiting a strong architectural dimension – for the Barcelona residents were going to be addressed.

Bohigas and his team responded via a multitude of immediate initiatives, breaking with a logic of global urban planning visions that would take years to materialize.[5] This expeditious strategy led some observers to speak of a city perceived more as a system, a puzzle, rather than a unitary and theoretical entity.[6] But for the critic Peter Buchanan, who observed this metamorphosis in 1984, urban design – as opposed to planning – was the tool needed to define an identity for the Catalan capital:

"The most effective way of saving cities is by reinterpreting and reinforcing the identities of them and their parts. This can only be achieved through form and image, by coherent design endowing meaning and symbolism – that is by urban design projects of high quality and never by planning."[7]

The question of identity, which Buchanan raises here, was also advocated as one of the objectives for future development projects. Each designer of public space would be responsible for contributing to urban legibility by taking up existing elements of language, and for redefining a local and social identity specific to each neighborhood.[8] This ambition found its answer in the principle of monumentalizing the city and its public spaces,[9] in particular for sites located outside the historic center that lacked character. In this respect, architecture and sculpture were to play a dominant role in the design of public spaces in the eighties.

The reign of the architects

Barcelona's policy was characterized by the decision to delegate the design of projects to external agents, most of whom were architects recently graduated from the Escuela Técnica Superior de Arquitectura de Barcelona (ETSAB).[10] Among the designers commissioned were Roser Amadó, Andreu Arriola, Jaume Bach, Joan Busquets, Manuel de Solà-Morales, Lluís Domènech, Beth Galí, Jordi Garcés, Enric Sòria, Oscar Tusquets, and the duo Albert Viaplana, and Helio Piñón. According to Buchanan, the advent of these Catalan architects in the creation of public spaces is attributable to the fact that Bohigas was the director of the aforementioned institution at the time (1977–80) and had "access to a group of talented young architects" to whom he awarded many direct contracts.[11]

In the search for form and identity that characterized Barcelona's public space policy, several projects also involved collaborations between artists and architects.[12] Thus we see a proliferation of creations by local and international artists such as Richard Serra (Plaça de la Palmera de Sant Martí, 1985), Eduardo Chillida (Parc de la Creueta del Coll, 1986), Roy Lichtenstein

2.1–2.4 In the historical center of Barcelona. *(1) Plaça de la Mercè, Municipality of Barcelona – Lluís Mestras – Ramon Sanabria – Pere Casajoana –Rosa Maria Clotet; (2) Plaça Reial, Federico Correa – Alfonso Milá; (3) Plaça Trilla, Jaume Bach, Gabriel Mora; (4) Plaça de la Concòrdia, Municipality of Barcelona – Lluís Mestras – Ramon Sanabria – Carmen Fiol*

2.5

2.6

2.7

2.5–2.7 Neighborhood and infrastructural squares. (5) *Plaça de Mossèn Clapés, Miquel Vidal;* (6) *Plaça Sóller, Municipality of Barcelona – Lluís Mestras – Ramon Sanabria – Josep Julià –Josep Lluís Delgado – Carme Ribas – Andreu Arriola;* (7) *Plaça dels Països Catalans, Viaplana – Piñón – Miralles, 1983* **2.8–2.9** Artists' interventions. *(8) Parc de l'Estació del Nord, Andreu Arriola – Carmen Fiol – Beverly Pepper, 1992;* (9) *Plaça de la Palmera de Sant Martí, Pedro Barragán – Bernardo de Sola – Richard Serra, 1985*

2.8

2.9

(Moll de Bosch i Alsina, 1987), Beverly Pepper (Parc de l'Estació del Nord, 1992), and Claes Oldenburg and Coosje van Bruggen (Parc de la Vall d'Hebron, 1992)[13] (Fig. 2.8–2.9).

Bohigas and his team thus forged a real climate of experimentation throughout the 1980s, encouraging innovative and singular proposals from the various commissioned designers. This climate produced very heterogeneous creations, while at the same time revealing "in the multiplicity of approaches and personal positions of the architects put to work by the municipality, a sensitivity to materials and mineral or vegetable textures, an attention to the built form and to physical requirements – to channel water, to host signs and lighting," observed the theorist Jean-Louis Cohen.[14] Several critics have pointed out another common trend despite this diversity of production: a minimalist attitude, attributed to a typically Catalan architectural posture.[15]

With nearly two decades of hindsight, Cohen recalls another aspect of the Barcelona experience: "the renunciation by many architects, not of forms, but of narcissism and their awareness of specific urban conditions."[16] He thus demonstrates that formal experimentation is not necessarily opposed to the integration of the project into its local and material context, provided that it does not cater to a baseless gesture of design. This point seems essential to bear in mind for analysis of the more recent production of public spaces that follows.

THE LYON MODEL

Because of its novel and convincing character, the pioneering experience of Barcelona rapidly became a reference whose success transcended national borders. Elected officials, urban planners, and public space designers from all over Europe flocked to the site to see the many emblematic achievements. Among the curious were Michel Noir, Mayor of Lyon, as well as Henry Chabert, Vice President of Greater Lyon, and Deputy Urban Planner in charge of urban planning for the City of Lyon.[17] These two figures were behind the implementation of another operation that would also become an internationally renowned reference: Lyon's policy for the development of public spaces.

The first change undertaken was institutional: in order to get away from the segmentation by fields of competence that so often characterizes municipal technical services, a multidisciplinary body within the Urban Community was created in 1990 to coordinate future developments. Called the Public Space Department, it was directed by Jean-Louis Azéma.[18] This upheaval of the established municipal bureaucracy contributed to the constitution of a real "urban culture" within Lyon's urban services.

Three basic principles then guided the implementation of the policy undertaken by this new department.[19] The first was to treat all public spaces in the city with the same attention according to a "principle of solidarity." The second was to consider "creation" – entrusted to external agents – as the only contemporary way to address sometimes contradictory issues. Finally, the third approach advocated a unity of treatment of Lyon's public spaces, with the ambition of revealing the identity of the agglomeration.

Agglomeration solidarity

The Lyon public space policy led by Chabert and his team emerged during a period of urban crisis marked by the suburban riots of the early 1980s. This operation thus established itself as "one of the important levers of a policy of recomposition and urban solidarity," which consisted in particular in affirming "an equity of urbanistic treatment between the central, and the peripheral spaces."[20] The principle of planning unity by means of a common vocabulary, which will be discussed later, contributed to this ambition. In order to coordinate the multiple interventions planned throughout the city, a series of thematic plans were also developed at the scale of the agglomeration: a *Color Plan* identifying the characteristics of each place, a *Green Plan* for landscaped areas, a *Blue Plan* for river areas, and finally a *Lighting Plan* relating to night-time lighting.[21]

In accordance with this principle of urban solidarity, equal attention was paid to the development of the city center and the suburbs, whether they were large housing estates or peripheral localities (Fig. 2.10–2.11). In spite of this effort made by Lyon's services, the critics of the specialized magazines would focus particularly on the developments of the Presqu'île, "placed under the sign of the embellishment of the urban heritage."[22] The major challenge for the historic center was therefore to reclaim traffic and parking spaces in favor of pedestrians. Thus, several developments were to be preceded by the creation of underground parking lots, to which particular care was given[23] (Fig. 2.12–2.14).

The era of the landscape architects

The second notable element of Lyon's approach was to entrust the creation of public spaces to external agents, as in Barcelona. One of the objectives of Henry Chabert's policy was in effect to distance itself from the technocratic vision that dominated the urban planning department's services. That is without doubt the reason why in 1989 he called upon Jean-Pierre Charbonneau, a multidisciplinary engineer and urban planner, to become technical advisor on public spaces.[24] In 1993, Charbonneau

2.10

2.11

2.12

2.13

2.14

2.15

2.16

2.10–2.11 Public spaces in the suburbs. *(10) Place des Bleuets, In Situ, 1992. (11) Place de la Mairie Solaize, Ilex – Roland Jéol, 1992* **2.12–2.14** The public spaces of the Presqu'île. *(12) Place des Célestins, Michel Desvigne – Christine Dalnoky – Michel Targe – Jean-Michel Wilmotte – Daniel Buren; (13) Place de la République, Alain Sarfati – Pierre Vurpas – François Morellet; (14) Place des Terreaux, Daniel Buren – Christian Drevet, 1994* **2.15–2.16** The era of landscape architects. *(15) Place de la Bourse, Alexandre Chemetoff, 1993; (16) Place Antonin-Poncet, Michel Bourne, Didier Repellin, Jean-François Grange-Chavanis, 1990*

published a text entitled *Plaidoyer pour l'art urbain* (Plea for Urban Art), which restored the theme of "creativity" as a way of responding to the many issues crystallized by public spaces.

From this perspective, the design of such installations was entrusted to external practitioners "capable of bringing a capacity for creation and innovation while respecting the past."[25] In deciding to relieve the municipal service technicians of this task, the architects and urban designers, whose responses were considered "often too formal,"[26] would also be somewhat sidelined in this vast operation, to the benefit of landscape architects. "The experience is all the more exceptional in the panorama of France's large cities because it called upon all the renowned landscape architects of the 'French school,'" noted the theorist Jacques Lucan in 1993[27] (Fig. 2.15–2.16). This laboratory would indeed reveal a whole generation of landscape architects, such as Alexandre Chemetoff, Christine Dalnoky, Michel Desvigne, Alain Marguerit, as well as the agencies Latitude Nord, Ilex and In Situ, to name only the main ones. Through the implementation of its *Lighting Plan*, Lyon would also contribute to the recognition of the profession of lighting designer, calling on the skills of Louis Clair, Pierre Bideau, Roland Jéol, Alain Guilhot, Laurent Fachard, and Philippe Hutinet.[28]

Unity of development

The last distinctive point to be retained from the Lyon model is the search for a unity of development, which affirmed itself from the outset of this vast urban renewal operation. This objective was reflected firstly in the creation of a line of furniture specific to the Lyon area, entrusted to Jean-Michel Wilmotte in 1990 following an international competition.[29]

The second decision was to define a common language to be used for all future developments in Greater Lyon. To this end, in 1994 the Public Space Department published a reference catalog entitled *The Vocabulary of Public Spaces, the References of Greater Lyon*.[30] This catalog lists a limited range of components considered essential to the design of a development, detailing four themes: the treatment of boundaries, the treatment of the ground, the furniture, and the vegetation. This desire for moderation was part of a search for coherence aimed at improving the legibility of the urban landscape, but it also responded to considerations of cost and maintenance.

The different testimonies of the actors involved in the definition of this reduced vocabulary claim an ambition of "simplicity" and "sobriety" as founding values that allow one to guard against "spectacular" and "aestheticizing" attitudes.[31] In the introduction to the reference catalog, Chabert also emphasizes the intention to reveal through this vocabulary a sort of *genius loci* for Lyon.[32] It is thus clear that the challenge was not only to achieve a formal unity between all the public spaces of Greater Lyon according to the principle of "agglomeration solidarity" stated above. It was also a question of reflecting on the identity of Lyon, in the hope that it would be reinforced by each future development. The tones, materials, and mineral surfaces recommended in the document resonate with the distinctive colors of the agglomeration and in particular with its architecture. The ambition of a local anchorage was thus firmly asserted.

TURN OF THE CENTURY: THE EMERGENCE OF A FIELD OF DESIGN

MID-NINETIES: GENERALIZATION OF THE SUBJECT

The Barcelona and Lyon urban policy models contributed to widespread recognition of the fundamental role of public spaces. In the years following, throughout Europe, localities of every status, size, and influence embraced the subject.[33] Innovative designs proliferated in small remote villages as well as in the largest urban areas. The abundance of projects in cities such as Berlin, Bordeaux, Amsterdam, Zurich, London, or, even more conspicuously, Copenhagen, testifies to the proactive public space development policies implemented by their leaders. This enthusiasm for the subject was quickly boosted by numerous publications, which in turn contributed to consolidation of the emerging field (see pp. 32–34).

The Barcelona and Lyon laboratories thus contributed to the recognition of a new field of intervention and to the constitution of a climate favorable to experimentation in design. In particular, they encouraged the appearance of new designer profiles in the field of public spaces. They also contributed to the acceptance of a redistribution of space for the benefit of the citizens. From these models, the idea persists that the peripheries are as deserving of quality development as the urban centers. It is no longer a question of pedestrianizing and embellishing only the historical core of a locality; every free space in the city center and the periphery is now considered to be a place conducive to urban life.

But the generalized infatuation with the issue of public spaces seems to have led to the loss of a fundamental element. The ambitious and coordinated policies of the time have disappeared, replaced by more diffuse strategies, illustrated by a profusion of isolated operations carried out according to opportunity or necessity.[34] The planning of public spaces no longer seems to be on the scale of multiple operations carried out simultaneously and coordinated by an overall policy: action is taken on a piecemeal basis, possibly abandoning any idea of coherence or formal unity.

CONCERNS AND VECTORS FOR CHANGE

To take a critical look at the development of public spaces at the turn of the 21st century requires an understanding of the context in which they were produced.[35] This period of widespread reclamation of public spaces indeed saw a certain number of major evolutions of very different orders, all of which would have an impact on the emerging field of design. The evolution of forms of contract, the arrival of new promoters, the diversification of the types of open spaces treated, the profiles of emerging designers, the expression of new concerns, and finally the development of design tools in the digital age, are all vectors that influenced the production of public spaces during this period. The articles, reviews, and books dealing with the design of public spaces that appeared from the mid-1990s onward also reveal a series of themes that concerned practitioners, critics, and theorists of the period. As such, these new subjects of reflection were to influence the understanding of the design of the public realm. Indeed, these spaces remain places that express the characteristic social organization of a given time.

Predominant concerns

The topics emerging in the specialized literature at the turn of the 21st century[36] concern general issues: mobility, infrastructure, heritage, ecology, biodiversity, food, energy, time management, information technology, urban tourism, the cult of the body, and so on. More specifically they concern the role attributed to public spaces such as urban regeneration, the creation of living and democratic space, symbols of identity ... Nevertheless, some recurrent and predominant themes appear to stand out in the panorama of concerns of the time.

The first is that of the design project in its relationship to the existing. In the early 1990s, many operations still consisted of reclaiming the history of localities by pedestrianizing them. Indeed, the question of mobility, which is at the origin of the repositioning of public spaces at the heart of urban concerns, still occupied many minds. The architectural and urban heritage was then asserting itself as a major theme of reflection.[37] At that time, critics such as the architect-urbanist Bernard Huet[38] tended to make practitioners attentive to the history of the places in which they intervened, rejecting a logic of *tabula rasa* associated with the modernist period and ideology. In this context of reflections, the notion of site became prevalent, affecting all disciplines of urban design.[39] The project began to be understood in terms of "transformation."[40] An idea of dialogue with the existing, rather than of preservation, emerged from this conception of the project, which acted as a revealing factor for the site on which it was based.

While the countries of southern Europe were particularly focused on these questions of site, and more specifically on the relationship to heritage, environmental concerns began to be expressed in the countries of the north.[41] Ecological awareness emerged in the seventies and progressively imposed itself over the following decades as a major and global issue. It also affected urban professionals. Indeed, these environmental concerns called into question the excessive and harmful use of the automobile, a subject that naturally found a resonance in the reclamation of public spaces. Designers approached the ecological question in extremely varied ways.

Some addressed it by providing practical solutions: the developments they proposed aimed to combat global warming or to diversify the fauna and flora in the urban environment. Still in an operational perspective, it is sometimes a question of dealing with natural disasters linked to the ecological crisis. Thus, the management of rainwater *in situ* was becoming a central theme in the development of the early 21st century. Faced with this passion for environmental issues, some researchers and critics were worried about a potential simplistic and promotional recycling of the subject.[42]

A third subject gradually grew in importance until it became, without doubt, the major preoccupation of the discussion on public spaces at the beginning of the 21st century. It was the consideration of users and urban practices in all their diversity. This attention responded to a growing concern for the quality of life in the city. The reclaiming of public spaces has been accompanied by a major reassignment of importance to pedestrians, and therefore to city dwellers, who are now at the heart of design concerns. The desire is not only to reallocate generous surfaces to these users, but also to design them to best meet their many needs. Numerous discussions also support the idea of a resurgence of public space as a democratic platform and a social condenser.

2.17–2.18 Temporary interventions. *(17) Rue du Beulet, Untitled, Alain Vaucher – Thierry Treppey, Les yeux de la ville, Geneva, 2003; (18) Rue de l'École de Médecine, Canal, Robert Ireland – Pierre Bonnet, Les yeux de la ville, Geneva, 2005* **2.19–2.20** Corporate landscapes. *(19) Evolution Square – Campus Rotkreuz, Vogt Landschaftsarchitekten, 2011; (20) Unter den Linden 32–34, Berlin, Topotek 1, 2006*

2.21

2.22

2.21–2.22 Large recreational parks. *(21) Riemer Park, Riem-Munich, Latitude Nord, 2005; (22) Cultuurpark Westergasfabriek, Amsterdam, Gustafson Porter + Bowman, 2005* **2.23–2.24** Reclaiming riverfronts. *(23) Quays of the Garonne, Bordeaux, C. Corajoud – M. Corajoud – P. Gangnet, 2008; (24)* Banks of the Rhône, *Lyon, In Situ / Jalbert – Tardivon, 2007*

2.23

2.24

There has been an increase in the interest of designers in adapting developments to new urban uses, particularly for leisure and recreation, which are frequently discussed in specialized journals.[43] This interest is manifested in the proliferation of new types of spaces dedicated to urban games and sports. It is also illustrated in more traditional spaces by the use of devices and materials that encourage hedonic and playful activities that, until recently, might have been considered marginal, provocative, or disrespectful, such as climbing, sliding, tumbling, and bathing, or even just relaxing.[44] There is also interest in more mundane uses, such as walking, to which special attention is given by developing appropriate features. Finally, some are focusing on questions related to the size of the human body, to perception, to feelings and emotions experienced by users of urban spaces.[45]

Designers: new profiles in the spotlight

To meet these new urban challenges, this period of renewed interest in public spaces is marked by the emergence of new professional profiles among designers, not without occasionally causing some tension. Traditionally, open spaces were the responsibility of public works engineers, who were in charge of the development and maintenance of roads. Breaking with this tradition, the architecture profession initially asserted itself as dominant, in the context of reclaiming public spaces. The urban reconstruction of Barcelona in the 1980s was the prerogative of this profession, both on the side of the clients and of the designers, associated in more exceptional cases with artists.

Later on, landscape architects, formerly relegated to the creation of parks and gardens, broadened their field of intervention and in turn invested in the design of public spaces.[46] The Lyon experience described earlier undoubtedly contributed to the European influence of this profession, which became increasingly interested in urban environments. Several theorists, such as Rem Koolhaas, Sébastien Marot, and Jacques Lucan, associate this breakthrough with a decline of architecture, or an urban planning context in crisis.[47] They point to a culture, know-how, and operating modes that are more adapted to the challenges of the time.

Profiting from this attention, European landscape architects started to campaign for the recognition of their profession.[48] With this impetus, events, books, and magazines, then websites, were created in order to engender a landscape debate on a continental scale.[49] Inevitably, these specialized media willingly covered the development of public spaces and contributed to their influence. Moreover, it seems important to underline the synchrony between the recognition of a field of design (that of public spaces) and a discipline (that of landscape architecture), sometimes leading to confusion.

Accepting the rise of landscape architects at the forefront of public space design, it is also important to qualify its extent. Over the years 2000–2015, architects and landscape architects seem to have shared the projects relatively equally.[50] Moreover, it would seem appropriate to gradually abandon the Manichean vision that consists of opposing these two disciplines, since urban professionals now appear to be developing their own concerns and project intentions, which are above all independent of their training. Indeed, we note that the recognition of public spaces as a field of design in its own right has really contributed to blur the disciplinary boundaries.

This blurring of identity of urban professionals is reinforced by a tendency for firms dealing with urban issues to become multidisciplinary, that is, to bring together complementary backgrounds and expertise within the same team. We are also seeing an increasing number of collaborations between firms, either on an ad hoc basis, driven by a set of specifications, or simply by a desire to embrace other disciplines.

It is notably within the framework of such collaborations that visual artists and product designers have in turn made a place for themselves in the creation of public spaces. This is often the only way for them to contribute to the realization of a project, since the clients usually require them to join forces with architects or landscape architects capable of the overall management of a construction site. In this broadening of the design team's skills, a rise in the profession of lighting designer has emerged to address issues of security, ornamental enhancements, and to extend use by offering a framework for city night-life. More recently, other specialists (sociologists, economists, historians, biologists, ecologists, etc.) have begun to be integrated into the design teams with a view to dealing with increasingly complex urban issues. All of these new professional profiles have thus come to shake up established traditions, not without calling into question the pre-established professions.

Contracts: international competition and a climate of experimentation

From the beginning of the 1990s, a major change has influenced the way in which contracts are awarded. This is the establishment of European directives and bilateral agreements concerning public contracts, which for those exceeding a certain value require the issue of international invitations to compete. This opening of markets could explain the export of styles and know-how from one country to another. In reality, the current production of public spaces is still predominantly undertaken by local architectural and landscape design firms.[51] On the other hand, in what is a highly competitive context, the principle of international collaborations seems to be of increasing interest to designers. These collaborations undoubtedly contribute to the export of ideas and methods across borders.

Agreements concerning the award of contracts at a European level have also led to a generalization of competitive procedures, adopting different forms depending on the situation (open competitions, invited competitions, parallel study contracts, etc.).[52] These many forms of competitive procedure have undoubtedly contributed to fostering a climate of experimentation, encouraging the development of unusual project concepts.[53] They are also opportunities for important debates on the subject of public spaces, participating in the establishment of a form of criticism of their design.

A final aspect concerning contracts could be considered as a vector for the evolution of public space design. Since the beginning of the 21st century, there has been a pronounced fashion for temporary interventions, which is reflected in the organization of "ephemeral design festivals" in urban space[54] (Fig. 2.17–2.18). These pilot projects make it possible to rapidly animate underused or monofunctional spaces, temporarily and with few resources. They are an effective way of verifying the potential of a spatial configuration, freeing it from the administrative, normative, and political constraints of a definitive project, while deconstructing prejudices or unfounded fears. This type of operation has undoubtedly contributed to the exploration of new materials and forms of development, as well as to the active involvement of artists and city dwellers in the creation of public spaces.

Clients: the emergence of private operators

Changes in the client profile also seem to have affected the design of public spaces at the end of the 20th century. An increasing number of private clients, large companies, or institutions call upon architects, landscape architects, or urban designers to design their outdoor spaces, with the aim of contributing to the definition of their identity. If some of these spaces remain freely accessible to the public, they remain private from a property point of view and their owners keep total control of them. As such, they cannot be considered true public spaces.

However, their design allows for real experimentation, particularly in terms of form, which certainly has an influence on the resulting product. Being a reflection of a brand or an institution, such spaces conceived as unique places often take on an iconic dimension. One can also see a strong influence of the decorative arts and graphic design expressed in particular paving designs and bright colors. Alternatively, the designs are inspired by natural landscapes, with the aim of shaping attractive exteriors. These commercial strategies and the striking images they produce are widely published in the trade press (Fig. 2.19–2.20).

In the same vein, public-private partnerships have also appeared, especially in the context of large-scale urban development projects or the conversion of industrial or port sites.[55] It is indeed rare for sites of a significant size to be totally in public hands, and the authorities sometimes have to unite concerned private owners around a project aimed at a particular urban quality. Although this form of partnership may seem obvious today, one may wonder about the excessive power acquired by private actors, favoring spectacular projects that contribute above all to shaping their own image.

Notwithstanding that changes in client profile play an undeniable role in the creation of new forms of urban space development, public commissions still seem to dominate the production of the early 2000s. In the context of exacerbated global competition of the period, public space in its capacity to promote the identity and attractiveness of a city nevertheless becomes, for some, a perfect medium for urban marketing.

A diversity of open space types

In addition to developments relating to contracts and clients, the scope of public spaces has been broadened by the appearance of new types of space. If, because of their size, their function, or their land status, some of these developed spaces do not fit precisely into the definition of public urban space as discussed here,[56] they nevertheless constitute contexts that are conducive to experimentation by designers. Widely disseminated in specialized publications, these examples and the formal innovations they present undoubtedly have repercussions on the designs studied in this book.

In particular, the 1990s saw the widespread creation of very large-scale parks occupying wastelands or sites characterized by derelict infrastructure, such as abandoned freight stations or airports (Fig. 2.21–2.22). The design of these large recreational spaces has given the opportunity for many planners to develop the theme of leisure use by seeking to provide conducive spatial and material configurations. These particular sites also push the designers to develop new landscape expressions in connection with contexts strongly marked by past industries or infrastructures. Following the same impetus, reclamation of hitherto neglected spaces, transformed into places of recreation, spaces linked to river, lake, or maritime areas, has also been the subject of numerous interventions (Fig. 2.23–2.24).

2.25–2.26 Institutional public spaces. *(25) Taxingeplan, Tensta, LLP – Front Design, 2006; (26) Abidjplein Averbode, Montaigu-Zichem, Omgeving Landscape Architecture, 2010* **2.27–2.28** Building courtyard. *(27) Choorstraat, Hertogenbosch, Buro Lubbers, 2008; (28)Classensgade, Copenhagen, 1:1 Landskab, 2010*

2.29–2.30 Playgrounds and playscapes. *(29) Potgieterstraat, Amsterdam, Carve NL, 2010; (30) Gärten der Potenzen, Riem-Munich, Rainer Schmidt Landschaftsarchitekten und Stadtplaner 2005* **2.31–2.32** Large polyvalent squares. *(31) Sechseläutenplatz, Zurich, Vetschpartner Landschaftsarchitekten AG, 2014; (32) Turbinenplatz, Zurich, Atelier Descombes Rampini, 2003* **2.33–2.34** Streets as places to stay. *(33) Passeig de Sant Joan, Barcelona, Lola Domènech architect, 2011; (34) New Road, Brighton, Landscape Projects – Gehl, 2007*

At the same time, many public institutions have begun to perceive the potential of undeveloped spaces as city showcases. So there has been an increase in forecourts of museums, historic buildings, universities, or even religious buildings redesigned with the aim of inviting citizens to occupy them daily (Fig. 2.25–2.26). These include distinctive surfacings, innovative furniture, and interactive fountains.

This type of solution can also be found in courtyards of certain apartment buildings – private spaces for collective use. In these cases, the designers have to imagine friendly and welcoming layouts that act as shared extensions for the dwellings that border them. Their interest is particularly focused on the design of the furniture intended to provide opportunities for neighbors to meet. In these layouts, we observe the hijacking of a domestic language, which is given a more robust and collective character. A strong ornamental dimension is also illustrated by the meticulous choice of colors and by the development of ornamental motifs (Fig. 2.27–2.28).

Finally, playgrounds have also undergone significant formal and material changes in recent years, which have been widely publicized in the professional media (Fig. 2.29–2.30). These sites show particular attention paid to the choice of ground modeling and surfacing, which feature quite unusual colors. The designs also display variations of traditional equipment (slides, swings, turnstiles, sandboxes, etc.), innovative water games, and climbing structures, thereby becoming real adventure courses. In recent years, these facilities inviting free play have tended to spread to all urban spaces, even the most ordinary ones, according to a new phenomenon of the "ludic city."[57]

Apart from the aforementioned emergence of these new types of space, conducive to formal and material experimentation, urban public spaces in the most conventional sense of the term, that is, squares and streets, remain the places that largely dominate current design production. However even these "traditional" spaces seem to be changing to adapt to new practices. In particular, there is a tendency to develop very large squares, embodying places dedicated to urban life of a scale that seemed to have disappeared from European cities, particularly since the advent of the automobile (Fig. 2.31–2.32). Streets are also evolving as they are no longer considered only as places of transit or of strolling. They now include artifacts – street furniture, fountains, night lighting – judiciously designed and arranged to provide opportunities for relaxation, amusement, social interaction, or simple contemplation of urban activity. In this way, they lose their purely functional character to become real places for living and for extended stay (Fig. 2.33–2.34).

Design tools in the digital age

Before concluding this chapter, it is necessary to mention one last evolution that may have played a role in the development of new forms of public space, namely the appearance of computer-aided design tools. Assuming that progress in terms of visualization techniques has always had a direct influence on the way architecture and landscape are conceived,[58] it seems necessary to look at the design tools that have recently become popular.

In effect, the architectural and landscape production of these last decades has been marked by the development of a series of novel computerized tools. Computer-aided design and drafting software (CAD) developed in the 1980s and democratized over the following decade has completely changed the design and construction of our urban landscapes. Subsequently, three-dimensional design software allowing the development, analysis, and realization of increasingly complex geometries has undoubtedly contributed to the appearance of new sculptural forms.

These new digital tools have thus profoundly modified the ways of working for architects, landscape architects, and urban designers, extending their field of possibilities. The development of image processing and rendering software has also had an impact in terms of representation and visual narratives, putting the emphasis back on "a renewed exploration of the scenic, narrative and perspective image."[59] The popularization of Photoshop software (1988) has played a significant role in this renewed interest in scenography and connectivity in design, through collage or photorealistic illustrations.

Perhaps in reaction to this new digital wave, many designers have recently returned to more traditional representational techniques. Hand-drawn models, sketches, and perspectives are making a comeback at competition presentations and in trade magazines. These manual supports have a more sensitive and less fixed dimension – because of their abstraction – than the photorealistic synthetic images that some people are beginning to tire of.

We have just outlined a series of significant changes from the turn of the 21st century. They can be considered as vectors of evolution that have influenced the way in which public spaces are designed. They explain the context in which formal and material characteristics, as well as completely new fields of reference, have emerged in our landscapes. The resulting new expressions are the most striking elements of this period's production. Among them, we identify five planning strategies that serve respectively, to *animate, ornament, construct, model*, and *naturize* the public space.

1 Allaman, Martine, "Espaces publics: liberté, identité, continuité," *Diagonal*, n° 112, April 1995, p. 14.

2 Plan Urbain, *Espaces publics*, Paris, Ministère de l'Equipement et du Logement-DAUDRI, 1988, pp. 31, 47.

3 In parallel, the Barcelona municipality carried out an urban policy focused on the rehabilitation of housing in the historic center, and a few years later launched large urban development operations to host the 1992 Olympic Games.

4 Oriol Bohigas, who confided in Alexandre Chemetoff in 1983, spoke of "remaking the city from what we find there." Alexandre Chemetoff, "Entretien avec Oriol Bohigas," *AMC – architecture*, n° 2, October 1983, p. 46.

5 Bohigas, Oriol, "Un programma per Barcelona/A Program for Barcelona," *Casabella*, n° 483, September 1982, pp. 14–15; Oriol Bohigas, "Ten Points for an Urban Methodology," in Tim Marshall, *Transforming Barcelona*, London/NewYork, Routledge, 2004, pp. 94–95.

6 Bohigas, *op. cit.*, 1982, p. 14; David Mangin, "Les trottoirs de Barcelone," *L'Architecture d'aujourd'hui*, n° 260, December 1988, p. 2; Hanno Rauterberg, "Der Aufbruch hält an/Reconquering Barcelona," *Topos: The International Review of Landscape Architecture and Urban Design*, n° 29, 1999, p. 6.

7 Buchanan, Peter, "Regenerating Barcelona with Parks and Plazas," *The Architectural Review*, n° 1048, June 1984, p. 36. It should be noted that Jean-Louis Cohen qualified the oversimplified opposition between "urbanism of projects" and "urbanism of plans" made by many critics of the Barcelona model at the time, underlining the fact that all the actions undertaken on an ad hoc basis were inevitably part of a global vision prepared upstream. Jean-Louis Cohen, "Learning from Barcelona: Twenty Years of Urban Projects and their Reception," in Pep Subirós (ed.), *Ciutat real, ciutat ideal (Real City, Ideal City)*, Barcelona, Centre de Cultura Contemporània, 1998. Available online: https://www.publicspace.org/multimedia/-/post/learning-from-barcelona-twenty-years-of-urban-projects-and-their-reception [accessed February 23, 2022].

8 Bohigas, *op. cit.*, 2004, pp. 92–94; Jean-Louis Cohen also notes this preoccupation with identity, which is implicit in an article published in 1983: Jean-Louis Cohen, "La Barcelone de Bohigas: Identité d'une ville," *AMC – architecture*, n° 2, October 1983, pp. 42–45.

9 Casanovas, Miquel Martí, "Barcelone (1979–2004). Monumentalité et renouveau de la voie publique," *Urbanisme*, n° 346, January–February 2008, p. 56.

10 Several authors point out the prerogative of architects in the creation of Barcelona's public spaces. Jordi Farrando Sicilia, "Vom Wandel der Formen und Konzepte/The Changes in Forms and Concepts," *Topos: The International Review of Landscape Architecture and Urban Design*, n° 29, 1999, p. 75; François Tomas, "L'espace public, un concept moribond ou en expansion," *Géocarrefour*, vol. 76, n° 1, 2001, p. 81.

11 Buchanan, *op. cit.*, 1984, p. 33.

12 Gehl, Jan, and Lars Gemzøe, *New City Spaces, Strategies and Projects*, Copenhagen, The Danish Architectural Press, 2001, p. 29.

13 Miles, Malcolm, *Cities and Cultures*, London, New York, Routledge, 2007, p. 83

14 Cohen, "La Barcelone de Bohigas ...," *op. cit.*, 1983, p. 45.

15 To name but a few: Alexandre Chemetoff, Jean-Louis Cohen, "Le droit à la ville: les espaces publics de Barcelone," *AMC – architecture*, n° 2, October 1983, pp. 46–47, p. 51; Buchanan, *op. cit.*, 1984, p. 33; Rauterberg, *op. cit.*, 1999, p. 8. The author claims purity or restraint; Karl H. C. Ludwig, "Die Inszenierung des öffentlichen Freiraums/La mise en scène de l'espace libre public," *Anthos*, n° 3, 2000, pp. 6–7.

16 Cohen, *op. cit.* 1998.

17 Foret, Catherine, "La création d'un service 'espace public' au sein de la Communauté urbaine de Lyon (1990): une initiative pionnière en France," *millénaire3*, Centre de Ressources Prospectives du Grand Lyon, May 2008, p. 18.

18 *Ibid.*

19 Azéma, Jean-Louis, "Les espaces publics du Grand Lyon," in François Tomas (ed.), *Espaces publics, architecture et urbanité de part et d'autre de l'Atlantique*, Saint-Etienne, Université de Saint-Etienne, 2002, pp. 239–240.

20 Foret, "La création ...," *op. cit.*, 2008, pp. 13, 5.

21 The *Color Plan* is also sometimes referred to as the *Reference Plan for Public Spaces*. Azéma, *op. cit.*, 2002, p. 239; Henry Chabert (ed.), *Espaces publics, espaces de vie ... Les réponses lyonnaises*, Lyon, Horvath, 1993, pp. 49–55.

22 Betin, Christophe, "La construction de l'espace public. Le cas de Lyon," *Géocarrefour, revue de géographie de Lyon*, n° 76, 2001, p. 53.

23 Houzelle, Béatrice, "Entre Saône et Rhône ... Les aménagements de la Presqu'Île," *Techniques & architecture*, n° 419, May 1995, p. 38.

24 Foret, "La création ...," *op. cit.*, 2008, p. 4.

25 Interview with Henry Chabert by Jacques Lucan, "Entretien avec Henry Chabert. Reconquérir les espaces publics," *AMC – architecture*, n° 44, September 1993, p. 33.

26 Remarks by Jean-Pierre Charbonneau reported in Catherine Sabbah's "Espaces publics. L'invention d'une politique," *Techniques & architecture*, n° 419, May 1995, p. 47.

27 Lucan, Jacques, "Les espaces publics du Grand Lyon," *AMC – architecture*, n° 44, September 1993, p. 28.

28 David, Brigitte, "Le Plan Lumière. Lyon vit aussi la nuit," *AMC – architecture*, n° 44, September 1993, p. 39.

29 On the subject of Lyon's urban furniture, see Catherine Foret, "Un nouveau mobilier urbain pour l'agglomération lyonnaise (1991)," *millénaire3*, Centre de Ressources Prospectives du Grand Lyon, May 2008, Available online : http://www.millenaire3.com/ressources/un-nouveau-mobilier-urbain-pour-l-agglomeration-lyonnaise-1991 [accessed October 10, 2017].

30 *Le vocabulaire des espaces publics, les références du Grand Lyon*, document edited by the Communauté urbaine de Lyon, Service Espace Public, 1994.

31 *Ibid.* Jean-Pierre Charbonneau speaks on this subject in the document. Similar remarks by Jean-Louis Azéma are recounted by Catherine Foret, "L'invention d'un vocabulaire des espaces publics (1990–1994) ou comment renforcer l'unité de l'agglomération par 'l'harmonisation des signes du territoire,'" *millénaire3*, le Centre de Ressources Prospectives du Grand Lyon, May 2008, p. 7. Finally, Charbonneau and Azéma are quoted in Martine Allaman, "La griffe du Grand Lyon," *Diagonal*, n° 112, April 1995, pp. 15–18.

32 *Le vocabulaire des espaces publics, les références du Grand Lyon*, *op. cit.*, 1994, p. 5.

33 In 1999, Miquel Vidal Pla, in an article on the impact of the "Barcelona model," noted that it had spread to all Spanish cities – large, medium, and small. With a certain amount of hindsight, we can say that this phenomenon has affected the whole of Europe. Miquel Vidal Pla, "Spanien: Weiterarbeiten am Modell Barcelona/Spain: Developing the Barcelona Model," *Topos: The International Review of Landscape Architecture and Urban Design*, n° 27, 1999, p. 41.

34 Testifying to this phenomenon, in 2011 the journal *'scape* devoted a dossier to the topic of acupuncture as an urban development strategy. "Feature: Acupuncture," *'scape*, n° 1, 2011, pp. 18–43.

35 This contextualization is based in particular on the analysis of a selection of books (see notes 10, 11, and 13, p. 38), of reference sites (ArchDaily, Landezine, European Prize for Urban Public Space) and of specialized magazines (period covered 1992–2015 – *AMC – architecture, Arkitekten, Arkitektur DK, Anthos, Garten + Landschaft, JoLA, Paisea, 'Scape, Topos, La revue Urbanisme, a+t*). This survey has fed into a census of nearly 180 open space projects realized between 2000 and 2015. The systematic categorization of these projects in a multi-criteria table made it possible to cross-reference various types of information (designer profile, design period, geographic location, urban context, type of space, initial condition, etc.) in order to identify new design trends and investigate their potential origins.

36 *Ibid.*

37 As an example, in Lyon Catherine Foret mentions the principle of "reclaiming the heritage of city centers" which has generated a number of public space redesign interventions since the 1970s. Comments recounted by Foret, "La création ...," *op. cit.* 2008, p. 3.

38 Huet, Bernard, "Une génétique urbaine," *Urbanisme*, n° 303, November–December 1998, pp. 56–59.

39 See also: Carol Burns and Andrea Kahn (eds), *Site Matters. Design Concepts, Histories and Strategies*, New York, Routledge, 2005.

40 Marchand, Bruno, "Preface," in Bruno Marchand, Julien Descombes and Marco Rampini (eds), *Common Grounds. Atelier Descombes Rampini 2000–2015*, Basel, Birkhaüser, 2017, p. 21. [French version, *Lieux Communs*, Gollion, Infolio 2017].

41 Fleury, Antoine, *Les espaces publics dans les politiques métropolitaines. Réflexions au croisement de trois expériences: de Paris aux quartiers centraux de Berlin et Istanbul*, doctoral thesis, Paris, Université de Paris 1 Panthéon-Sorbonne, UFR de géographie, 2008 [version February 29], in particular p. 29.

42 Let us quote as an example Caroline (Mollie-)Stefulesco, "De quelques impostures," in the introduction of Catherine Seron-Pierre, "Détails: l'arbre dans la ville," *AMC – architecture*, n° 162, June–July 2006, p. 112.

43 As evidence of this interest, several journals have been looking at the issue of urban and sports recreation since the late 1990s: Eric Adamkiewicz, "Les pratiques récréatives autonomes urbaines," *Urbanisme*, n° 302, September–October 1998, pp. 44–47; "Dossier: loisirs urbains," *Urbanisme*, n° 319, July–August 2001, pp. 52–87; Jean-Pierre Augustin, "Espaces publics et cultures sportives," *Géocarrefour*, vol. 76, n° 1, 2001, pp. 27–30; François Ascher, "Loisirs," *Urbanisme*, n° 330, 2003, pp. 70–71; and more specifically on the question of urban bathing: Thorbjörn Andersson, "Badkultur kring sundet," *Landskap*, n° 7, 2005, pp. 162–167.

44 Crunelle, Marc, "La ville à pratiquer," in Jean-Paul Thibaud, Cristiane Rose Duarte (eds), *Ambiances urbaines en partage. Pour une écologie sociale de la ville sensible*, Geneva, MétisPresses, 2013, p. 107. On the subject of the recreation possibilities of public spaces, see also: Quentin Stevens, *The Ludic City: Exploring the Potential of Public Spaces*, London, Routledge. 2007.

45 The journal *Urbanisme*, for example, addresses the question in the special report "Dossier: Corps à corps avec la ville," *Urbanisme*, n° 325, July–August 2002, pp. 31–70. Several authors raise a general interest in the urban sciences for the questions of bodily, sensory, and emotional feelings of users, articulating around the notion of atmosphere: Pascal Amphoux et al., *La notion d'ambiance. Une mutation de la pensée urbaine et de la pratique architecturale*, Lausanne, IRECDA/EPFL, 1998; Michèle Grosjean, Jean-Paul Thibaud (eds), *L'espace urbain en méthodes*, Marseille, Editions Parenthèses, 2001, p. 7; Ariella Masboungi, "Un urbanisme des ambiances," in Alain Bourdin, Ariella Masboungi, *Un urbanisme des modes de vie*, Paris, *Le Moniteur*, 2004, pp. 67–85 and more recently: Jean-Paul Thibaud, Cristiane Rose Duarte (eds), *Ambiances urbaines en partage, pour une écologie sociale de la ville sensible*, Geneva, MétisPresses, 2013.

46 We also notice a reverse movement, in the sense that architects and urban designers have recently claimed the design of green spaces, producing a real blurring of disciplinary boundaries. Paola Viganò points this out for example in "I territori dell' urbanistica/The Territories of Urbanism," *Lotus International*, n° 150, 2012, p. 112.

47 Koolhaas, Rem, "Singapore Songlines: Thirty Years of Tabula Rasa," in O.M.A., Rem Koolhaas, Bruce Mau, *S,M,L,XL*, New York, The Monacelli Press, 1995, pp. 1008–1087. Sébastien Marot, "L'alternative du paysage," *Le Visiteur*, n° 1, 1995, pp. 54–80. Jacques Lucan,"L'irrésistible ascension des paysagistes," *AMC – architecture*, n° 44, September 1993, p. 41.

48 In 1999, the magazine *Topos* drew up an overview of the situation in terms of training and status of landscape architects in a selection of European countries; this overview shows the general growth of the profession and its recent orientation toward urban issues "Europa – Der Stand der Dinge/Europe – The State of Affairs," *Topos: The International Review of Landscape Architecture and Urban Design*, n° 27, 1999.

49 The *Biennal Europea de Paisatge* of Barcelona was created in 1999 with the aim of serving as a platform for European debate. The triennial albums of the Landscape Architecture Europe (LAE) foundation from 2006 onward confirm this intention of joining forces on a continental scale, see p. 32. The main magazines and websites that emerged at that time include *Topos: The International Review of Landscape Architecture and Urban Design* (Germany, 1992) and *Landskab* (Denmark, 1997), and more recently *'scape* (the Netherlands, 2006), *Journal of Landscape Architecture* (*JoLA*, Europe, 2006), *Paisea* (Spain, 2007), *Landezine* (online, 2009).

50 According to survey, see note 35.

51 *Ibid.*

52 Directive 92/50/EEC and subsequent adaptations.

53 Some people also denounce a drift in the system of competitions, organized in close proximity to one another at intervals of a few years, without a more global guiding vision, resulting in a juxtaposition of public space designs, each more singular than the last. Svava Riesto, Jan Støvring, "Stories under your Feet: Renovation of Købmagergade in Copenhagen," *Topos: The International Review of Landscape Architecture and Urban Design*, n° 89, 2014, p. 42.

54 For example, *Paris plages* (since 2002), *En ville, sans ma voiture!* (Geneva 2001 and 2002), *Les yeux de la ville* (Geneva, 2003 and 2006, Fig. 2.17–2.18, p. 49) and *Lausanne jardins* (since 1997).

55 Let us also underline the case, unique to our knowledge, of the philanthropic institution Realdania based in Denmark, which supports projects related to the built environment, particularly in the field of public facilities and spaces, by encouraging innovation and exemplary interventions, see the Superkilen and Måløv Aksen projects.

56 See definition p. 31.

57 See on this subject: Sonia Curnier, "Programming Play into Public Space?," *Metropolitics*, March 20, 2015. Published online: https://metropolitics.org/Programming-play-into-public-space.html [accessed March 20, 2015].

58 Silvestre, Federico López, "Técnicas de representación y proyectos de intervención: breve historia de une relación cuestionada. Representation Techniques and Intervention Projects: A Short History of a Questioned Relationship," *Paisea*, n° 14, 2010, pp. 11–17.

59 De Jong, Erik, "Vistas of the Imagination," *'scape*, n° 1, 2008, p. 46.

PORTRAITS

Each chapter that follows corresponds to a family of projects and is structured identically. A brief introduction provides a summary defining the characteristics that distinguish the family of projects and helps to clarify the selection of the two chosen case studies. This is followed by a monograph analyzing each example. The chapter then ends with the main conclusions drawn from the cases studied.

A METHOD FOR CRITICAL ANALYSIS OF THE PROJECT'S GENESIS

The monographic analyses are based on a comprehensive method, developed specifically for this study, which combines four complementary approaches.

The first consists of acquiring a good knowledge of each project by reviewing the *specialized literature* (articles, thematic, or monographs). Often produced by the designers themselves, the texts and iconography that make up these presentations are useful for understanding how the project narrative has developed over the years. Insofar as it is accessible, the *official literature* ((competition) brief, possible annexes, the competition jury report, and press releases published throughout the process) allows for a better understanding of the issues and constraints set by the client and the other parties involved in the process.

In a second phase, this basic documentation is completed by *on-site project visits* in order to confront the constructed reality of the work. These visits provide some distance from the often idealized, or at least biased, version of a project as presented in publications. The on-site observations allow one to form a personal, precise, and tangible idea of the materials and uses of each case study. Whenever possible, the spaces are surveyed at different times of the day or week, to study them in changing circumstances of lighting, climate, and occupancy.

The third and perhaps most novel approach is to delve into the genesis of each project. Common public space analyses usually study the design intentions at a given moment, most often when the work is completed. They do not take into account the hesitations, constraints, methods, and developments that led to these results, which are then considered definitive. Genetic analysis, borrowed from the field of textual criticism,[1] makes it possible to go back to the origins of each project's conception and retrace all the ensuing changes. In practice, this approach consists of studying archival documents that reveal the experiments, continuities, and reversals that contributed to the final result. In this case, the most informative documents are the figurative elements: sketches, technical and illustrative project drawings, photographs, 3D visualizations, collages, models, etc.[2] When available, certain texts (exchanges between team members and personal design notes) also make it possible to explain certain project changes.

The three approaches detailed above leave much room for interpretation. In an effort to capture the reality of the design as closely as possible, the analysis of each case study was supplemented by a guided interview with at least one of its authors. The main objective of these exchanges was to learn more about the initial intentions and the major project evolutions, in order to help understand its genesis. They also served to bridge the more or less intentional and conscious distance that always exists between the project reality and the "narratives aimed at legitimizing the work."[3] The exchanges also made it possible to question the architects or landscape architects on their way of approaching certain theoretical themes on which this research is based.

THREE INVESTIGATIONS

In order to verify the hypothesis of a possible increase in formal, material, and semantic autonomy of public spaces at the beginning of the 21st century and its consequences on urban landscapes, three critical angles shape the monographic analyses.

Firstly, for all case studies, the initial intentions of the designers must be identified. What were the concerns that generated their original concept? What are they trying to encourage or emphasize? Are the considerations more related to use, heritage, climate, or the environment? Or are they more in line with purely sculptural or artistic intentions?

Pursuing this angle of analysis, the spatial translation of the initial intentions is assessed in detail; what are their consequences in terms of the design's composition, formalization, and materialization? The aim is to identify the inspirations and references that guide the project's development, as well as the operating methods implemented by the designers, and the tools they use. How are the imagined forms generated? Do the project authors establish rules, or do they opt for random forms that reflect a freer artistic gesture? What determines the size of the different elements of the layout? What choices of materials and plant species are made, and what motivates them?

Secondly, we will look at the relationship to the material context. What relationship do the analyzed projects have with the surrounding buildings and public spaces? Does the development serve more to differentiate the public space or, on the contrary, to underline certain elements of the urban or landscape context in which it is located. How is the perimeter of a project delimited? Does the design tend to make this delimitation visible? Is the urban morphology taken into consideration in the development of the project? The designers' view of the architecture that borders the public space is also of interest. Do the built frontages have any influence on the design, orientation, rhythm, vocabulary, materiality, or color of the proposed development? What about the physical and visual continuity with adjacent public spaces? The ambition here is to understand if new concerns push the designers to make choices that break with this material context.

Thirdly, the question of the local or universal dimension of the proposed development will be raised. Do the design of the public space, the materiality given to it, and finally its implementation, stem from a desire to anchor the project locally or are they transposable to other environments? Which elements seem specific to the site? Which, on the contrary, seem to respond to universal concerns or references? Does the project take on a particular narrative? If so, does this narrative result from an interpretation of the site? Do the adopted fields of reference recall distant settings, or are they locally inspired? What about the translation of these ideas into the design? Is it more of the order of a metaphor, an evocation, a reinterpretation, or an illusion? Does it consequently call upon globally shared perceptions? Without further delay, let's dive into the case studies to answer all these questions.

1 This approach appeared in the literary field more than forty years ago. In 2000, the literary critic Pierre-Marc de Biasi, one of the main contributors to the emergence of the discipline, devoted a special issue of the journal *Genesis* to the application of this method to the field of architecture. This text has largely inspired the development of this methodological field. Pierre-Marc De Biasi, "Pour une approche génétique de l'architecture," *Genesis*, special issue "Architecture," n° 14, 2000, pp. 13–65.

2 In some of the portraits, it seemed useful to complement the archival documents with graphic analyses produced by the author in order to better understand the reading of the projects. A green background has been added to distinguish these external contributions from the documents drawn from the designers' archives.

3 Huet, Bernard, "Les enjeux de la critique," in Agnès Deboulet, Rainer Hodde, André Sauvage, *La critique architecturale. Questions-frontières-desseins*, Paris, Editions de la Villette, 2008, p. 80. [Orig. ed., *Le visiteur*, n° 1, fall 1995]. Here the narratives are to be understood as the words expressed by the designers during conferences and interviews, but also as the texts of the working documents and the various publications of the project.

ANIMATE

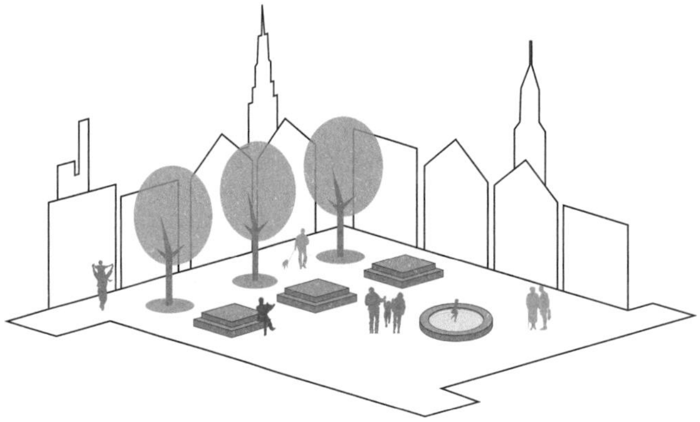

3.1.1

3.1.2

3.1.3

3.1.4

3.1.1–3.1.4
Welcoming urban furniture
Furniture design explicitly encourages idle and convivial practices that were previously uncommon in cities. The seating elements are more collective, comfortable, mobile, and interactive. Long tables allow groups to sit down for a picnic or even to work. *(1) Choorstraat (private courtyard), Hertogenbosch, Buro Lubbers, 2008; (2) HafenCity – public spaces, Hamburg, Miralles Tagliabue EMBT, 2010; (3) Enzi – Museumsquartier, Vienna, PPAG Architects, 2004, (4) Turbinenplatz, Atelier Descombes Rampini, 2003*

3.1.5–3.1.6
Dry and interactive fountains
Following the trend of updating traditional urban design elements, aiming to encourage a recreational and diversified appropriation of public spaces, fountains are available in the form of large basins or interactive and reversible water games. *(5) Bundesplatz, Berne, Stauffenegger + Stutz – Stephan Mundwiler, 2004; (6) The mirror on the Place de la Bourse, Bordeaux, J-M. Llorca – C. Corajoud – M. Corajoud – P. Gangnet, 2006*

3.1.5

3.1.6

A large majority of public space designs of the turn of the 21st century include few substantial innovations in terms of ground treatment, furniture design, lighting, or vegetation. In general, these designs are still subject to the surrounding buildings, which they enhance through a certain sobriety. In this sense, they are more part of a continuity and not representative of hitherto unseen evolutions in the field.

Among these projects, however, we can identify examples that present an evolution by focusing attention on uses during the design process. They propose new and meaningful experiences to city dwellers, stimulating convivial, playful, and leisurely activities. This approach translates into a spatial arrangement concerned primarily with the creation of uses. The project's design focuses notably on certain components, which we will call artifacts (furniture, equipment, fountains, etc.), suggesting new urban practices. In short, the approach aims to *animate* public space, abandoning its symbolic and embellishment role in favor of a certain domesticity and playfulness.

Being part of an urban space design tradition, the *animated* public spaces do not assume a form of singular expression as pronounced as other developments of the early 21st century. Nevertheless, one can wonder about the impact that a strong consideration of uses, and in particular of more convivial and recreational uses, can have on such schemes.

SELECTED CASE STUDIES

The two squares selected for this chapter were inaugurated at the time this research began. The choice was first made from the work of the Atelier Descombes Rampini (ADR), which was not yet internationally recognized at the time, but whose preoccupations and creative ideas had long been focused on the question of use. The small Place Simon-Goulart (2003–2013) in Geneva immediately stood out as an example to be studied because of the wealth of activities that pervaded the public space following its inauguration, testifying to the skill with which the authors had addressed the question of uses.

The Place de la République in Paris (2009–2013) emerged as a second case study. The team led by TVK had to deal with a gigantic square dominated for more than a century by heavy road traffic. The streamlined approach of the new pedestrian esplanade responds to a profound reflection on the reversibility and cohabitation of uses. This preoccupation explains the immediate use of the redesigned square by many people from different backgrounds. The Place de la République has thus rapidly imposed itself on the international scene as an original development, emblematic of what a 21st-century public space could be.

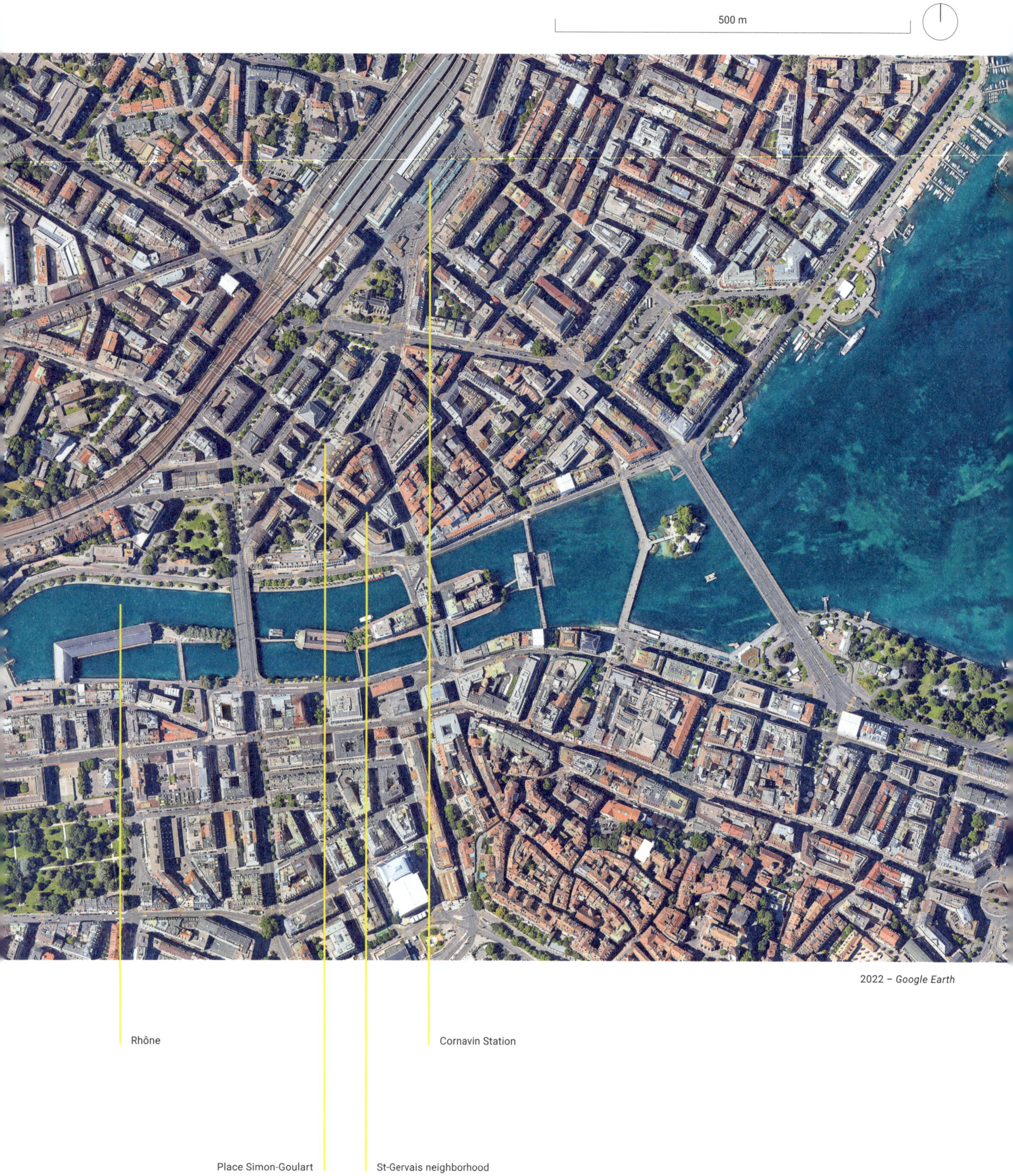

2022 – *Google Earth*

3.1.7 Location of the Place Simon-Goulart

PLACE SIMON-GOULART
GENEVA 2003–2013

Location Geneva, Switzerland **Client** Municipality of Geneva **Lead designers** Atelier Descombes Rampini (Geneva) **Type of commission** Parallel study contracts [MEP] (2003) **Construction** 2012–2013 **Former status** Public space used as a parking lot **Area** 0.4 ha

In the early 1990s, the Geneva authorities launched a program entitled "Place!" aimed at enhancing a certain number of emblematic city *places* (public squares).[1] The reclamation operation would lead to the redevelopment of nearly a dozen public squares, including Place Simon-Goulart, located halfway between the Cornavin train station and the Rhône at the level of the Ponts de l'Île, at the junction of the medieval district of Saint-Gervais and the so-called Ceinture Fazyste (Fazyist belt) built in the 19th century.

The open space that the square occupies was created in the 1950s, as part of a large-scale transformation of the faubourg of St.-Gervais.[2] The creation of the new void coincided with the construction of a group of buildings by Pierre Cahorn, which would form the major frontage of the square.[3] The historical architecture of this ensemble contrasts with the gabled facade of the modernist block that Marc-Joseph Saugey built at the same time (1951–1955) on the north side of the future square. At the foot of these two residential buildings are shops, cafés, and restaurants with the capacity to animate the public space. To the south, Place Simon-Goulart is defined by the 15th-century temple of Saint-Gervais. The fourth side of the square is bounded by the Rue des Terreaux-du-Temple, beyond which two schools are located (Fig. 3.1.10).

Despite its appearance, the Place Simon-Goulart is thus a relatively recent public space. Qualifying it with the term "public space" seems somewhat incongruous, given that only six years after its creation, in 1962, the square was transformed into a parking lot, a function that it would retain for nearly fifty years. The decisive turning point came in the summer of 2002, when a temporary pedestrian arrangement was tested and led to the decision to transform the existing parking lot into a pedestrian, user-friendly, urban square. This redevelopment was a godsend in the dense neighborhood of Saint-Gervais, which lacks recreational spaces (Fig. 3.1.9).[4]

The following year, the City of Geneva launched a competition in the form of parallel study contracts (*mandats d'étude parallèles*), with the aim of giving a new face to the square and its surroundings[5] (Fig. 3.1.8). The very synthetic objective expressed in the brief was simple: "to make Place Simon-Goulart pedestrian-friendly and to integrate the temple and its surroundings into the project."[6] The young Geneva firm, Atelier Descombes Rampini, took part in this selective procedure and won the contract in June 2003 with a project entitled "Aline."[7] In the eyes of the jury, it distinguished itself from the five other competing teams by the attention paid to the different uses of the square's proposed transformation.[8]

This concern is reflected in the project by a subdivision of the space into places defined by a differentiated treatment of the ground, suggesting varied functions and activities. The temple is highlighted by a slightly elevated square made of light-colored stone. A large gravel rectangle occupies the heart of the square and serves as a place of entertainment. A wooden terrace equipped with furniture elements allows for more leisurely activities and is itself bordered by an alignment of maple trees that act as a screen from the street. These different surfaces are unified by concrete paving, applied to the entire perimeter of the block, which marks the continuity of the sidewalk and the flow of movement. The only added elements are a circular fountain implanted in the square, which echoes the bench of the same shape placed in the southern part of the perimeter, and at the centre is a tree (Fig. 3.1.11–3.1.13).[9]

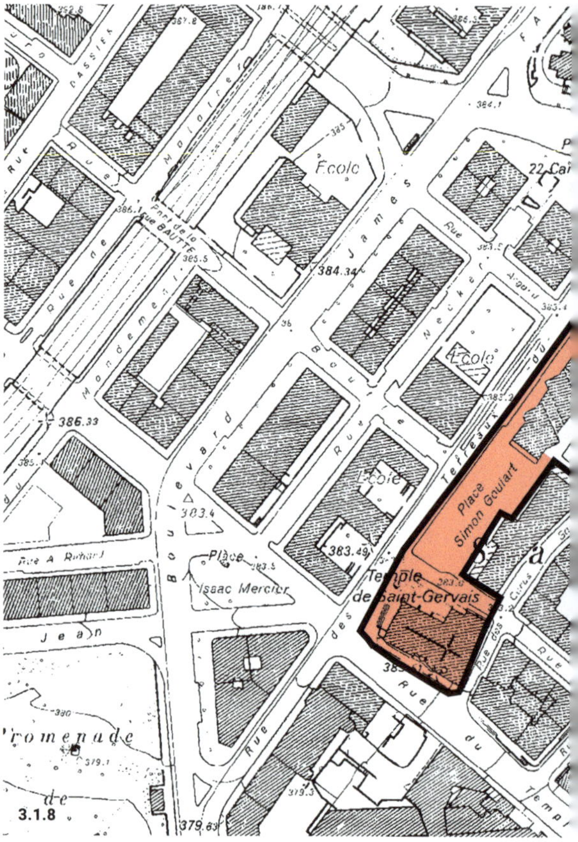

3.1.8

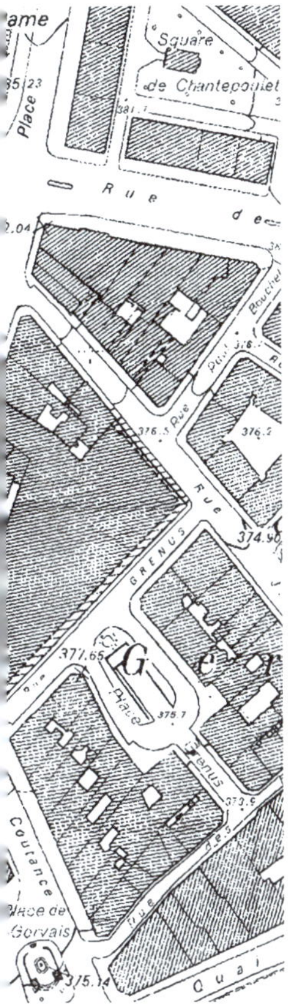

3.1.9

3.1.8 Parallel study contracts perimeter
In red – final intervention perimeter
3.1.9 Event "En ville sans ma voiture!," September 2002 **3.1.10** Photograph of the square before the redevelopment

Temple de Saint-Gervais

Group of buildings by Pierre Cahorn

Slab by Marc-Joseph Saugey

Rue des Terreaux-du-Temple

3.1.10

A HOMOGENEOUS ISLAND

Among the scarce preliminary sketches of the project, a preparatory digital drawing seems to be at the origin of the winning proposal, almost taking on an original conceptual quality. This working drawing testifies to the intention to make uniform the entire block targeted by the competition. On a cadastral plan they received, the architects schematically apply a regular, unidirectional pattern over the entire surface of the allotted perimeter (Fig. 3.1.14). This distinctive Geneva surfacing is characterized by a bush-hammered cement screed on which are applied false metal joints, oriented perpendicularly to the sidewalk edge, which simulate slabs of 1 m by 500 mm.[10] The reproduction of this style, specific to the city, immediately gives the space to be redesigned continuity with the city's larger scale network of public spaces.

The designers use this surfacing to unite the disparate textures and buildings that characterize this particular site, which they are careful to place in a larger context in two analytical diagrams (Fig. 3.1.15–3.1.16). They are interested in this site shaped by different urban and architectural developments, without adopting a nostalgic attitude toward its history, as the jury emphasized in its report: "The 'famous' historical analysis or filiation, leading to a project stance, is here supplanted by the simple desire to relate built elements that the vagaries of history have juxtaposed."[11]

This way of approaching the project, by taking an interest in the constitution of the target site while accepting it as a given state, is recurrent Geneva practice. The researcher Thierry Maeder identifies this particularity: "their projects are based (and forge themselves) on a preexisting substratum. Rather than replacing this substratum, they simply transform it."[12] Bruno Marchand also underlines this principle of "transformation," which is distinguished by "the taking into account of time periods, strata and the relationship to history,"[13] as being characteristic of the operating mode of Julien Descombes and Marco Rampini. He explains this in particular by the two architects' postgraduate training at the University of Geneva's Institute of Architecture (IAUG), which made this a "central teaching and project theme."[14] The geological terms "substratum" and "sedimentation" used by Maeder and Marchand suggest that the project of the public space or architectural project is superimposed, as an additional layer onto an existing context.[15]

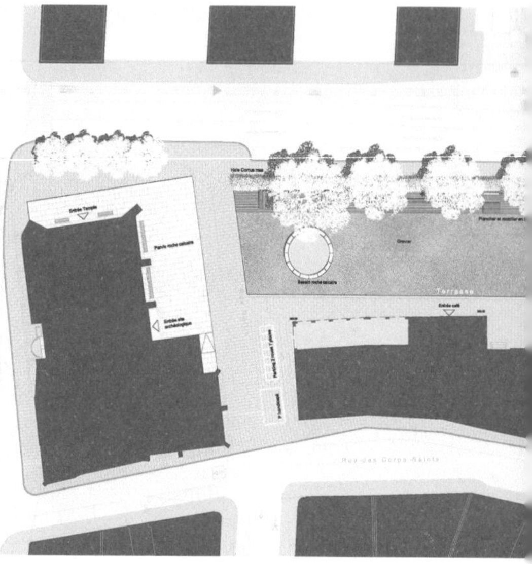

3.1.11–3.1.13 Plan and study model of the winning project. *(11) Atelier Descombes Rampini et al., "Aline," MEP presentation boards, June 2003; (12–13) Atelier Descombes Rampini et al., photographs, June 2003;* **3.1.14** Pavement pattern applied to the whole block. *Atelier Descombes Rampini, preparatory drawing, May 14, 2003* **3.1.15–3.1.16** Situation diagrams of the square in a wider context. *Atelier Descombes Rampini et al., "Aline," MEP presentation boards, June 2003*

PARTITIONING THE SPACE FOR DISTINCT FUNCTIONS

Within this common surfacing, the designers distinguish three subspaces that they list in the project presentation text: "a very wide sidewalk" on the Cornavin-Coutance street side will be mainly dedicated to movement and parking;[16] "a temple forecourt" aims to highlight the religious building; finally, in the center "a square" will host multiple activities. With these three denominations, the team recognizes the diversity of the block in terms of function and the different potential uses that it offers.

While the first of the three identified subspaces, the sidewalk, blends into the pre-established layout, the other two, defined as "major spaces,"[17] will be physically delineated to make them recognizable. This project stage, which the architects describe as "reworking the surface,"[18] is an opportunity to precisely define the shape and scale to be given to the square and to the temple forecourt. In a first variant, the delimitation of the latter already corresponds practically to its final form. On two sides of the religious building, a surface defined by lines parallel to the facades completes the whole to form an almost perfect rectangle (Fig. 3.1.17).

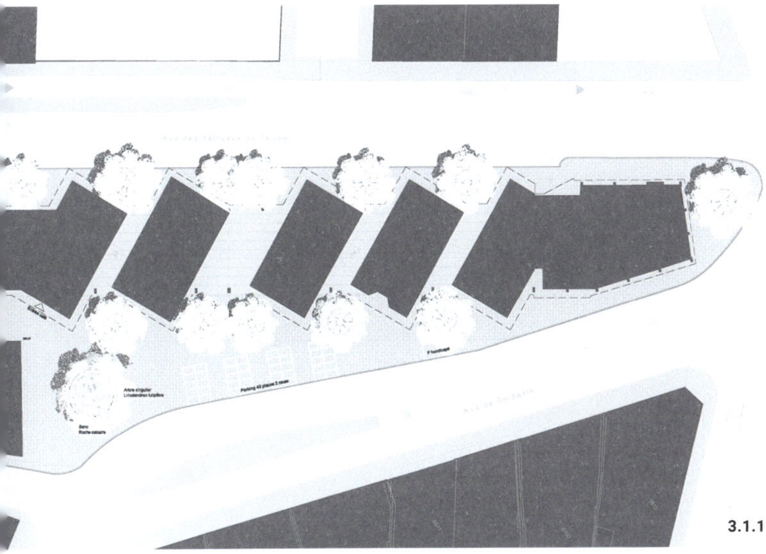

3.1.11

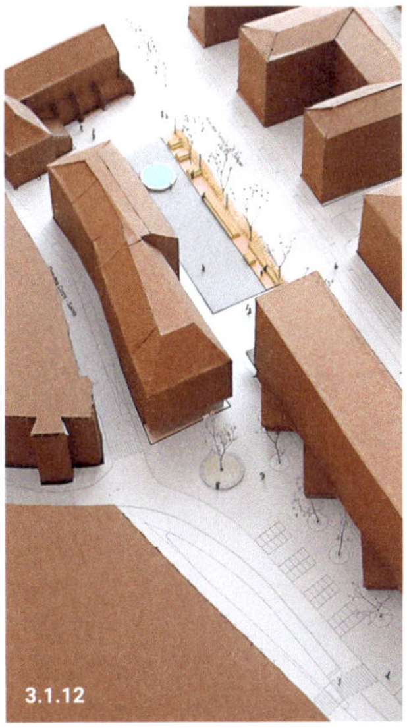

3.1.12

3.1.13

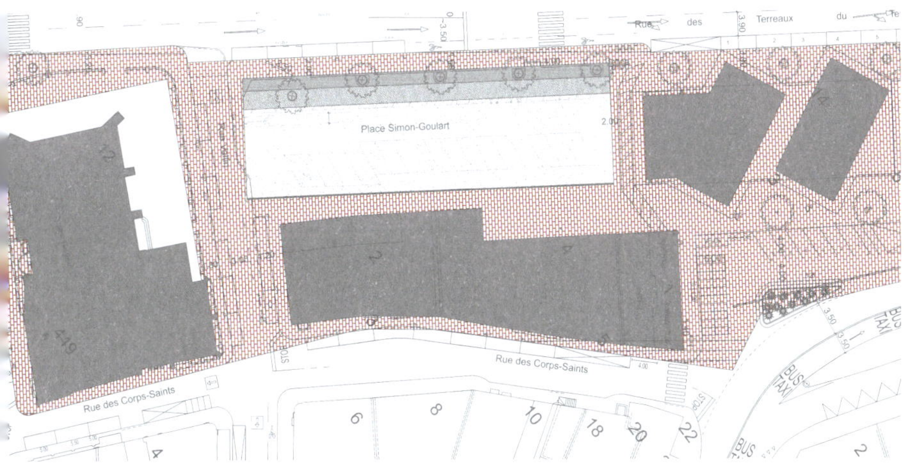

3.1.14

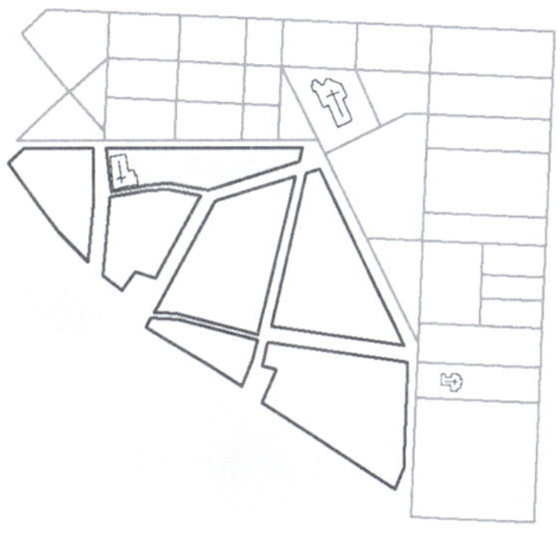

1 STRUCTURE DE LA VILLE
LE RHONE
- LE QUARTIER DE ST GERVAIS
- LA CEINTURE FAZYSTE

3.1.15

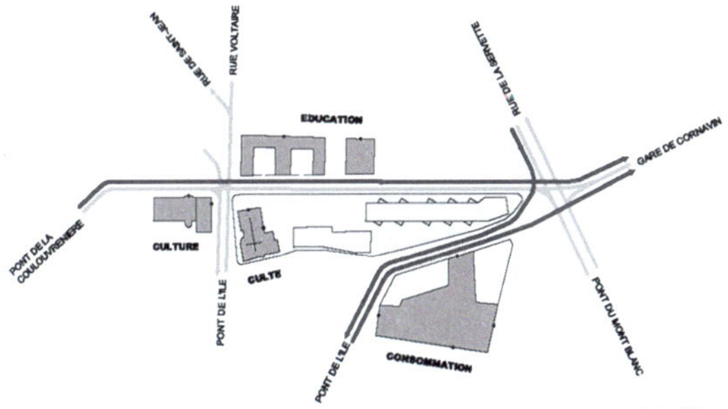

3.1.16

2 CONTEXTE URBAIN
EQUIPEMENT PUBLIC, TRAFIC, RESEAU TRANSPORT PUBLIC

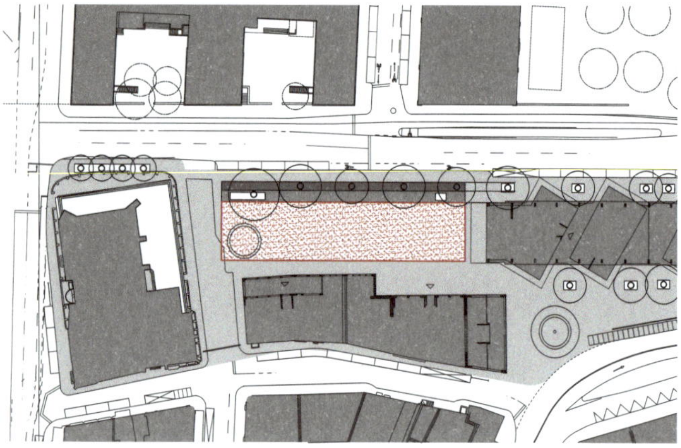

3.1.17

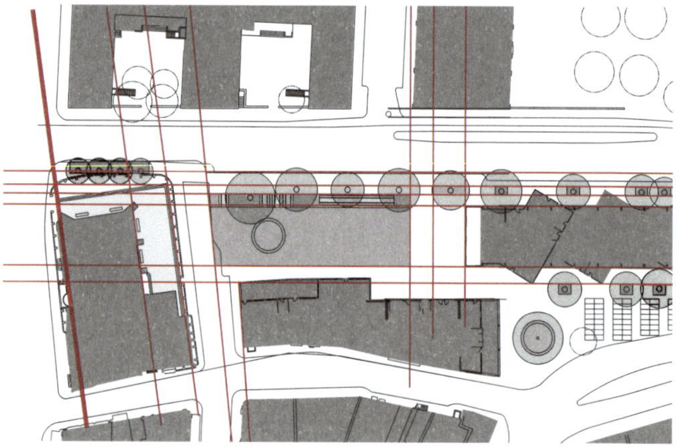

3.1.18

3.1.19

3.1.20

The square itself takes the form of a perfect quadrilateral, which at present occupies the largest possible area. The aim is to give it an "identifiable geometry"[19] in the words of the Geneva architects. In a later design, the strict orthogonality of the space is abandoned in order to orientate more clearly the movements to the south: the small side is now angled to align geometrically with the street and the temple of Saint-Gervais (Fig. 3.1.18). The square is also reduced on the northern side to ensure a passageway at the foot of the Marc-Joseph Saugey block.

This design document also reveals the construction features on which the architects rely to compose the public space. These features seem to be meticulously copied from the surrounding buildings. They testify to a desire on the part of the designers to guarantee continuity, both physical and visual, in order to offer a clear reading of the space. The ADR team nevertheless establishes a certain hierarchy between the different buildings: the temple of Saint-Gervais, the Saugey block, and the Necker elementary school predominate in dictating the geometry and dimensions of the future square.

3.1.17 A large quadrangle as a square. *Atelier Descombes Rampini, working drawing, May 20, 2003* **3.1.18** Composition derived from the surrounding buildings. *Atelier Descombes Rampini, working drawing, May 27, 2003* **3.1.19** Construction of the paved temple forecourt. *Atelier Descombes Rampini, site photographs, October 2012* **3.1.20** Reinterpretation of the Turbinenplatz bench. *Atelier Descombes Rampini, site photographs, May 2013* **3.1.21** Appropriation by skaters

Continuing their quest to define the space, the designers would focus on designing the fourth side of the square. Instead of the opaque wall planned in an initial working model, they finally opted for a planted hedge aimed solely at reducing "visual contact with traffic,"[20] without cutting themselves off from the other side of the street. The schoolchildren and students of the two schools who frequent the public space in large numbers as they leave school confirm the success of the project's development.

From this analysis of the square's composition, we finally note that the architects like to use simple geometric figures, most often quadrilaterals. These formal choices induce a certain abstraction of the layout and facilitate the spatial legibility of the square for future users. In the same spirit, the designers would install two circular furniture elements to serve as landmarks for passersby. The fountain in the square is identical in size and echoes the round bench at the foot of a tulip tree on the Coutance street side (Fig. 3.1.11–3.1.12, p. 72–73).

MATERIALITY AT THE SERVICE OF SPATIAL ORGANIZATION

To this division of space is added the choice of surfacing intended to specify the role and value of each subspace. The Atelier Descombes Rampini seeks to combine materials, colors, and patterns to further characterize the different areas. The temple's forecourt is covered with paving slabs of limestone, a noble material worthy of the religious building. Cut in multiple large formats, its light color recalls that of the temple's plinth[21] (Fig. 3.1.19).

The square itself will be subdivided into two areas. The larger to be left free except for the circular fountain planned to the south. This is bordered by a smaller area comprising a wooden terrace, where there is a large banquet table surrounded by three large platforms, reinterpreting the banquette developed by the architects for their Turbinenplatz project (Zurich, 2000–2003) (Fig. 3.1.20, and Fig. 2.32 p. 54).[22]

As for the square's ground cover, it was initially envisaged as a gravel surface. However, in terms of maintenance, the crushed material was considered "not very compatible with a place of passage"[23] by the competition jury and also not suitable for the possible markets or one-off events envisaged for the square at the time of the selection procedure. Therefore, the designers decided to cover the surface with anthracite colored concrete as homogeneous as possible, to ensure that the surface is perceived as a single and unique element.[24] Tango dancers and skaters, among others, now enjoy this particularly smooth surface (Fig. 3.1.21–3.1.23). The anthracite color of the concrete was chosen to contrast with the light-colored surface that covers the rest of the block, as the architects explain: "We suddenly have this very smooth concrete surface that stands out in a world more attentive to finding connections with its surrounding structures."[25] It is a question of materially defining the square to affirm its importance.

The designers carefully choose, develop, and reinterpret specific materials and forms to clarify the spatial organization of the previously defined plot and to encourage the citizens to appropriate the space. Sometimes the choice of materials is subject to a reading of the built context, sometimes it is distinguished by privileging a question of perception and use. The design is nevertheless discreet and adopts a resolutely urban vocabulary by using common mineral surfacings – poured concrete, slab patterned concrete and stone paving – equipped with mainly wooden furniture.

URBAN STORYTELLING AS A PROJECT TOOL

In these different choices of materials, the designers are content to distinguish places for various practices: active or passive, mobile or static, collective or individual, exceptional or everyday. Nonetheless, they show restraint, being careful not to freeze the spaces by establishing precise uses. The economy of the proposal's project elements should not, however, lead to a reduction in the efforts made by the designers to achieve this openness to multiple uses. On the contrary, the design process reveals the extent to which anticipation of uses takes on a central role and is far more elaborate than it appears. It is already illustrated at the stage of the selection procedure, in a text outlining the urban life to take place in Simon-Goulart:

"Morning, noon and evening, day and night. For the neighborhood or the passers-by, because we also pass by frequently. On the way down to the city center, between two courses, after a show at the Saint-Gervais theater, during Saturday shopping, at four o'clock after school, on the way to the Cornavin train station, to the Saint-Gervais temple or to a party at the Salle du Faubourg. For a drink, for a snack, for a neighborhood party, to splash around in the water, to eat on the go, to discuss current events or exchange banalities. At the edge of the city, along the city's boulevards, the opportunity for a break for the urban center's inhabitants and users."[26]

The square appears as a place for everyday life, where the designers take the trouble to describe the moments that define it. The narrative of the urban life there is mainly about moments of meeting and sharing. Public space is undeniably a place for gathering in small or larger groups. We can also imagine a more solitary configuration, where individuals could simply witness the scenes described and thereby have the feeling of "belonging,"[27] in a collective dimension specific to urban environments.

The narrative part of this presentation text goes beyond the sole objective of a communication statement intended to sway the competition jury. It proves to be a valuable working tool, which feeds the designers' project development. Imagining the range of possible appropriations and real-life experiences of a place allows a response that is as close as possible to the future expectations. To do this, they also explore scenarios that emerge from working models used to test spatial configurations. They will thus stage: a convivial meeting around the large "banquet table," a furtive nap on a bench, a chance encounter while crossing the square, a more introspective moment, such as a "street ballet" told by Jane Jacobs[28] (Fig. 3.1.24–3.1.27).

3.1.22

3.1.23

3.1.22–3.1.23 Materiality at the service of spatial organization. *(23) Atelier Descombes Rampini, site photograph, May 2013*

COMMUNAL PLACES, BETWEEN BANALITY AND COMMUNITY

This approach allows the designers to conceive the benches in such a way as to guarantee a wide range of possible uses. Larger than the archetypal Turbinenplatz that serves as a model, they will easily accommodate an after-school group of students from nearby schools. With this seating, appearing as large sofas, people are encouraged to relax comfortably, as in a living room. Thus the authors of the project succeed in giving a community scale to domesticity. Such domestic conviviality is also found around the long banquet table, which evokes a large family reunion or a country feast.

In terms of language, the essence of this project lies in the search for a subtle mix between the banality of the forms, materials, and plant species used and the desired conviviality of the layout, tinged with domestic or village references. This aspiration is expressed in the term "*Des lieux communs*" (communal and common places) with which the winning team begins its project presentation text in June 2003. The French adjective "*commun*" can indeed be interpreted as a synonym for ordinary. The architects, who like to play with the meaning of words, probably also associate it with the meaning of collective or community. These two terms combined seek to inscribe the Place Simon-Goulart as somewhere that would stand out in the network of public spaces in Geneva, more by its practices than by its form and materials. In this sense, the users will remember the uses that can be made of it more than its spatial characteristics. The fact remains that the conceptual stripe of uses constituted by the furnished wooden terrace here, when pushed to its extreme, becomes a sort of icon of the square, which cannot be found anywhere else.

3.1.24

3.1.25

3.1.26

3.1.27

3.1.24–3.1.27 Staging of urban scenes in a model. *Atelier Descombes Rampini, photographs of model, June 4, 2003*

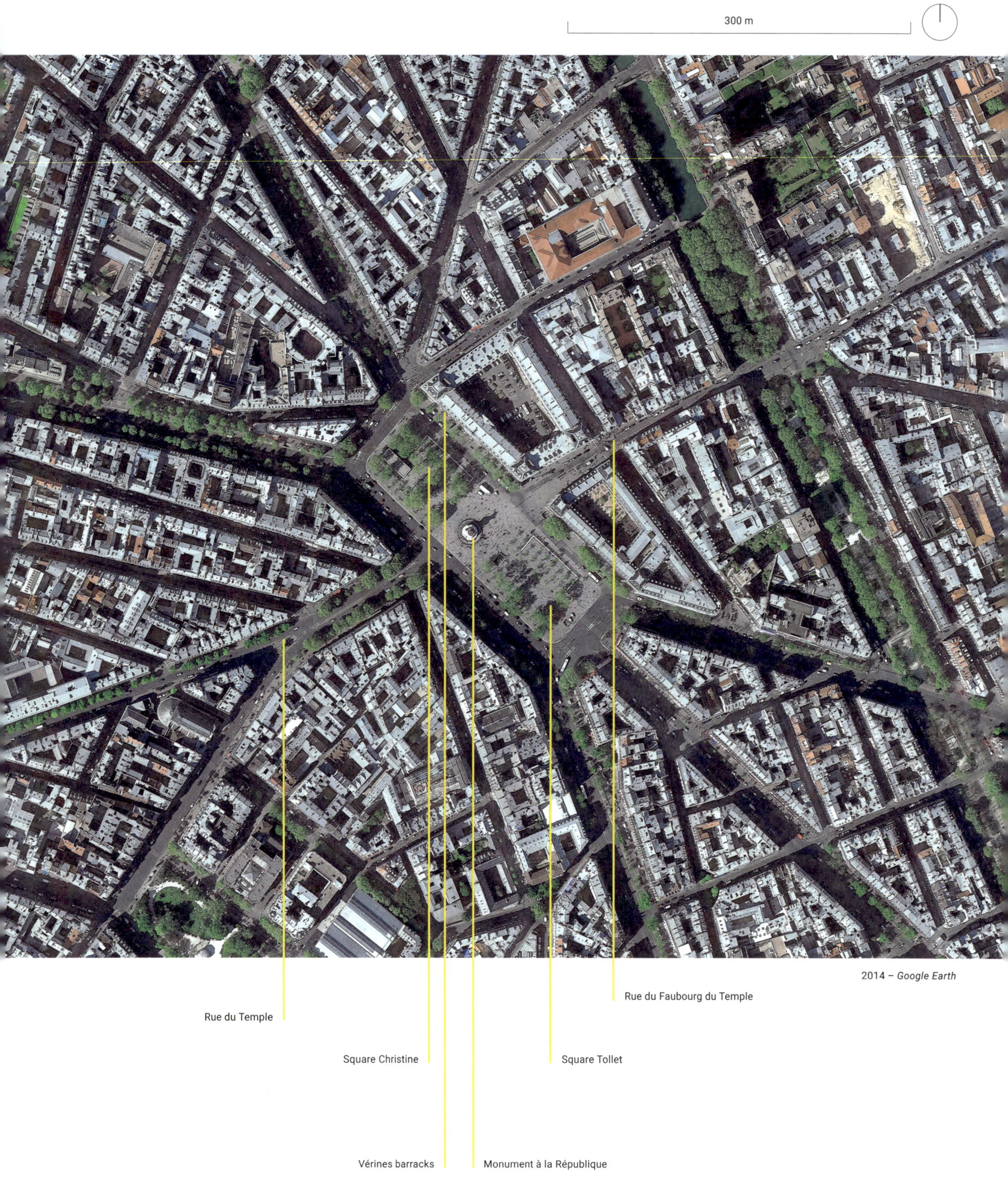

3.1.28 Location of the Place de la République at the intersection of seven major axes of the capital

PLACE DE LA RÉPUBLIQUE PARIS 2009–2013

Location Paris, France **Client** City of Paris – Roads and Transportation Department (DVD) **Lead designers** Trévelo & Viger-Kohler Architectes Urbanistes (project leaders – Paris) / Areal (landscape architects) – Martha Schwartz Partners (landscape architects) **Type of commission** Selected competition (2009–2010) **Construction** 2012–2013 **Former status** Square consisting of a double roundabout essentially dedicated to traffic **Area** 3.4 ha including 2 ha of pedestrian area after redevelopment

In April 2009, the city of Paris launched an international design competition for one of the capital's most emblematic public spaces: the Place de la République. The Place de la République stands out because of its size; its surface area of nearly 3.4 hectares (120 × 280 m) makes it one of the largest squares in Paris. Initially occupied by a water tower, at around 1865 under the Haussmann administration, it was to take the shape we know today. Its composition was the subject of many reflections before the inauguration of its final layout in 1883 (Fig. 3.1.29–3.1.31). The installation of the monument to the Republic by Charles and Léopold Morice, erected on this occasion, gave its name to the square, which then acquired a symbolic value, becoming the site of numerous political events.[29] More than a century later, according to the town councillors who decided to undertake its transformation, the almost unchanged layout of the Place de la République no longer reflected this symbolic status.

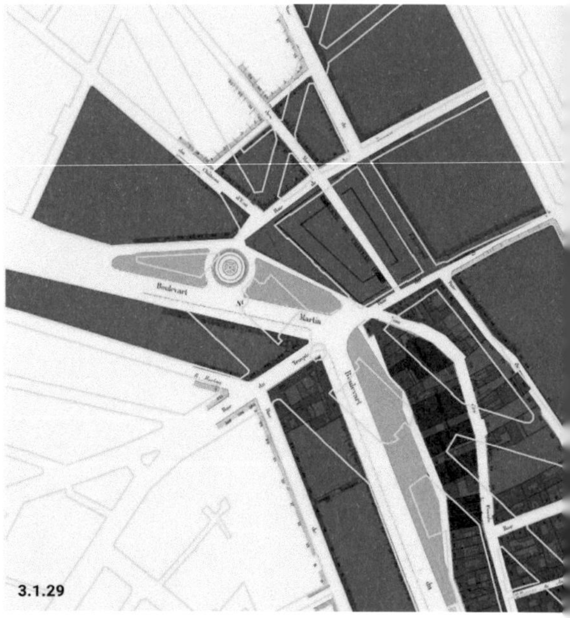
3.1.29

The public space qualifies as a "square" only in that it possesses the qualities of a hard surfaced area defined by four built facades. In fact, the void it occupies is totally subservient to the traffic flowing through the seven major arteries that converge there in a star-shaped plan dominated by the Morice brothers' monument. The square itself is presented as a double roundabout, each of which is occupied by a public space, respectively named Tollet and Christine. These two island spaces, while devoted to pedestrians, are difficult to access because of the six traffic lanes to be crossed, and hence are little used (Fig. 3.1.32–3.1.33).

From among 72 international bids submitted in response to the Paris City Council's call for entry in 2009, the jury selected five teams to submit a development proposal.[30] The brief is based on a prior consultation conducted with residents and users of the square.[31] One of the main objectives highlighted in the document is to generate "a popular and convivial square that creates social links and embodies the values of the Republic."[32] Competitors are invited to consider the notions of suitability, versatility, and multiplicity of uses. These uses should relate to the neighborhood and daily life, implying thinking in terms of openness and conviviality, but also of large political, festive, or cultural gatherings on the scale of the capital. Strongly focused on this question of practices and uses, the text nevertheless mentions the importance of dialogue with the square's built heritage, taking particular care to highlight "its architectural composition and major urban alignments."[33]

The Parisian agency Trévelo & Viger-Kohler (TVK), in association with the landscape architect Martha Schwartz and her Luxembourg colleagues AREAL,[34] won the competition in early 2010. The team proposes to radically pedestrianize the intersection by creating a vast pedestrian esplanade (2 ha) attached to the northeast front of the square. While seeking unity of space through this layout plan, the designers propose a bipartite division of the area lengthwise, to accommodate different uses through distinct ambiences. The esplanade is to be bypassed by a reduced seven-lane roadway. The southern sidewalks will be widened to encourage pedestrian movement, while allowing for outdoor extensions of existing shops and cafés (Fig. 3.1.34–3.1.35).

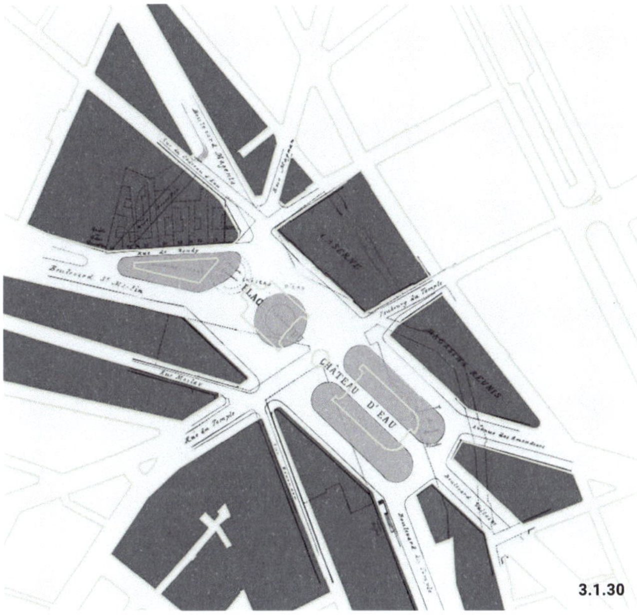

3.1.30

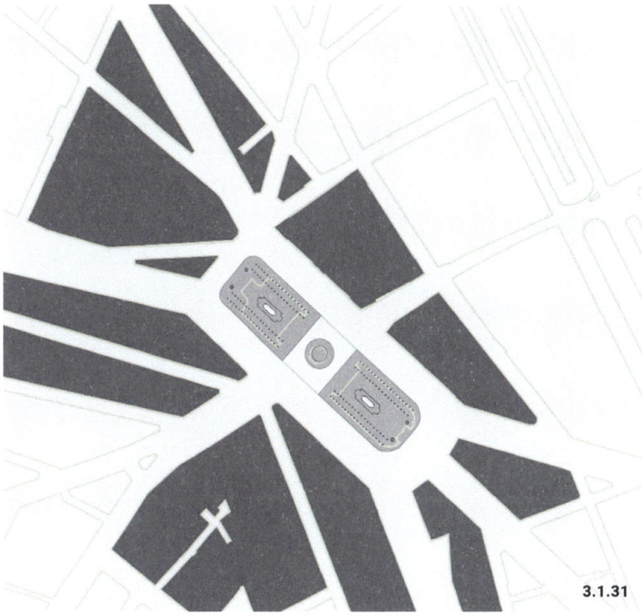

3.1.31

3.1.29–3.1.31 Evolution of the square 1811 / 1867 / 1884 **3.1.32–3.1.33** State of the Tollet and Christine squares in 2009

3.1.32

3.1.33

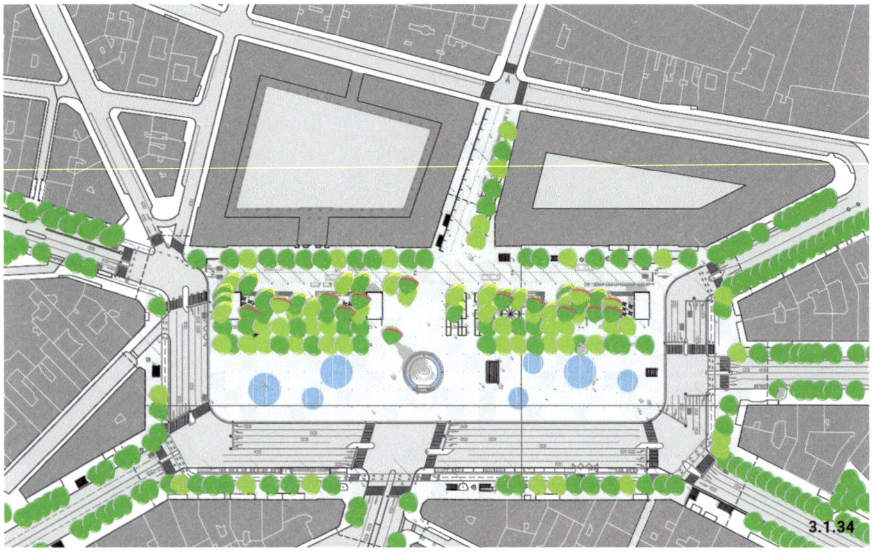

3.1.34

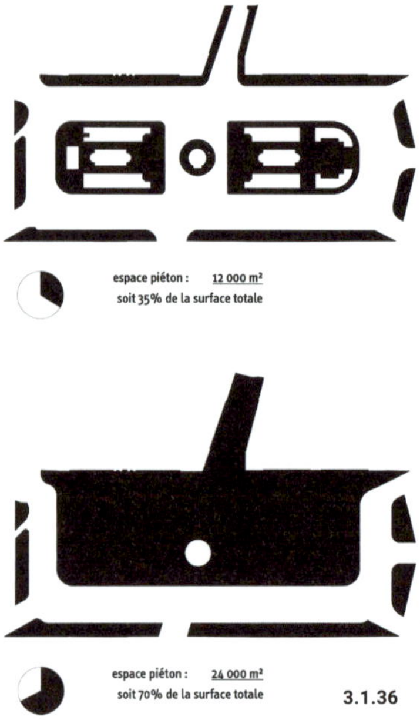

3.1.36

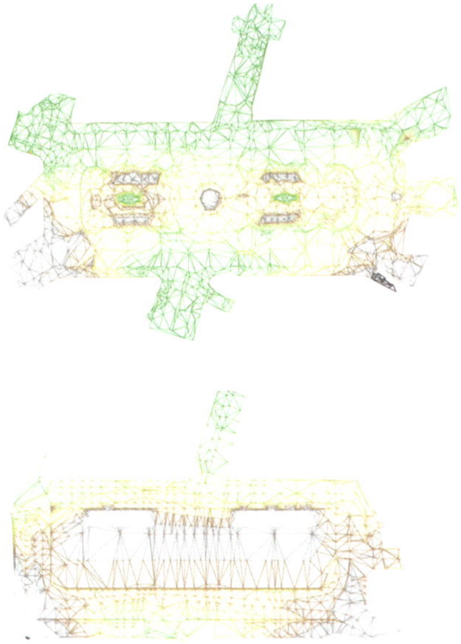

3.1.37

3.1.34–3.1.35 General plan and aerial view of the winning project. *TVK et al., competition entry, November 2009*
3.1.36 Pedestrian areas doubled by the project. *TVK et al., diagram, n.d.*
3.1.37 From fragmentation to unity of space. Representation of the levels of the square before and after the intervention. *TVK and Atec, diagram, n.d.*

3.1.35

A LARGE PEDESTRIAN ESPLANADE

In the notice that accompanies its competition boards, the team led by TVK makes the following observation: "The road surface is enormous and its structure (two traffic circles, one beside the other) dictates its terms. On the other hand, the pedestrian space is illegible, fragmented, and static. There is no unity." The designers continue, "To elevate the square to its full potential, a radical transformation is required."[35] This will be achieved by creating a vast esplanade, removing the site's road traffic character, and doubling the pedestrian area (Fig. 3.1.36). The quest for unity will be ensured by this new platform, which it is hoped will be homogeneous in its form as well as in its materiality.

In terms of form, two aspects of the square are to be addressed: its continuity and its flatness. Indeed, the designers observe that the overall surface of the old square is not only fragmented into several functional surfaces but that it is also domed. To make it a recognizable entity, they will not only try to unify it but also make it decidedly flat, allowing a reading of the public space as a continuous surface from one side to the other, in the longitudinal sense. Transversely, steps are to correct the difference in level along the northeast side (Fig. 3.1.37).

Through this careful groundwork, the TVK team manages to create a continuous plateau that will contribute to "making the exceptional dimension of the space of the square perceptible, offering it the monumentality that it had never managed to generate," as the critic Emmanuel Caille points out.[36] Applying this leveling to the entire public space will also make it possible to appreciate the homogeneity of the composition of the Haussmann facades that border it. In this sense, the project includes a dimension of embellishment that is in keeping with the tradition of French urban design.

It remained for the TVK team to determine the extent and especially the exact form that this esplanade will take. In a first variant, it explores the idea of joining the two squares to form a single one in the center (Fig. 3.1.38). A second option is to completely eliminate the squares by extending the northeast and southwest sidewalks to the road to form four separate esplanades. Two road axes intersect in the center of the void around the Republic monument, which retains its function as a roundabout (Fig. 3.1.39). These two drawings respond to a strictly symmetrical rationale for composition that confirms the desired principle of spatial unity. But these sketches do not appear to satisfy the designers, who seek to more clearly affirm the change in status of this intersection.

A DIFFERENCE DICTATED BY USES

In the course of formal research, the TVK team comes up with the solution we know today, a vast rectangle connected to the northeast front of the square, ensuring pedestrian continuity from the Rue du Faubourg du Temple to the Canal Saint-Martin (Fig. 3.1.40). They thus decide both to occupy the center of the public space and to connect it to the city by extending it along this long side. The radical choice of asymmetry, which some attribute to a contribution by Martha Schwartz,[37] responds to interpretations of the context that are new and emblematic of new concerns surrounding the question of public space development.

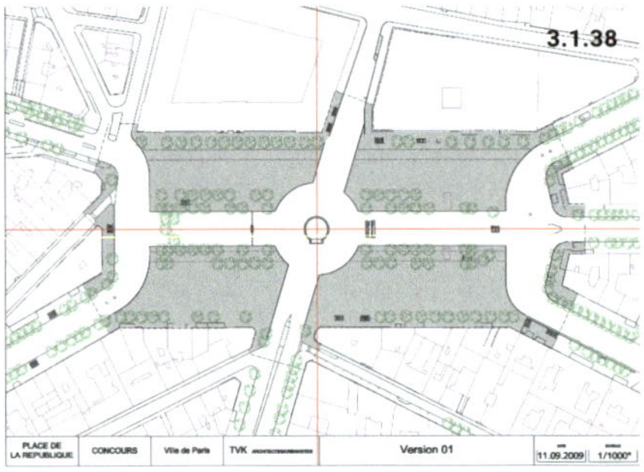

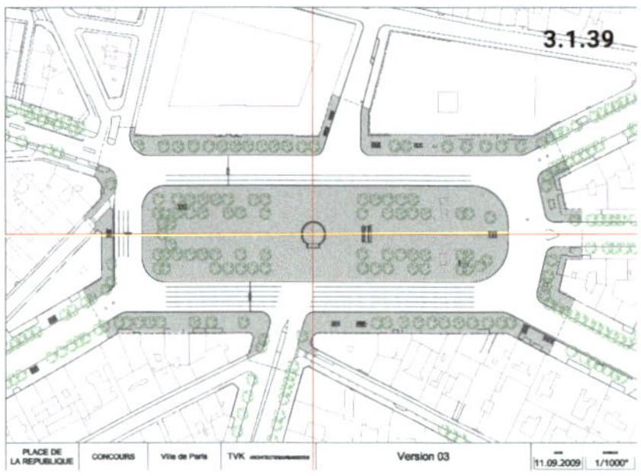

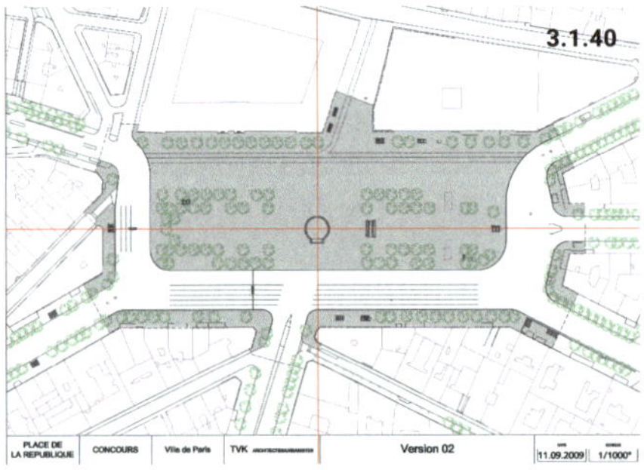

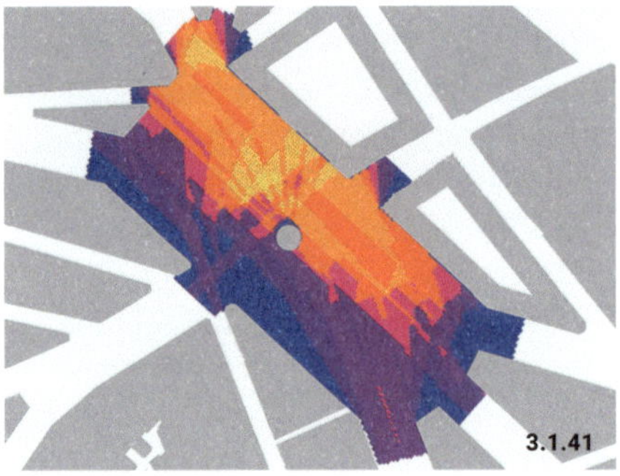

3.1.38–3.1.40 Some variations explored by the TVK team before finding the final shape of the square. *TVK et al., plan, September 11, 2009. Added symmetry axes and pedestrian surface highlighted by Sonia Curnier* **3.1.41** Study of sunlight on the square. *TVK and Transsolar, diagram, s.d.* **3.1.42** Aerial view of the plaza after restoration of the plane tree alignment. *TVK et al., new version of the square, September 2010*

3.1.42

On the one hand, it is the result of the designers recognizing a "functional dissymmetry" [38] of the square. In effect, they identify distinct occupations of the buildings, and in particular of their first floors, which border the two long sides of the space. To the southwest, the sidewalks are animated by small shops, cafés, and restaurants, while the northeast is distinguished by two large courtyard blocks occupied respectively by a few department stores and the imposing Vérines barracks, which according to the designers could be redeveloped.[39] In addition to these curricular differences, there is an "environmental and climatic dissymmetry"[40] that the authors of the project identify with the help of the Transsolar agency specialized in climatic engineering. Because of its orientation, the square has distinct zones in terms of sunlight and wind exposure. To maximize the comfort and use of the esplanade, the designers therefore will decide to favor the northern surface, which is more pleasant from a climate perspective (Fig. 3.1.41).[41]

By prioritizing the functional and environmental conditions of the place, the designers openly reject the Haussmann-style symmetrical composition of the square and the continuity of the great urban arteries – two factors to which the competition brief had nevertheless drawn attention.[42] Through this gesture to asymmetry, they affirm a new reading of urban morphology, no longer considered as a heritage ensemble to be imperatively enhanced, but rather as a context to be analyzed from different angles, with particular reference to current concerns. The conviviality of the square and the user's comfort are to take precedence over its relationship to the built fabric.

HESITATIONS BETWEEN MODULATION AND UNITY

In a second stage, the designers will try to modulate this large unitary space to make it more easily usable. At the competition stage, it is proposed to divide the square in two along its length, categorically confirming its asymmetry. The northeastern half, qualified as a "garden," is to be mainly dedicated to daily and local uses. It is to be covered by a dense mass of vegetation and structured by steps creating terraces with pavilions. An empty "square" complements this structured area, acting as a multipurpose and metropolitan space, suitable for large gatherings. At the center of, and enhanced by, this vast empty space will be the statue of the Republic.

But this spatial and functional modulation was to gradually disappear in favor of a more homogeneous layout. The most important change would be the sudden abandonment of the bipartite division of the square, which was to occur directly after the end of the competition. At the request of the client,[43] the TVK team would be required to re-establish the double tree line to the south of the square (Fig. 3.1.42).

Other simplifications of the project would emanate from the will of the designers or from more technical constraints (Fig 3.1.43–3.1.45). The originally planned circular pools were to be transformed, with the help of the fountain designer Jean Max Llorca, into a large rectangular mirror located to the north of the statue of the Republic. A wooden "deck" available for various uses was to serve as the southern counterpart. The winning team would also decide to simplify the area delimited by steps to the northeast. The four initial terraces were to be transformed into two; more generous and freely adaptable. Of the multiple kiosks originally planned on each terrace, only one pavilion would remain, moved to the central axis of the square due to the subway's right of way.[44]

Thus, from a clear two-part composition, the designers finish with a more complex and stratified approach. The metropolitan and local scale, to which the initial dichotomous division referred, will be reconciled in an overall project, where the square in its entirety symbolizes the urban character and diversity of Paris. The different zones thus characterized will encourage a multitude of uses on this large site, but "the permanent continuity of the ground"[45] will always guarantee the square's unity.

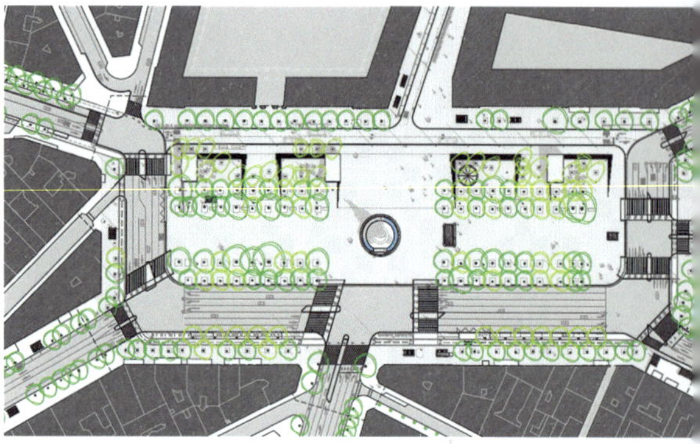

3.1.43

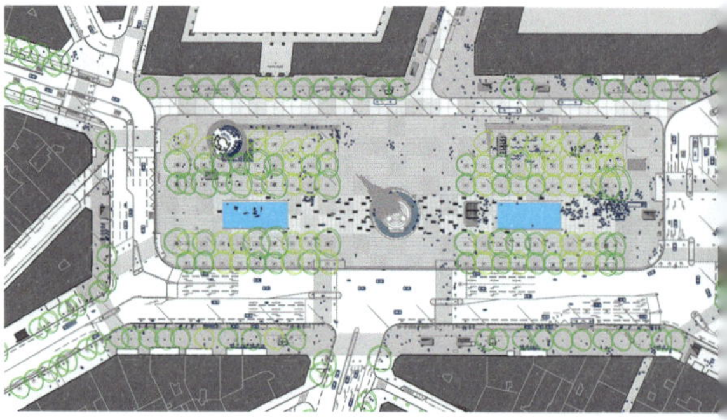

3.1.44

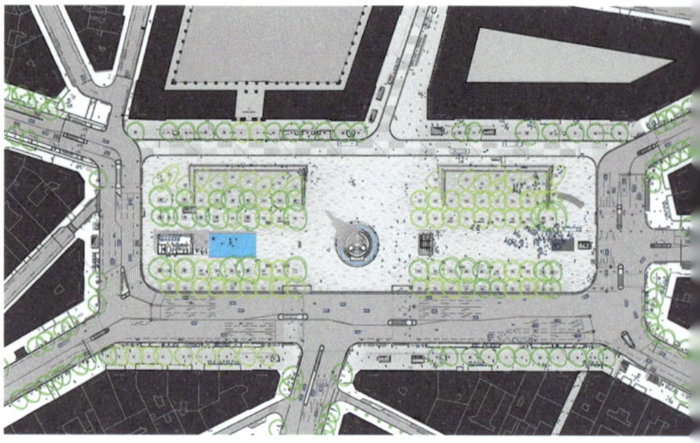

3.1.45

A SURFACE, SIMULTANEOUSLY SPECIAL AND COMMONPLACE

The idea of a large, continuous surface remained and became simpler as the project developed. The layout of this central component of the development occupies the designers' attention during the three years that separate obtaining the commission from the square's inauguration. The choice of prefabricated, textured concrete slabs measuring one meter by two meters had already been made at competition stage. There was talk of using them to create a large checkerboard. This singular pattern, which is to prevail for several years, is finally abandoned in favor of a random texture according to a principle of "pixels," producing a subtle texture (Fig. 3.1.46–3.1.47). By abandoning the idea of a recognizable graphic pattern, the designers endow the square with a more ordinary character than originally expressed, without, however, rendering it totally neutral and insignificant.

The project constantly oscillates between this desire to make the square distinctive while at the same time inscribing it in the Parisian context. This ambiguity has already been observed in the composition of public space, which seeks to make the place and the surrounding facades legible while denying the symmetry inherited from the Haussmann period. The paving material also reveals this ambiguity. By its minerality, concrete assumes something relatively banal. But this material is at the same time distinctive, given that its use in Parisian public space is not at all common. Its formulation is developed specifically for the Place de la République,[46] to respond both to sensory considerations – texture inviting people to sit directly on the ground, reflective qualities – and to the practical consideration of robustness (Fig. 3.1.48–3.1.50).

For Pierre-Alain Trévelo, partner at TVK, this choice of a distinctive covering is not insignificant. It creates a relationship between the ground surface and the Haussmann facades. In his opinion, this is a requirement of the enhancement, offering "a new point of view on the late 19th-century architecture by the effect of a very strong contrast between concrete and stone."[47] But in an older text, the designers made other statements, claiming a search for belonging in terms of tones, describing concrete as a material that allows "the use of monochrome tints that integrate into the colorimetric continuity of Parisian paving and roofs."[48] The concrete of the Place de la République will thus be both special and commonplace, absolute and contextual, depending on how one reads it (and how the architects' narrative is updated).

ABSTRACTION AND SIMPLIFICATION OF THE AREA

Though the developed paving is specific to the Place de la République, it is nevertheless almost abstract and minimal in its expression. For Trévelo, it is indeed fundamental to transform a space by avoiding recourse to "things too easily visible, too easily transferable, too easily dated or too directly related to its author."[49]

This sought-after abstract characteristic is also expressed in the references summoned by the architects. In a late collage, we find models such as Philip Johnson's Glass House (1949), whose thin structure and transparency are to be used to

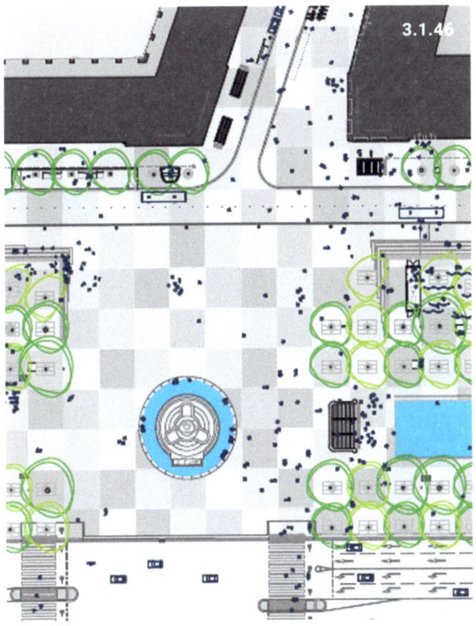

3.1.46

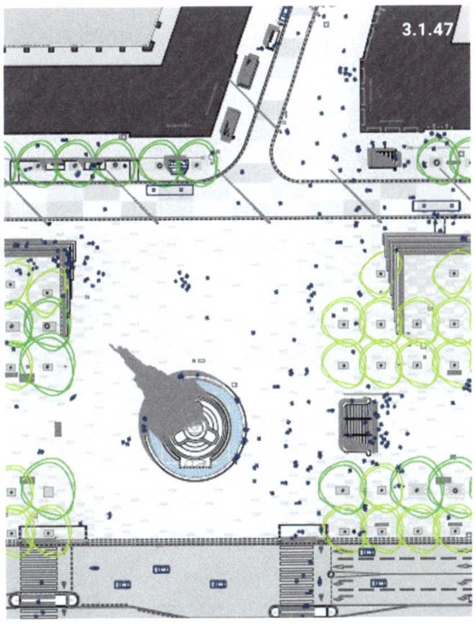

3.1.47

3.1.48

3.1.49

3.1.50

3.1.43–3.1.45 Successive simplifications of the leveling and layout of the square. *(43) TVK et al., general plan, September 2010; (44) TVK et al., general plan, June 2011; (45) TVK et al., general plan, May 2013* **3.1.46–3.1.47** Evolution of the design of the square's surfacing. *(46) TVK et al., general plan, July 2011; (47) TVK et al., final plan, June 2013* **3.1.48–3.1.49** Prototypes of concrete slabs studied in the workshop for the tactile and aesthetic qualities of the material. *TVK et al., prototype photographs, April and June 2011* **3.1.50** A simultaneously specific and common ground

design the pavilion in the square (Fig. 3.1.51). In the same drawing, the Superstudio collective's Supersurface (1971) is evoked by the group of hippies in the foreground. This formal analogy later appears repeatedly in the documents of the TVK team, who juxtapose their completed project with the visionary one of the Florentine architects.[50]

In the design of the square, the geometric figures used by the designers, the rectangles of the slabs and the pavilion, as well as the circular fountain-base of the monument, are emblematic of the simplicity to which they aspire. This desire for effacement will also be achieved by an economy of constructive details, which implies careful design work. All the "added" elements – ventilation grids for the metro station, tree planting containers, bus shelters, pavilions, and fountains – will fit as much as possible into the grid defined by the square's paving. As for the furniture, it will be as sparse as possible, with only a few large wooden benches placed at the foot of the plane trees.[51]

The new Place de la République is thus resolutely displayed as a pure and abstract space. Moreover, several critics have pointed out this "minimal" character of the layout,[52] probably appearing to be a sufficiently exceptional aspect in the production of public spaces at the beginning of the 21st century to be noteworthy. For Emmanuel Caille, this restraint would have an effect on the general perception of the public space: "All of the installations – the inevitable water mirror, the benches, the pavilion-cafe – deliberately sober, appear to strive to escape the anecdotal (perhaps overly so in the case of the pavilion) in order to give the square its monumental status."[53] Landscape architect and theorist Tim Waterman believes that this "simple austerity allows the warmth of human activity to fill the space," thereby associating it with qualities of use and atmosphere.[54]

Widely acclaimed by the local and international specialized press, the new uncluttered Place de la République was nevertheless the object of more virulent criticism by the architect Françoise Fromonot. The latter feared that the pared-down layout would make the place "conducive to permanent congestion by an intense program of events and the material supports attached to it [...]" and that, conversely, "when not much happens there or when there are not many people there – there are still 2 hectares of flat surfacing that does not succeed in validating an area of such scale."[55]

AMBIGUITY OF LAYOUT

In the eyes of the project authors, this purification of the layout is nonetheless essential to guarantee the principle of *reversibility* of use guiding its conception. They readily describe the square as "a vast open field,"[56] "an open stage for multiple urban uses," "an available and adaptable platform," or "a vast usable space."[57] With these designations, they aim to describe the openness of their project to all possibilities.

To affirm this goal, the TVK team seeks to illustrate the versatility of the envisioned public space in its competition presentation. It then calls upon the draftsman Martin Etienne to create sketches to demonstrate the capacity of the site to host successively different types of festive, political, and cultural events, while guaranteeing a coexistence with more ordinary uses (Fig. 3.1.52–3.1.55).

Subsequently, the TVK team again solicits the illustrator to freely imagine possible uses of the future public space (Fig. 3.1.56–3.1.57). This time the catalog is no longer used as a communication narrative intended to convince a competition jury,

3.1.51

3.1.52

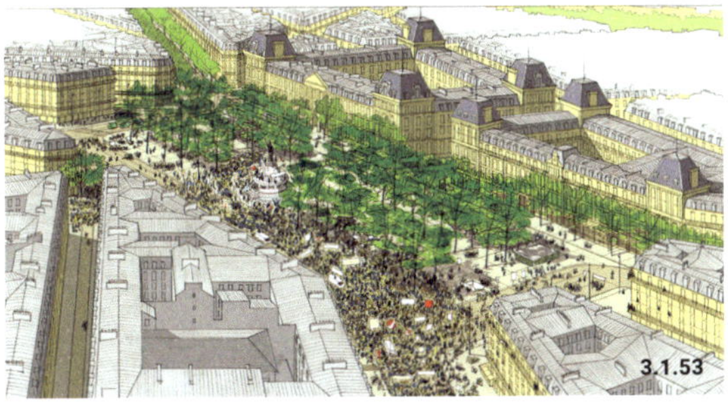

3.1.53

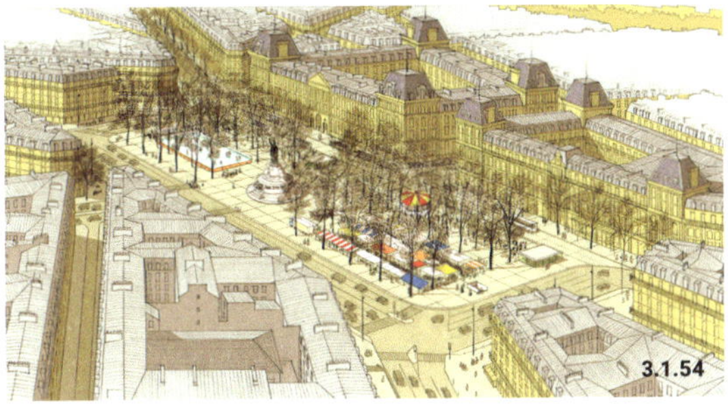

3.1.54

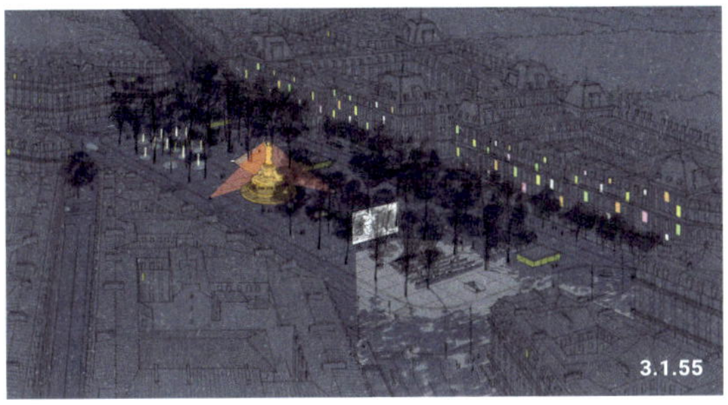

3.1.55

3.1.51 Illustration of the future square with Philip Johnson's Glass House (far left) and the hippies living in Superstudio's Supersurface (center). *TVK et al., perspective-collage, n.d. [video tracing the construction of the collage, dated 2010]* **3.1.52 –3.1.55** Illustrations of the reversibility of uses on the square by Martin Etienne. *Martin Etienne, TVK et al., competition entry, November 2009*

but as a working tool. The drawings are intended to feed into the design process. Indeed, even if the designers imagine the accommodation of a multitude of uses, they wish to ensure that others are not excluded.[58]

They have to find a balance between defining the public space sufficiently to encourage its use, while avoiding over-characterizing or freezing it. As Trévelo explains, "What we can do is not only allow the possibility of new currently unimaginable uses, but also encourage them. The more one puts oneself in a position to accept them, to make oneself available to them, the more one arouses them, the more one makes the design capable of allowing them to appear of their own accord."[59] Through its purification and abstraction, the design of the Place de la République is thus deliberately "equivocal."[60] The designers were content to define the framework conditions of a square, which would subsequently be appropriated, diverted, and sometimes even abused by a multitude of users. In this way, they show a certain letting go, presenting their work not as a finished piece,[61] but as an initiating gesture, leaving room for unexpected creativity by the city's inhabitants.

3.1.56–3.1.57 General panorama and details of potential occupations of the square envisaged by Martin Etienne. *Martin Etienne, TVK et al., panorama of uses, November 2011*

3.1.56

3.1.57

CREATING THE COMMONS

Restore value to public space

Analysis of the two projects confirms that the question of use is indeed foremost in the designers' minds at all stages. This preoccupation is principally illustrated by the desire to affirm the predominance of pedestrians over cars. The Place de la République approaches this re-conquest in a radical manner, even going so far as to use numbers to prove it. In Simon-Goulart, it is not so much maximizing pedestrian space (the block to be treated becomes inaccessible to vehicles as a whole), but more defining a square with an "identifiable shape." In both cases, the aim is to define a place that city dwellers will feel comfortable in.

It is also a question of ensuring that the place they create will be adopted by the citizens. The aim is to enhance a banal and routine urban practice, by inviting users to linger in the public space through social and recreational activities. In the Place de la République, the role of the public space as a place for civic gathering, debate, and protest is also taken into account. The strategies and working methods developed by the Atelier Descombes Rampini and TVK teams to ensure and encourage this multitude of uses reveal strong similarities. In particular, they use the realities of urban life in the form of text, staging of models, or even drawings to describe the versatility and capacity of the public space they wish to develop. These tools are used to convince the various external actors as well as for internal assurance of the proposed development's usage value.

A changing relationship between the surfacing and the material context

In both projects, the spatial formalization of these objectives begins with a ground plan, which is then developed with the help of design elements. If these approaches seem similar at first glance, the detailed study of their formulation reveals quite different paths, particularly with regard to the adjacent buildings. In Simon-Goulart, the composition of the ground is dictated by the location of the buildings, thus facilitating the spatial reading of the public space for passers-by. On the other hand, the layout of the design elements responds above all to a logic of use, with the furnishings serving to orient the trajectories and appropriations of the users. At the Place de la République, the opposite is observed. The concrete paving with its assumed asymmetry is more subject to a logic of comfort of use and trajectory. As for the design elements, the central strip of the square is flanked by a double alignment of trees, which is in keeping with the Haussmann symmetry of the Parisian square. In terms of landscape strategy, there is thus a dissociation or, on the contrary, a symbiosis with the given urban morphology, depending on the approach.

As for the materiality of these surfaces, we find in both projects a narrative on the relationship between vertical and horizontal surfaces. At the Place de la République, the project authors contrive a careful reflection on the paving, highlighting the surrounding architecture, by way of contrast. In Geneva, the limestone of the Temple de Saint-Gervais forecourt recalls the color of the base of the building, this time in a search for unity. As for the relationship to the network of adjacent public spaces, continuity is the watchword here, by retaining the Geneva paving design for the project area. The central square, on the other hand, stands out as a singular element with its anthracite concrete covering. In Paris, a clear break with the adjacent streets is also assumed, in order to underline the exceptional character of the square.

In both cases, the materials are developed to encourage certain uses and characterize each square. Nevertheless, they remain in a relatively traditional public space design style, by their minerality and by the chosen colors. At once banal and singular, the ground materials and the fittings are more robust than noble, perhaps foreshadowing the idea of a new urban aesthetic of the unfinished, more focused on the quality of suitability.

These two projects demonstrate that by reinterpreting a traditional design language, it is possible to provide a utility value that responds to the current needs of city dwellers, while inscribing each square in the continuity of the urban public space network to which it belongs. These *animated* spaces encourage convivial and hedonistic practices, without drifting into a playful aesthetic. Moreover, through more figurative arrangements, their designers manage to create singular places without referring to new or distant universes. These projects thus appear to distinguish themselves from certain trends that will be discussed in the following chapters of this book.

Minimalism and abstraction

The simplicity that characterizes these designs is undoubtedly due to the fact that both public spaces are in prominent urban and architectural contexts. This is not the case for all the examples that follow. But this simplicity also stems from an attitude of restraint toward public space that their designers seem to share. This restraint is both minimalist and abstract. A few elements, carefully designed and judiciously placed in the space to accomplish their function, are enough to define the framework conditions that allow urban life to benefit. To this parsimony is added a formal simplicity characterized by the use of elementary geometric figures that appears almost unique in the production of public spaces at the beginning of the 21st century. The designers thus seem to want to protect themselves from formal gestures of ungrounded creativity. The way they look at the city integrates simplicity as a founding value of the project, guaranteeing a preserved and enhanced urban landscape. It is also presented as a means of creating a common space, that is, places where the ideas of community and conviviality dominate.

However, the idea of a total minimalism must be qualified. Indeed, the latter is primarily intended to be formal and expressive, whereas the design effort deployed to achieve this is far from minimal, quite the contrary. The composition of the space, the choice of materials, and the constructive details are made at the cost of painstaking developments. Their approach thus does not testify to an economy of means that characterizes artistic minimalism, or even Arte Povera and the conceptual art that resulted from it. By this revealed sophistication, the architecture of the public space does not efface itself completely in front of the uses and reveals interests, even fixations, formal and aesthetic on the part of the designers.

Finally, we can wonder about the consequences of this deliberate abstraction. Does it lead to the creation of arrangements that are not very contextualized, which in fact could be transposed elsewhere? The analysis of each project partially proves the contrary. In terms of composition and materiality, both projects react directly to the morphologies or elements of facades and surfaces present at the site. On the other hand, some of the materials used and especially the furniture developed by the two teams take on a more transferable dimension through universal qualities centered on the human being – on sensory, anthropometric, and ergonomic levels – that their creators seek to attribute to them.

PLACE SIMON-GOULART

1 On this subjet see, Marcos Weil, "Aménagement des places publiques à Genève," *Interface*, n° 18, 2013, pp. 8–14.

2 For the history of the site, see: City of Geneva, Department of Urban Planning and Public Lighting, *Connaissance du site Simon-Goulart. Quelques éléments d'histoire*, April 2003 [annex to the MEP [Mandat d'études parallèles, or Parallel Study Contracts] brief]. On the development of the square and the construction of the Saugey building discussed below, see Isabelle Charollais, Bruno Marchand, "De l'opacité à la transparence. 1951–1955. La reconstruction des Terreaux-du-Temple à St-Gervais," *Faces*, n°21, fall 1991, pp. 40–45.

3 Huber, Werner, "Platz da!" *Hochparterre*, n° 10, 2013, p. 73.

4 City of Geneva, Municipal Department of Construction and Roads, *Mandat d'études parallèles. Réaménagement des places Longemalle, Pré-l'Evêque, Simon-Goulart. Règlement et cahier des charges*. Geneva, n.d., p. 17. City of Geneva, *Aménagement espace public. Place Simon-Goulart*, documentary triptych, Geneva, June 2013.

5 The city in fact conducted three simultaneous procedures, each covering one square, the other two being Place de Longemalle and Place du Pré-l'Evêque. The three sites would be allocated randomly among the bidders selected during the call for competition. The six teams selected for Place Simon-Goulart were: Paysagestion – ACAU – Bourquin + Stencek – JEOL; ADR – O+U – LEA; Mayor + Beusch – SD Ingénierie; LRS – Jundt – Oxalis; Francis Goestchmann et partenaires; Urban Issue (BRS – ESM – In Situ). City of Geneva, *Réaménagement des places ... Règlement et cahier des charges, op. cit.*, n.d., pp. 3–5.

6 *Ibid.*, p. 18.

7 The architects joined forces with the civil engineers B. Ott and C. Uldry and the lighting designers from Lyon, LEA.

8 City of Geneva, Municipal Department of Construction and Roads, *Mandat d'études parallèles. Réaménagement des places Longemalle, Pré-l'Evêque, Simon-Goulart. Rapport du groupe d'experts*, Geneva, June 24, 2003, p. 23.

9 The development of Place Simon-Goulart proposed by the winning team in 2003 would not be inaugurated until ten years later. This delay is explained firstly by the implementation of a tram line on the Rue de Coutance, south of the Saugey building. Because of this, the area around the tram stop was removed from the intervention's area, which was consequently reduced to the square and its immediate surroundings.

10 See on this subject, Philippe Bach, "Le trottoir à la genevoise, une AOC qui s'ignore," *Le courrier*, August 6, 2011; David Ripoli, "Pavé, caillou, ciment. Histoire matérielle du revêtement de sol à Genève," *k+a, Art+architecture en Suisse*, n° 3, 2012, pp. 30–36.

11 City of Geneva, *op. cit.*, June 24, 2003, p. 23.

12 Maeder, Thierry, "An Approach through Milieu," in Bruno Marchand, Julien Descombes and Marco Rampini (eds), *Common Grounds. Atelier Descombes Rampini 2000–2015*, Basel, Birkhaüser, 2017, p. 200. [French version, *Lieux Communs*, Gollion, Infolio 2017].

13 Marchand, Bruno, "Preface," in Marchand, Descombes, Rampini (eds), *op. cit.*, 2017, p. 21.

14 *Ibid.*

15 These notions echo the reflections of the historian of architecture and urbanism from Geneva, André Corboz, who deals with the historical depth of territories and places by using terms like "substratum" or "stratification." André Corboz, "Le Territoire comme palimpseste," in André Corboz and Sébastien Marot, *Le Territoire comme palimpseste et autres essais*, Besançon, Les éditions de l'Imprimeur, 2001, pp. 209–229. [Orig. ed. in *Diogène*, n°121, January–March 1983, pp. 14–35].

16 This is the space that will finally be removed from the scope of intervention of the team Atelier Descombes Rampini (see Fig. 3.1.8, p. 70, and note 9).

17 Atelier Descombes Rampini et al., *Note de présentation courte*, descriptive text of project, September 27, 2013 [Archives ADR].

18 Julien Descombes, Marco Rampini (associates of Atelier Descombes Rampini), Lausanne, interview with the author in French, July 14, 2016.

19 *Ibid.*

20 Atelier Descombes Rampini et al., "Aline," MEP competition boards for the redevelopment of Place Simon-Goulart, June 2003 [Archives ADR].

21 Bussien, Gregory (project leader at Atelier Descombes Rampini), Geneva, interview with the author in French, March 24, 2015.

22 On the links between the development of the two squares, see Sonia Curnier, "Embracing the Ordinary. Behind the Design of Public Spaces," in Marchand, Descombes, Rampini (eds), *op. cit.*, 2017, pp. 189–196. [French version, *Lieux Communs*, Gollion, Infolio 2017].

23 City of Geneva, *Réaménagement des places ... Rapport du groupe d'experts, op. cit.*, June 24, 2003, p. 23.

24 Bussien, Gregory, interview cited above.

25 Descombes, Julien, and Marco Rampini, interview cited above.

26 Atelier Descombes Rampini et al., "Aline," *op. cit.*, submission illustrations, June 2003.

27 Pattaroni, Luca, "The Urban Art of Possibility," in Bruno Marchand, Julien Descombes and Marco Rampini (eds), *op. cit.*, Basel, Birkhäuser, 2017, p. 119.

28 Jacobs, Jane, *Déclin et survie des grandes villes américaines*, Marseille, Parenthèses, 2012, pp. 54–55. [Orig. ed. *The Death and Life of Great American Cities*, New York, Random House, 1961].

PLACE DE LA RÉPUBLIQUE

29 Concerning the history of the Place de la République, see the notices: Mairie de Paris, Direction de l'Urbanisme, *République, histoire d'une place*, Paris, n.d. [annex to the competition brief]; Mairie de Paris, Atelier Parisien d'urbanisme (APUR), *Concertation. Projet d'aménagement de la Place de la République. Diagnostic. Pistes de réflexion pour le programme du concours* (Consultation. Development Project of the Place de la République. Diagnostic. Food for Thought for the Competition Program.), n.d. [annex to the competition brief].

30 The chosen teams are led by the following firms: Agence Bruno Fortier, Agence Catherine Mosbach/Mosbach Paysagistes, Agence Josep Lluís Mateo/ Mateo Arquitectura, Agence Alexandre Chemetoff and Atelier Trévelo & Viger-Kohler / TVK. Mairie de Paris, *2010 DVD 112 Signature du marché de maîtrise d'œuvre pour l'aménagement de la Place de la République à Paris, (3e), (10e), et (11e) avec le groupement Trevelo et Viger-Kohler (mandataire), Martha Schwartz Partners, AREAL, ATEC, AIK Yann Kersalé* (2010 DVD 112 Signature of the Project Management Contract for the Development of Place de la République in Paris, (3rd), (10th), and (11th) with the Trévelo and Viger-Kohler consortium (TVK), Martha Schwartz Partners, Areal, ATEC, AIK Yann Kersalé), n.d.

31 The minutes of the procedure are to be distributed to the bidders. Mairie de Paris, *Bilan de la concertation sur le projet d'aménagement de la Place de la République du 15 December 2008 au 15 mars 2009* (Assessment of the Consultation on the Development Project of the Place de la République from December 15, 2008 to March 15, 2009), Paris, document, n.d., p. 4 [annex to the competition brief].

32 Mairie de Paris, *Aménagement de la Place de la République. Le programme d'aménagement* (Development of the Place de la République. The Development Program), Paris, June 9, 2009, p. 3

33 *Ibid.*, p. 4.

34 Hertenberger, Vincent (project leader at Trévelo & Viger-Kohler), Paris, July 22, 2015, interview with the author in French. Martha Schwartz's office contributed primarily to the conceptual phase of the competition. For the development of the project, the architects would rely more on AREAL's landscape skills.

35 Trévelo & Viger-Kohler et al., "Aménagement de la place de la République à Paris 3ème, 10ème et 11ème arrondissements. Notice de présentation architecturale, technique et financière," competition boards, November 12, 2009, p. 3 [Archives TVK].

36 Caille, Emmanuel, "Place de la République/berges de Seine. Paris, pour le meilleur et pour le pire," *D'architectures*, n° 221, October 2013, p. 85.

37 Waterman, Tim, "At Liberty: A Piece of Paris has been Recivilized for Walking (or Skating, or Scootering, or Protesting)," *Landscape Architecture Magazine*, n° 104, 2014, p. 112.

38 Trévelo & Viger-Kohler et al., *op. cit.*, November 12, 2009, p. 7.

39 In 2012, Jean-Pierre Charbonneau expressed reservations about this functional dissymmetry considering that it does not correspond to the capacity of the buildings to generate activity on the square. Jean-Pierre Charbonneau, "A propos de la place de la République à Paris," *Tous urbains*, n° 0, 2012, pp. 24–27.

40 Trévelo & Viger-Kohler et al., *op. cit.*, November 12, 2009, p. 7.

41 These aspects are detailed in the notice that accompanies the competition proposal. *Ibid.*, pp. 3–4, 6 (Archives TVK).

42 Mairie de Paris, *op. cit.*, June 9, 2009, p. 4.

43 This demand is the result of pressure exerted by the Mayor of Paris, Bertrand Delanoë and the Architectes des Bâtiments de France (ABF). Vincent Hertenberger, interview cited above.

44 *Ibid.* As the project developed, the designers had to adapt many components of the initial concept to the reality of a highly constrained site. Beneath the surface, five metro lines serve the eponymous station. From an administrative point of view, the square straddles three 'arrondissements' (3rd, 10th and 11th), leading to numerous negotiations concerning the project itself or its future maintenance.

45 Trévelo & Viger-Kohler et al., *op. cit.*, November 12, 2009, p. 5.

46 Concerning production of the concrete slabs, see Sélène Agapé, "Place de la République. Paris opte pour le béton," *Techniques & architecture*, n° 47, 2003, pp. 34–35.

47 Trévelo, Pierre Alain (partner of Trévelo & Viger-Kohler), Paris, interview with the author in French, July 22, 2015.

48 Trévelo & Viger-Kohler Architectes Urbanistes, *Dossier de presse – Place de la République*, press kit, June 2013, p. 11.

49 Trévelo, Pierre Alain, interview cited above.

50 In a critical article about the square, Françoise Fromonot attacked the *Supersurface* reference, which she considered a weak distortion on the part of the winning team, and which, according to her, disregards the ideological scope and the historical-political context of the Superstudio proposal. Françoise Fromonot, "Surface de réparation," *Criticat*, n° 14, 2014, pp. 59–61. We will qualify this criticism by noting that the TVK team shares with Superstudio a vision of spatial design as a way to create an appropriable, informal, and popular living environment, through an economy of means.

51 This minimalism of furniture was debated among critics. For some the benches are superfluous, Waterman, *op. cit.*, 2014, p. 125. While others lament the insufficient seating offered in the plaza, Fromonot, *op. cit.*, 2014, p. 50.

52 Darrieus, Margaux, "TVK: Place de la République, Paris 3e," *AMC architecture*, n° 226, 2013, p. 56; Waterman, *op. cit.*, 2014, pp. 122, 125.

53 Caille, *op. cit.*, 2013, p. 86.

54 Waterman, *op. cit.*, 2014, p. 122.

55 Fromonot, *op. cit.*, 2014, pp. 50, 59.

56 Trévelo & Viger-Kohler et al., *op. cit.*, November 12, 2009, p. 4.

57 Trévelo & Viger-Kohler Architectes Urbanistes, *Dossier de presse – Place de la République*, press kit, June 2013, p. 5. And in a revised version of the text Trévelo & Viger-Kohler Architectes Urbanistes, *Place de la République*, press kit, 2013, p. 39.

58 Hertenberger, Vincent, interview cited above.

59 Trévelo, Pierre Alain, interview cited above.

60 This neologism, which seems to have become widespread in current urban discourse, was used in particular by the sociologist Marc Breviglieri: "Une brèche critique dans la 'ville garantie'? Espaces intercalaires et architectures d'usage," in Elena Cogato Lanza, Luca Pattaroni, Micha Piraud and Barbara Tirone (eds), *De la différence urbaine. Le quartier des Grottes/Genève*, Geneva, MétisPresses, 2013, p. 215.

61 Vienne, Véronique, "In Paris, a Celebrated Place for Protest Gets a Quietly Radical Facelift," *Metropolis Magazine*, October 7, 2014, http://www.metropolismag.com/ideas/paris-place-protest-gets-quietly-radical-facelift/ [accessed April 29, 2015, when the title was "Place for Protest"]. Original quote attributed to the architects: "Our work is unfinished, on purpose. We wouldn't want it any other way."

ORNAMENT

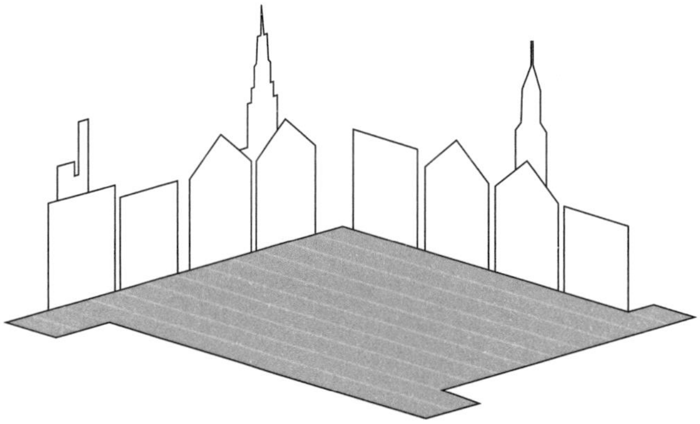

3.2.1–3.2.2
A pictorial approach to ornament
The use of avant-garde materials, such as the paint used for road marking, encourages designers to explore new forms of expression of public spaces. This redeployment gives rise to pictorial and graphic explorations, in the form of abstract or figurative motifs. *(1) DKV-Versicherung, Berlin, Topotek 1, 2000; (2) Taxingeplan, Tensta, LLP – Front Design, 2006*

3.2.3–3.2.4
Solid surfaces ornament
Large, brightly colored surfaces allow the characterization of a place by a simple gesture and with relatively few means, radically affirming the new status of a public space. *(3) Geelhandplaats, Antwerp, Omgeving Landscape Architecture, 2011; (4) Stadtlounge, St-Gallen, Carlos Martinez Architekten – Pipilotti Rist, 2005*

3.2.5–3.2.6
Ornament with modules
Paving stones or slabs – more traditional surfacing – deviate from conventional practice, giving rise to expressive innovations. The modules then become like pixels forming more complex and sometimes symbolic ornamental designs. *(5) Classensgade, Copenhagen, 1:1 Landskab, 2010; (6) Købmagergade, Copenhagen, KBP.EU, 2013*

Public space design can be summarized as a ground work (surfacing and topography) on which elements (furniture, vegetation, fountains, shelters, etc.) are placed. Some projects focus primarily on the surfacing, which is distinguished by a recognizable pattern. These carpet-like strategies reinforce the unification of a space, making it clearly identifiable by a material, sometimes a color, but most often by a specific pattern. As such, we call this type of development *ornamented*.

Ornamented surfacing has long been exemplified in the implementation of cobblestone or flagstone paving that adorns many historic public spaces. For nearly two decades, this tradition has evolved into more complex ornamental patterns, possibly characteristic of the digital age. These patterns can range from highly figurative designs to more abstract evocations, depending on the intervention. The development or redeployment of new materials, such as tartan or road paint, has opened up fresh avenues for pictorial experimentation. Finally, in some cases, the surface ornament has been enriched by a strong narrative dimension added to the project's formal presence.

SELECTED CASE STUDIES

The choice of case studies first oriented toward a local project (Switzerland), the Place du Molard in Geneva. Developed in 2004 by a multidisciplinary group of architects, landscape architects, and artists, including 2b architectes, Stéphane Collet, Cécile Albana Presset, and Christian Robert-Tissot, this public space is distinguished by its ambivalence between day and night. During the day, its paving displays a certain sobriety, while at night its innovative lighting makes it far more spectacular. It is this ambivalence that caught our attention. Moreover, the developed motif seems to answer a desire to inscribe the project in the history of the location, despite a final appearance that appears easily transferable.

At the beginning of this research, the newly opened (2012) Superkilen development by BIG, Topotek 1, and Superflex was widely publicized in the international trade press, giving it an almost iconic dimension. It was almost impossible to talk about the subject of *ornamented* public space without referring to it. This example is distinguished by the use of paint, both in the form of flat areas and pictorial motifs. These features are implemented on two very distinctive squares, one red, the other black. Unlike the Place du Molard, the ornamental strategy is applied this time in a more depreciated urban context. The question of the relationship to the adjacent buildings and public spaces thus takes on another dimension.

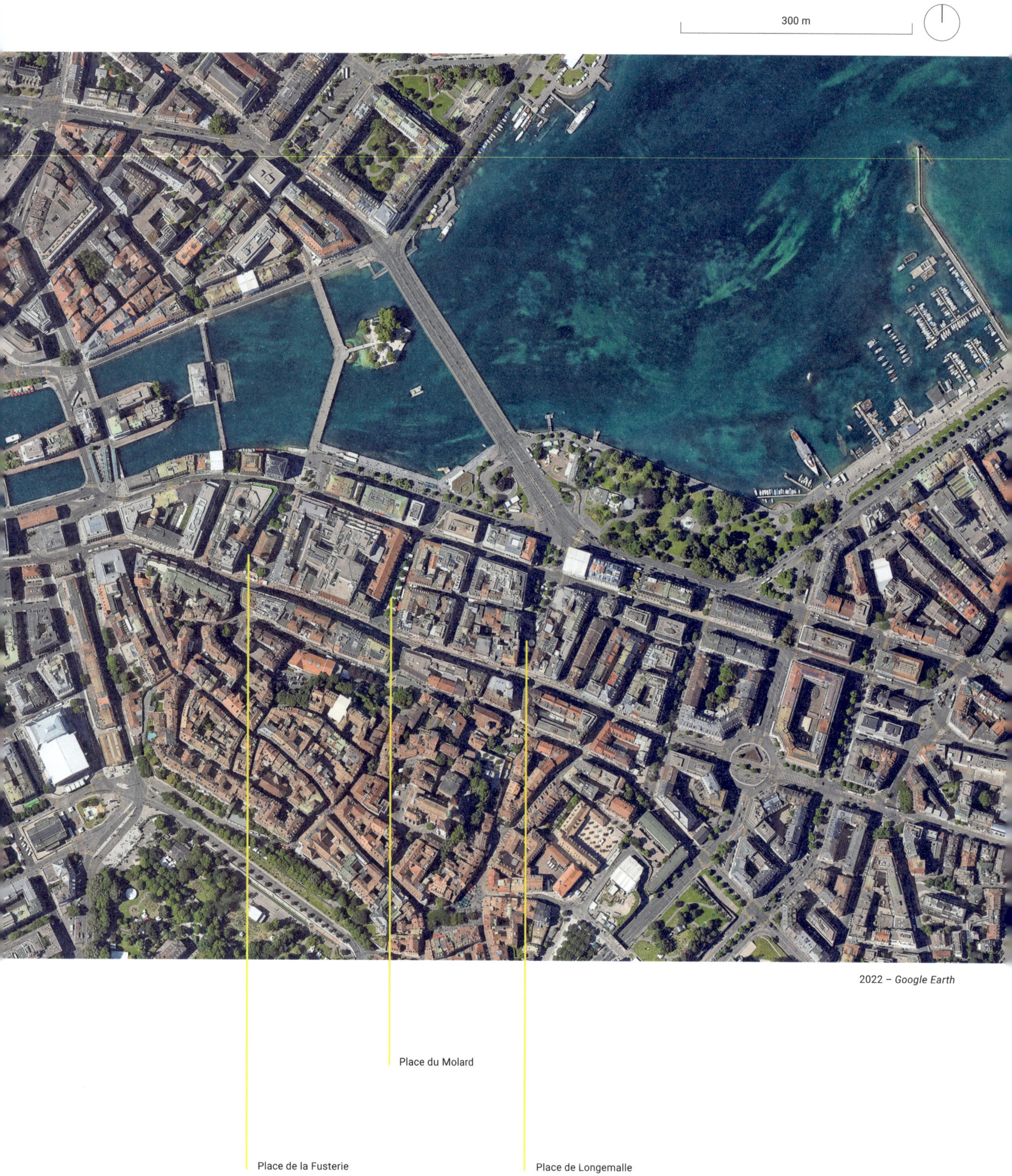

2022 – *Google Earth*

3.2.7 Location of the Place du Molard

PLACE DU MOLARD GENEVA 2002–2004

Location Geneva, Switzerland **Client** Municipality of Geneva **Lead designers** 2b architectes / S. Bender – Ph. Béboux (architects and urban designers – Lausanne) / S. Collet (architect) / CA. Presset (landscape architect) / Ch. Robert-Tissot (artist) **Type of commission** Parallel study contracts [MEP] (2002) **Construction** 2003–2004 **Former status** Pedestrian square formerly used as a traffic and parking area **Area** 0.3 ha

At the end of 2001, the partners of 2b architectes, Stephanie Bender and Philippe Béboux, their colleague Stéphane Collet, and the landscape architect Cécile Albana Presset, decided to join forces to respond to a call for entry – launched by the city of Geneva – for the competition for the redevelopment of the Place du Molard. The regulations encouraged the formation of teams including engineers, but the Lausanne group enriched itself with the contribution of the artist Christian Robert-Tissot, out of "intellectual interest" and "a desire to open up the practice."[1]

The collective was selected, alongside five other teams from French-speaking Switzerland, to compete for parallel study contracts (*Mandats d'étude parallèles*) and to submit a proposal a few months later. According to the brief, the challenge was to "enhance the value of the square, in its historical context, by renewing the surfacing, by a layout that would reinforce its open and pedestrian character, and by better spatial and technical management of the various activities that take place there throughout the year"[2] (Fig. 3.2.8). The Place du Molard is in the historical, commercial, and pedestrian sector of the Rues-Basses of Geneva, an area heavily frequented on a daily basis. The objective was therefore not to further animate the square by creating new uses, but to facilitate existing practices by offering a space that is as open as possible. The competition brief also insisted on a few points that will resonate with the winning team: respect for the history of the site, whose spatial configuration dates back to the 14th century;[3] the enhancement of the remarkable quality of the architectural ensemble bordering the square; the encouragement of simple solutions; and finally the development of the theme of night-time lighting. It is also specified that "the main object of the development project [...] is the repair of the ground surfaces, from facade to facade."[4]

Following this demand to the letter, the Béboux-Bender-Collet-Presset group won the competition with its "Chuchotements" project, of which the competition jury appreciated both "the idea's simplicity and strength."[5] The winning proposal consists of standardizing the entire square with a flat surface and a uniform covering – sandstone paving – that extends from facade to facade. As the only volumetric elements, it is proposed to complete the alignment of existing plane trees, under which the terraces of bistros, installed until then on the eastern edges of the square, will cluster. To this clear spatial gesture is added an ornamental dimension that takes the form of backlit resin paving stones, randomly arranged on the square. The artist Christian Robert-Tissot would superimpose a poetic dimension by inscribing everyday expressions in different languages on these luminous paving stones (Fig. 3.2.9–3.2.12).

3.2.8 The Place du Molard before the redevelopment **3.2.9–3.2.10** Project at the competition stage. *2b / S. Bender–Ph. Béboux, S. Collet, C.A. Presset, Ch. Robert-Tissot, "Chuchotements," MEP entry boards, March 19, 2002* **3.2.11** A unified design from facade to facade **3.2.12** The Place du Molard glowing at night

UNCERTAIN LIMITS

The simplicity of a uniform, ordinary paving confirming priority for pedestrians, and the concentration of the leisure activities and plane trees in the center of the square, are justified by a desire to recover the "unique character" of the location.[6] It is therefore the pre-existing void, defined by a remarkable architectural ensemble, that seems to take precedence in the eyes of the designers. The numerous models and three-dimensional representations of the square that will accompany the project process, testify to the importance given to the understanding of this hollow volume and its defining elements.[7]

The proposal therefore focuses on the ground surface, "on its physical nature as well as on its form."[8] At this stage, it is already important to note a discrepancy between the perimeter on which the intervention will focus and the spatial void under

3.2.9

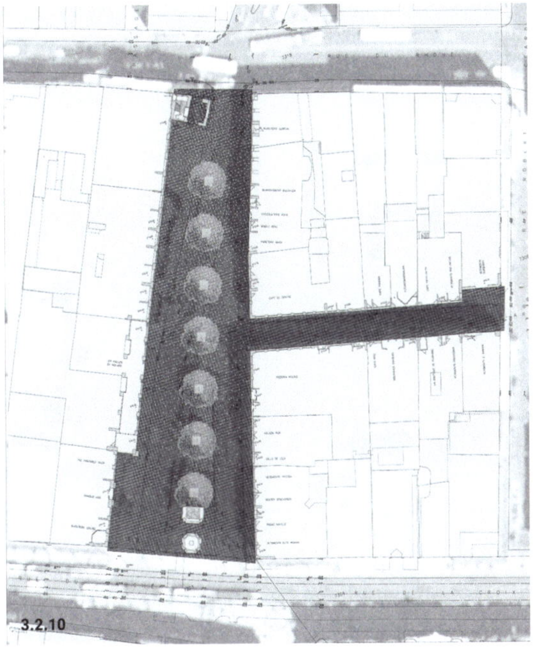

3.2.10

3.2.11

3.2.12

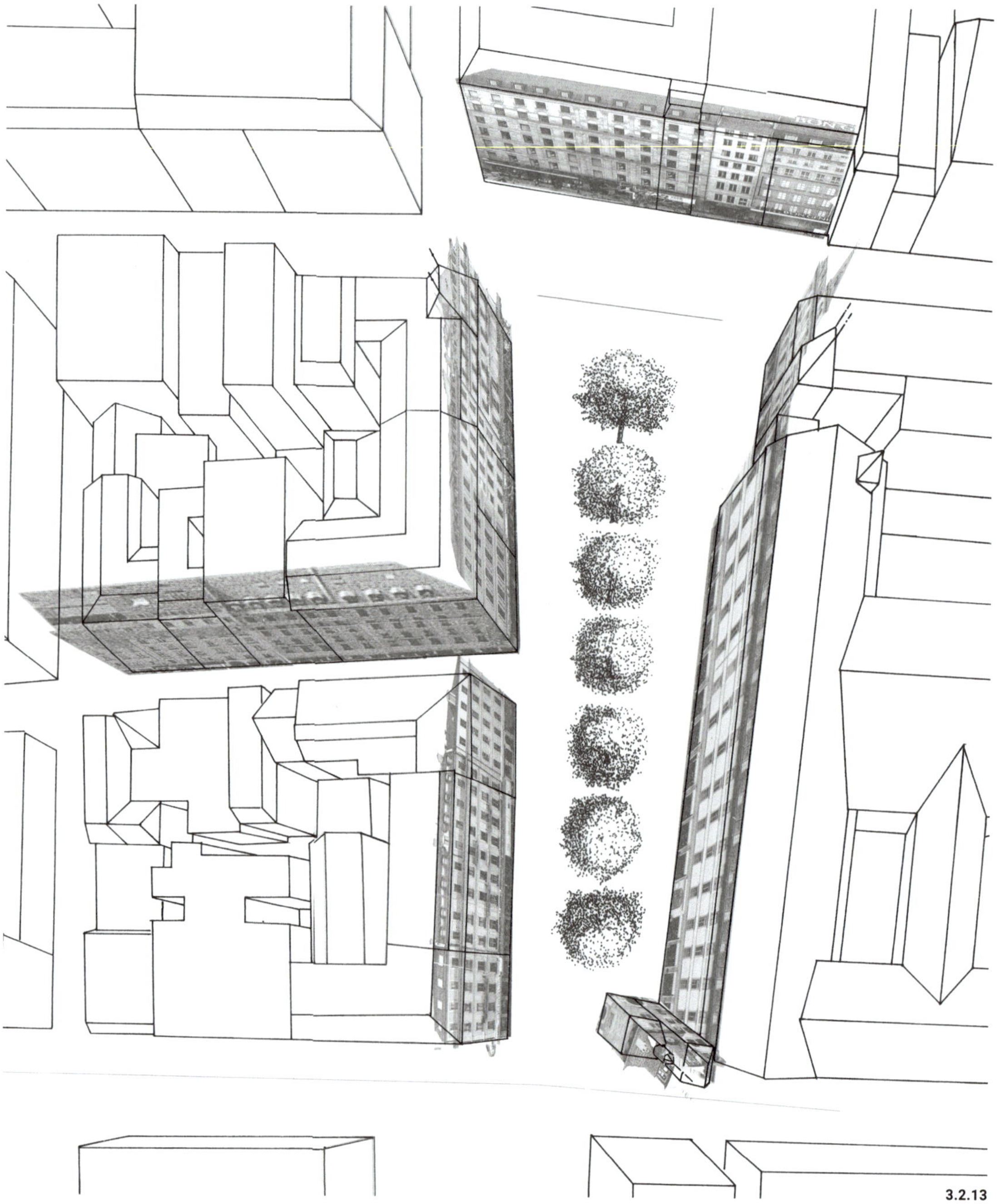

3.2.13

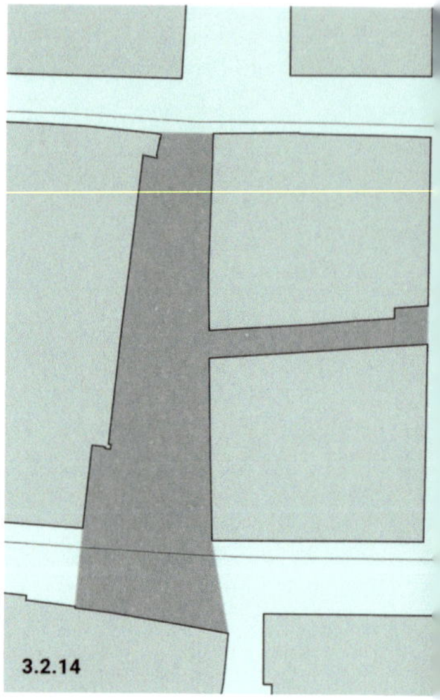

3.2.14

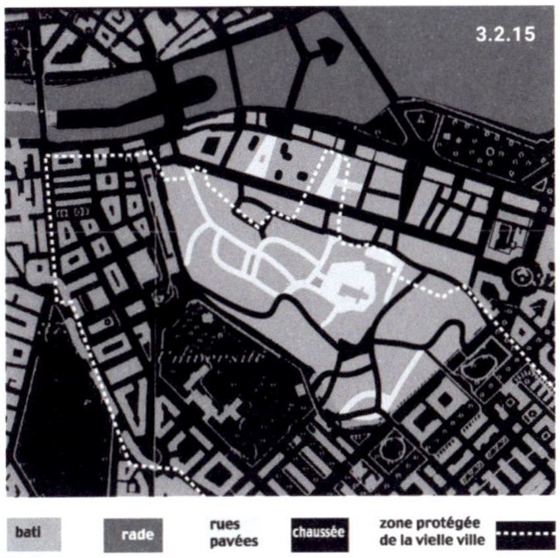

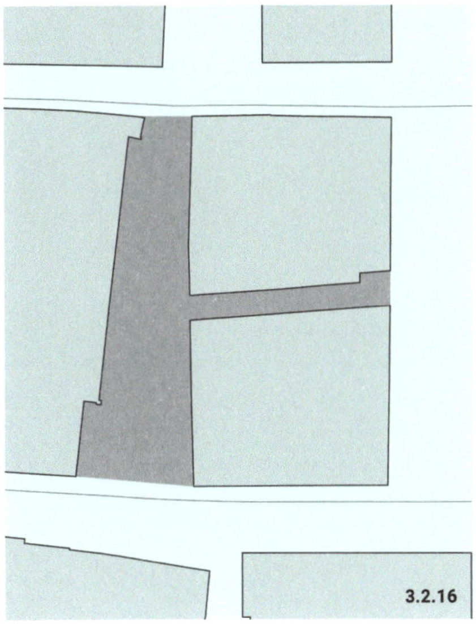

3.2.13–3.2.14 Aerial perspective of the square – an "idealized void." *(13) 2b / S. Bender–Ph. Béboux, S. Collet, C.A. Presset, Ch. Robert-Tissot, "Chuchotements," MEP entry boards, March 19, 2002; (14) redrawing showing the idealized void* **3.2.15–3.2.16** Site plan and surrounding surface materials. *(15) 2b / S. Bender–Ph. Béboux, S. Collet, C.A. Presset, Ch. Robert-Tissot, "Chuchotements," MEP entry boards, March 19, 2002; (16) redrawing showing the actual perimeter of the project*

consideration. Indeed, the first drawing on the competition board is an aerial perspective (Fig. 3.2.13) – a mode of representation that would have been inspired by Toyo Ito[9] – that shows an "idealized void" oriented toward the southern facade of the square. This viewpoint was probably favored because it magnifies the void in question. The delimitation of the trapezium thus represented undoubtedly corresponds to the limits of a space that would be perceived by an individual standing in the square. But the void considered does not coincide with the perimeter of intervention determined by the competition, which in fact ends at the right of the Rue du Marché. It is therefore difficult to make the "idealized void" correspond to the "developed surface." A demarcation faintly indicated on the drawing by a thin black line ... but clearly marked by the abrupt transition between two surfaces in the realized project. The southern delimitation of the square thus appears ambivalent between narrative and reality.

This uncertainty can also be read by comparing the abovementioned image with the second drawing that appears just below it in the competition submission (Fig. 3.2.15). To justify the choice of paving stones, the designers insist that the Place du Molard belongs to the perimeter of the old town, and this time they assume that there is a break with the adjoining road. In the explanatory text, they advocate "continuity with the adjacent public spaces."[10] However, the diagram clearly shows that it is not the adjacent spaces – that is, directly contiguous – that serve as a reference, but rather the surrounding network, considered on a larger scale. Thus depicted, the Place du Molard appears as an isolated figure in the middle of a continuous dark labyrinth. The desire to link it to the past, to mark its belonging to the protected perimeter of the old town, seems to take precedence over the physical continuity of the paving with the adjoining network of spaces. This ambivalence of definition between the void and the ornamented surface is thus used differently according to the elements of the narrative that the authors wish to support.

A NEED TO FIND A LOGIC SPECIFIC TO THE SITE

As the space is already very much in use and strongly defined by some remarkable existing facades, the team decides to be as restrained as possible in its intervention, as stipulated by certain expressions inscribed in the competition submission: "the challenge of almost nothing" or "an intervention in minor mode."[11] 2b architectes compare this approach to the project for development of the Place Léon Aucoc (1996, Bordeaux), for which the architects Lacaton & Vassal proposed to allocate the entire budget to the maintenance of a space considered sufficiently qualitative that they refused to intervene more heavily.[12] Despite a similarly reserved attitude, it must be admitted that the Geneva intervention is much more substantial. Indeed, the leveling of the Place du Molard to confirm its exclusively pedestrian use and to erase the borders of the old roadway, as well as the choice of a uniform historical paving that would be totally in accord with its surroundings, seems not to satisfy the designers. They therefore apply themselves to developing a more sophisticated ground covering that will assume its own identity.

The archives show numerous attempts to find the appropriate language and the degree of design impact that would endow the square with a greater character than its spatial definition alone. In the few weeks leading up to the competition submissions, the authors will explore different graphic motifs based on simple geometric shapes that structure the square and determine suitable sub-areas (Fig. 3.2.17–3.2.18). Other more figurative proposals, such as this sketch clearly materializing the word

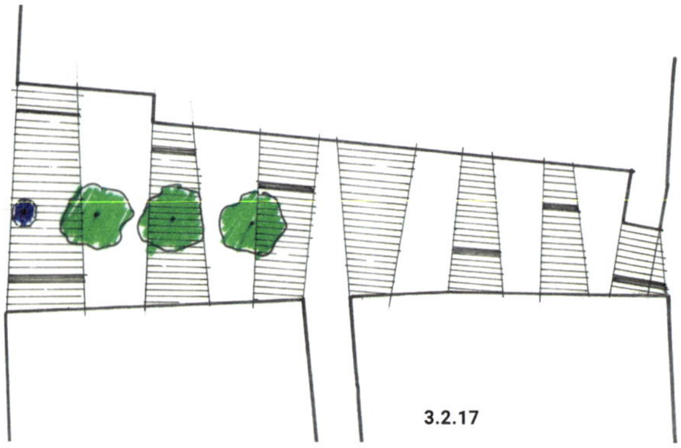

3.2.17

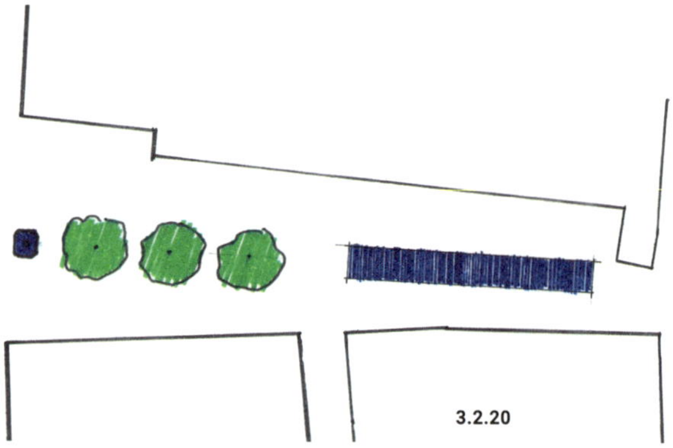

3.2.20

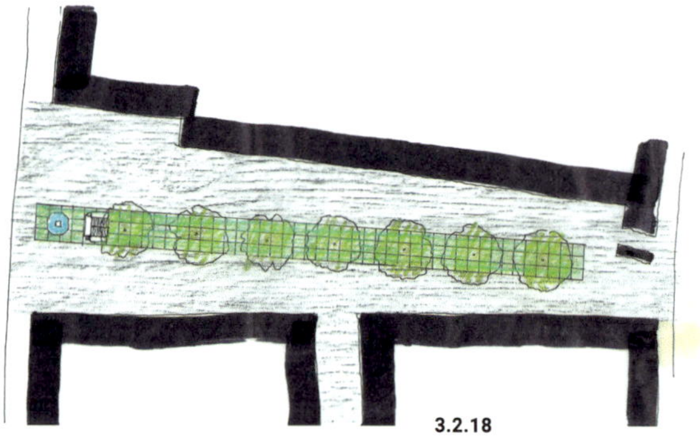

3.2.18

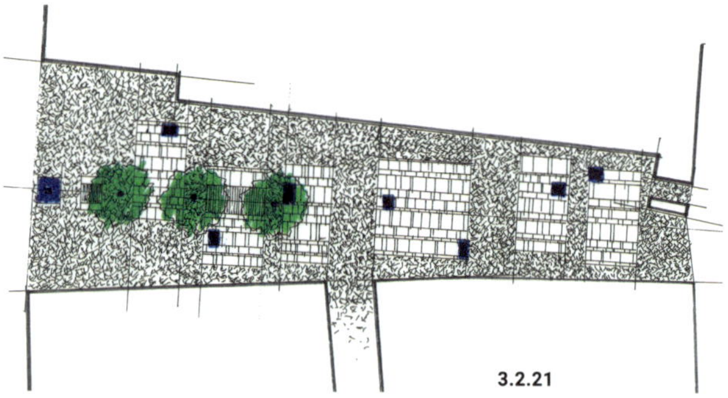

3.2.21

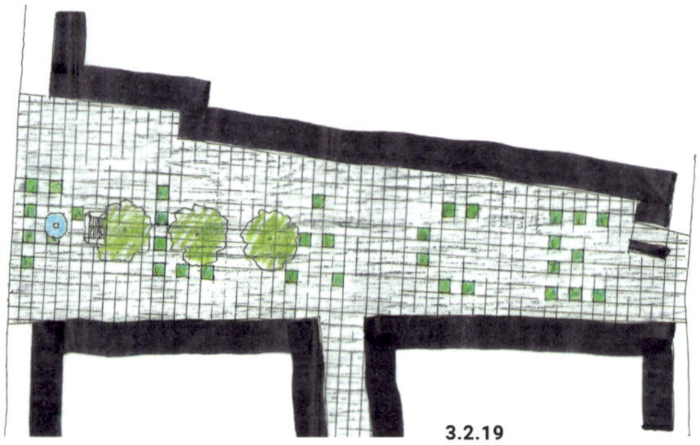

3.2.19

3.2.22

3.2.17–3.2.22 Exploratory sketches produced during the MEP process. *2b / S. Bender–Ph. Béboux, S. Collet, C.A. Presset, Ch. Robert-Tissot, sketches, n.d.* **3.2.23** Historical plan illustrating the presence of water in the square as a reference **3.2.24** Reference image illustrating the shimmering water. *2b / S.Bender–Ph.Béboux, S. Collet, C.A. Presset, Ch. Robert-Tissot, photography, n.d.*

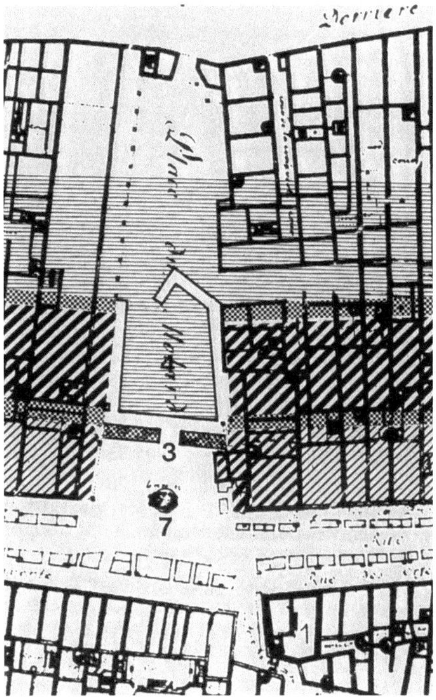

3.2.23

"place" (Fig. 3.2.19), are content to simply individualize the square. But the team is not satisfied with these variants, perhaps overly detailed and finally abandoned in favor of a more discreet effect. At this stage, "the objective is a motif, not a drawing. [...] it's almost a texture, an image" as the architects describe it.[13] The turning point in the process seems to occur at the moment when the historical trail is explored.

HISTORY REVISITED BY A UNIVERSAL SYMBOL

While researching the history of the square, the group discovered that the name "Molard," derived from "Moullard," probably comes from "*môle*," which means dike or pier (Fig. 3.2.23). There would therefore have been a port at this site, and the team wondered about the most appropriate way to represent this past. It is the second subject that will be the object of thorough development, by exploring several variants during the competitive process.

A few drawings testify to these attempts to represent water at the square. For example, there is a simple rectangular body of water in the alignment of the three plane trees (Fig. 3.2.20), or there is the idea of "water stones," a sort of parallelepipedic emergence over which a thin stream of water would flow (Fig. 3.2.21–3.2.22). But redundancy with the existing fountain, of these too literal and visible transpositions, does not do the job ...

It is then that the idea arises of referring to the flickering of the sun or moon on the water (Fig. 2.2.24). This image is translated by the architects into a computerized photomontage that appears "as small pieces of white paper on the ground"[14] (Fig. 3.2.25). This rapidly sketched illustration will serve as a reference for the further development of the project. It is decided that these glowing paving stones would not simply be made of lighter stones but would actually be made of glass and would become luminous after dark. They are to be placed randomly on the square, and their proportion will increase toward the north, producing a gradation from dark to light that intensifies the relationship to the lake. A durable evanescent phenomenon is thus created on the ground.

The reference remains rooted in local imagery, through its historical anchorage, but its design translation takes a universal form. This transferable feature of the design solution is such that it will be found in Copenhagen, a few years later, in the context of the redevelopment of Købmagergade, an axis punctuated by three squares (2007–2013, Fig. 3.2.27–3.2.28). The KBP.EU consortium, which apparently did not know about the existence of the Place du Molard,[15] decided to distribute light sources randomly on the Trinitatis Kirkeplads. In this case, the device, identical to that in Geneva, symbolizes a starry sky to recall the presence of an astronomical observatory formerly attached to the church that sits in the middle of the square. In the same way as in the Place du Molard, the story is locally anchored, yet the effect is quite universal, producing striking formal similarities between the two projects.

In both cases, the symbolic dimension is such that the original inspiration is not obvious, and many in Geneva also perceive a Milky Way or simply a purely ornamental motif without meaning. However, this freedom of interpretation does not bother the architects, who assume the universal scope of the imagined device, as long as the vision of the square gives pleasure to its users.[16] The narrative dimension thus becomes more of a development tool for the project, rather than a message that must necessarily be understood by all.

3.2.24

This sensory approach to the project also reflects another concern that seems to absorb the designers, that of the perception of the square. This can be seen, for example, in the way the density of the luminous elements is tested in perspective in a Photoshop file to measure the impact of the resulting effect (Fig. 3.2.25–3.2.26) or in the different samples constructed to find the right materiality and implementation of the paving stones (Fig. 3.2.29). Note that this question of perception is approached with a certain romanticism, rather than motivated by pragmatic considerations, such as the spatial orientation of future users.

Poetry is in fact a theme that appears several times in the designers' narrative. It is certainly evoked to describe the idea of scintillation, but 2b architectes also speak of the "poetics of the non-control of the final image" by explaining how the arrangement of the paving stones in no way emanates from an "arbitrary architect's drawing."[17] In reality, the authors have simply divided the square according to a theoretical grid of 2 × 2 m, specifying the number of luminous stones that the pavers should place in each square (Fig. 3.2.30–3.2.31). It is a question of getting rid of an overly subjective and deterministic attitude, in order to let oneself be surprised by a real randomness. Thus, the ornament no longer becomes a pattern totally controlled by the designers.

BACKGROUND-FIGURE AMBIVALENCE

Having established the paving stones and their implementation leads us to consider the night-time view of the square. While during the day, the design is almost imperceptible to the lay visitor, it becomes inescapable once night falls. When the 1,857 resin paving stones are illuminated, the ground surface suddenly takes on a dominant presence against the void and the buildings that structure it. The square, previously serving as a background, is thus metamorphosed to a leading role. The impression of entering a unique space is no longer determined by its spatial nature, but by its paving, simultaneously an enchanting visible presence and a support for the narrative of the lake's past.

The equivocality is quite intentional, according to Philippe Béboux: "Here, the installation is ambivalent. By day, it simply marks the continuity. On the other hand, at night it has total autonomy and appears as a real object. And that's what has always interested us, this sort of absence and then bold presence. The development finds its balance between the two."[18] But the architect does not necessarily justify the need to highlight the public space more at night.

On the other hand, the discussion will lead to a discussion of the redevelopment of the adjoining Place de Longemalle (2003–2013), imagined by 2b architectes at the time of the Molard's construction. Completed by the Place de la Fusterie to the west, they constitute a series of three squares that once marked the boundary between the lake and the city of Geneva. In Longemalle, the architects focused on the paving too, although the design also includes several distinctive furniture elements (circular benches, street lamps, etc.). Here, the design of the paving – which is based on a sketch made in 2002 for the Molard (Fig. 3.2.32) – is much more pronounced: alternating bands of concrete and paving stones clearly structure the square (Fig. 3.2.33–3.2.34).

3.2.25

3.2.25–3.2.26 Variations in the density of luminous paving stones. *(25) 2b / S. Bender–Ph. Béboux, S. Collet, C.A. Presset, Ch. Robert-Tissot, photoshop photomontage, study alternative produced during the preparatory phase of the MEP, February 23, 2002; (26) 2b / S. Bender–Ph. Béboux, S. Collet, C.A. Presset, Ch. Robert-Tissot, "Chuchotements," MEP entry boards, March 19, 2002* **3.2.27–3.2.28** A similar design in Copenhagen based on a completely different narrative. *(27) Købmagergade, Copenhagen, KBP. EU (Karres en Brands – Werk Arkitekter – Sangberg Architects), 2008–2013; (28) KBP. EU, "Fra Kultorvet til Mælkevejen," perspectives, entry for first round of competition, February 22, 2008* **3.2.29** Prototype for illuminated paving stones. *2b / S. Bender–Ph. Béboux, S. Collet, C.A. Presset, Ch. Robert-Tissot, photography, 15 April 2003*

3.2.26

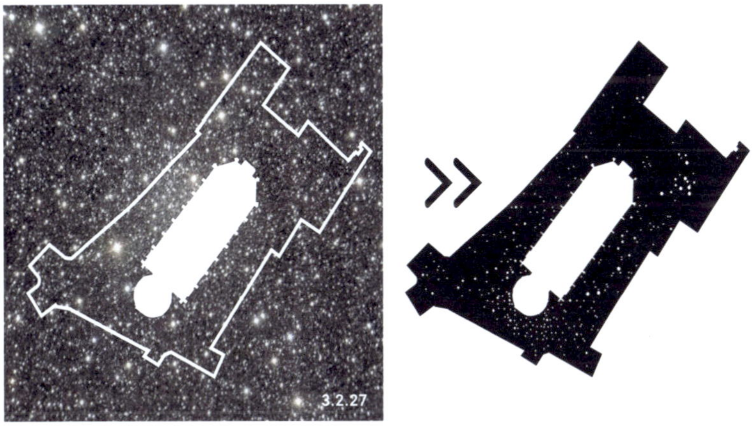

3.2.27

3.2.28

3.2.29

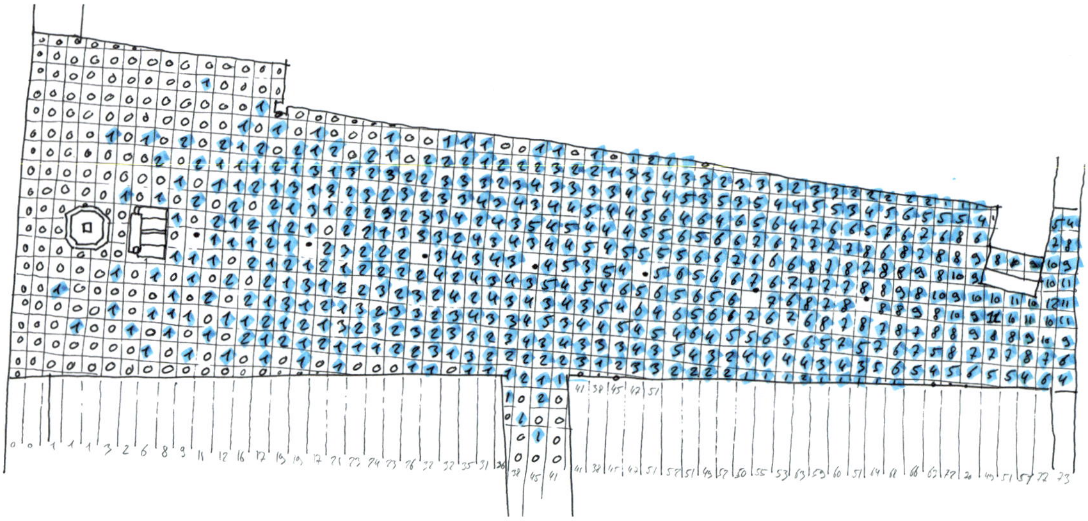

3.2.30

3.2.30 Variation of distribution of the illuminated paving stones set on a grid of 2 × 2m. *2b / S. Bender–Ph. Béboux, S. Collet, C.A. Presset, Ch. Robert-Tissot, study plan, February 27, 2002* **3.2.31** Electrical plan of the completed design. *2b / S. Bender–Ph. Béboux, S. Collet, C.A. Presset, Ch. Robert-Tissot, publication drawing, n.d.* **3.2.32** Sketch made for the Place du Molard, details see fig. 3.2.17, p. 110. *2b / S. Bender–Ph. Béboux, S. Collet, C.A. Presset, Ch. Robert-Tissot, sketch, n.d. [MEP phase]* **3.2.33–3.2.34** General plan and photograph of the Place de Longemalle. *Place de Longemalle, Geneva, 2b / S. Bender–Ph. Béboux, 2013*

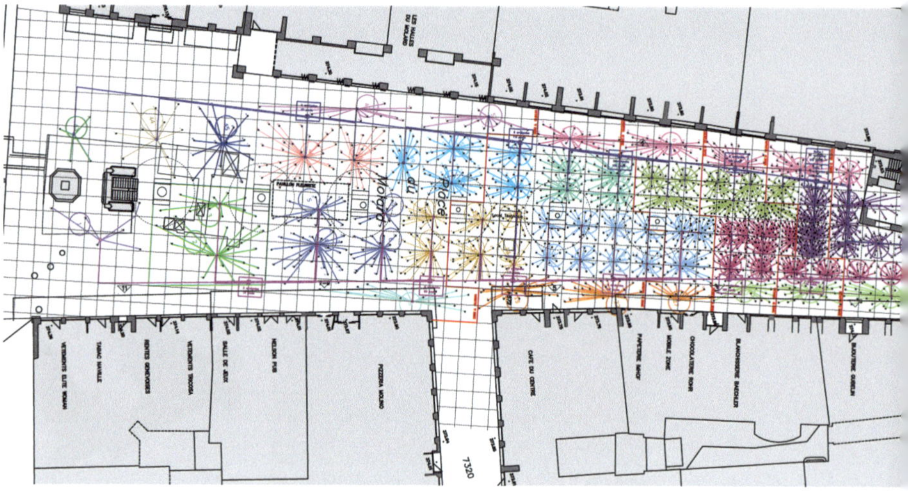

3.2.31

3.2.32

According to 2b architectes, one of the reasons for this difference in stance is that the success of a public space depends essentially on two parameters, which are not only beyond the responsibility of the public space designer, but can also change: the quality of the architecture, which generates the void, and the design, which determines the degree of activity. Depending on the inherited context, the designer can then adopt a strategy that is more or less "marked," "characterized," "instrumentalized."[19] In Longemalle, the need to produce a more present surface, endowing the space with a certain autonomy, is justified by a "more diffuse" context, not in its spatial definition, but in the architectural and functional quality of the buildings that border the square.

One might therefore suppose that the need to characterize the Place du Molard, when the majority of the shops are closed, would reside in a desire to ensure night-time activity in the square. However, 2b architectes affirm that this was not the real intention at the time and that the night was above all an opportunity to evoke the lake's past.[20] Sometimes, therefore, the need to *ornament* the surfacing appears to emanate from a narrative rather than a spatial or functional desire.

3.2.33

3.2.34

2022 – *Google Earth*

3.2.35 Location of Superkilen

SUPERKILEN
COPENHAGEN 2007–2012

Location Copenhagen, Denmark **Client** Københavns Kommune – Realdania **Lead designers** BIG – Bjarke Ingels Group (architects – Copenhagen) / Topotek 1 (landscape architects – Berlin) / Superflex (artist collective – Copenhagen) **Type of commission** Selected competition (2007) – second round for two finalist teams (2008) **Construction** 2010–2012 **Former status** Former industrial transportation route turned into a residual space **Area** 2.7 ha

Nørrebro is a popular, young, and multi-ethnic neighborhood of Copenhagen, with a reputation as a sensitive area. Its urban fabric can be described as heterogeneous and mixed, including housing, offices, small shops, workshops, cultural and leisure facilities. After neglecting the area for several decades, the Municipality of Copenhagen decided to address its urban renewal. The envisaged program emphasized a series of targeted interventions, public facilities, and open space developments, as evidenced by the redevelopment of Nørrebrogade, Nørrebroparken (2008), BaNanna Park (2010), and the construction of a subway station in connection with a new circular line. In 2003, the construction of a bicycle path, integrated into a city-wide network, began the metamorphosis of the Superkilen site.[21]

The organization of the Superkilen competition is characterized by a public-private partnership between the Municipality of Copenhagen and the private institution Realdania,[22] with the area to be developed occupying a linear strip of about 700 meters in length, spatially very articulated and poorly defined by a disparate built fabric. It is a former railroad site whose activities ceased in 1920 and which has since been an open, unused space. The objective of the competition is "to architecturally improve the area by changing its current status from a monofunctional transit area to a multifunctional living and activity space for recreational practices, reflecting and bringing together the diversity of the neighborhood's residents and promoting integration. At the same time, Superkilen must be an attraction for all of Copenhagen."[23] The project brief insists several times on the exceptional character to be conferred on the future public space by emphasizing the need to design "a beacon for Nørrebro, with its own character" and "an innovative urban project."[24] The ambition of a unique interpretation is thus clearly proclaimed.

The competition is aimed at architects or landscape architects, who are strongly encouraged to work with other professional disciplines.[25] The Danish office BIG (Bjarke Ingels Group) decided to invite the Berlin landscape designers Topotek 1 and a local artists' collective, Superflex, to join their working group. They were to be selected with four other teams to participate in the competition, and then selected together with GHB Landskabsarkitekter to submit a proposal for the second round, which they went on to win.

Their project entitled "Superkilen, 3 zones, 3 colors – a global neighborhood"[26] is based on the idea of dividing this indeterminate place into three subspaces singled out by colored treatment of the ground. Each part has its own atmosphere and vocation. Thus, the red square is dedicated to active uses in connection with the adjacent sports hall; the black square, nicknamed "the black market," brings together commercial, exchange, and social activities; finally, the linear park with its artificially shaped terrain is intended for family, recreational, and sports uses. Appropriations, some of which are deliberately unprecedented, are encouraged by furniture from all around the world. This reflects the immigrant population that, according to the authors, represents the most distinctive element of the neighborhood (Fig. 3.2.36–3.2.39).

3.2.36

3.2.36–3.2.39 "Superkilen, 3 zones, 3 colors – one global neighborhood." *BIG, Topotek 1, Superflex, "Superkilen, 3 zoner, 3 farver – et globalt kvarter," competition entry, October 5, 2007*

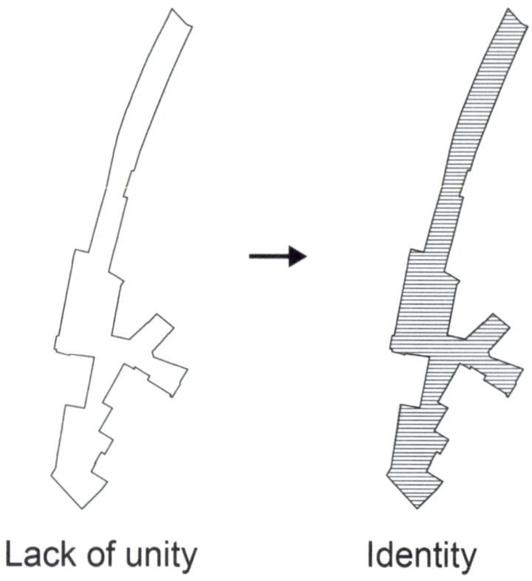

3.2.40

3.2.41

3.2.42

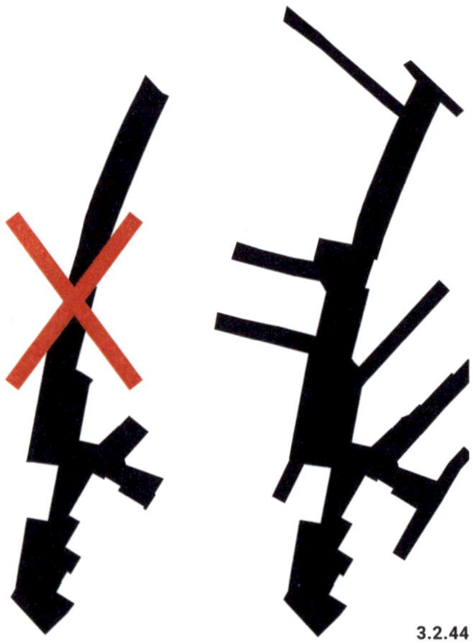

3.2.44

3.2.45

3.2.46

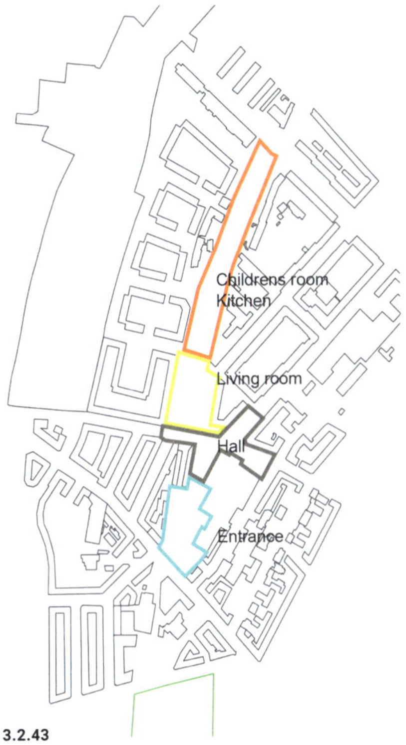

3.2.43

3.2.40–3.2.41 A unified surface. *(40) BIG, Topotek 1, internal study diagram, September 11, 2007; (41) BIG, Topotek 1, internal study diagram, September 10, 2007* **3.2.42–3.2.43** Structuring of the space into sub-areas. *(42) BIG, Topotek 1, internal study diagram, September 6, 2007; (43) BIG, Topotek 1, internal study diagram, September 12, 2007* **3.2.44** Diagram of intent, with caption: "We propose to extend the site borders so the connected streets are a part of the site." *BIG, Topotek 1, internal study diagram, September 19, 2007* **3.2.45–3.2.46** Evolution of the synthetic diagram of the project. *(45) BIG, Topotek 1, Superflex, "Superkilen, 3 zoner, 3 farver – et globalt kvarter," competition entry, October 5, 2007; (46) BIG, Topotek 1, Superflex, presentation document, November 9, 2011*

GIVE THE PLACE AN IDENTITY BY A RADICAL TREATMENT OF THE SURFACING

While the final design appears to have a certain complexity that we'll attempt to unravel in the following pages, the initial concept is simple and focuses on the ground. It stems from an initial desire to unify this residual space and give it an identity of its own, by proposing a ground covering that is both uniform and distinctive (Fig. 3.2.40). This approach, which could be described as a "carpet strategy,"[27] is literally depicted in an exploratory sketch by Topotek 1 (Fig. 3.2.41), who have been working on this approach since the firm was founded in 1996.[28]

But Superkilen, standardized in this way, still looks too big, too long, or perhaps simply too confusing. The designers then turn their attention to finding an internal structure. They consider a fluid division of the space by the main pathways or a subdivision into places with different ambiences and functions recalling the rooms of an apartment (Fig. 3.2.42–3.2.43). Eventually, the designers were to retain the idea of sequences but revert to a more obvious articulation of three spaces, as suggested in the competition brief[29] (Fig. 3.2.45).

The spatial division responds not only to a desire for structure but also to a desire to diversify user experiences. Each part should therefore offer complementary opportunities and above all possess a singular character assured by the choice of a color. As Nanna Gyldholm Møller, project leader at BIG, explains: "The idea of the three colors was to clearly subdivide this long park by creating spaces that would add identity to the area."[30] This way, the project will not only assert its singularity in the face of the adjacent network of public spaces, but each subpart will clearly assume independence from the other two.

A SUPERLATIVE PROJECT

This singularity through color reflects a search for immediate visual effect. Martin Rein-Cano, co-founder of Topotek 1, justifies this primacy of the visual by the need to disrupt the district's image, in the eyes of its own inhabitants as well as those of the outside world.[31] But the visual effect apparently was not enough to define the new identity of Superkilen, which was enriched by new project intentions throughout the process.

Since the beginning of its redevelopment, Superkilen seemed destined to overdo it. When the time came to name this undefined and residual space, the clients opted for the name "Superkilen," whose prefix – super – already reflects the desire of the competition organizers to make this place a true "emblem for the neighborhood."[32] This vocation was well grasped by the winners, who followed the request to the letter, imagining a project to which a "profusion of signs and symbols"[33] would be superimposed as the development progressed, until reaching a final image that was quite dazzling.[34]

The designers assume this visual and symbolic bludgeoning that they consider necessary, once again, to reconstruct the image of the place and the neighborhood in general. Bjarke Ingels, the founder of BIG, describes the project as "excess, saturation, and congestion"[35] and Rein-Cano says that depending on the situation "it is important sometimes to be loud."[36]

To intensify the project, a layer of narrative is deployed to reinforce the formal proposal of the three colored spaces. In order to anchor their intervention in the neighborhood, the designers revisit its multi-ethnic dimension and the theme of immigration by developing the space with furniture elements from the countries of origin of Nørrebro's residents.[37] They hope to create a sense of belonging and to reverse the negative image of a neighborhood with a high level of immigration. By treating the furniture elements as transposed ready-made,[38] the project is inspired by English landscape design, which incorporated garden constructions – pastiches of ancient Greek ruins or Asian pagodas – as the team's landscape designers like to recall in their presentations and publications.[39]

AMBIVALENCE TOWARD THE CONTEXT

All the aspects mentioned so far contribute to an autonomy of Superkilen from the surrounding context, be it by origin, form, or expression. It is true that the buildings that border Superkilen do not qualify the open space much, either in spatial or programmatic terms. The site's railway history has resulted in the majority of the adjacent buildings turning their backs on it and being located at a distance.

Rein-Cano believes that when dealing with public space, it is necessary to seek a relationship with the adjacent architecture, provided that the latter exhibits qualities.[40] In this case, a posture of contrast was justified: "It is not a clear space, which creates a certain autonomy. Also, it is worthwhile to continue a story, if it is interesting. There was nothing interesting to continue, so we had to create something of our own."[41] The undefined environment thus legitimizes the creation of what he describes as "anti-space," which would be neither contextual nor one of continuity. However, two aspects of the project show that this indifference claimed in the narrative is not in fact total. The first concerns the way in which the paving of the two squares will be delimited, the second relates to the evolution of the motifs that cover them.

In a sketch of intent from the first weeks of work, the designers sought to extend the scope of the competition, with the aim of intensifying the continuity between Superkilen and the surrounding public spaces (Fig. 3.2.44). They ultimately stuck to the boundaries given for the competition submission. At this stage, both the black and red squares had an undefined form (Fig. 3.2.45). But as the project developed, the designers realized that the built ensembles bordering the two spaces are not comparable. The black square is bordered by two parallel bands of housing with regular facades of similar height. The red space occupies a residual gap, resulting from the meeting of two skewed orientations. It is bordered by heterogeneous forms, including simple garages, garden pavilions, or walls marking a property line. Moreover, several of these frontages present a gabled facade to the square.

Consequently, the team decided to interrupt the design of the black square at a distance from the harmonious fronts that border it, thus showing a certain reverence for the built environment. Conversely, the red cladding was to extend over the entire area, even covering some gable walls. The black square is thus treated as a defined and delimited object, while the red surface integrates the building in an unprecedented way (Fig. 3.2.46). This difference in the treatment of the two squares demonstrates that the spatial configuration and the nature of the surrounding buildings are not totally suppressed by the authors of the project. So is Superkilen not completely acontextual?

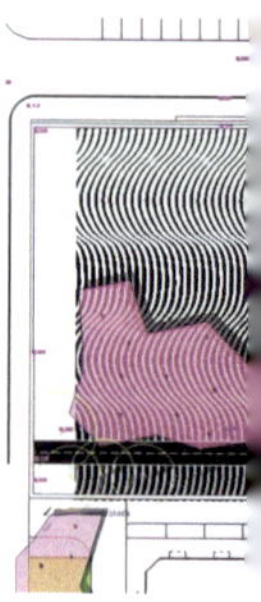

3.2.47–3.2.48 Two monochrome squares. *BIG, Topotek 1, internal study diagram, September 26, 2007* **3.2.49** Circular graphic pattern. *BIG, Topotek 1, Superflex, "Superkilen, 3 zoner, 3 farver – et globalt kvarter," competition entry, October 5, 2007* **3.2.50** Undulating graphic pattern. *BIG, Topotek 1, internal study document, February 27, 2009* **3.2.51** Final surfacing of the square. *BIG, Topotek 1, Superflex, publication drawing, April 2009* **3.2.52–3.2.53** Pattern variant at the competition stage. *(52) Redrawing highlighting the elements of the context on which the pattern is based.; (53) BIG, Topotek 1, Superflex, "Superkilen, 3 zoner, 3 farver – et globalt kvarter," competition entry, October 5, 2007*

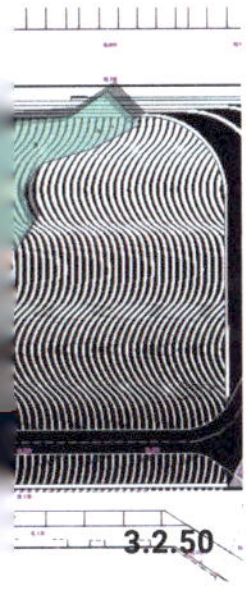

3.2.50

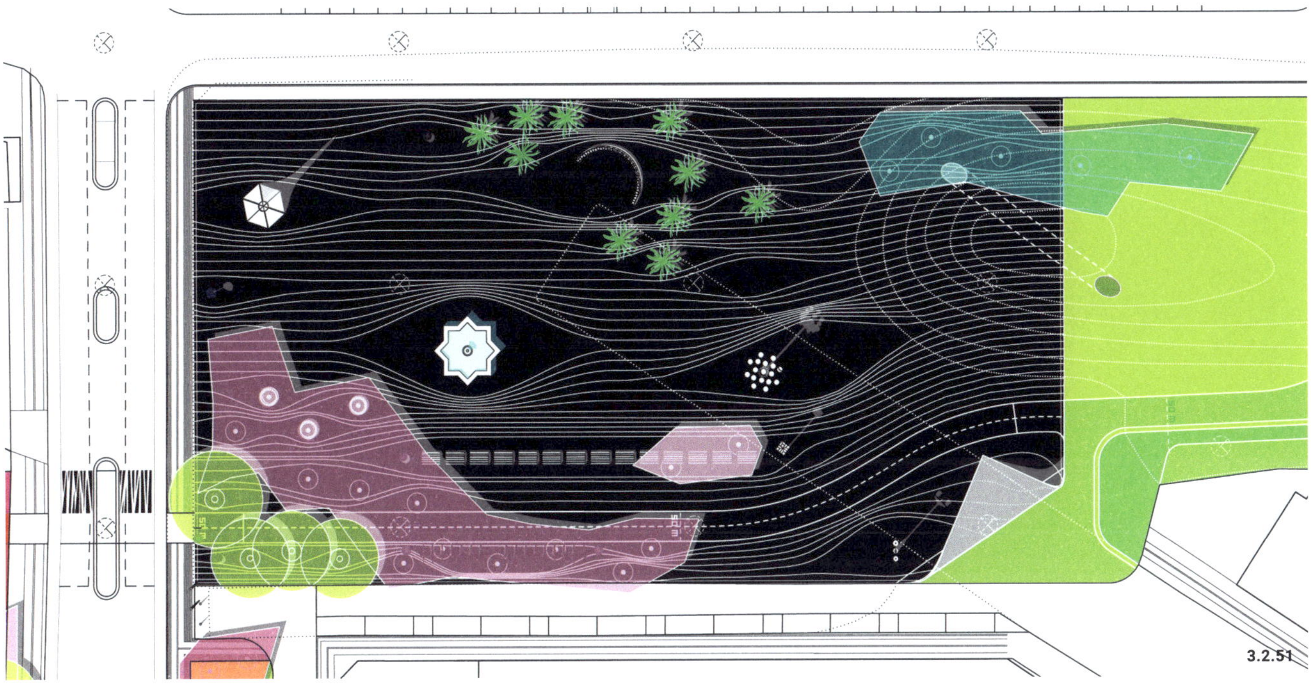

3.2.51

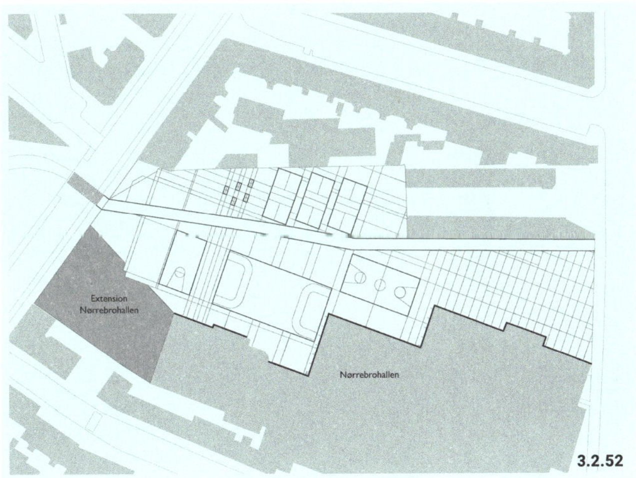

3.2.52

3.2.53

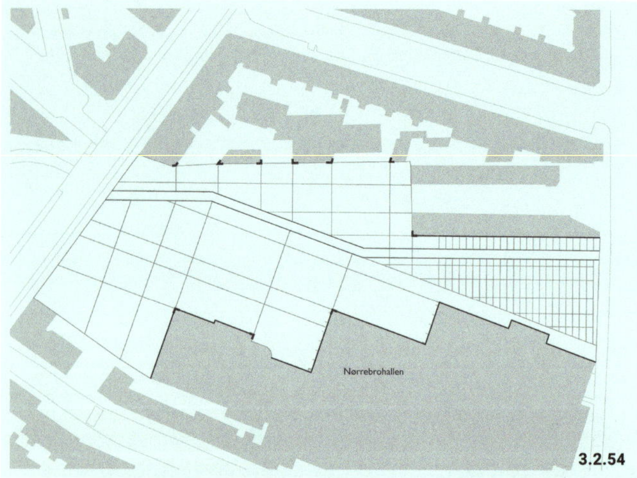

3.2.54

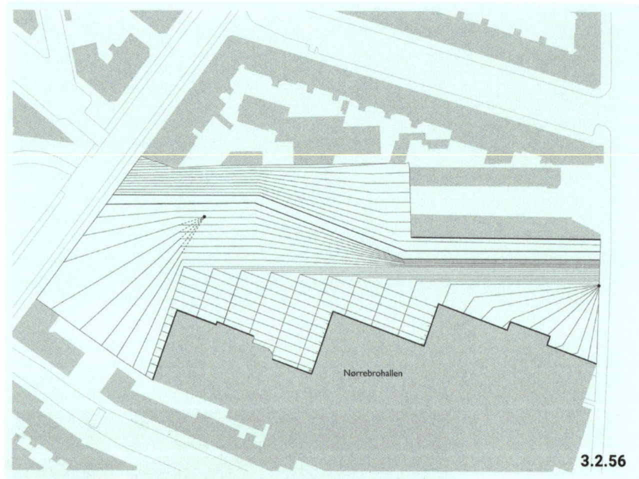

3.2.56

3.2.55

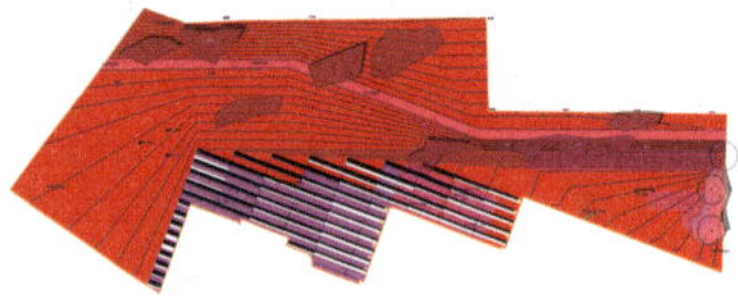
3.2.57

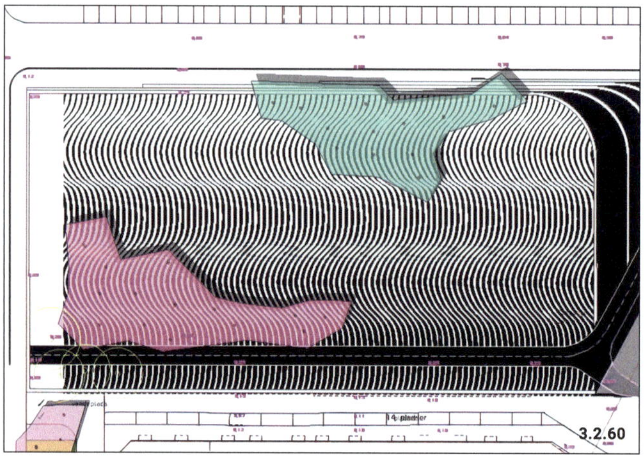
3.2.60

3.2.61

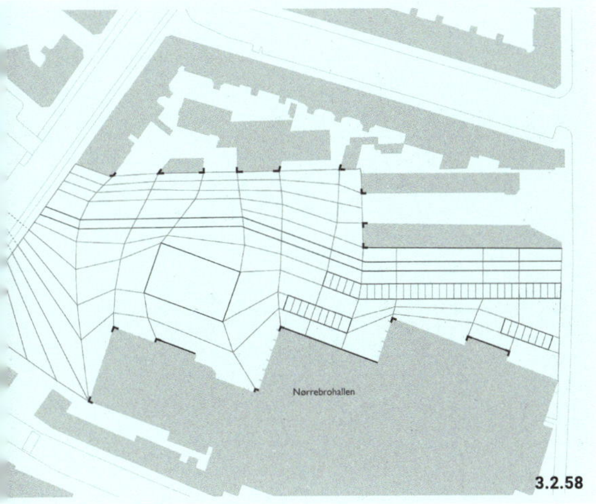

3.2.58

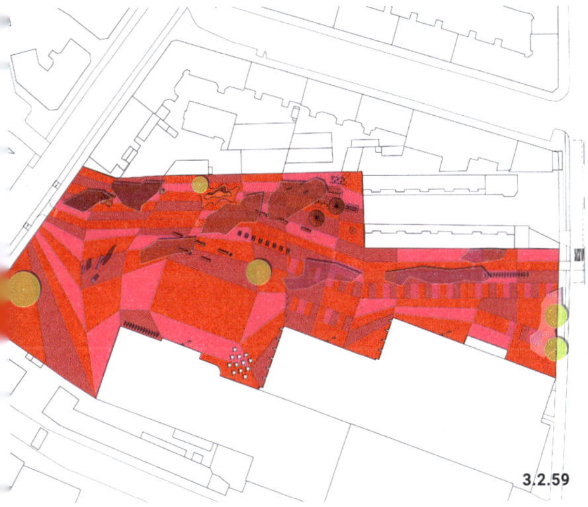

3.2.59

3.2.54–3.2.55 Pattern variant, orthogonal to the two fronts. *(54) Redrawing highlighting the elements of the context on which the pattern is based.; Based on (55) BIG, Topotek 1, study plan, 2009* **3.2.56–3.2.57** Fluid pattern variant. *(56) Redrawing highlighting the elements of the context in which the pattern is based.; (57) Based on BIG, Topotek 1, study plan, February 27, 2009* **3.2.58–3.2.59** Selected variant. *(58) Redrawing highlighting the elements of the context in which the pattern is based.; (59) Based on BIG, Topotek 1, Superflex, publication drawing, April 2009* **3.2.60** Graphic pattern. *BIG, Topotek 1, study plan, February 27, 2009* **3.2.61** *Fall*, 1963, Bridget Riley. © Bridget Riley, photo Tate

THE DESIGN OF THE RED SQUARE AS AN EXAMPLE

The ground surfaces are a second illustration of the designers' ambivalence toward the built context. Initially conceived as monochromatic (Fig. 3.2.47–3.2.48), these colored backgrounds will eventually be ornamented with patterns. In the black square, a repetitive circle motif, more abstract or very figurative graphic lines will be tested as the project develops (Fig. 3.2.49–3.2.50). The final design is made up of a network of parallel lines that spread like waves around each piece of furniture or tree implanted in the square (Fig. 3.2.51).[42] The black square thus very quickly integrates a logic indifferent to the context, which corresponds to the formal autonomy conferred on it by its strictly rectangular delimitation.

The red square will maintain, as the project develops, a more ambiguous relationship with the buildings that border it. During the competition, the team clearly asserted the dominance of the Nørrebrohallen, on which the orientation and geometry of the motif are based (Fig. 3.2.53). The paving is presented as a programmed surface integrating parking spaces and sports fields (field hockey, basketball, badminton, volleyball) that dictate the rhythm of a strictly orthogonal grid.

In a second phase, the primacy of the sports hall will be counterbalanced by a consideration of the front that faces it (Fig. 3.2.55). The matrix, still orthogonal, adopts this time the main orientation of the two edges, accepting their equivalence. Perpendicular lines are drawn from the angles of the adjoining buildings. In the center of the square, the meeting between the two geometries is moderated by the dedicated cycle path. In another intermediate sketch, it is precisely this circulation element that generates a more fluid design, with some lines radiating from a focal point (Fig. 3.2.57). Consideration of the viewpoint of pedestrians and cyclists on the move seems to take over the logic of layout plan that has dominated until now.

The final design is a distorted grid (Fig. 3.2.59). Three programmatic elements – the bike path, a multi-use plaza, and the parking lot – respond to the main orientations of the space. A net of lines connects the corners of these three elements and to existing buildings, producing irregular polygons. These alignments with the adjacent buildings provide a visual coherence to the square, despite its complexity. Note that the plan representations and aerial photographs of the project are the only means of apprehending this sought-after motif of the red square. The perceived reality is quite different. On site, it is difficult to grasp the design in question, in contrast to the black square, which is presented in extreme clarity.

A PICTORIAL TREATMENT OF THE PUBLIC SPACE

To explain the motifs of the two squares, the designers present them as imported components, just like the furniture elements from around the world scattered throughout the space. Although transplanted, they have a geographical anchor, a country, a region, a city, from which they originate. The ground motifs have no identifiable origin; they are in a way universal or stateless. It is stated on the competition's illustrations that the choice of colors was motivated by their neutrality "in terms of culture, nationality, or language." While there is no reference to a place for the ground treatment, the team seems to draw its inspiration from the artistic field.

Rein-Cano believes that "painting and color are inherent elements of composition" in his practice as a landscape designer.[43] He thus attests to a pictorial approach to public space, to which he devotes a genuine interest observable in the production of Topotek 1. In the case of Superkilen, this approach is enriched by the intention to create visual illusions, whether through the blurring of horizontal and vertical surfaces in the red square, through the vibration produced by the juxtaposition of the colors lilac, purple, red, and orange, or through the lines on the ground in the black square, which "create a sensation of topography."[44] These optical effects stem from an intention to offer users a true sensory experience. The term "sensation" appears repeatedly in the designers' narrative, as if to insist on the ambition to provoke physiological stimulation through their development project.

These preoccupations recall the approach of certain Op Art (or Optical Art) artists of the 1950s, which has recently been the object of renewed interest in Europe.[45] One of the first intentions of the current movement, strongly influenced by *Gestalt* theory, is to transform the rapport to the work and "to suggest the movement virtually using optical devices, such as retina effects, to destabilize the observer's perception of lines, forms, and color."[46] To our knowledge, the authors of Superkilen were not explicitly inspired by Op Art, which appears neither in the reference images and presentations, nor in the partial archives consulted. The juxtaposition of the project and some of the works seems nevertheless surprising, and the narrative supported by some optical artists is curiously close to the concerns expressed by the designers.

For example, one of the intermediate variants of the black square motif, mentioned above, echoes Bridget Riley's 1963 painting *Fall* (Fig. 3.2.60–3.2.61). In this painting, the artist proceeds by strictly identical repetition of an undulating line to produce an effect of instability and movement. The final layout of the square is reminiscent of works by the French-Hungarian painter Victor Vasarely, which he defined as "undulatory" (Fig. 3.2.62–3.2.63).[47] In his *Naissances* and *Manipur*, the artist draws on a rational/random dialectic by disrupting the rigor of a grid of parallel lines to reveal geometric patterns suggesting a form of volumetry. The line pattern applied to Superkilen also undergoes inflections by adapting to the layout of the cycle path or elements of furniture and vegetation, intensifying the topographical perception of the square. The processes of the planners and the optical artist seem comparable, in their constitutive rules as in their produced effects.

As far as the red square is concerned, links can also be woven with V. Vasarely's production according to two themes in his work. During his *"gonflages"* (swellings) period, the artist experimented with principles of deformation similar to those implemented in Superkilen (Fig. 3.2.64–3.2.65). Pure geometric shapes – often squares – are linked, generating irregular polygons. These patterns are reminiscent of the polygons that connect the rigorously delineated programs of the red square – plaza, bike path, parking lot – to the ties of the existing context. In terms of color, Superkilen's hues are similar to some of Vasarely's early paintings, such as the *Alphabet AR* (Fig. 3.2.66–3.2.67), or to Bridget Riley's more recent production in some of her works from the *Fragments* series.

Even if these relationships between Superkilen and Op Art are only suppositions, they partially confirm the artistic, pictorial, and graphic treatment that the designers have dedicated to the development of these two squares. Thus, the public space clearly moves away from a purely functional role, to become a sensory environment, in which art seems to present itself as a legitimate inspiration.

3.2.62

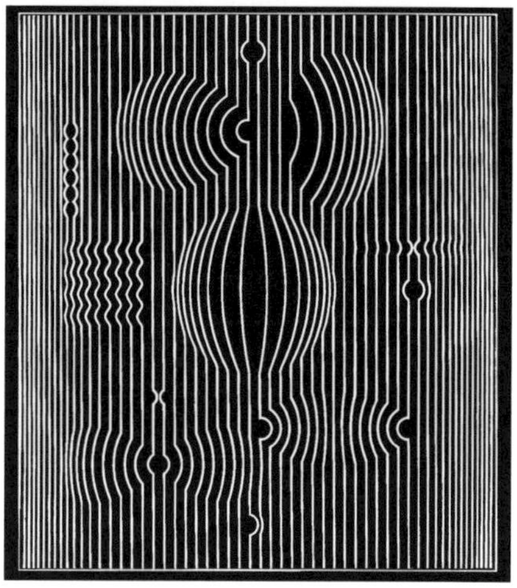
3.2.63

3.2.64

3.2.65

3.2.66

3.2.62 Final design of the black square. *BIG, Topotek 1, Superflex, simplified plan, n.d.* **3.2.63** *Manipur -Neg,* Victor Vasarely, 1957 **3.2.64** *Cheyt-J,* Victor Vasarely, 1970 **3.2.65** Aerial view of Superkilen **3.2.66** *Alphabet VR,* Victor Vasarely, 1960 **3.2.67** Detail of the surfacing of Superkilen

3.2.67

PICTORIAL FIGURES

Ambivalent relationship to the built environment – between narrative and project reality

By emphasizing an in-depth treatment of the ground, the two *ornamented* projects analyzed question by definition the relationship of the public space to the adjacent built volumes. However, two almost contradictory attitudes can be observed in the presentation of the designers' intentions.

In Place du Molard, the theme of emphasizing the void tends to make one believe that the public space will take on a unitary and discrete background value. However, it can be seen that the initial desire for sobriety is counterbalanced by a growing need, as the project develops, to define the ground in order to further mark the redevelopment. It is not enough to standardize the space with an ordinary covering, as the narrative could imply, it is necessary to underline the quality of the place by a singular solution. This translates into a theme for the public space and the definition of a language of its own, without opting for an exuberant design.

In Superkilen, the narrative is quite different, and this right from the start. It is stated that the adjacent buildings are completely disregarded, which, it is true, have little architectural substance and play a lesser role in defining the space to be developed. The public space is thus conceived in a striking manner and deliberately takes precedence over the rest, thus becoming a feature. A careful study of the project's development shows, however, that the designers are not as inattentive to the context as they claim, given the different treatment of the two squares in relation to their spatial configuration. An analysis of the evolution of the red carpet motifs will also reveal the increasing role played by the built environment on the ground design.

Whatever the point of view stated at the outset, there is in each case a disparity between radical statements and a more complex project. Restraint toward the built environment is not absolute in the Molard project that sets out to be self-effacing. Conversely, the more striking design of Superkilen, based on a supposed initial indifference, eventually incorporates some surrounding built features.

A literally poché surfacing

Affording a specific character to each *ornamental* project not only influences its relationship with adjacent buildings. The unique identity conferred on them also helps to detach these squares from the public spaces that border them. With their singular and clearly delineated surfacing, the Place du Molard and the two squares of Superkilen are in fact like real entities, whose background is not only the building but the urban environment as a whole. This is also confirmed in the iconography of the two projects.

In the case of Superkilen, the layout is often represented as a succession of monochrome shapes devoid of any contextual elements. The case of the Place du Molard is less obvious, but some representations also show the square as isolated, notably the overall plan of the public spaces in the old town. In this way, the public space seems to be *poché*;[48] a way of giving it a pre-eminent position in the network of public spaces. From a conceptual point of view, these spaces seem to be treated as singular elements, objects *per se*.

But in the case of Superkilen, emphasis does not stop at the conceptual and representative stages. The strategy of delineation, infill, and contrast is faithfully reflected in the physical development. The red and black squares are uniformly filled in with paint or asphalt. The ground is quite literally *poché*.

A new definition of local identity

As for the question of local anchorage, these two *ornamental* designs are intended to be contextual; but, for their designers, this term seems to encompass new interpretations. The materialization of the Place du Molard is inspired by the physical context in which the space is located, the designers seeking to link the project to the cobbled street network of the old town. But the proposal is also based on a historical reading of the space to be developed. Its past becomes the theme for developing the paving motif, in reference to the port that once occupied this urban space.

The local anchoring is also, in both proposals, cultural. In Geneva, it is the cosmopolitan nature of the city that is highlighted. Its many international organizations serve as inspiration conveyed in the words of everyday life etched in the glass paving stones on the ground. In Superkilen, the cultural reference perimeter is more restricted. The designers are specifically interested in the project's neighborhood population. The 57 nations from which the inhabitants of Nørrebro come are to be represented by the furniture and plants that occupy the public space. Thus, it becomes global and guarantees the designers a certain freedom in imagining the layout. The globalization phenomenon that seems to have affected the architectural discipline at the turn of the century[49] is thus extended to the design of public spaces, here taking a rather positive turn.

Whatever the form finally given to the space – form sometimes expressed in a very global language – the designers always strive to justify the contextual dimension of their proposal. The unusual definition that they give of a local identity seems, however, to legitimize the use of a novel formal language, one doubtless more distant than the specific qualities found in the immediate surroundings. Thus, the planners are free to draw on new referential fields, of which art seems to be the most influential.

Art as a referential field, and lack of control

The influence of art is unmistakable in the way the designers tackle these public spaces. It is notable that both groups voluntarily call upon an artist or a group of artists to complete their skill-sets. Although the artists in question do not initiate the *ornamental* design of the ground cover, this choice of collaboration testifies to the sensitivity of the architects and landscape designers to art.

This influence translates into a pictorial treatment of the ground, whether it be through light, textures, surfaces, shapes, or colors. There are many analogies with the decorative arts, such as mosaics, and with the visual arts, notably Op Art, and with graphic design. Finally, the question of visual perception is clearly embraced in both projects, by a dynamic perspective that attracts passersby to exploration of their spaces.

It should be noted that, concerning the Place du Molard (which is located in a historical context), the designers wish to detach themselves from an excessively arbitrary and subjective role, which would result in a static design for the paving. They favor the idea of an effect – a gradation in this case – in which lack of control is expressed by the random implementation of the paving on site. In the case of Superkilen, on the other hand, the designers master every detail of the design, thus fully assuming the subjectivity of their proposal; but the choice of furniture is left to the free will of the local inhabitants. Are we witnessing a certain resignation on the part of the designers, who do not want to be seen as despotic creators? In any case, this principle of lack of control of the final image challenges the notion of design as a fixed and peremptory creative act.

PLACE DU MOLARD

1 Beboux, Philippe (partner at 2b architectes), Lausanne, interview with the author in French, June 29, 2015.

2 City of Geneva, *Mandat d'étude parallèle, Réaménagement de la place du Molard. Règlement et cahier des charges* (Parallel Study Contracts, Redevelopment of Place du Molard. Regulations and Brief), February 2002, p. 10.

3 The distribution to the participants of a detailed document tracing the history of the square bears witness to the importance attached to the heritage dimension: City of Geneva, *Connaissance du site: la Place du Molard, parcours historique* (Knowledge of the Site: Place du Molard, Historical Tour), January 2002 [annex to the Parallel Study Contracts brief]. The winning team furthermore used one of the document's images in its competition boards.

4 City of Geneva, *Place du Molard. Règlement et cahier des charges, op. cit.*, February 2002, p. 13.

5 City of Geneva, *Mandats d'étude parallèles pour le réaménagement de la place du Molard. Rapport du groupe d'experts* (Parallel Study Contracts for the Redevelopment of Place du Molard. Report of the Expert Group), March 26, 2002, n.p.

6 Béboux, Bender, Collet, Presset [BBCP], *Réaménagement de la place du Molard. Annexe au Permis de construire* (Redevelopment of Place du Molard. Annex to the Building Permit), March 3, 2003 [Archives 2b architectes].

7 Note also that the theme of the void occupies a central place in the approach of the 2b agency and to which Stephanie Bender will devote a thesis, defended in 2011 at the EPFL: Bender, Stephanie, *Le vide: nouvelles stratégies urbaines*, doctoral thesis n° 4841, Lausanne, Ecole Polytechnique Fédérale de Lausanne, 2011.

8 Béboux, Bender, Collet, Presset, "Chuchotements," competition boards, MEP Réaménagement de la Place du Molard, March 19, 2002 [Archives 2b architectes].

9 Based on discussion with Stephanie Bender (associate of 2b architectes), July 15, 2015.

10 Béboux, Bender, Collet, Presset, *op. cit.*, competition boards, March 19, 2002.

11 *Ibid.*

12 Lacaton & Vassal, "Place Léon Aucoc, Bordeaux," n.d., http://lacatonvassal.com/index.php?idp=37 [accessed March 16, 2016].

13 Beboux, Philippe, interview cited above.

14 *Ibid.*

15 Kock, Thomas (partner at Polyform/Werk, member of KBP.EU), Copenhagen, interview with the author, September 30, 2015.

16 Beboux, Philippe, interview cited above.

17 *Ibid.*

18 *Ibid.*

19 *Ibid.*

20 *Ibid.*

SUPERKILEN

21 Kuben, *Superkilen – Det urban liv. Konkurenceprogram*, n.d., p. 3 [competition brief].

22 The involvement of the philanthropic institution Realdania in public projects, and in particular in the case of Superkilen, is a matter of debate. See Brett Bloom, "Superkilen : Park med ekstrem borgerinddragelse!," *Kritik*, n° 207, April 2013, pp. 47–76; Jens Lenler and Torben Benner, "Borgere på Nørrebro: Det blev som Realdania ville," *Politiken.dk, Kultur*, July 14, 2010.

23 Kuben, *Superkilen – Det urban liv. Konkurenceprogram*, n.d., p. 6 [competition brief].

24 *Ibid.*, pp. 2, 8.

25 Public call for competition on: Competitionline, "Superkilen – future innovate urban space in the outer Nørrebro District. Restricted competition," February 6, 2007, http://www.competitionline.com/en/results/7445 [accessed March 2, 2016].

26 BIG, Topotek 1, Superflex, "Superkilen, 3 zoner, 3 farver – et globalt kvarter" [30057], public call for competition on: Competitionline, "Superkilen – future innovate urban space in the outer Nørrebro District. Restricted competition," February 6 [Archives Topotek 1].

27 This term has been used since the turn of the century to describe development strategies that consist of covering a given area with a singular surfacing, most often a solid color or a distinctive motif.

28 Rein-Cano, Martin (partner of Topotek 1), Berlin, interview with the author, February 11, 2016; on this topic, see also note 40.

29 Kuben, *op. cit.*, n.d., pp. 6–7 [competition brief].

30 Gyldholm Møller, Nanna (project leader at BIG), written interview, October 22, 2015.

31 Rein-Cano, Martin, interview cited above. Let us emphasize that color is a component frequently used in initiatives – citizen or artistic – for reclaiming public space or urban renewal. Generally carried out quickly and with few means, these initiatives often adopt a festive and original language allowing the introduction of a new look to the space.

32 Kuben, *op. cit.*, n.d., p. 7.

33 Bridger, Jessica, "Life on the Wedge: In Copenhagen, Superkilen Rolls out a Half-Mile Mash-Up of Global Culture," *Landscape Architecture Magazine*, n° 103, 2013, p. 96.

34 Reeh, Henrik, "Der Superkeil von Kopenhagen," *Stadt Bauwelt*, n° 193, 2012, p. 61.

35 Ciuffi, Valentina, "Il parco dei parchi/The Park of Parks," *Abitare*, n° 516, October 2011, p. 53.

36 Rein-Cano, Martin, interview cited above.

37 Following the competition brief to integrate the local population in the design process, the residents were invited by the project authors to propose objects and to contribute directly to the project definition in its uses as well as in its aesthetic dimension. This unusual approach totally monopolized the critical reception which essentially focused on these elements of furniture. See in particular Ciuffi, *op. cit.*, 2011; Robert Schäfer, "Der Park der Wunder – Superkilen," *Garten + Landschaft*, n° 122, 2012, pp. 15–19; Ralf Wollheim, "Vereinte Nationen," *DB – Deutsche Bauzeitung*, n° 10, 2013, pp. 14–15.

38 The designers compare the furniture to an "objet trouvé" from M. Duchamp. BIG, Topotek1 and Superflex, "Superkilen," *Landskab*, n° 93, 2012, p. 158.

39 Rein-Cano, Martin, interview cited above. This particularity of the Topotek 1 approach is frequently noted: Pietro Valle, "Riding a Fake Cow on a Movable Landscape, Heading to the Beach," in Thilo Folkerts (ed.), *Topotek 1 Rosemarie Trockel: Eine Landschaftsskulptur für München*, A Landscape Sculpture for Munich, Basel/Boston/Berlin, Birkhäuser, 2011, pp. 96–97; Barbara Steiner (ed.), *Creative Infidelities: On the Landscape Architecture of Topotek 1*, Berlin, Jovis Verlag, 2016, p. 217.

40 See Topotek 1 projects such as DKV-Versicherung (1996–2000, Fig. 3.2.1, p. 102), which is based on the composition of the facades; or Broderie Urbaine Innenhof: Unter den Linden 32–34 (2004–2006, Fig. 2.20, p. 49), which uses the colors of the adjacent buildings.

41 Rein-Cano, Martin, interview cited above.

42 *Ibid.*

43 Steiner, Barbara (ed.), *Superkilen. A Project by BIG, Topotek 1, Superflex*, Stockholm/Oslo, Arvinius + Orfeus Publishing, 2013, p. 14. And Rein-Cano, Martin, interview cited above.

44 Rein-Cano, Martin, interview cited above.

45 Several exhibitions in the early 21st century have focused on the theme: *L'œil moteur. Art Optique et cinétique, 1950–1975*, Musée d'art moderne et contemporain de Strasbourg, May 13–September 25, 2005; *Op Art*, Schirn Kunsthalle Frankfurt, February 17–May 20, 2007, cited in Montfort, Anne, "Rendre Visible" in Musée d'art moderne de la Ville de Paris, *Bridget Riley Retrospective*, Paris, Paris Musées, June 12–September 14, 2008, p. 13; and more recently *Eye Attack, Op Art and Kinetic Art 1950–1970*, Louisiana Museum of Modern Art, Denmark, February 4–June 5, 2016.

46 Dezeuze, Anna, "The 1960s: A Decade Out-of-Bounds," in Amelia Jones (ed.) *A Companion to Contemporary Art since 1945*, Oxford, Blackwell Publishing, 2006, p. 42.

47 See in particular: Marc Hallain, *Vasarely*, Paris, Fernand Hazan Éditeur, 1974, p. 15; Bernard Dahhan, *Victor Vasarely: ou la connaissance d'un art moléculaire*, Paris, Denoël/Gonthier, 1979, pp. 219–220, 235.

PICTORICAL FIGURES

48 In urban planning, the *poché* as a method of representing solids/voids, backgrounds/figures, goes back in particular to Giambattista Nolli's famous plan of Rome (1748) or to Camilo Sitte's analyses of open spaces (1889). It was more recently revived by Colin Rowe and Fred Koetter in *Collage City* (1978). According to Jacques Lucan, who explored the conceptual message supported by this representative process in 2004, the *poché* is a way of monumentalizing a particular element, thereby giving it a pre-eminent value in relation to the rest of the context. Jacques Lucan, *"Généalogie du poché®," Matières*, n° 7, 2004, p. 41.

49 See on this subject, Jacques Lucan, *Précisions sur un état présent de l'architecture*, Lausanne, Presses polytechniques et universitaires romandes, 2015, pp. 231–254.

CONSTRUCT

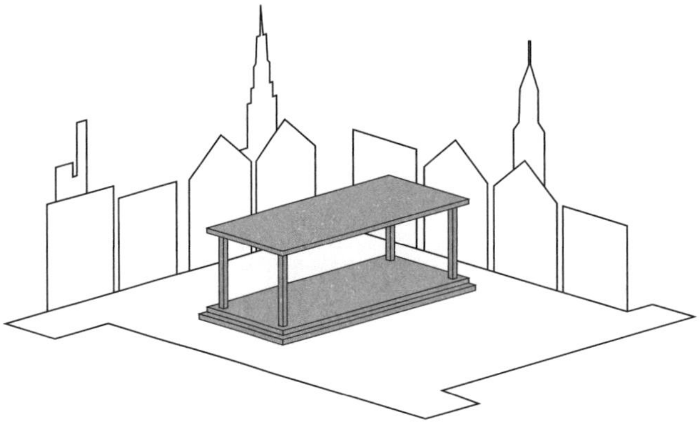

3.3.1
A prominent example
The Plaça dels Països Catalans, in Barcelona, is an example, if not paradigmatic, then at least striking, of the design strategy to follow when *constructing* public space. Widely published in professional journals, it has left its mark on a whole generation of architects and landscape designers. In addition to the grandeur of the two roofs and their value in articulating the space, their abstraction was a constitutive element of the character attributed to the square. *Plaça dels Països Catalans, Barcelona, Viaplana – Piñón – Miralles, 1983*

3.3.2–3.3.5
Various languages
The expression of the large roofs can vary from an abstract register to a more figurative language, inspired by various fields of reference. The three-dimensional structures sometimes take on a certain thickness, to become habitable. By their size and their presence, these constructions determine the character of the public space. *(2) Vieux Port in Marseille, Foster + Partners, Michel Desvigne, Tangram, 2013; (3) The Lantern, Sandnes, AWP Office for Territorial Reconfiguration, Atelier Oslo, 2009; (4) Metropol Parasol, Seville, Jürgen Mayer H. & Partner Architekten, 2011; (5) Centro Abierto de Actividades Ciudadanas, Cordoba, Paredes Pino, 2010*

Although still a marginal trend, some recent public space designs are made more intelligible by the construction of a large roof or structure visible from a distance. Public spaces usually free of construction, except for small structures of the pavilion or kiosk type, thus become truly *constructed*. They take on a three-dimensional scale creating a new relationship with the surrounding buildings and asserting a recognizable presence in the network of public spaces. The consequent dimensions in terms of size or surface of the built structures participate in this assumed manifestation.

The compositions so *constructed* not only make it possible to mark a public space in the urban fabric but in certain cases to articulate a place that lacks clarity. The *structures* sometimes have the function of hosting defined events, such as markets, but they can also simply have the vocation of offering a space protected from bad weather or sunlight, depending on their geographical location. These three-dimensional structures adopt very different languages depending on the situation, ranging from an affirmed abstraction to a much more rhetorical style in other cases. This choice of language can then testify to a desire for continuity or on the contrary to rupture with the surrounding context.

SELECTED CASE STUDIES

Two examples quickly stood out as case studies for this chapter. The first is the MFO-Park in Neu-Oerlikon, built by a team bringing together landscape architects Raderschall Landschaftsarchitekten and architects Burckhardt+Partner Architekten. The public space design is a true hybrid innovation in two respects: on the one hand, it combines the concepts of park and square, and on the other, open and built space. By its habitable dimension and its construction characteristics, this structure takes on a new value in the evolution of *constructed* public space.

The second case study, the Theaterplein in Antwerp redeveloped by Studio Associato Secchi-Viganò, was chosen for the exceptional dimensions and the value of articulation of the proposed roof in relation to the surrounding built environment. While the development structures are usually displayed as independent, here a relationship with one of the buildings defining the square, the theater, seems to be in evidence. This strong interdependence constitutes an evolution, which deserves to be studied. The unmistakably urban and abstract vocabulary of the Theaterplein, in contrast to the lush MFO-Park, also presents itself as an element worth investigating.

3.3.6 Location of the MFO-Park

MFO-PARK
ZURICH
1998–2002

Location Zurich, Switzerland **Lead designers** Planergemeinschaft MFO-Park (Burckhardt+Partner Architekten, Zurich, and Raderschall Landschaftsarchitekten, Meilen) **Type of commission** Two-round competition (1997–1998) **Construction** 2001–2002 **Former status** Former industrial area – private space **Area** 0.6 ha

At the end of the 1980s, the Maschinenfabrik Oerlikon firm (MFO), which had just been acquired by the ABB Group, was faced with an unavoidable restructuring. At that time, the factory occupied a large part of the industrial land in the north of the Oerlikon municipality. The question of converting this area of almost 60 hectares for a mixed-use district was soon raised; it was initially renamed Zentrum Zürich Nord (ZZN), then a few years later Neu-Oerlikon. The City of Zurich, in partnership with the site's main landowners, launched a competition in 1992 to define the broad outlines for the area's future urbanization.

A team of young local architects won, with the proposal to preserve the existing industrial area's structure together with some buildings. To give the district a strong identity, the project anticipated the construction of four large parks as drivers and guarantors of quality for the development of the district, to extend over 20 to 30 years (Fig. 3.3.8–3.3.10). The future Oerliker Park, MFO-Park, Louis-Häfliger Park, and Wahlenpark, would each be the subject of a specific public space project.[1]

The MFO-Park competition, launched at the end of 1997, covered a rectangular area of approximately 0.9 ha, which is part of the orthogonal grid of the industrial area.[2] The site was still occupied by buildings at the time and so inaccessible to competitors (Fig. 3.3.7). As its transformation depended on the demolition of existing buildings, the proposals were expected to integrate the principle of a park to be realized in two stages. In addition to these uncertainties, the design of the green spaces was done well before the district's conversion. The appearance and programming of the buildings to border the MFO-Park was still quite uncertain. Under these conditions, the designers had to work with a hypothetical context.[3]

The competition was to be held in two stages: the first focused on the conceptual idea, the second on a more finished project. The brief called for spatial flexibility and the integration of varied activities – sports, social, relaxation, meditation – plus movement due to the proximity of the station.[4] As for the character of the future green space, the program remained vague. Because of the changing urban context, however, it was stated that the MFO-Park should "provide an identifiable focal point" and that it could "assume an autonomous character."[5] This encouragement for singularity was also linked, due to its location, to its role as a gateway to the new neighborhood.

Faced with these multiple expectations, the multidisciplinary team of landscape architects Raderschall Landschaftsarchitekten[6] and architects Burckhardt+Partner imagined a space clearly divided into two distinct places: a gigantic green hall, nicknamed "Park-Haus,"[7] would occupy the northern part and would be completed, during the second stage of construction, by a square to the south. The parallelepipedic hall comprised a light metal framework to be covered by a multitude of climbing plants. The "facades" of this structure, designed as double walls of a certain thickness, form habitable spaces. As for the southern square, it would be occupied by 25 slender columns (*Ranksteelen*) following the template of the green hall, arranged in an orthogonal grid (Fig. 3.3.13–3.3.14).

Of the 72 designs submitted in the first round, 12 were selected by the jury for further development. Despite its very bold proposal, the Raderschall Landschaftsarchitekten and Burckhardt+Partner grouping was among the successful competitors. In the autumn of 1998, they won the second round of the competition. The northern part of the park was inaugurated four years later[8] (Fig. 3.3.11–3.3.12, 3.3.15).

3.3.7

3.3.7 The site at the beginning of construction. *Planergemeinschaft MFO-Park, collage of analog photos, n.d.* **3.3.8–3.3.10** Model of the development of the Zentrum Zürich Nord according to the vision of the Ruoss/Siress/Schrader team in 1992 and developed by the Büro ur, Ueli Roth **3.3.11–3.3.12** MFO-Park realized. *May 2015* **3.3.13–3.3.15** Evolution of the project's plan from competition to completion. *(13) Planergemeinschaft MFO-Park, "Parkhaus," entry boards for the first round "Konzeptphase," March 1998; (14) Planergemeinschaft MFO-Park, "Parkhaus," entry boards for the second round "Projektphase," August 1998; (15) Planergemeinschaft MFO-Park, final project plan, February 2002*

3.3.8

3.3.9

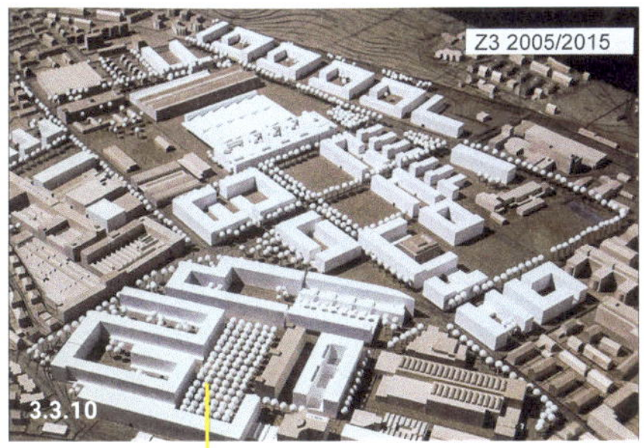

3.3.10

3.3.11

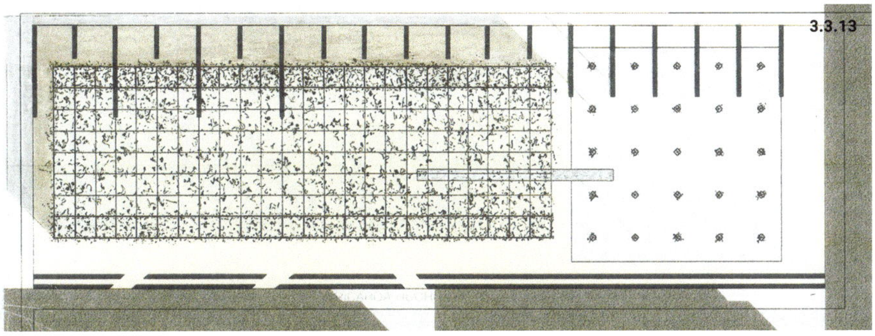
3.3.13

3.3.12

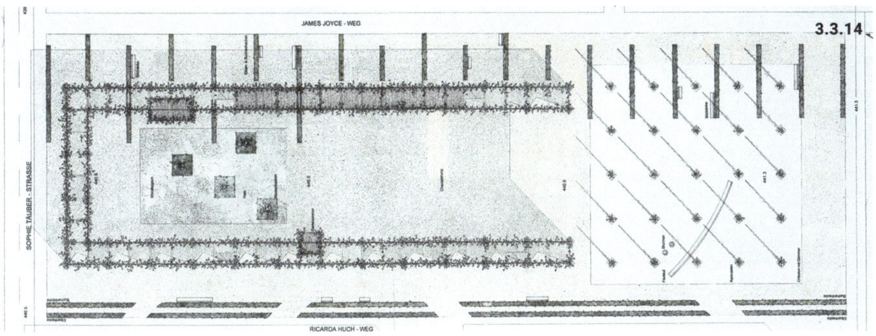

3.3.14

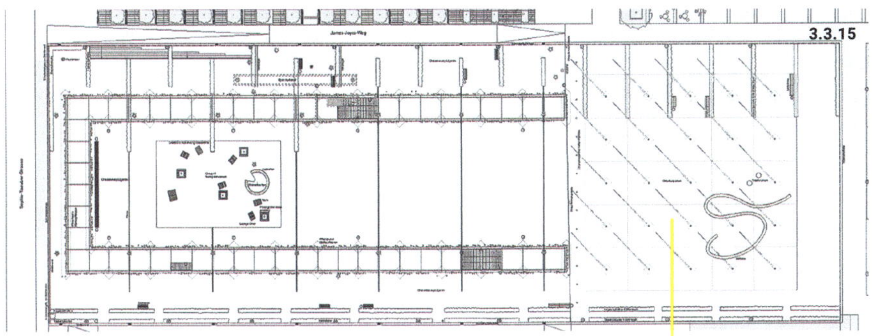

3.3.15

3.3.16

3.3.17

3.3.16–3.3.18 Preliminary sketches before the formation of the complete team. *Roland Raderschall, sketches, January 1998* **3.3.19** First sketch of the collective idea of Park-Haus. *Attributed to Heinz Moser, sketch, n.d. [approx. early 1998]* **3.3.20** Protagonists at work. *July 1998, at the Raderschallpartner office*

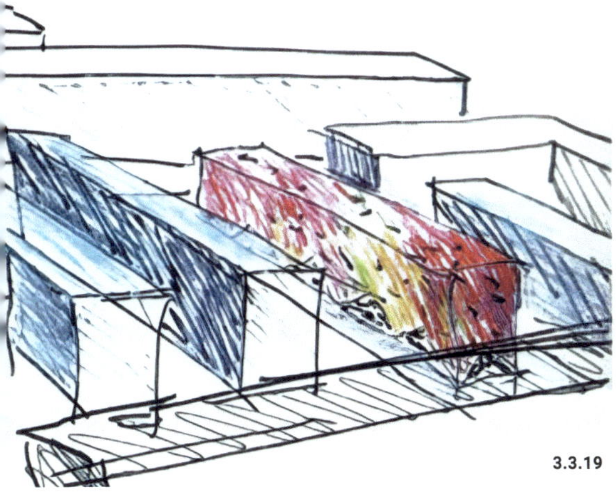

3.3.19

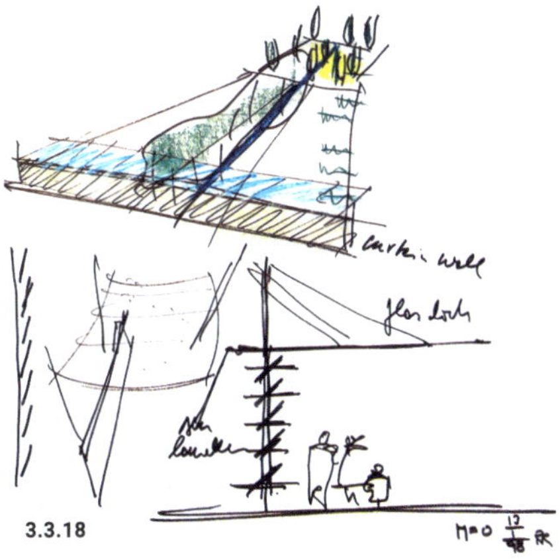

3.3.18

3.3.20

COMPETITION CONDITIONS AT THE ORIGIN OF AN EXTRAORDINARY CONCEPT

The Park-Haus, named for the park to which one attributes a building's volumetric dimension, appears as a true innovation. From the beginning of the project, the authors quickly became aware of the atypical character of their proposal, which they described on their submission illustrations as follows: "Nowhere today is there an urban garden such as the one proposed."[9] This creation would captivate the jury and also, once completed, the many specialized magazines would note the development's unique character.

According to Sybille Aubort Raderschall, partner at Raderschallpartner, this invention owes much to two factors, almost fortuitous, relating to the competition conditions. The first is the exclusive rights given to the landscape architects to take part in this park design competition,[10] which led the architect Heinz Moser of Burckhardt+Partner to contact the landscape design office, back then called Raderschall Landschaftsarchitekten, to propose a collaboration. The second is the rare, if not unprecedented, decision by the city of Zurich to hold a two-round competition that allowed the jury to integrate this bold proposal.[11]

With regard to the first factor, archived documents confirm the idea of a bi-disciplinary invention. Prior to collaboration with Burckhardt+Partner, the landscape designers first imagined a relatively traditional green space, as evidenced by some sketches by Roland Raderschall (Fig. 3.3.16–3.3.18). Shortly thereafter, Moser, with whom the landscape designers regularly associate, and his team join the venture. Raderschall and Aubort Raderschall enthusiastically accepted the proposal to collaborate, both because the north of Oerlikon is tinged with a particular architectural atmosphere, but also because they are attached to the idea of surrounding themselves with contributions from complementary disciplines.[12]

As soon as the architects joined the team, the project took a different direction. Moser quickly expressed the intention of echoing industrial halls. During the first joint session, he produced the famous original sketch of what was to become the MFO-Park: a three-dimensional structure on the scale of the surrounding buildings, covered with bright vegetation (Fig. 3.3.19).[13] From this point on, an intense and fruitful collaboration began. The project's six collaborators[14] met in the landscape architects' workshop to collectively develop their proposal, inducing a unique vision and an intertwining of disciplines that will be discussed below (Fig. 3.3.20).

While participation limited to that of landscape architects is thus at the origin of the Park-Haus creation, it is nevertheless the principle of a two-round competition that allowed this original idea to see the light of day.[15] During the first-round deliberations, the bold proposal was in effect quickly discarded. In the end, it had a last-minute reprieve thanks to two members of the jury, Jürg Altherr and Robin Winogrond, who insisted on giving the competitors a chance to demonstrate the feasibility of their extravagant proposal.[16] For the second submission, the team therefore focused on proving the feasibility of the Park-Haus, by rationalizing the structure, documenting the climbing plants, specifying the materials envisaged and delivering a detailed cost calculation. This pragmatic demonstration convinced the jury, who between the two submissions had had "time to get used to the idea."[17]

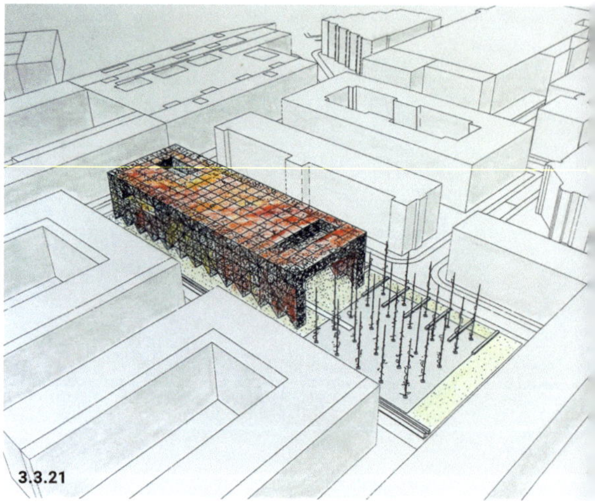
3.3.21

A VOID, DESIGNED AS A SOLID

To return to the question of collaboration between architects and landscape architects, several aspects of the project reflect a dialectic between the two disciplines and their modes of thought. For example, a temporal dichotomy arose in the implementation of the project: the slow growth of the natural covering to be superimposed on the rapidly constructed prefabricated architecture.[18] Through the seasonal evolution of the project, another contrast appeared: the fixed aspect of the built structure as opposed to the fluctuating appearance of the vegetation over the year. Finally, in terms of design, the totally controlled character of the built structure contrasts with the uncertainty of the climbing vegetation, which constitutes a true experiment.

Thus, throughout the project, a dialectic between architecture and landscape, short term and long term, control and uncertainty, was established, which explains the complexity and the unusual character of this development. In this disciplinary interaction, the *constructed* dimension nevertheless seems to have imposed itself throughout the project's development, giving new value to the public space.

Faced with an uncertain urban context, the designers decided to rely on two constants: the strictly orthogonal fabric of the neighborhood and the architectural qualities of its industrial halls. During the competition, this interest was clearly expressed: "Oerlikon Nord is today dominated by enormous volumes of industrial buildings. The Park-Haus makes reference to these translucent halls and this historical urban tradition in a completely new poetic way. By analogy with the new large buildings, this is done with contemporary (garden) architectonic expression."[19] Beyond a sensitivity for the lighting of these halls, the question of their scale seemed particularly fascinating to the project's authors. Consequently, the MFO-Park structure would be dimensioned to echo these industrial remains taking on a similar value to that of the surrounding buildings (Fig. 3.3.21).

A second project element, brought by Roland Raderschall, quickly consolidated this conceptual twist.[20] The landscape designer proposed to render this structure habitable thus making it more than a simple roof. It was therefore decided to double the envelope of the parallelepiped to integrate a series of paths and living spaces within the framework, giving it a new functional dimension. This addition had a direct effect on the formal expression of the project, which moved away from a landscape approach that is nevertheless widely conveyed in the competition's references.

One illustration in particular seems to run counter to this new order. It shows a gigantic barrel-vaulted arbor set in an 18th-century colonial garden in India (Fig. 3.3.22). The MFO-Park authors refer to the geometric properties – symmetry and monumental proportions – of this utopia, as evidenced by the caption "a grandiose perspective"[21] accompanying their representation. The confrontation of the aerial layout of the Park-Haus and the historical reference is, however, unsettling. In terms of scale effect, the two structures clearly resonate with each other. Yet, the duplication of the envelope contradicts the image of the arbor – a traditional element of garden design – which remains above all a light device for staging the space. With its strictly parallelepiped shape and added thickness, the Park-Haus moved away from the graceful impression of the arched horticultural arbor, becoming a real structure, like the buildings that surround it.

3.3.22

3.3.23

3.3.26

3.3.21 Axonometric of the MFO-Park showing the integration into the built environment. *Planergemeinschaft MFO-Park, "Parkhaus," entry boards for the first round "Konzeptphase," March 1998* **3.3.22** "Eine grossartige Perspektive." A grandiose perspective. *Reference presented on the competition boards: Planergemeinschaft MFO-Park, "Parkhaus," entry boards for the first round "Konzeptphase," March 1998* **3.3.23–3.3.25** Sainsbury Centre for Visual Arts, Norwich, Foster + Partners, 1978. *Construction site photos* **3.3.26–3.3.28** MFO-Park. *April 2015*

3.3.24

3.3.27

3.3.25

3.3.28

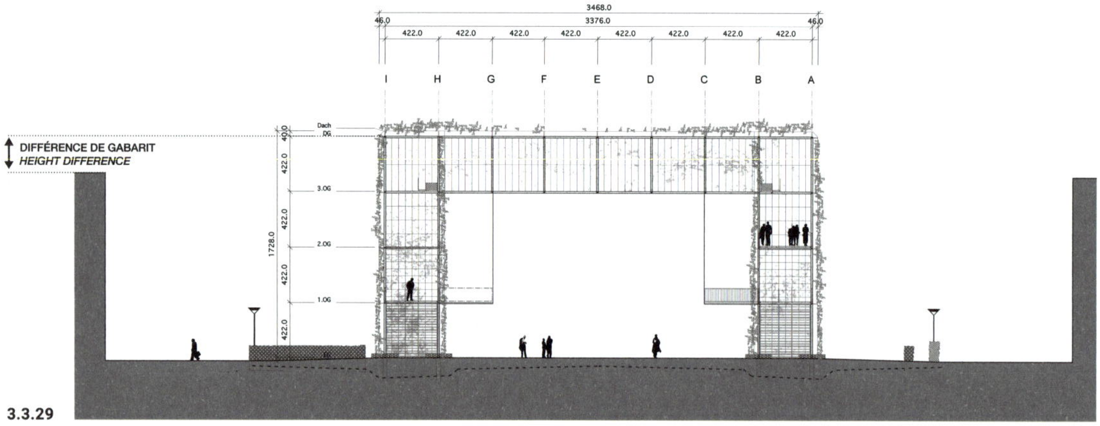

3.3.29

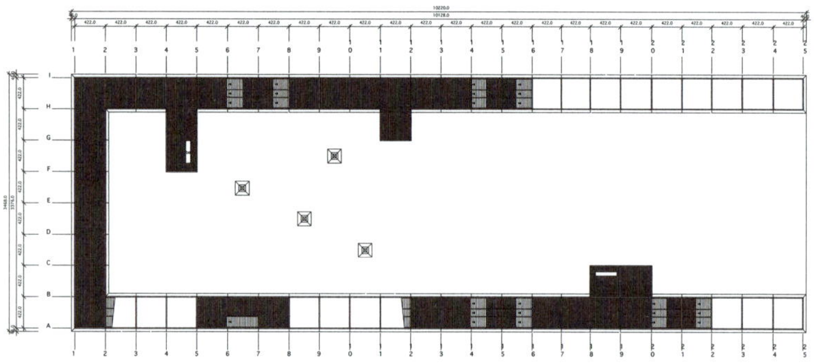

3.3.30 2.Obergeschoss

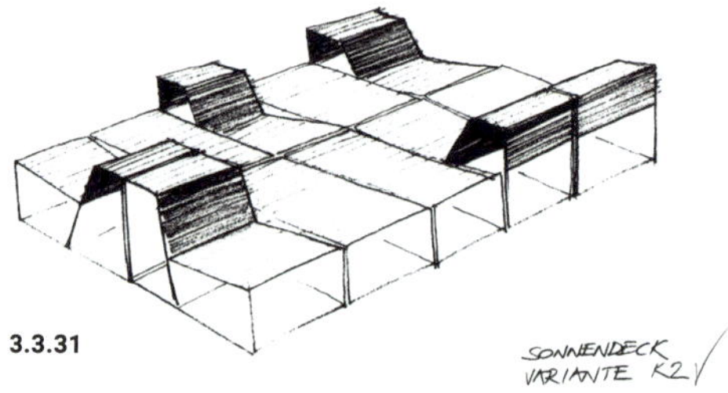

3.3.31

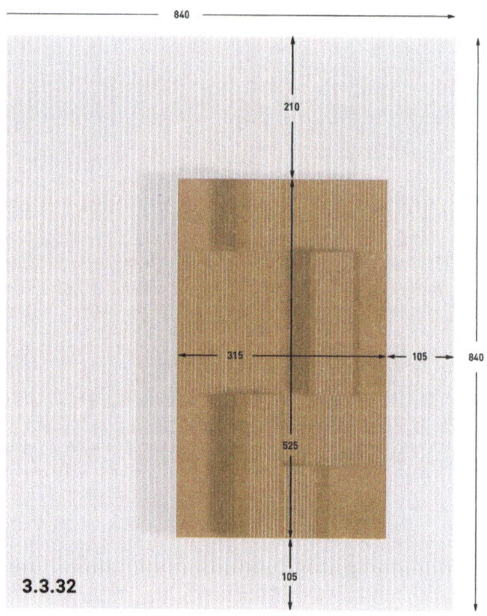

3.3.32

3.3.20–3.3.30 Composition in accordance with a predefined orthogonal grid. *Planergemeinschaft MFO-Park, working plans and sections, Baueingabe, June 27, 2000. [Section edited and annotated by Sonia Curnier]* **3.3.31–3.3.32** Development of furniture according to the park's reference unit. *Planergemeinschaft MFO-Park in collaboration with Frédéric Dedelley, work sketches, n.d.* **3.3.33–3.3.34** References displayed on the competition boards. *Planergemeinschaft MFO-Park, "Parkhaus," entry boards for the first round "Konzeptphase," March 1998; (33) "Ein uralter Traum." An ancient dream. F. Colonna,* Hypnerotomachia Poliphili, *Venice, Aldus Manutius, 1499, n.p.; (34) "Malerin im Sonnenschein," Frank Buchser, 1862, Kunstmuseum Solothurn, Depositum des Kunstvereins Solothurn.*

3.3.33

3.3.34

A PREDOMINANTLY CONSTRUCTIVE RATIONALITY

Although the Park-Haus was conceived by an extremely close collaboration between architects and landscape architects, it is difficult to attribute the predominance of its *built* character to the influence of the Burckhardt+Partner team in the project's development. This hasty assumption can, moreover, be disproved by the fact that R. Raderschall was responsible for the doubling of the structure and that he was subsequently inspired by a major architectural reference for the project: the Sainsbury Centre for Visual Arts (Foster + Partners, 1974–1978).[22] The similarities between the two metal skeletons indeed reflect the fundamental influence of Foster's building from an expressive and structural perspective (Fig. 3.3.23–3.3.28). In terms of proportions, the Park-Haus reproduces a similar span and static height to the three-dimensional latticework of the visual art center. The English architect's design seems above all to have inspired the team by its technical and rational character.

This rationality is confirmed in another element of the project: its dimensions. If the orthogonal shape and proportions of the Park-Haus refer to the industrial buildings on the site, it's a project-specific metric that explains its intriguing height of 16.88 m. Analysis of the drawings reveals that this surprisingly precise height is in reality but a multiple of the hall's double wall depth. Research of comfort of use, thus of human scale, initially defined this habitable thickness. The measurement was then refined for static reasons to result in a reference unit of 4.22 m (Fig. 3.3.29–3.3.30). On this basis, an orthogonal grid would dictate the entire internal composition of the building, from the proportions of the total framework (8 × 24 modules). Various subspaces were defined and added as the project developed, to give the structure added flexibility in use (staircases, corridors, balconies, terraces, and loggias). Even the furniture elements, developed specifically for the park with Frédéric Dedelley, were based on a division of this unit of measurement (Fig. 3.3.31–3.3.32). Through this modularity, which clearly recalls a manufacturing logic, the MFO-Park expresses itself as a fundamentally rational built project.

AN ONEIRIC PROJECT NARRATIVE

Looking at the competition submission illustrations from an iconographic point of view, it is nevertheless surprising to find no obvious allusion to this industrial rationality, nor to Foster's Sainsbury example. These layouts are, however, covered with pictorial references from all spheres, as if a design imaginary at an almost polar opposite to this posture of extreme rationality had been added to the project.

In the first phase of the competition, the illustrations had a primarily evocative function, serving both to anchor the project's concept and to depict the desired ambience. The first reference that appears is an engraving taken from *The Dream of Poliphilo,* accompanied by the caption "an ancient dream," which clearly expresses a nostalgic and dreamlike accent (Fig. 3.3.33). Other reproductions appear to collaborate in defining such an atmosphere, for example, the summoning of a painting by Swiss artist Frank Buchser (Fig. 3.3.34). The latter shows an interest on the part of the design team in developing more sensitive aspects of the project, through the play of light and shadow, coolness and warmth. In the second round, this interest indeed took a more practical turn, with the construction of a model used to trial the density of vegetation to be provided and the positioning of the structural openings – the "windows" – to admit light to the covered space.

In the text that accompanies the competition submission illustrations, we are given a description of this changing climate and play of light, also evoking other senses such as smell or hearing: "Atmospheres: In a region rich in rain – shadows dance on the gravelly ground – birds chirping in the arcades – a cyclist in the hall – a walk via the fragrant green stairs – a summer night in the opera box – a swaying as if under a big top."[23] A similar desire to depict the very special atmosphere of the Park-Haus can be found in some of the almost impressionistic perspectives (Fig. 3.3.35). These elements testify to the thematic spectrum of sensory perceptions in the MFO-Park development project, far removed from the rationalism revealed above.

AUTONOMOUS OR CONTEXTUALIZED OBJECT?

It is perhaps this dialectic between constructive rationality and dreamlike atmosphere that caused some critics to focus on the singular character of the development. In an article devoted to analysis of the Park-Haus, Axel Simon, who depicts it as a true "event in itself," considers that "the strength and unity of this space make it relatively autonomous in relation to its future neighbors."[24]

It is true that some elements, beyond their form, suggest that the built structure is a radically autonomous undertaking. Regarding the ground treatment, for example, leveling the land has the effect of producing a slightly raised base at the northern part of the park (Fig. 3.3.36–3.6.37). The plant-covered structure thus comes to rest on this plinth, resembling an artistic object mounted on a pedestal. For the remainder, involvement as an artistic gesture is clearly assumed by the designers: "the space appears as a sculptural object,"[25] we are informed by one of the first competition submission illustrations. Seen from this angle, the Park-Haus would thus be a singular intervention, an object *per se*.

Moreover, the distinctive treatment of the built volume's facades allows us to qualify the vision of the Park-Haus as a purely autonomous gesture. The relationship to the built environment is key and is illustrated in the asymmetry of the structure as dictated by the surrounding context. On the south side, the large hall opens generously onto the square that was to have been built at a later date. The two longitudinal sides, covered with vegetation, act as filters with respect to the buildings that face them, but remain permeable at ground level. Finally, on the north side, the treatment is much more hermetic: with no possible views or passage. Indeed, at the time of the development's competition, an entertainment complex (casino or cinema) was planned, from which the designers clearly wished to exclude themselves.[26]

In terms of materiality, the context's importance is even more clearly expressed in certain development choices. The steel structure and the steel grating are of course echoes of the site's industrial past. In the same vein, all the differences in level, such as the risers or the edge of the fountain, are materialized in corten steel. Finally, the floor of the large hall is covered with crushed yellowish marl reminiscent of the chromatic atmosphere of the existing industrial brick buildings.[27]

3.3.35

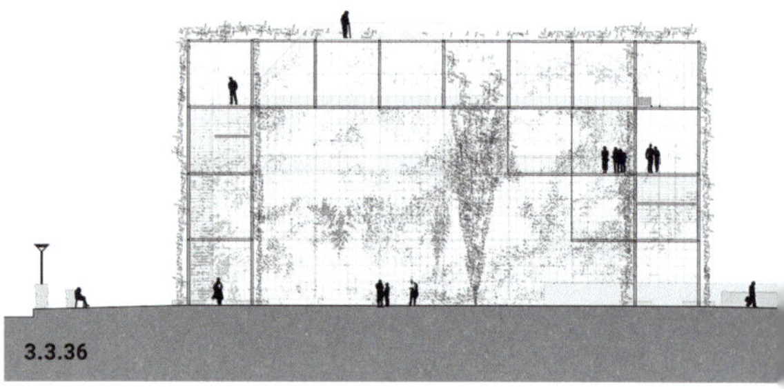

3.3.36

Because it was conceived as a solid building, the Park-Haus could at first glance be seen as an autonomous object enhanced by a plinth. However, the asymmetrical treatment of the volume's envelope, as well as the choice of materials in relation to the industrial context, call this autonomy into question. On the contrary, these elements reinforce the analogy with the built environment and the anchoring of the project in the existing fabric. The resulting monumental hall must therefore be considered as a *constructed* object, which remains contextualized.

3.3.35 A pictorial mode of representation. *Planergemeinschaft MFO-Park, "Parkhaus," entry boards for the second round "Projektphase," August 1998* **3.3.36–3.3.37** Cross-section and longitudinal section showing the differentiated treatment of the facades. *Planergemeinschaft MFO-Park, publication drawing, n.d., reproduced unscaled*

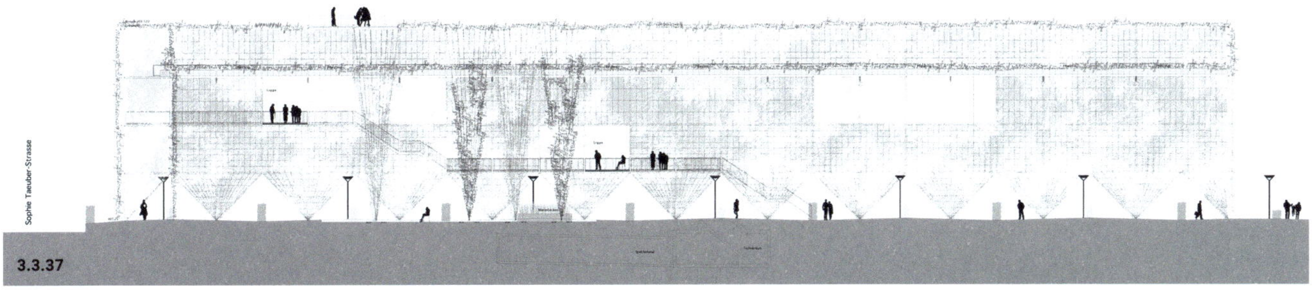

3.3.37

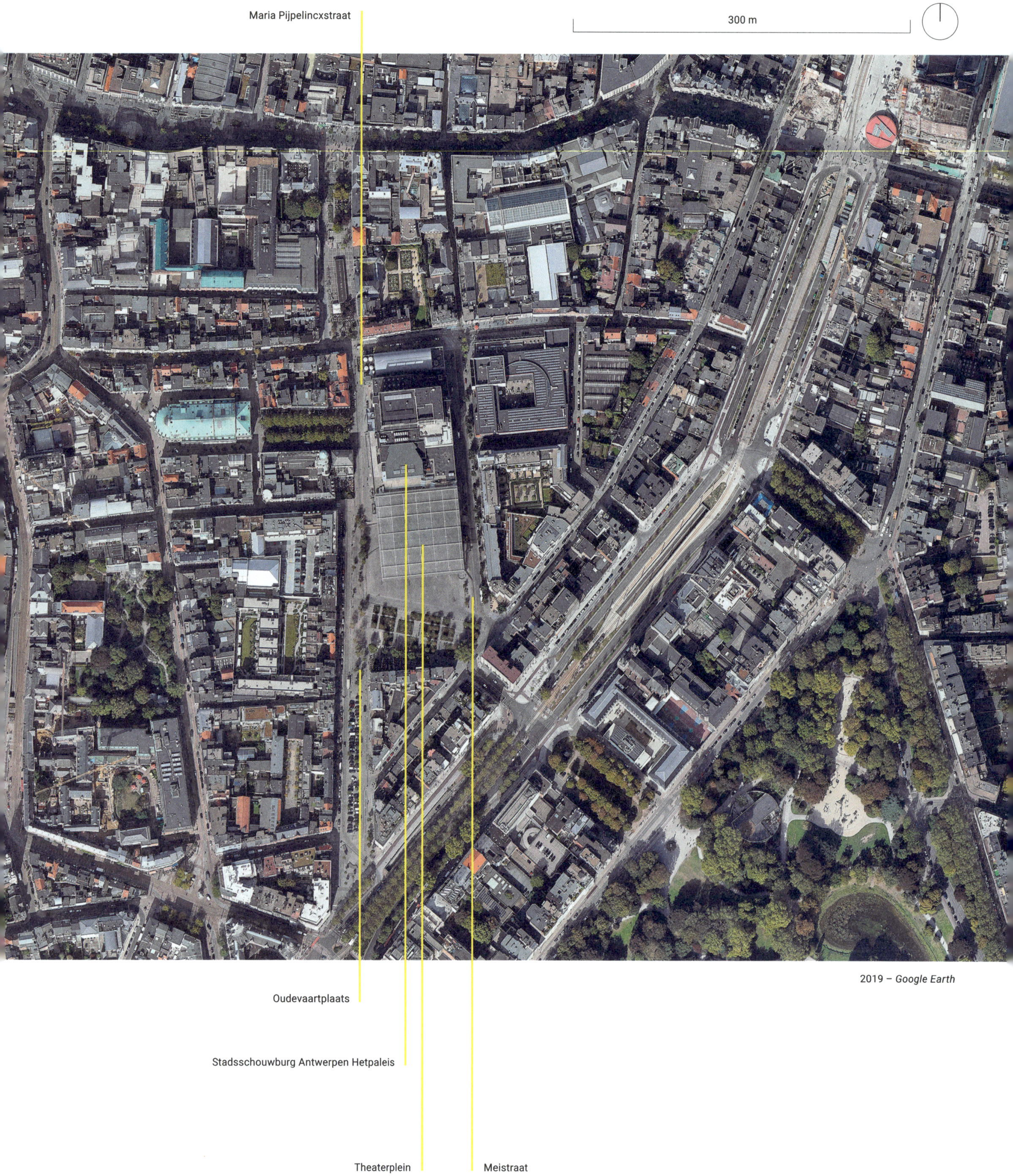

3.3.38 Location of the Theaterplein

THEATERPLEIN
ANTWERP
2004–2008

Location Antwerp, Belgium **Client** Stad Antwerpen **Lead designers** Studio Associato Bernardo Secchi Paola Viganò (Milan) / Dirk Jaspaert (local structural engineer) **Type of commission** Open Oproep – invited competition (2004) **Completion** 2008 **Former status** Open space, poorly designed and outdated **Area** 3.4 ha

In 2004, the city of Antwerp, supported by Flemish Master Architect (Vlaams Bouwmeester) Bob Van Reeth, launched a competition in the form of an "Open Oproep"[28] for the development of the Theaterplein. This square, totally neglected for several decades, occupies a strategic position in a city center undergoing major changes. The area to be redeveloped, of approximately 3.4 ha, also includes the two streets bordering the square on both sides. The square is dominated by a large theater dating from the 1970s, whose imposing but outdated red fire-escape stairs would be replaced. The building houses two main facilities, the Hetpaleis, a theater for young people and children, and the Stadsschouwburg Antwerpen performing arts theater. An underground parking lot, beneath the square, seems to be the project's only real constraint (Fig. 3.3.39).

3.3.39

In effect, the competition's very open brief does not define precise objectives for the design of these public spaces.[29] Nevertheless, it points to the regrettable spatial characteristics of the square, "too wide" and "without obvious boundaries," to which the proposals must respond. Regarding future uses, the designers are expected to transform the space into a place of activity, in addition to the famous weekend market that attracts a significant population.[30]

At the time, the Milanese office Studio Associato Secchi-Viganò[31] had been working in the Antwerp area for more than a year, both on the city's Structure Plan and on the design of the Spoor Nord park. So the partners decided to respond to this call for competition for a strategic area of a city that they were beginning to know well, and invited Flemish civil engineer Dirk Jaspaert to join their team. Their candidacy was accepted alongside four other internationally renowned firms,[32] and the project they developed convinced the jury to award them the commission.

In examining the site, the prizewinners identified two fundamental problems to be solved in the new development: the theater facade, little appreciated by the people of Antwerp, and the fragmented nature of the space. Their proposal was summarized in a few simple principles, starting with the realization of as continuous a surface as possible – in the form of a plane sloping toward the theater – in order to create a coherent square bordered by two streets. The second measure concerns the articulation of this vast space to give it structure. The Theaterplein would therefore be subdivided into a hard surface intended for collective and active uses and a garden area for calmer and more introverted activities. The Pijpelincxstraat/Oudevaart-plaats axis that borders the square to the west was to be dedicated mainly to strolling, while the Meistraat to the east would be used as a service road. Finally, the imposing square roof that covers the hard-surface area is the most striking element of the design. It distances the much-criticized theater facade while giving it a presence in the square (Fig. 3.3.40–3.3.42).

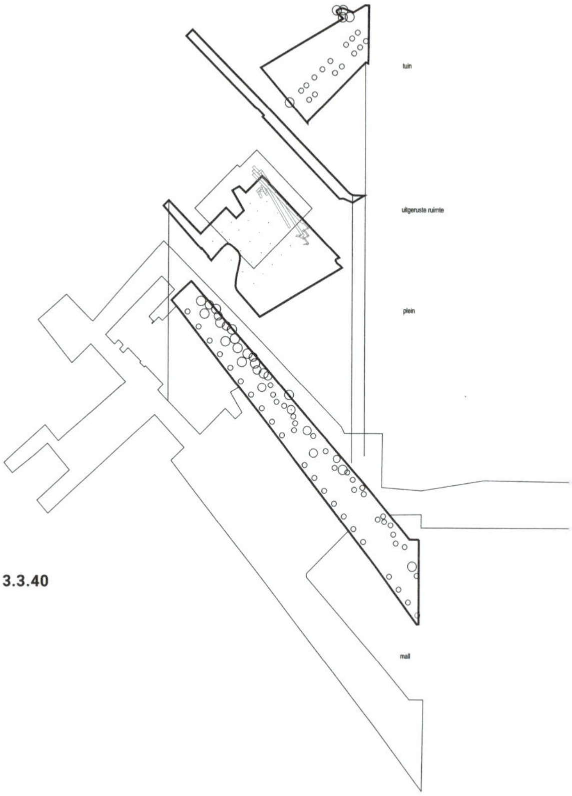

3.3.40

3.3.41

3.3.39 Photo of the site before redesign. *March 2004* **3.3.40** Exploded axonometric illustrating the four subspaces. *Studio 04 Secchi and Viganò et al., "Spazio s-misurato," album accompanying the Open Oproep competition boards, n.d. [estimated date December 2004]* **3.3.41** Axonometric of the winning project. *Studio 04 Secchi and Viganò et al., "Spazio s-misurato," album accompanying the Open Oproep competition boards, n.d. [estimated date December 2004]* **3.3.42** Aerial view of the project. *Studio 04 Secchi and Viganò et al., "Spazio s-misurato," album accompanying the Open Oproep competition boards, n.d. [estimated date December 2004]* **3.3.43** Large-scale representation of the meeting of two systems. *Studio 04 Secchi and Viganò et al., "Spazio s-misurato," album accompanying the Open Oproep competition boards, n.d. [estimated date December 2004]*

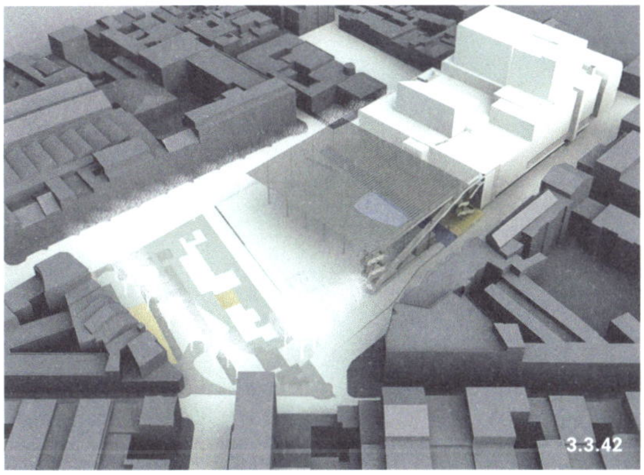

3.3.42

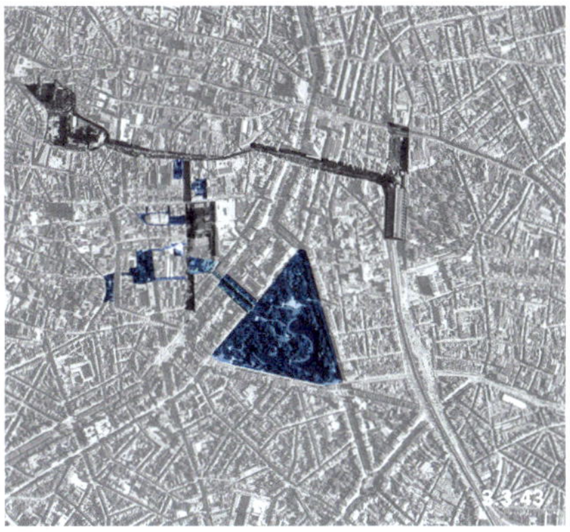

3.3.43

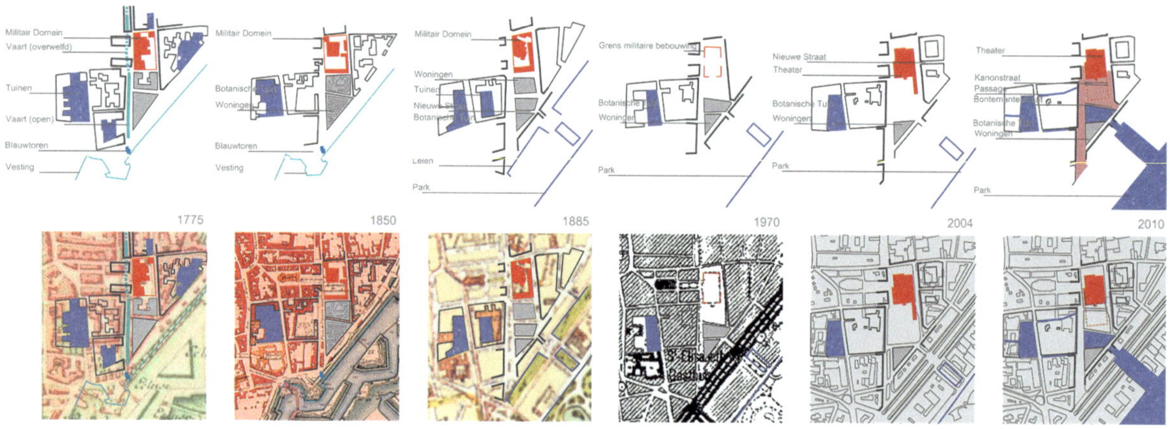

3.3.44

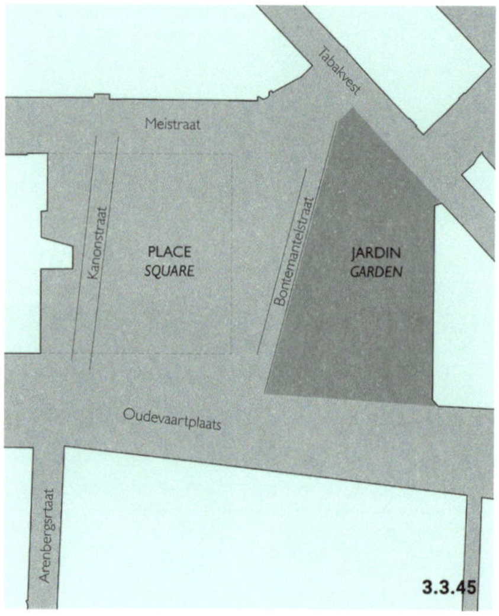

3.3.45

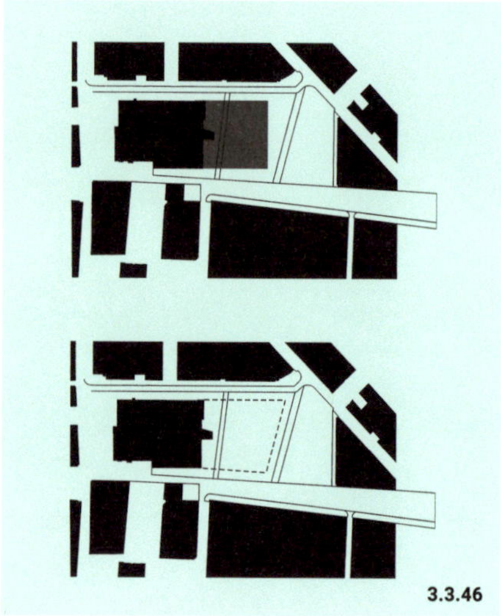

3.3.46

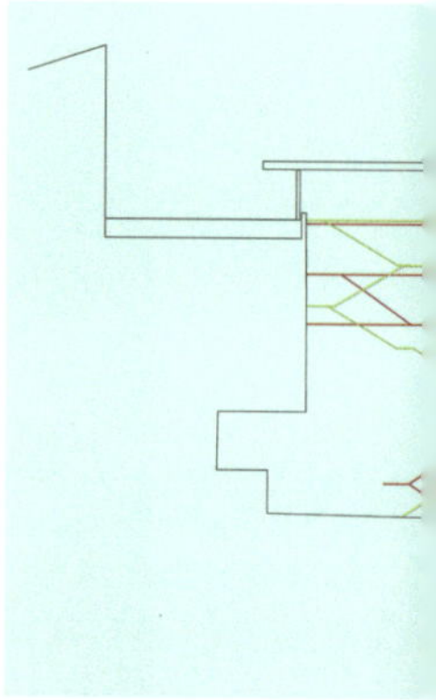

3.3.44 "Micro-history" of the Theaterplein. *Studio 04 Secchi and Viganò et al., "Spazio s-misurato," album accompanying the Open Oproep competition boards, n.d. [estimated date December 2004]* **3.3.45** Project articulated around the historical axes **3.3.46** Potential variation of roof in relation to the ground lines. *Unscaled redrawing, Sonia Curnier* **3.3.47** Cross-sectional drawing of the emergency staircases planned at two stages of the project. Yellow: stairs as realized; red: stairs at the stage of the Open Oproep. *Based on Open Oproep phase (December 2004) and publication drawing (December 2009)* **3.3.48** Relationship between the roof, the theater, and the surrounding buildings

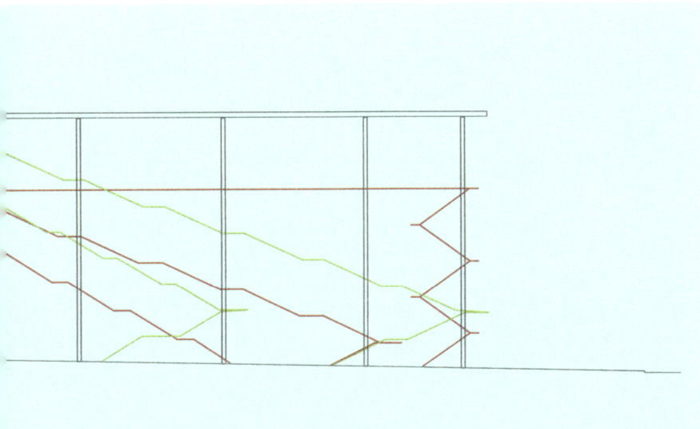

3.3.47

3.3.48

INTELLECTUAL JUSTIFICATION FOR THE COMPOSITION OF THE SPACE

The project proposed by the architects for Open Oproep 2004 is called "Spazio S-misurato." A disproportionate space, which they describe as follows:

"A 'spazio s-misurato' is a large immeasurable space, difficult to gauge, where distances are hard to read, where one feels disoriented, dimension appears absent, the space devoid of it. [...] From our point of view, this immeasurable space is not to be filled, but to be made comprehensible."[33]

The team does not use the expression "Spazio S-misurato," in the sense of a gigantic space but of a place devoid of measure. It is therefore a question of giving it structure to achieve a certain clarity and a tangible scale.[34] To do this, the Italo-Flemish team decided to divide the area into four subspaces – a covered square, a garden, a promenade, and a street – which, by their own characteristics, respond to differentiated uses (Fig. 3.3.40). This spatial redefinition is not, however, established as an act of composition without foundation. It is based on both a historical and an urban reading of the Theaterplein that allows us to understand the constitution of this vast, undefined void.

A larger-scale interpretation allows the designers to position the site to be treated at the meeting of two networks of urban space: a series of streets and squares on the one hand and a series of green spaces on the other (Fig. 3.3.43). This first element of contextualization justifies the division of the vast area into two entities, a square and a garden, allowing the two systems to be reconnected. But it is the identification of a number of historical developments that had contributed to the constitution of the Theaterplein that would serve to define the precise geometry of the garden.

A series of archived plans assembled by the architects allowed them to trace what they call a "micro-history" (*microverhaal*) of the square, whose emptiness is revealed as a recent development. Indeed, the present Theaterplein would have been occupied by buildings dating at least as far back as the 18th century (Fig. 3.3.44). The oddity of the vast, undefined urban void of the Theaterplein would thus be the consequence of the demolition of these buildings. Based on these old documents, the project authors used the position of two former roads that have since disappeared, the Kanonstraat and Bontemantelstraat, to trace the passages that articulate the development: the first runs transversely across the square, while the second delimits the area devoted to the garden (Fig. 3.3.45).

Drawing on the past, the designers defend themselves from a purely formal and historical approach: "If we accept these measures, it is not because of their legitimacy or because they are more 'real,' but because they provide pragmatic answers to the demands of today and of the future." [35] The history of the place is thus not a simple theme supporting the project narrative, but a way to capture and make legible the spatial characteristics of the square, erased by the vagaries of the past.

This intellectual justification of the project through historical archives was to have an even more fundamental consequence for the development of the square: the idea of occupying this vast void once filled by a three-dimensional volume. "What if the space between these two streets, and between them and the theater, became a clearly defined and covered square?" the team asked in the initial phase of the competition.[36]

AN AIR CUBE AS A THEATER EXTENSION

With its impressive size, the roof is of course the Theaterplein's most prominent design element. The leap in scale directly connects this large roof with the surrounding built environment. In its spatial definition, however, it seems to have a privileged relationship with the theater in particular. Seen from above, in plan, the roof is square-shaped, the sides of which take up the width of the cultural institution (about 70 m). Rather than reflecting the shape of the roof to that of the ground, with the aim of reinforcing certain perspectives or guidelines, through the pure form of the square the designers asserted solidarity with the theater, thus assuming a true architectural posture (Fig. 3.3.46).

The volumetric characteristics of the 1970s theater were also decisive for the size of the new building. Nothing seems to justify its roof height (22.1 m at the foot of the theater facade, 23 m at the lowest point on the square), except pure function; the construction of new fire escapes from the theater's upper level seems to be at the origin of the dimensioning of the cover (Fig. 3.3.47–3.3.48). Its scale is thus determined by the scale of the theater and not by the scale of the given public space.

The roof, on the other hand, displays a certain independence, even indifference, to the other buildings bordering the square. The authors adopted this distancing from buildings which, according to them, were of little interest to the public space.[37] They even sought to reinforce it. Thus, the proposed new sculptural fire escapes, which replaced the obsolete red ones, were deployed as a filter redefining the square without totally concealing the facades in the background.

This idea of giving a new reading of the built context is also illustrated in the effect that the large roof has "in establishing a new hierarchy, in terms of proportions, between the theater and the void onto which it opens."[38] This gesture distanced the much maligned brutalist edifice, while restoring its value through a framing that offers a new perspective of its facade.

Through the various strategies listed, the designers define a volume of air delimited by four sides – the floor, the roof, the stairs, and the theater – of which the other two remain non-materialized. This "virtual cube," as they call it, thus assumes a certain autonomy from the surrounding context, but "confronts the scale of the theater."[39] In terms of expression, the parallelism of the roof, which resonates with the uprights of the theater facade, further strengthens the link between the two structures.

3.3.49

3.3.50

ROOF SPAN REINFORCED BY THE GROUND TREATMENT

The three-dimensional perception of the public space is not limited to the stature of the roof. In the Secchi-Viganò-Jaspaert proposal, the once very uneven ground is reworked to ensure continuity of the square's central space. A slightly inclined plane (2% slope) connects the lowest point, at the garden level, to the highest, at the entrance to the theater. The lateral borders that follow the slope are sculpted to best meet the various needs and uses of the site: stairs and bleachers, curbstones to accommodate skateboarders, and a ramp for market delivery vehicles (Fig. 3.3.49–3.3.53).

By removing the theater's front stairs and shifting the slope to either side of the plaza, the designers restored coherence to the Theaterplein's central space. The streets are thus treated as the "lower sides" of this space, which thus becomes prominent. Approaching the theater facade, this difference in level assumes the value of a plinth, not only for the theater but also for the new roof on the square. Similar to the

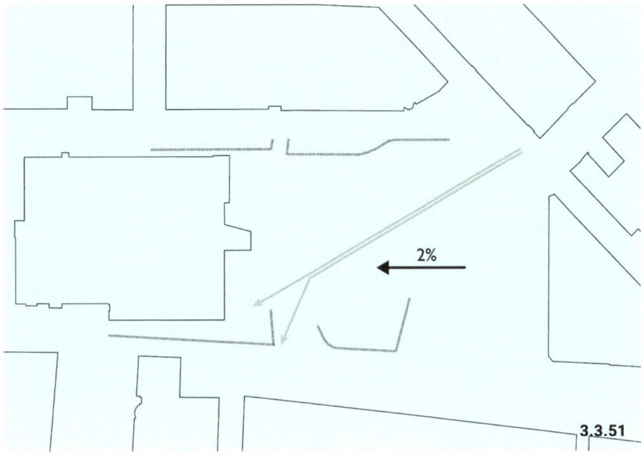

3.3.51

3.3.49–3.3.50 Bleachers and stairs of the completed project **3.3.51–3.3.53** Topographic principles of the project in plan and section

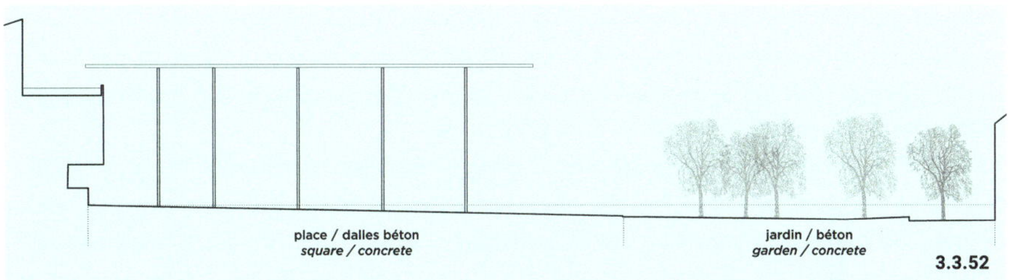

3.3.52

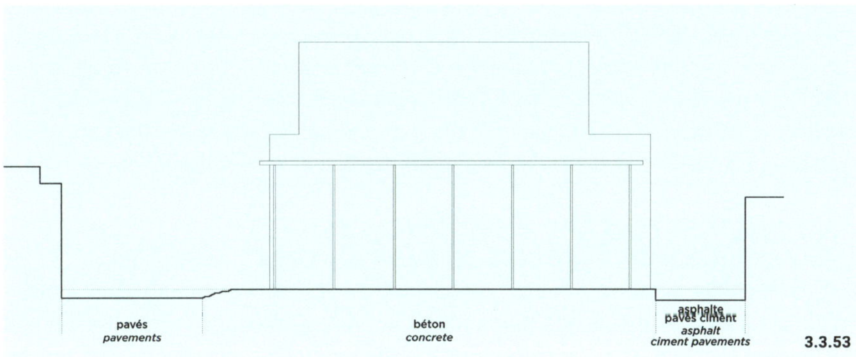

3.3.53

MFO-Park, the structure takes on the appearance of an object of value placed on a pedestal. The monumental role of the roof was to be further enhanced by another aspect relating to the ground treatment.

If Paola Viganò, co-founder of the Studio Associato Secchi-Viganò, believes that the project has changed little since the Open Oproep[40] competition submission, it is probably because the most striking element, the roof, is a faithful realization of the original design. However, a careful study of the development's ground works, in terms of composition and materials, reveals alterations that go far beyond simple project refinement. The evolution is evident in the garden space, where the relatively complex forms and proliferation of materials imagined in 2004 were gradually abandoned in favor of a calmer composition of the finished project.

This quest for purification extends over the entire design. The juxtaposition of the ensemble's successive plans testifies to a reduction of the ground finishes, but above all to an evolution of an almost conceptual nature that tends more and more to unite the two central elements, garden and covered square. On the layout plan of the Open Oproep submission, these two elements are still explicitly distinct: the square merges into the system of surrounding streets and public spaces, while the garden exists as an autonomous entity (Fig 3.3.54). Wooden terraces are planned at the foot of the theater as well as along the southern front of the square. A transverse passage under the large roof is defined by tinted concrete.

These heterogeneous elements disappeared as the project progressed, but the most profound change was the choice of a unique materiality covering the whole of the Theaterplein, in order to link the square and the garden (Fig. 3.3.58–3.3.60). The concrete chosen was applied differently to the two entities. Under the roof, it formed large slabs aligned with the theater's facade, while in the green space, it formed a grid of smaller slabs that follow the geometry of the sloping road axis. Despite this subtle distinction in the size and direction of the grid, the material continuity gives the space a sense of grandeur and uniformity. This spatial and conceptual clarification has the effect of amplifying the relationship of the roof and the theater to the vast area. The open space is thus in keeping with its primary Theaterplein function.

3.3.54–3.3.55 Distinct subspaces. *Studio 04 Secchi and Viganò et al., "Spazio s-misurato," album accompanying the Open Oproep competition boards, n.d. [estimated date December 2004]* **3.3.56–3.3.57** Towards a ground unity. *Studio 04 Secchi and Viganò et al.,* Bovengrondse voorzieningen/Aanvullingen aanbesteding, *February 10, 2006* **3.3.58–3.3.60** Continuity of color and materiality between the square and the garden. *Studio 04 Secchi and Viganò et al.,* Bovengrondse voorzieningen, *January 8, 2007*

3.3.60

ABSTRACTION AND MONUMENTALITY: SYMBOLS OF A "SOCIAL INFRASTRUCTURE"

While the treatment of the surfacing is the object of a real effort of simplification, a search for abstraction and a will to avoid any unfounded formalist attitude can be read everywhere in the project. Two of the designers' concerns explain this desire to reduce the project to its essentials: the primacy of the functional question and the desire to contextualize the design through the absence of signs and references of its own.

Paola Viganò does not deny an occasionally subjective attitude in the development of a project. For example, the architect chose apple trees for the garden purely for aesthetic considerations. On the other hand, it is important for her agency that such formal decisions are never made at the expense of the use of a place. Each project feature must, according to her, "resist the criticism of the user" in order to "avoid formalism [...] or a kind of autonomy of the architecture, of autonomy of the symbol."[41] In addition, the project must be as abstract as possible in order not to freeze uses and to allow the greatest diversity of usage. Similarly, regarding primacy

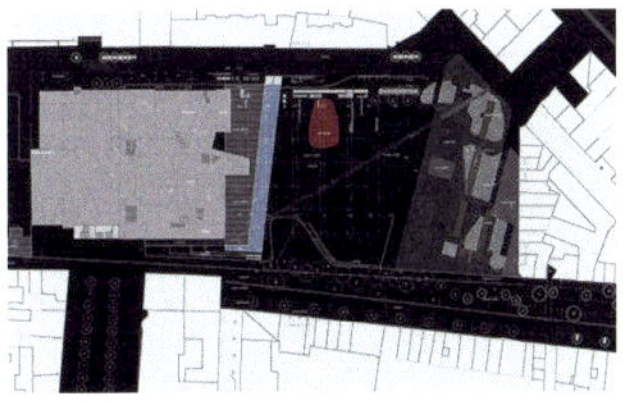

3.3.54

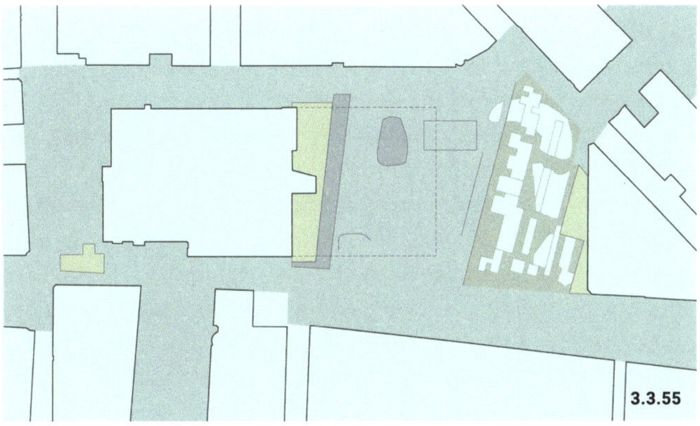

3.3.55

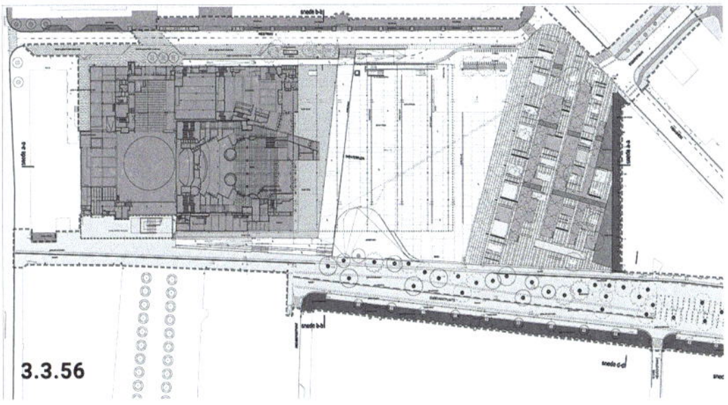

3.3.56

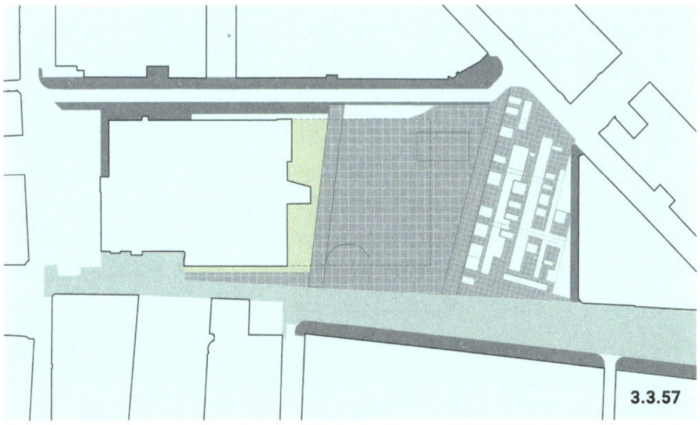

3.3.57

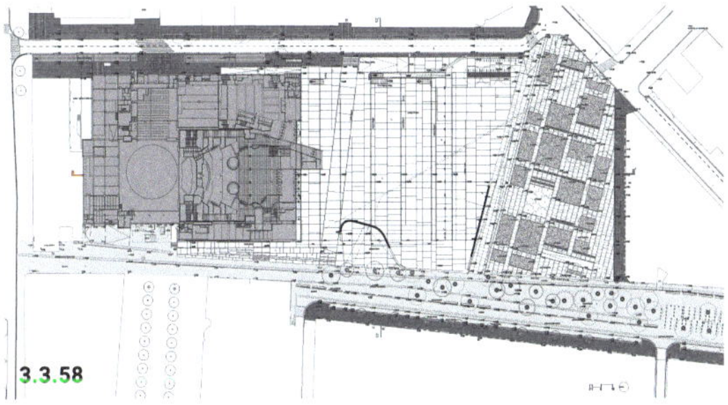

3.3.58

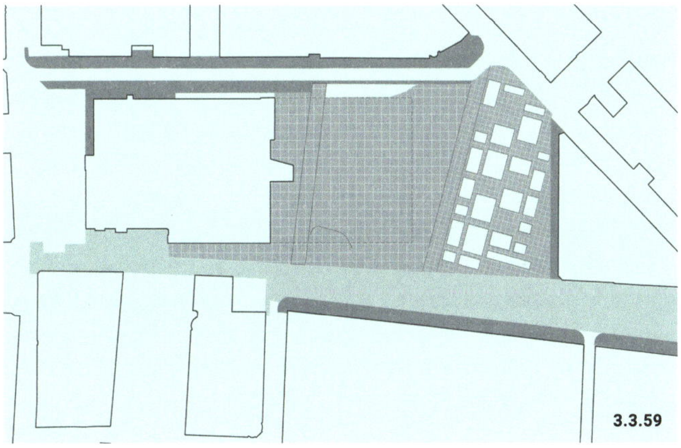

3.3.59

of function, in the sense of uses, this abstraction stems from a search for robustness in the materials and the layout details. All these elements contribute to the pure, almost raw character of the Theaterplein.

The search for abstraction is also reflected in the simple geometry and airy character of the transparent roof, which, supported by a series of slender columns (350 mm in diameter!), seems to float above the passersby. To reinforce this effect of lightness, the structure was deliberately concealed over the grid of thin parallel beams, whose interstices left the sky visible from the square. Finally, the structure was painted white, producing an immaterial character that confirmed the desire to create a volume of air (Fig. 3.3.61). The pursuit of this sober and ethereal language inevitably raises the question of anchoring the project in its context, from a formal point of view. However P. Viganò does not consider the abstract and the context as antinomic notions, the first one being, according to her statements, a means of revealing the second.[42] The contextual dimension would not be so much a question of language, but would be expressed more by a simple composition, allowing articulation of a given state.

Despite the formal restraint expressed in the Theaterplein design, some critics will readily describe the intervention as an "iconic object."[43] The placement of the monumental roof on a pedestal, its gigantic dimensions in relation to the open space, and the distancing from the surrounding buildings may indeed justify the comparison with a singular object, which would depart from the restraint proclaimed by P. Viganò. Drawing a parallel between Mies van der Rohe's concept of *beinahe nichts* and the Antwerp project, theorist Roemer van Toorn brings an original point of view to the question. He considers that the simplicity and minimalism of the details, repeated indefinitely on the Theaterplein, lead to a dematerialization of the form, which is in line with the notion of virtuality regularly invoked by the designers of the layout. But for him, "the urban design, in spite of its radical scale, displays austerity, an appropriate neutrality and even modesty."[44]

R. van Toorn develops an interesting dialectic between modesty and scale, according to a new form of monumentality: "The deployment of the overwhelming canopy, the infinite staircases and the meticulous materiality create a form of monumentality that makes space for city life, for the most part beyond monumental forms of self-glorification."[45] The monumentality created here would thus serve a collective, varied, and free reappropriation of space, and is in fact distinguished from a singular arbitrary gesture, so feared by the Milanese architects. Thus, with its radical dimensions and minimal language, the monumental roof can be interpreted above all as a "social infrastructure,"[46] a symbol of Antwerp's rediscovered urban life (Fig. 3.3.62–3.3.63).

3.3.61

3.3.62

3.3.61 An ethereal and abstract language **3.3.62–3.3.63** An infrastructure for a renewed urbanity. *(63) Studio 04 Secchi and Viganò et al., "Spazio s-misurato," album accompanying the Open Oproep competition boards, n.d. [estimated date December 2004]*

3.3.63

CHARACTERIZED VOLUMES

The constructed void: a new attitude toward the built environment

By building a three-dimensional structure as the main element of the scheme, the two public spaces analyzed are affirmed as true constructed voids. In both cases, the term "volume" to qualify these constructions seems more justified than that of simple cover. However, the volume's design process clearly differs between the two examples. In Neu-Oerlikon, the extreme rationality, the strictly orthogonal geometry, but even more obviously the thickness given to the structure, pushes one to interpret the gesture as a void taking on a value of solid. By contrast, at the Theaterplein, this theater extension is presented as an immaterial volume, which the designers describe as a "virtual cube."

If we look more closely at the modus operandi of each project, the process seems almost reversed. In the first case, the original reference of a threadlike arched pergola gradually bends to a built logic by becoming strictly parallelepipedic. Then, the structure thickens with a double wall and is covered with climbing plants, to finally become habitable. In the second public space, it seems that the idea of a volume of dimensions equivalent to the theater is the starting point of the reflection. The cube is then dematerialized until only the essential elements for its interpretation remain. Whatever the conceptual path adopted, these two constructions raise the question of the relationship to the solids and voids that surround them.

As a foreword to this chapter, constructed spaces have been defined as being made intelligible by the construction of a structure whose purpose is to signify or articulate a place. By their size, these structures resemble true urban-scale pieces and thus redefine the relationship between public space and built space, the former sometimes taking precedence over the latter. This presupposition must be nuanced with regard to the two cases studied. The analyses reveal a much stronger relationship between the built environment and the constructed public space.

In the MFO-Park, this attitude is illustrated above all by the strictly orthogonal form of the structure and its implantation in the alignment of the adjacent buildings, confirming the orthogonal logic that governs the entire Neu-Oerlikon district. In Antwerp, the large roof responds to a different reasoning. It is clearly a building, that of the theater, which defines its orientation, its form, its dimensions, and its size. The two elements thus become interdependent. As a result, the structures of the MFO-Park and the Theaterplein become extremely contextualized. Their built value, which could be perceived as competing with the surrounding built environment, actually reinforces it.

The heritage dimension in focus

The strong relationship to the built environment highlighted above testifies to a heritage sensitivity on the part of both design teams. At MFO-Park, this is reflected not only in the confirmation of the district's industrial structure but also in the materials used, which reprise the colors and elements of the old halls. The industrial past is also reinterpreted in the principle of modularity that will define the metal skeleton as well as in the fine metalwork, which stands as a tribute to the Maschinenfabrik Oerlikon of the past.

In Antwerp, this interest in the history of the place proceeds from an almost archaeological search through archived plans to understand the origin of the vast void. The uncovered "micro-history" will serve as an intellectual justification for the composition of the space, but also to justify the construction of a large roof in place of a block that once occupied this void. The designers also show a certain sensitivity to the much-maligned 1970s theater architecture, to which they wish to bring a renewed perspective. The added roof acts as a new facade for the theater while redefining its relationship to the square in terms of scale.

It should be noted that the existing built environment is not, however, taken as a sovereign value in the design of the two projects. Through the asymmetrical treatment of the vertical faces of their built volume, the developers clearly establish a hierarchy between the buildings they wish to highlight and those that it is preferable to conceal. The development thus becomes a real mediator of a state of affairs to which it gives a new appreciation.

A language in line with the vocation of the space

While the strategy of constructing the public space is therefore part of an approach that resonates with the surrounding buildings, the same cannot be said of the expression of the structures erected, which distances itself more readily from this context. The language seems above all to be defined in relation to the vocation of the space to be treated – park on the one hand, urban square on the other.

In the case of the MFO-Park, the formal and material choices respond above all to a conception of the park as a natural place for leisure far removed from its immediate urban environment. This feature is reflected in the landscaping of the ground, covered with crushed stone, contrasting with the asphalt of the adjacent streets. As far as the built part is concerned, the primary structure certainly adopts a language typical of the local factory buildings. However, it is clothed in lush vegetation, which is the most striking element of its appearance. The development thus clearly asserts an expressive autonomy characteristic of a park.

At the Theaterplein, the designers refer to universal themes that define their entire production: abstraction, minimalism, and geometry. The composition of the development is essentially based on simple forms and a limited number of materials. The search for abstraction finds its apogee in the realization of the virtual cube, which responds to both rational and aesthetic concerns. The refined language and the very urban materials respond this time to the vocation of the square located in the heart of the city.

These significantly different expressions can also be explained by a different sensitivity on the part of the authors of each project. Obviously, the designers of the MFO-Park (architects and landscape architects) seem to pay particular attention to the effects and sensations that the park will have on its future users, while the designers of the Theaterplein (architects and engineers) seek above all a certain robustness and abstraction symbolizing an idea of community.

Whatever their justification, these obviously different appearances between the two projects confirm the idea of a dissociation between the fact of building, to be considered as a project strategy, and the language given to the public space design through a theme, more oneiric or Cartesian, evocative or abstract, sensitive or conceptual, depending on the case. While the project strategy clearly demonstrates a desire to set the scheme in a given context, the language defined can, on the contrary, contribute to singling it out in the urban fabric and more specifically in the network of public spaces to which it belongs.

MFO-PARK

1 On the topic of the historic development of Zentrum Zürich Nord/Neu-Oerlikon: Hochbaudepartement der Stadt Zürich, "Neu-Oerlikon/Bahnhof Oerlikon," n.d., https://www.stadt-zuerich.ch/hbd/de/index/entwicklungsgebiete/neu-oerlikon.html [accessed May 16, 2016]; Andreas Steigmeier, "Asea Brown Boveri (ABB)" and Peter C. von Salis, "Maschinenfabrik Oerlikon (MFO)," in *Dictionnaire historique de la Suisse (DHS)*, Hauterive, Attinger, vol. 1, 2002, pp. 534–535 and vol. 8, 2009, p. 312; Ueli Roth, "Neuer Stadtteil Zentrum Zürich Nord," *Topos: The International Review of Landscape Architecture and Urban Design*, n° 3, 2002, pp. 31–35; "Industriegebiet und Bahnhofareal Zürich-Oerlikon, Überarbeitung," *Schweizer Ingenieur und Architekt*, Competitions, n° 48, 1992, pp. 918–922; Benedikt Loderer, "Zentrum Zürich Nord," *Hochparterre*, n°11, 1994, p. 31; Benedikt Loderer, "Die Heimliche Hauptstadt," *Hochparterre*, n°10, 2001, pp. 14–21; Benedikt Loderer, "Neueste Masche: Kein Gewebe," *Hochparterre*, n°6–7, 2005, pp. 10–11.

2 Gartenbau- und Landwirtschaftsamt der Stadt Zürich, *MFO-PARK/Zentrum Zürich Nord. Zweistufiger Konzept- und Projektwettbewerb. Wettbewerbsprogramm* (Two-Stage Concept and Project Competition. Competition Program), November 25, 1997, p. 10.

3 Simon, Axel, "Das grüne Park-Haus," *Garten + Landschaft*, n° 112, 2002, p. 32.

4 Gartenbau- und Landwirtschaftsamt der Stadt Zürich, *MFO-PARK. Wettbewerbsprogramm, op. cit.*, November 25, 1997, pp. 12–13.

5 *Ibid.*, p. 12.

6 Registered business name today Radeschallpartner Landschaftsarchitekten.

7 "Park-Haus" (originally spelt Parkhaus) is the title given to the project by the team. The phrase thus coined combines the words "park" and "house," but also represents a play on words because in speech the term means "parking lot."

8 The second part has not been completed to date. The building occupying this area is still in place and may never be demolished. The rest of the analysis therefore focuses only on the *constructed* part, namely the large plant-covered structure.

9 Burckhardt+Partner Architekten, Raderschall Landschaftsarchitekten, (Arbeitsgemeinschaft), "Parkhaus," competition boards for the second round "Konzeptphase" of the MFO-Park competition, August 1998 [Archives Raderschallpartner].

10 An architect is therefore obliged to partner with landscape architects in order to participate. Note also that the competition is only open to Swiss landscape architects, but that in addition eight international offices will be personally invited to participate. Gartenbau- und Landwirtschaftsamt der Stadt Zürich, *MFO-PARK. Wettbewerbsprogramm, op. cit.*, November 25, 1997, p. 3.

11 Aubort Raderschall, Sibylle (associate of Raderschallpartner), Meilen, interview with the author in French, August 26, 2015.

12 As the project progressed, the team would be enriched by the contribution of the Ticino horticulturist Fritz Wassmann for the choice of climbing plant species, and the industrial designer Frédéric Dedelley for the design of the urban furniture. An interesting collaboration was also set up with the company Jakob SA, specialized in the production of cables, who developed the complex structure to support the climbing plants.

13 Aubort Raderschall, Sibylle, interview cited above.

14 In addition to the three protagonists already mentioned, Roger Nussbaumer and Oliver Gilbert developed the project on behalf of Burckhardt+Partner; Jessica Gilbert, at that time the only employee of the Raderschall Landschaftsarchitekten office, would also be involved in the competition.

15 In addition to these competition characteristics, the Swiss-German context of the project explains the possibility of realizing such a utopia. The city of Zurich presents itself as a daring client encouraging the conception of innovative projects. On the other hand, in terms of budget, this project is among the most expensive of the corpus of projects analyzed here.

16 Aubort Raderschall, Sibylle, interview cited above.

17 *Ibid.*

18 Barman-Krämer, Gabriela, "Der MFO-Park in Zürich-Oerlikon: ein zukünftiger Parktypus auf dem ehemaligen Industrieareal," *Topiaria Helvetica: Jahrbuch*, 2004, p. 53.

19 Burckhardt+Partner, Raderschall, *op. cit.*, August 1998.

20 Aubort Raderschall, Sibylle, interview cited above.

21 Burckhardt+Partner Architekten, Raderschall Landschaftsarchitekten (Arbeitsgemeinschaft), "Parkhaus," competition boards for the first round "Konzeptphase" of the MFO-Park competition, March 1998 [Archives Raderschallpartner].

22 Aubort Raderschall Sibylle, interview cited above.

23 Burckhardt+Partner, Raderschall, *op. cit.*, August 1998.

24 Simon, *op. cit.*, 2002, pp. 32, 33.

25 Burckhardt+Partner, Raderschall, *op. cit.*, March 1998.

26 Aubort Raderschall, Sibylle, interview cited above. Finally it is a residential building that will occupy the plot, and whose occupants can enjoy the use of balconies facing south without being overlooked.

27 *Ibid.* The marl chosen during the competition phase is replaced in the realized project by crushed yellow limestone, mixed with gravel of similar color.

THEATERPLEIN

28 This instrument is a typically Flemish form of open competition, developed with the aim of guaranteeing a certain quality of the public domain and facilities. The procedure consists of an open call for competition, followed by a restricted selection of teams invited to present a project that will be discussed by a jury, initially anonymously and then with the design teams. See on this subject, Hans Ibelings, *Designing for the Public*, Amsterdam, Sun Architecture Publishers/Flemish Government architect, 2009, p. 5; Vlaams Bouwmeester, "De Open Oproep," n.d., http://www.vlaamsbouwmeester.be/nl/instrumenten/open-oproep/info [accessed June 20, 2016].

29 Without access to the full competition brief, this information comes from David Vanderburgh and Carlo Menon, "The Finger and the Moon. Belgian Competitions in their Representational Context," in Jean-Pierre Chupin, Carmela Cucuzzella, Bechara Helal, *Architecture Competitions and the Production of Culture, Quality and Knowledge. An International Inquiry*, Montreal, Potential Architecture Books, 2015, pp. 49–50.

30 According to the summary of the brief, Vlaams Bouwmeester, *Heraanleg van het Theaterplein en omgeving te Antwerpen*, (Reconstruction of the Theaterplein and Surroundings in Antwerp), n.d., available online: https://www.vlaamsbouwmeester.be/sites/default/files/opencallprojectfilesnotstarted/55dfcf5ed48445359d6089fc78595fdf.pdf, [accessed June 20, 2016].

31 In 2015, Studio Associato Secchi-Viganò became Studio Paola Viganò, following the death of Bernardo Secchi. The interview with Paola Viganò and the consultation of the archives were conducted after this change of name. In the text, however, the original name of the office is referred to, which was in force at the time of the project's development.

32 Baumschlager & Eberle Ziviltechniker; TV SWK Studiebureau voor Wegen en Kunstwerken/Johan Van Reeth BVBA; West 8 – Landscape Architecture & Urban Design; Zaha Hadid Architects/Stephane Hof.

33 Studio 04 Bernardo Secchi and Paola Viganò, Dirk Jaspaert, "*Spazio s-misurato*," album accompanying the Open Oproep competition boards, n. d. [estimated date December 2004], p. 1 [unnumbered], [Archives Studio Associato Secchi-Viganò].

34 Twenty years before the design of the Theaterplein, Bernardo Secchi was already theorizing about the need to articulate an urban space, in relation to its purpose, regardless of its scale. Bernardo Secchi, "Progetto di suolo," *Casabella*, n° 520, 1986, p. 22: "The quality of an urban space is proportional to its articulation; the articulation of a space must be always justified and legitimized. The articulation of urban space and functions must coincide; a space can be too articulated for the functions it accommodates, generating perceptive difficulties; more often by being under-articulated, it can hinder the correct functioning of activities; it can interrupt point of contact."

35 Studio 04 Secchi Viganò et al., "*Spazio s-misurato*," *op. cit.*, n.d., p. 3.

36 *Ibid.*

37 Viganò, Paola (partner of Studio Associato Secchi-Viganò/Studio Paola Viganò), Lausanne, interview with the author in French, July 1, 2015.

38 "Piazza del teatro ad Anversa, Belgio/Theater square, Antwerp, Belgium," *Industria Delle Costruzioni*, n° 46/428, 2012, p. 27.

39 Studio 04 Secchi Viganò et al., "*Spazio s-misurato*," *op. cit.*, n.d., p. 6.

40 Viganò, Paola, interview cited above.

41 *Ibid.* The architect defines her practice, and this project in particular, as "sober" and "minimalist."

42 *Ibid.*

43 Bravo, David, "Theater Square," n.d., http://www.publicspace.org/en/works/f116-theater-square [accessed June 22, 2016].

44 Van Toorn, Roemer, "The Ultimate Value of Beinahe Nichts," in *The Specific and the Singular: Architecture in Flanders,* Antwerp, Flemish Architecture Institute, 2010, p 119.

45 *Ibid.*

46 Paola Viganò uses this expression to describe the Theaterplein project and the Spoor Noord Park. Paola Viganò, "I territori dell'urbanistica/The Territories of Urbanism," *Lotus International,* n° 150, 2012, p. 112.

MODEL

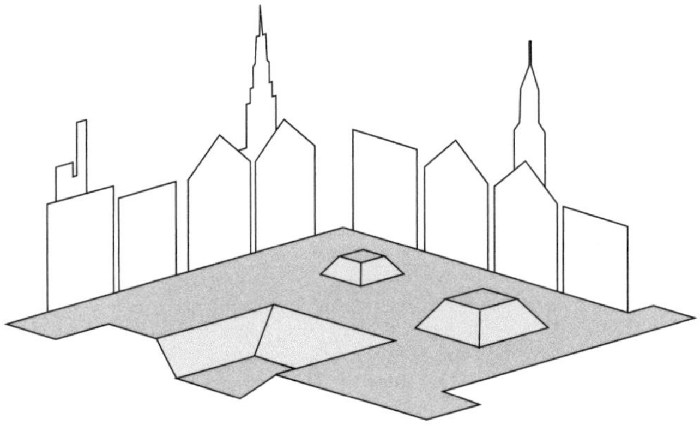

3.4.1

3.4.1
Parks and gardens
Modeling of the ground – a determining component of the work of landscape designers – has always been deployed in the design of green spaces. The creation of an artificial topography can sometimes take on a more playful and corporeal dimension in certain park and garden designs. The modeled ground instills an idea of movement. *Exterior spaces of the Laban Dance Centre, London, Vogt Landschaftsarchitekten, 2003*

3.4.2

3.4.2–3.4.3
Hybrid buildings
Some hybrid buildings, in the form of buildings and public spaces combined, attest to the topicality of topography and sculptural gestures in the field of architecture. Modeling is exploited to fluidify the relationship between exterior and interior spaces, and to provide additional public or collective spaces. *(2) Yokohama International Ferry Terminal, Yokohama, Foreign Office Architects, 2002; (3) Norwegian National Opera and Ballet, Oslo, Snøhetta, 2008*

3.4.3

3.4.4

3.4.4–3.4.5

Public spaces and playscapes
The playful dimension of topography is one of the reasons for the frequent creation of artificial modeled grounds in playgrounds and playscapes. These often have an assumed artificial character, by their geometrical aspect or by the materials and colors associated with them. Public spaces in the strict sense of the word that make use of modeling remain an exception. *(4) Charlotte Ammundsens Plads, Copenhagen, 1:1 Landskab, 2008; (5) Kalvebod Bølge, Copenhagen, JDS Architects – Urban Agency, 2013*

3.4.5

Some projects of the beginning of the 21st century affirm a form of three-dimensionality of public space, not built like examples of the "construction" family but of the order of shaping the ground. These spaces, which we call *modeled,* are distinguished by the creation of a very marked artificial relief.

This *modeled* treatment is sometimes used to stage an existing slope or the transition from one urban level to another. The notion of staging is important here, in the sense that the designers deliberately emphasize and exaggerate the topography of the site. In other cases, the *modeling* is created *ex nihilo* and results solely from a desire to design a three-dimensional surface.

Whatever the reasons behind the creation of such developments, their recent appearance in our urban landscapes is surprising. In particular, if the *modeled* spaces sometimes refer to local landscape conditions, they seem to have little connection with the built environment and the surrounding public space networks. In fact, by their unusual morphology and the imagery they conjure up, at first glance they display a desire to break with the urban context.

SELECTED CASE STUDIES

Although the trend toward *modeling* begins to be widespread in the early 21st century, public spaces (in the strict sense that we mean it here) that use this modus operandi are still relatively exceptional. Among them, the Paseo Marítimo de la Playa de Poniente – designed by the firm Office of Architecture in Barcelona – is a development for a seaside promenade in the resort of Benidorm. The complex shape imagined for this place testifies to a plastic development, which at first glance appears to be a decontextualized formal gesture. This singular morphology, enhanced by a colored surface, participates in the interpretation of the public space as an object *per se,* capable of competing with the distinctive skyscraper silhouette of Benidorm. For this reason, it seemed appropriate to study this project in detail.

The second example, in a less prestigious environment, is the Måløv station square, developed by ADEPT in collaboration with landscape architects LiW Planning. Located in a town on the outskirts of Copenhagen, it occupies a partially cut-off site bordered by two transport infrastructures. This project attracted our attention because it is openly inspired by a local natural reference. Indeed, the question of *modeling* stems from a larger-scale interpretation of the territory. Moreover, it was developed by a multidisciplinary team that includes a firm of landscape architects. The participation of this discipline may be seen as an alternative approach to *modeling* the land.

3.4.6 Location of the Paseo Maritímo de la Playa de Poniente

PASEO MARÍTIMO DE LA PLAYA DE PONIENTE BENIDORM 2002–2009

Location Benidorm, Spain **Client** Generalitat Valenciana – Ajuntament de Benidorm **Lead designer** OAB Office of Architecture in Barcelona **Type of commission** Invited competition (2002) **Construction** 2006–2009 **Former status** Seafront– four-lane street and parking area – design dating from 1970 **Area** 1.82 ha

Located on the Costa Blanca between Valencia and Alicante, the town of Benidorm was, until the end of the 1940s, a small fishing village with a few thousand inhabitants. In the early 1950s, it was decided to reorient its economic development toward mass tourism. The future seaside resort would be built on both sides of the historical village, along the two main beaches of Levante (*rising sun*) and Poniente (*setting sun*). The urban model is distinguished by an unusual aspect: within a previously defined road network, the future buildings will be able to be set up freely, and above all, without any limits in terms of height. Thus, Benidorm would develop according to speculative opportunities, reaching a staggering density of skyscrapers that was to bring much criticism[1]. Paradoxically, this model, which was once disparaged, is now a reference in terms of sustainable mass tourism due to economic land use, which implies a reduction in individual motorized vehicles.[2] However, one element runs counter to the standards of our time: the almost total absence of public spaces, except for the central shopping streets and the beaches.

3.4.7

Aware of this shortcoming, in the late 1980s, the municipality began to redevelop the promenade along the Levante beach, a very busy area lined with a continuous front of shops and cafés. The project entrusted to the Barcelona firm MBM Arquitectes is characterized by a sober language. It consists of standardizing the public space with a few simple elements: leveling the sidewalk and the road to form a continuous plane, introducing a slight difference in level to delimit the beach from the city, and providing the promenade with a clear identity along its entire length by means of palm trees and fairy lights[3] (Fig. 3.4.7).

A few years later, the construction of a new inland bypass road decongested the avenue bordering Benidorm's secondary beach, known as the Poniente. This was seen as an opportunity to redevelop the seafront promenade, the Paseo Marítimo, over approximately 1.5 km in order to revitalize this less developed area of the city. An ideas competition by invitation, without precise brief, was launched in 2002 by the Generalitat Valenciana, Ajuntament de Benidorm.[4] The Office of Architecture in Barcelona (OAB)[5] took part and won the competition by proposing a striking public space.

The Barcelona architects envisaged a wide promenade intended to become a real social hub for tourists and locals. This interface between the urbanized area of Benidorm and the beach 4m below was to be treated in a sculptural way, as an artificial relief. The shaped retaining wall integrated the different vertical accesses to the vast expanse of sand, while defining spaces, sometimes protected, sometimes exposed to the sun and to the gaze of passersby. On the upper level, the three-dimensional treatment allowed for a wider sidewalk, which would cantilever over the beach, creating rest areas along the promenade. Finally, the promenade would be covered with a colored surface to give the waterfront a clear identity (Fig. 3.4.8–3.4.10).

A CONCEPTUAL GESTURE

The question of an interface between city and sea seems to be at the origin of the architects' first sculptural formulations for this project. Above all, they wanted to give a certain depth to this boundary to create an intermediate space. Thus, as far as he can remember, Xavier Martí Galí (responsible for the project alongside Carlos Ferrater) began by cutting a sheet of *modeling* board, creating a random sinuous line to symbolize the indeterminacy of this interface. The undulating shape was then able to break free from the administrative and land boundary – between the maritime territory of state responsibility and the urban space in the hands of the municipality –

3.4.8

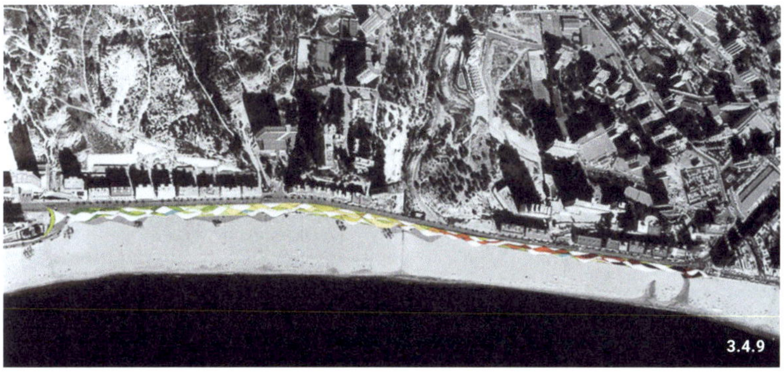

3.4.9

3.4.10

3.4.7 The Playa de Levante promenade. *MBM Arquitectes, 1986–1996* **3.4.8** Realized project for the Playa de Poniente promenade **3.4.9–3.4.10** Design project for the Playa de Poniente promenade. *OAB, photomontages, n.d. [2004]*

usually materialized by a clear vertical wall (Fig. 3.4.11). This first formalization, without scale, synthesizes, according to him, the conceptual idea that was to guide the project from beginning to end.[6] More commonly expressed in a two-dimensional way, by a sketch, the initial intention modeled here already testifies to a sculptural approach to public space.

Soon, the architects would transcribe the concept of undulation into drawings, producing the famous widely published sketches of sinuous lines intertwined in a skein-like pattern (Fig. 3.4.12). In some illustrations, these drawings take on a three-dimensional form already featuring the idea of a complex system of interlocking membranes. OAB also quickly exploited the principle of modeling to define three main levels of public space for different uses (Fig. 3.4.13). The highest level, bordering the road, was to be used for brisk walking (as opposed to strolling), taking the form of a straight line. Slightly below, a second level of promenade was to be widened from time to time by cantilevering over the beach. Finally, at the lower beach level, an undulating strip materialized by a wooden floor would welcome the seaside activities. It would act as a minimally designed threshold, beyond which the expanse of sand would unfold in its "natural" state. The three floors were connected by low sloping ramps and stairs, making the new promenade a flowing landscape.

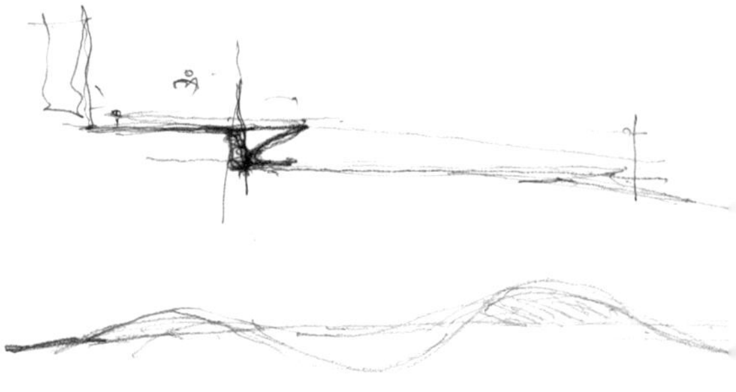

3.4.11

These initial formal principles gave rise to a sculptural evolution of the Paseo Marítimo that gradually became more complex, as the two levels of the promenade evolved toward a sophisticated interweaving of surfaces. But the most laborious and notable development would be the shape of the retaining wall separating the city from the beach.

A SCULPTURAL FORM OF EXTREME COMPLEXITY

Several variants of *modeling* could have been envisaged in order to break free of the land line delimiting Benidorm from the sea. One of the initial sketches showing a perspective of the future public space presents this wall as a sinuous but rigorously vertical section, whose cornice line corresponds point by point to that of the base (Fig. 3.4.14b). An alternative would have been to undulate only the upper part of the walk, in order to strictly respect the straight property line at the level of the wall's base (Fig. 3.4.14c). In the end, the architects undulated both the cornice and the foot of the wall independently, to create "tension"[7] (Fig. 3.4.14 d).

To intensify the effect, they added a sculptural dimension to this section by inflecting it, in cross-section, to result in a variable double-curved surface of great complexity (Fig. 3.4.14e–3.4.15). The wall thus adopts a sculptural form, sometimes concave, sometimes convex. These combined geometric principles served not only to define a variation of spatial situations but also to create fascinating plays of light and shadow, reinforced by the white paint that covered the entire element in the realized version of the project (Fig. 3.4.16–3.4.19).

To achieve this result, OAB initially worked from physical models, but it was soon a matter of refining the envisioned modeling in preparation for its construction. OAB describes this as a process from "the abstraction of the first idea to concretion and physicality."[8] At this stage, the manual modeling work began to show limitations, and they decided to move to digital drawing to allow the sculptural construction to continue[9].

3.4.12

3.4.11 Sketches in section and plan of the principle of freeing the property line. *Produced by Xavier Martí Galí during the interview in Barcelona, February 17, 2016.* **3.4.12** First sketches of the project. *n.d., OAB, unidentified author.* **3.4.13** Sketch of the three main levels of the public space. *Produced by Xavier Martí Galí during the interview in Barcelona, February 17, 2016*

3.4.13

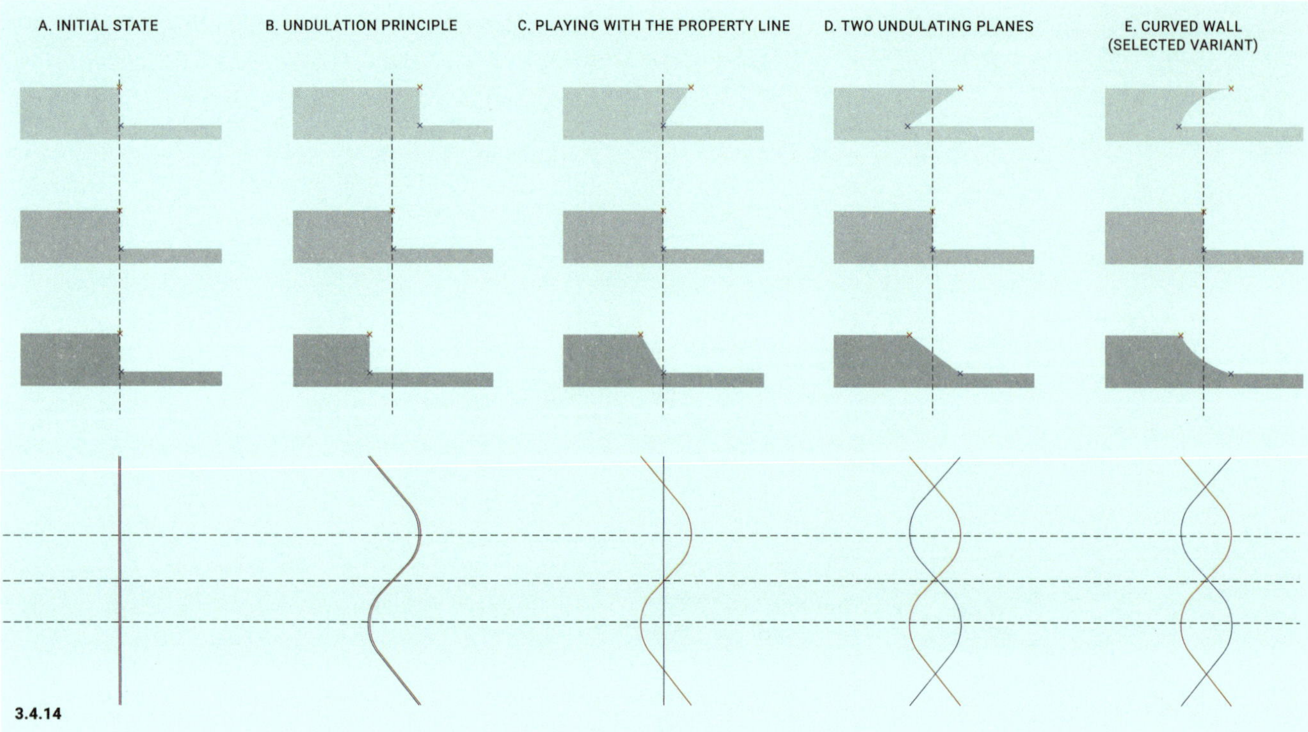

3.4.14

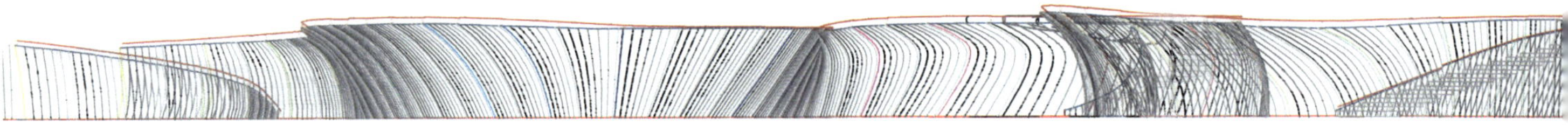

3.4.16

3.4.17

3.4.18

3.4.14 Schematic representation of different possible modeling alternatives **3.4.15** A curvilinear strip **3.4.16–3.4.19** A variation of spatial situations and shadow effects

FROM GEOMETRIC COMPLEXITY TO SITE RATIONALITY

In preparation for its realization, the second stage of the project had a direct impact on the development's final form. Indeed, the construction of such an unprecedented project was like a real experiment, which it was necessary to control by determining a certain number of pragmatic principles.

The first step was to define a grid of 6 m intervals to run perpendicularly along the entire length of the promenade, allowing it to be divided into identifiable segments. This reference system illustrates the passage from a totally free form, resulting from plastic considerations, to a certain rationality. Used as a working tool, this basic grid later materialized into load-bearing walls to support the Paseo and to stiffen the undulating retaining wall (Fig. 3.4.20).

The next task was to find an efficient and economical way to make the formwork elements for this ribbon of concrete of constantly varying curvature, which would extend for more than a kilometer and a half. To do this, the architects developed a principle that they call "serial."[10] A first segment of walkway, about 30 m long, was built at the western end of the Paseo. Elements of this typical section, which the firm calls "matrices,"[11] were then reused to compose the entire promenade. Thus, only about 60 formwork modules of nearly 5.5 m long by 4 m high were necessary to cast nearly one and a half linear kilometers of wall[12] (Fig. 3.4.21–3.4.25).

The implementation of a grid, and then of a serial logic, reveals the passage from a free design mode to a construction system regulated by pragmatic principles. It testifies, moreover, to an affirmed curiosity for geometry and a mastery of its implementation, which sets OAB's production apart.[13]

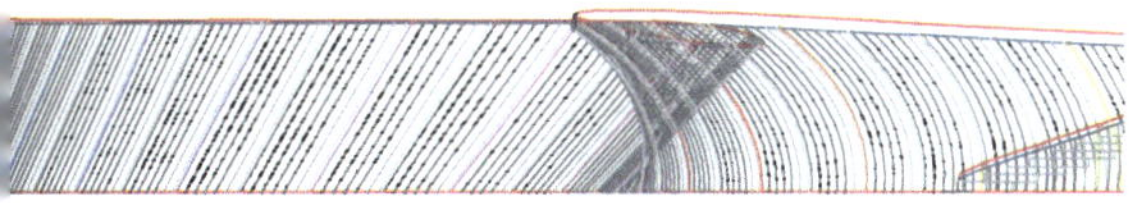

3.4.15

EQUIVOCAL ROLE OF THE NATURAL REFERENTIAL FIELD

So far, the Paseo Marítimo development seems to have followed its own logic, initially sculptural and unfettered, then based on a rational geometric system. The surrounding urban fabric does not appear to have played a role in defining the promenade's final shape, except perhaps in corresponding beach accesses with the ends of streets perpendicular to the seafront (Fig. 3.4.26). Questioned about this, Martí Galí says that he considers the buildings of Benidorm as "a front with which one must have a certain freedom"[14] because of their heterogeneity and their capacity to evolve very quickly in the absence of rules. As such, the project could be interpreted as a rather non-contextual intervention.

3.4.19

Nevertheless, the designers see this promenade as an interface between the city and the beach. If the urban environment was obscured in the formalization of the project, it seems that the "natural" space of the sea played a more marked role in defining the organic form of the promenade. When experiencing this public space, the mimicry of the waves, the foam, and the undulating tidal marks on the sand are indeed striking (Fig. 3.4.27–3.4.29).

Such maritime references, as well as images of cliffs or caves, systematically accompany the iconography of the published project (Fig. 3.4.30–3.4.32). This theme is also continued in OAB's narrative: "We conceived the project as being the generator of an architectural area [...] which adopts various natural and organic shapes, reminiscent of the structure of a cliff and also the movement of the waves and the tides."[15] Thus, the contextual dimension of the Paseo Marítimo, if it exists, would be illustrated more in relation to the natural landscape.

However, it is difficult to measure the role played by these imagineries in the evolution of the project. While some publications may suggest that these inspirations had formative value,[16] the genesis of the project as recounted by Martí Galí rather suggests that the formal and conceptual intention – the undulatory principle symbolizing an indefinite interface – precedes the later summoning of seductive natural imagery. As for the evolution of the *modeled* form, it primarily reveals geometric, ergonomic, perceptual, and flow-related concerns, rather than a search for mimicry with the surrounding landscape. The exploitation of the form for its symbolic and contextual qualities thus seems to have played a secondary role in the project's development.

Two elements support this hypothesis. Firstly, the natural phenomena evoked by the architects do not seem to have been the object of a careful study in terms of geometry and the natural laws that govern them, and which could have been transcribed in the design. As such, these references have more of a metaphorical than a formal value. The second point concerns the diversity of inspirations used, bringing together two types of referential fields: on the one hand, photographs of waves and foam, which refer to the sinuous form of the proposed walk, and on the other hand, representations of cliffs, caves, and canyons whose formal analogy would be translated into the effects of inflection of the retaining wall. However, while the sea is indeed a nearby natural element, the rocky landscapes sculpted by water to which OAB refers are much more distant imagery and therefore do not reflect a desire to anchor the intervention locally.

These observations allow us to presume that these reference images are rather intended to feed the narrative of the project by adding a poetic dimension to it after the design. The formal analogy of these images does not serve so much to inscribe the design into the landscape through its form, but rather to evoke attractive natural environments. It can be assumed, then, that the *modeled* form is primarily involved in characterizing the promenade as a clearly identifiable place through a language of its own rather than seeking a relationship to context. A final aspect of the project reinforces this desire to make the redesign of the Paseo Marítimo intelligible as an object *per se*.

3.4.20 The grid as a design tool materialized in the completed project **3.4.21** Artisanal formwork planted on the ground **3.4.22** Typical segment of the "matrix" **3.4.23** The serial principle applied to the whole length of the promenade **3.4.24–3.4.25** Repetition of a matrix, two similar staircases at two different places on the promenade **3.4.26** Rules and constraints – breakdown of vertical distribution. *R: ramp, E: staircase, in bold: existing wall sections preserved*

A DISTINCTIVE GROUND COVERING

While the retaining wall was to be painted white, in an effort to abstract and highlight the *modeled* form, the interwoven surfaces of the promenade are imagined from the beginning of the project as colored elements of varying hues in order to animate the linear intervention. At first, they were imagined in tinted concrete, but the limitation of rather dull tones that this material affords did not satisfy the designers in their search for a more assertive expression.[17] It was not until later, during construction, according to Martí Galí, that the idea of polychrome ceramic paving appeared. This material, developed specifically for the Paseo Marítimo,[18] allowed for the rendering of very vivid colors, an effect sought by the architects. A gradation of colors, corresponding to the spectrum of light, will progress in segments along the one and a half kilometers of promenade.

This atypical surfacing contributed to the singularity of the promenade, as did the shaped relief, intensifying its identification as an object *per se*. The ground treatment attracted a lot of critical attention, and several authors made a comparison – rather elementary – with the Avenida Atlântica (1970–71) of Roberto Burle Marx, Haruyoshi Ono, and José Tabacow.[19] Like the *ornamented* projects with which it has

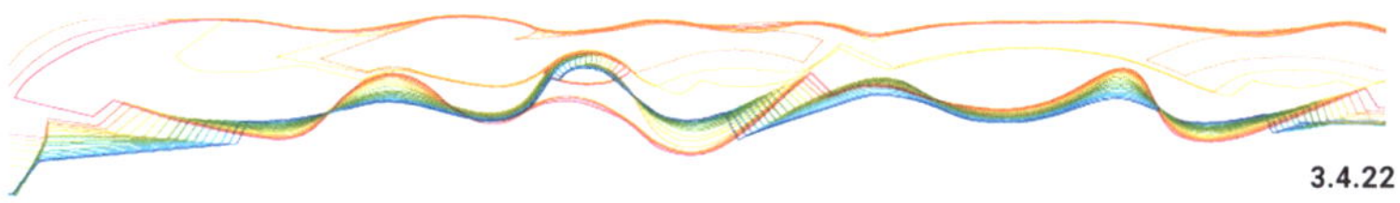

3.4.22

3.4.23

3.4.24

3.4.25

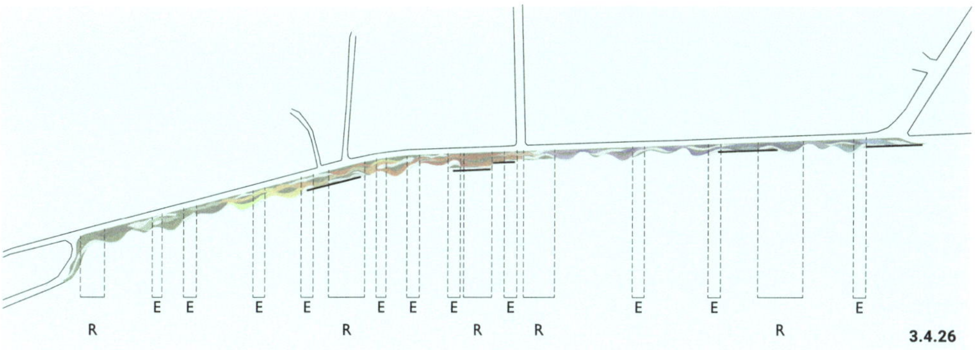

3.4.26

3.4.27

3.4.28

3.4.29

3.4.30

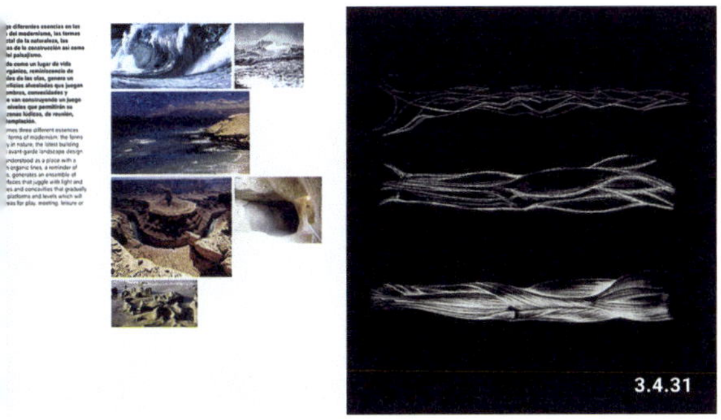

3.4.31

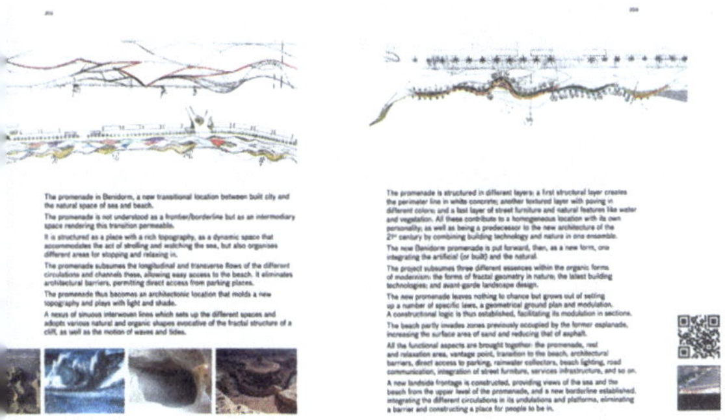

3.4.32

3.4.27–3.4.29 Formal analogy between the promenade and the sea **3.4.30** Reference image and model photo juxtaposed by OAB **3.4.31–3.4.32** Layouts of project publications featuring references as primary images. *Source: Ferrater Carlos, Xavier Martí Galí, Benidorm, Barcelona, Actar, 2011, p. 10–11; OAB, Office of Architecture in Barcelona. Carlos Ferrater & Partners, Barcelona, Actar, 2010, p. 202–203.*

many parallels, this project raises the question of the perimeter to which the characteristic surface is applied and the treatment of the boundary with the adjacent public spaces.

Along the length of the project, although the transition is abrupt, the boundaries appear justified, as the intervention corresponds to a recognizable spatial entity. Indeed, the project begins and ends with a notable change in the built fabric (Fig. 3.4.33). Along its width, however, the colored paving stops abruptly at the level of the asphalt roadway. The sidewalk at the foot of the buildings remained as is, due to land ownership issues (Fig. 3.4.34). OAB regrets not having been able to integrate it into a unitary project, which would have given the promenade a real value as a unifying base for this heterogeneous built environment.[20] On the contrary, this clear break now further dissociates this development from the built environment, intensifying its perception as an independent object.

THE NEED TO MAKE A DIFFERENCE

The architects of OAB seem to assume both this independence of the built environment and the unusual character of their intervention, which the critic Josep Maria Montaner describes as a space with "exuberant forms" and a "dominant character."[21] As described above, this marked identity is due as much to the molded profile of the *modeled* form as to the atypical surfacing of the promenade. It should be noted that depending on the point of view, the impact of the intervention is less pronounced. From the beach or from a distance, the white painted sculpted relief becomes a plinth, emphasizing Benidorm's distinctive skyscraper silhouette (Fig. 3.4.35). As such, it can be admitted that the singular character is expressed more by the colorful treatment of the promenade than by its *modeled* form.

While this iconic value seems to have fascinated the majority of critics, some, such as Julia Macher, were nevertheless challenged by it and noted the contrast with the Levante promenade redesigned in 1996.[22] The difference between the two public spaces is indeed striking: the Levante beach promenade is distinguished by a very sober, almost minimalist development, characterized by traditional materials and whose only rhetorical dimension is expressed in the lights in the form of garlands, recalling a harbor or open-air music venue environment (Fig. 3.4.7, p. 147).

When asked about this difference in attitude between the two projects, which were completed only a few years apart, Martí Galí suggests that it could be explained by a change of era or a difference in office strategy, but he insists above all on the distinction of the initial situations: "The Levante beach was already a popular and frequented place, lined with lively commercial first floors, which could be satisfied with merely light development, while the Poniente beach was a neglected site that needed an intervention capable of activating it, one that could attract people."[23] It was therefore crucial to interpret this redevelopment opportunity as the driving force behind a metamorphosis of this entire secondary sector of Benidorm. A few years after its completion, the iconic project seems to have initiated an urban regeneration, judging by the daily use of the promenade and the multitude of shops and terraces that have sprung up at street level.

In addition, the Barcelona architect draws attention to the fact that such a project would not have been possible in just any context: "We had an intellectual excuse to propose something rather liberal, because we were in an absolutely liberal city, lacking design."[24] He also emphasizes the conscious risk-taking of this experimental

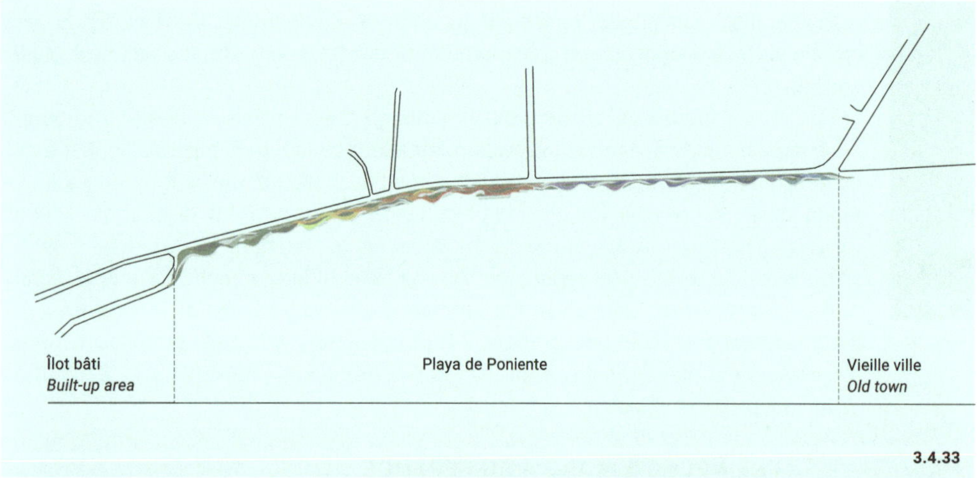

3.4.33

3.4.34

3.4.33 Clear limits of the pavement, corresponding nevertheless to a spatial entity **3.4.34** Promenade detached from the buildings **3.4.35** The project from a distance

3.4.35

project on different levels (formal, constructional, material, chromatic, etc.), which is also legitimized by the Benidorm context. Martí Galí considers the new and surprising expression of the initiative justified by the interpretation and understanding of a context capable of accepting it. In this sense, the project of the Paseo Marítimo de la Playa de Poniente becomes inseparable from Benidorm.

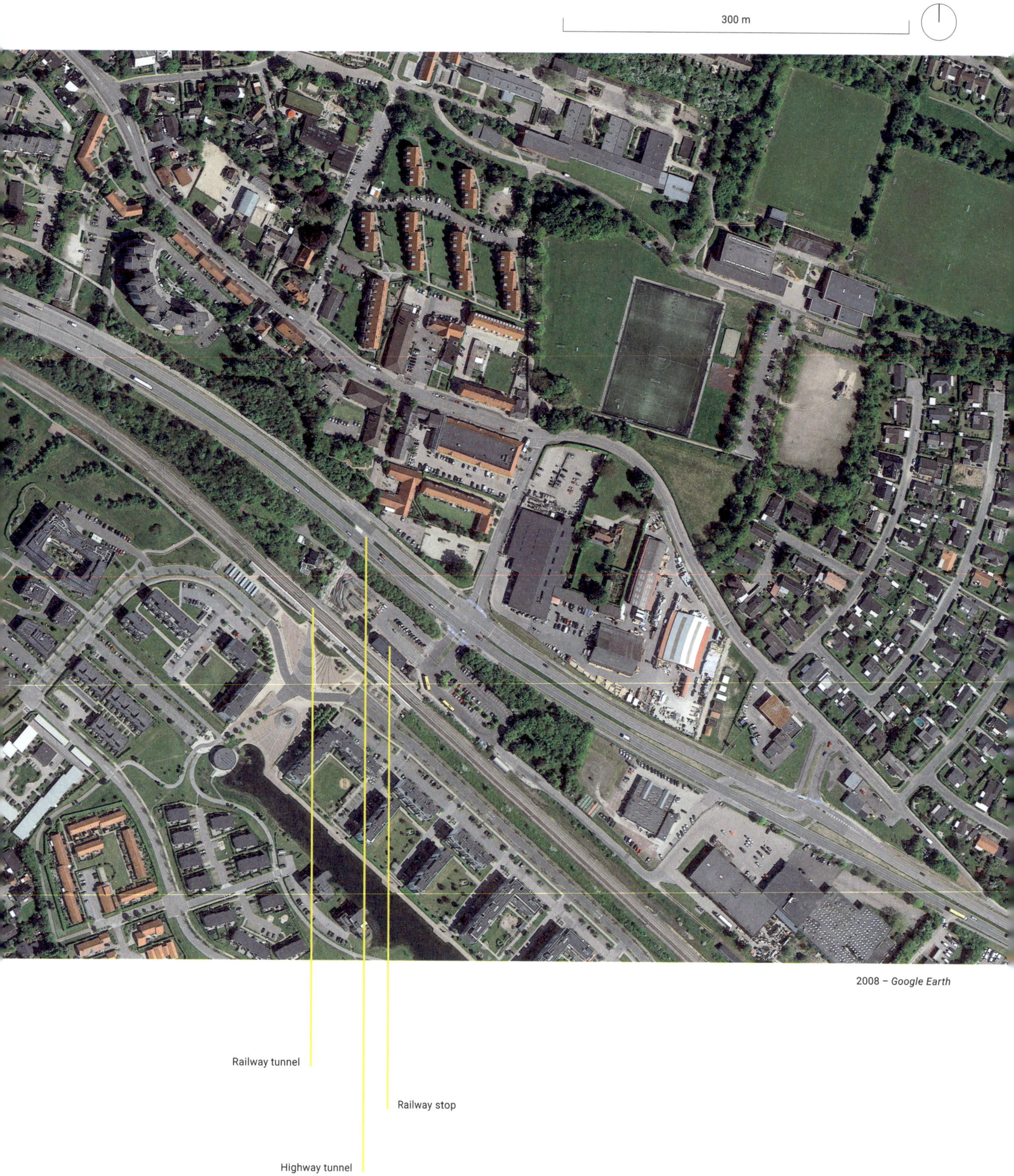

3.4.36 Location of Målov Aksen

MÅLØV AKSEN – THE STATIONSPLADS

MÅLØV 2008–2010

Location Måløv – Ballerup, Denmark **Client** Ballerup Kommune – Realdania **Lead designers** ADEPT (architects – Copenhagen) / LiW Planning (landscape architects – Copenhagen) **Type of commission** Invited competition (2008) **Construction** First stage completed in 2010 **Former status** Network of undesigned squares and underpasses **Area** 1.5 ha of which 0.4 ha realized

In June 2008, the municipality of Ballerup launched a competition for the development of a public space in the locality of Måløv on the outskirts of Copenhagen. This small town, which underwent its first major urban development in the 1970s and 1980s, has more recently expanded with the construction of the Søndergård district to the south of the municipality, completed in 2015.[25] The historic center of Måløv, which revolves around its main street lined with shops and public facilities, is cut off from Søndergård by a railway line and a viaduct. The objective of the competition is to develop the only pedestrian and bicycle axis that connects the two urban entities, passing by the municipality's railway station midway between them. A bent trajectory, a complex topography, and the existence of two tunnels crossing infrastructural obstacles make this artery difficult to deal with.

3.4.37

The competition brief is based on expectations expressed by the citizens during a participatory procedure launched in the autumn of 2007.[26] The main aim was to improve the safety, accessibility, comfort, appropriation, and aesthetics of this neglected, unwelcoming, and yet essential public space. The clients required the selected six teams of competitors[27] to define a masterplan for the entire site and to present a detailed project for a first phase of construction around the station.[28]

A multidisciplinary team consisting of young architects from ADEPT and landscape architects LiW Planning won the competition in the fall of 2008 with a project entitled "Måløv Axis – An Experience that Creates a Connection."[29] To address the lack of readability, the designers proposed firstly to give the connection a new, clear identity based on the theme of melting ice. Secondly, in order to make the public space more alive, they decided to punctuate the axis with small appropriable zones, creating a varied proposition for a wide range of users. Finally, the two tunnels were to be transformed into illuminated signs acting as landmarks and gateways to Måløv (Fig. 3.4.38).

The first stage of the project, carried out in 2010, covers a section that includes the tunnels, the square next to the station – the Stationsplads – and the grassed hillside known as Krogrunden (eventually developed in a manner quite different from the competition proposal). The following analysis focuses mainly on the Stationsplads, which has been *remodeled* and transformed into a recreational landscape.

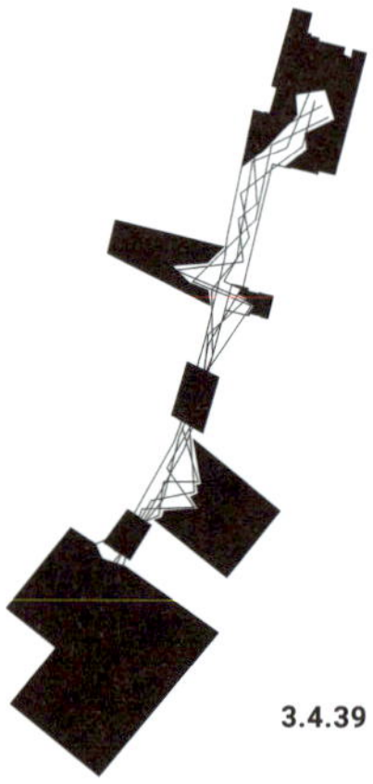

3.4.39

WIDE-SCALE SITE ASSESSMENT

When ADEPT and LiW Planning took on the project in June 2008, they quickly realized that the site lacked spatial definition.[30] They then decided to broaden their thinking to a perimeter wider than the strict limits of the municipality's center. This wider reading led them to reconsider the nature of the public space to be developed: Måløv Aksen should not be perceived solely as an urban connection linking the residential district of Søndergård, the railway station, and the heart of Måløv. The section is also part of a walking and cycling network, linking it directly to surrounding municipalities and natural areas (Fig. 3.4.41). The designers saw the need to reinforce the axis as an efficient, daily route but also to connect it with the surrounding landscape.

To do this, they intended to "create a more fluid continuous axis that is also more vibrant, and above all safe."[31] The fluidity of the connection would be guaranteed by a uniform and obstacle-free surface. Since Måløv Aksen's trajectory is both curved and hilly, this uniform treatment would also contribute to its interpretation as a continuous element. In terms of animation and safety, ADEPT and LiW Planning decided to transform the passageway into a place to be enjoyed. They used the adjacent

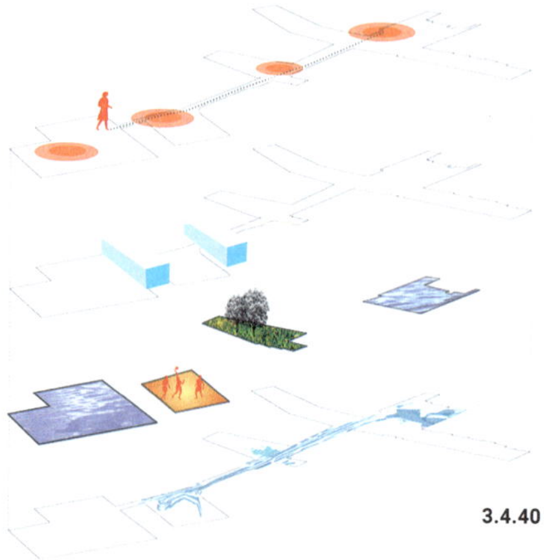

3.4.40

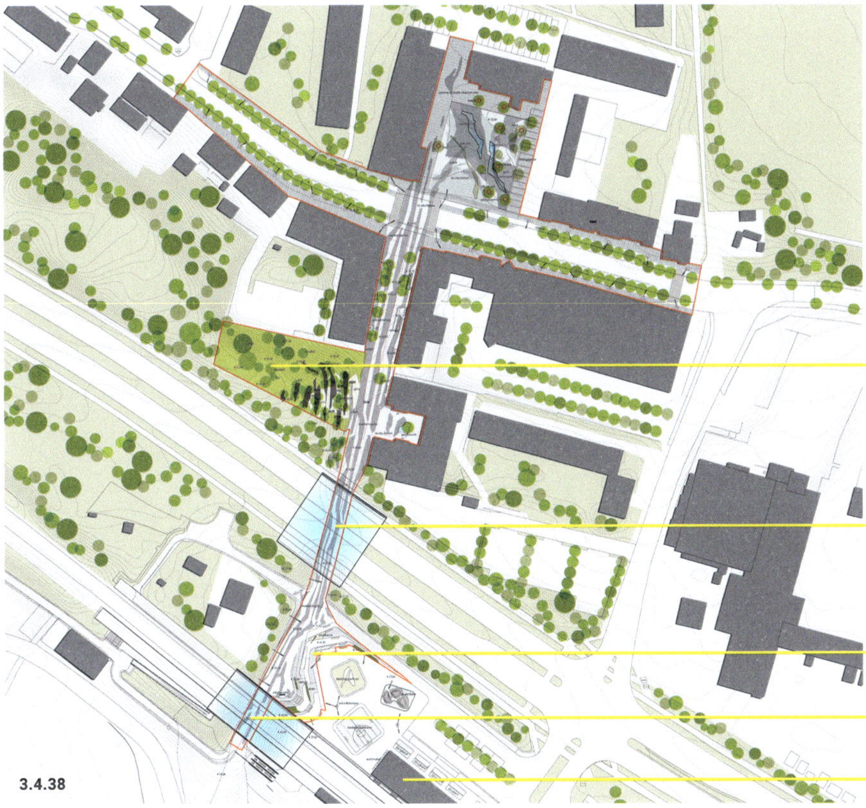

3.4.38

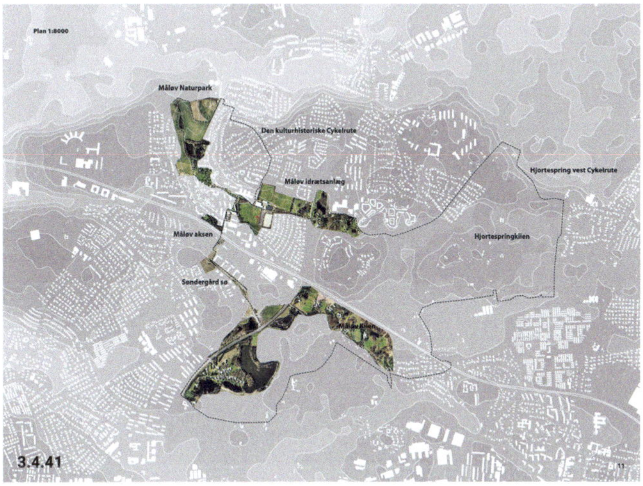

3.4.41

3.4.37 Reconnecting the historic center of Måløv with the new district of Søndergård **3.4.38** Overall project plan. *ADEPT, LiW Planning, "Måløv Aksen – En oplevelse der skaber sammenhæng," competition proposal, September 2008* **3.4.39–3.4.40** A fluid axis punctuated by spaces of different character. *ADEPT, LiW Planning, "Måløv Aksen – En oplevelse der skaber sammenhæng," competition proposal, September 2008* **3.4.41** Territorial analysis of Måløv Aksen. Section of a larger scale network of walking and cycling paths. *ADEPT, LiW Planning, "Måløv Aksen – En oplevelse der skaber sammenhæng," competition proposal, September 2008*

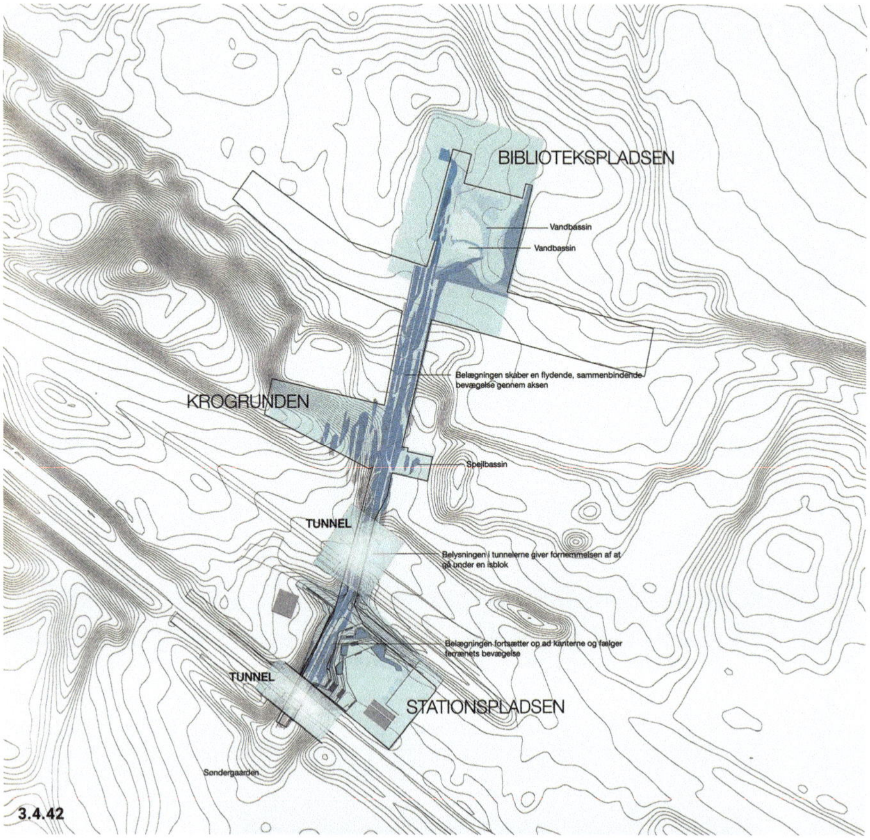

3.4.42

3.4.43

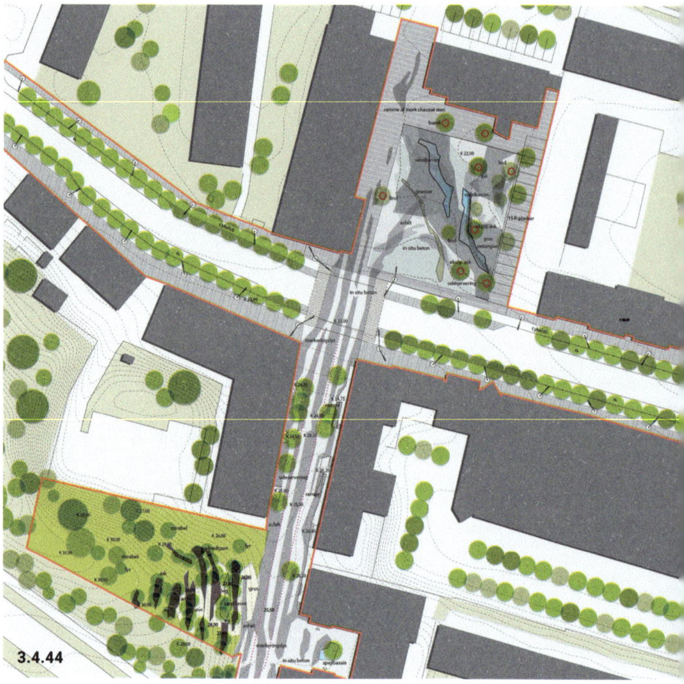

3.4.44

3.4.45

3.4.46

3.4.42 The theme of melting ice translated into the project. *ADEPT, LiW Planning, "Måløv Aksen – En oplevelse der skaber sammenhæng," competition proposal, September 2008* **3.4.43** One of the tunnels symbolizing a block of ice. *ADEPT, LiW Planning, "Måløv Aksen – En oplevelse der skaber sammenhæng," competition proposal, September 2008* **3.4.44** Pavement inspired by a riverbed. *ADEPT, LiW Planning, "Måløv Aksen – En oplevelse der skaber sammenhæng," competition proposal, September 2008. Extract from general plan* **3.4.45–3.4.46** Reference images of the project – anastomosing rivers and iceberg. *Reference presented in ADEPT, LiW Planning, "Måløv Aksen – En oplevelse der skaber sammenhæng," competition proposal, September 2008*

areas to create diverse usable spaces that guarantee activity and presence throughout the day. The section is punctuated at each end by the *Biblioteksplads*, the heart of the municipality, and the gateway to the new district of Søndergård. In between, the axis is marked by two complementary spaces: the planted hills of Krogrunden for quiet relaxation and the Stationsplads for more dynamic activities (Figs. 3.4.39–3.4.40).[32]

The integration of the development into a larger area also led the team to take a closer look at the surrounding natural environment and its genesis. During their investigations, ADEPT and LiW Planning discovered that the rugged terrain and moraine characteristic of the local landscape stem from its glacial past. They therefore decided to make the melting ice a unifying theme for the entire project, serving both to anchor the intervention locally and to reinforce the artery's identity.

THE MELTING ICE THEME EXTENDED

The glacial phenomenon thus established as the project's guiding image was spatially translated into each predefined subspace (Fig. 3.4.42). First, the axis and its adjacent spaces were associated with a river resulting from melting ice: "The river is the unifying element of the meltwater valley. It is the main movement of the axis [...] A movement that runs through a series of urban spaces, newly interpreted and active, that brings more life and safety to the axis. The river penetrates the edges and thus creates green pockets as places to stay."[33] By summoning this river imagery, the team plays on the notion of flow – of people and water.[34]

But the authors of the project did not stop at this poetic evocation. The river analogy directly took shape in the ground surface, inspired by the sinuous trajectory of intertwined channels. Starting with reference images, ADEPT and LiW Planning reinterpreted the organic forms into polygonal patterns to make a recognizable graphic motif (Fig. 3.4.44). Still related to the theme of water, the surfacing would be made of liquid materials – concrete and asphalt – poured directly on site.

The various locations along the axis were also inspired by the glacial world. The tunnels, which until now had looked like sinister subterranean passages, would resemble blocks of ice, materialized by a cladding of honeycomb polycarbonate panels giving them a special light (Fig. 3.4.43). As for the two public spaces, Krogrunden and the Stationsplads, the team wished to stage their existing relief, which it associated with the site's glacial past. The two slopes were sculpted in the image of moraine deposits, resulting in the distinctive *modeling* of the station square.

THE STATIONSPLADS: SHAPING A SPACE FOR WALKING AND EXPLORATION.

The specific challenge of the Stationsplads was to physically and visually connect two levels, respectively that of the railway station at track level and that of the axis below it. The ADEPT and LiW Planning team also wanted to make the station square an accessible place, imagined as a landscape, which would become a sort of "experience in itself."[35] To achieve this, the slope was *modeled* by large, irregularly shaped terraced platforms connected by a system of ramps and stairs (Fig. 3.4.47–3.4.48).

Regarding the elements that would have been used to shape this *modeling*, Martin Krogh, partner at ADEPT, nevertheless states, "If it has a logic, it is really related to flow. It sort of picks up the flow of people moving here and there. Sometimes we have created a little obstruction, so that you don't just have a direct trajectory, but you feel that the space is diverting you a little bit. But the *modeling* does not react in any way to the surrounding elements."[36]

The final form of the *modeling* would thus emanate from a reflection on the movements of people in the space. Without being directly linked to the tangible components of the site, the intervention is nonetheless contextual, according to the architect, in the sense that this *modeling* seeks to establish continuities with the station and the axis, from the point of view of passersby. This consideration of the human scale would also be used to size the platforms on which people can come to rest and sit.

However, the relationship to the human body was to be expressed in a more original way in this project. By treating the relief as a landscape, the team wanted to make the Stationsplads a space to be explored in a dynamic manner. This can be seen in the drawings presented on the competition illustrations, which feature various urban sports such as BMX, skateboarding, climbing, and parkour[37] (Fig. 3.4.49). Shortly after winning the competition, the team was contacted by a group of parkour practitioners intrigued by this artificial landscape. Curious to meet these unusual users, the designers decided to involve them in the project development. To meet their needs, they adjusted the height and width of the landings, offering different conditions for jumps and other stunts. They also decided to cover some platforms with a soft material that would allow for a comfortable landing. By integrating these unexpected participants, the authors demonstrate a flexibility toward their project, thus ensuring that it does not come across as a finished and unalterable creation (Fig. 3.4.50).

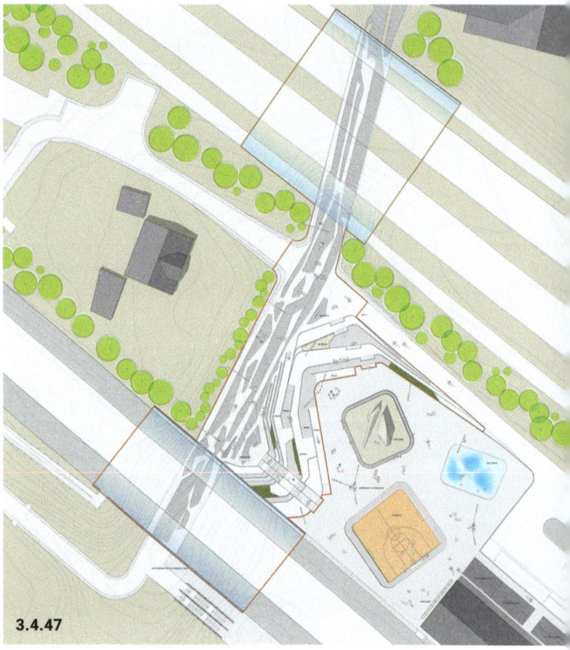

3.4.47

A GEOMETRIC AND ARCHITECTONIC LANDSCAPE

The undeniable influence of human scale and corporality in the shaping of the square thus revealed does not, however, explain the very geometric aspect of the modeling. The latter is indeed similar to polygonal lines extruded in order to create a relief. It is difficult to explain this exacerbated artificial character given to the *modeling*, but we can venture to put forward some suppositions.

The first observation that can be made concerns the close formal relationship that the angled platforms have with the very graphic design of the axis paving. These polygonal forms resonate in a surprising way with other projects by LiW Planning. One thinks in particular of some of the office's well-known projects, such as the City Hall Square in Viborg (2007–2011), Hannemans Allé in Ørestad (2007–2011), or the project for the Water Plaza in Reykjavik (2006–2010). This repetitiveness leads one to believe that it is the landscape design firm's in-house style reproduced in the course of the projects they develop.

Another element shows a formal interest during the development of the *modeling*. In the competition submission, the relief of the plaza has curved forms similar to the contour lines shown on the plan (Fig. 3.4.52). These curvilinear elements, which evoke natural forms, were abandoned in the final version in favor of strictly rectilinear walls (Fig. 3.4.53). It is possible that this change was made to intensify the echo of the paving design. One can also imagine that this adaptation was made during the transition to constructive reality, in order to simplify the construction and reduce costs.

Some photographs of the construction site remind us of the constructive reality of such a relief and allow us to qualify the term "*modeling.*" These images show retaining walls delimiting containers ready to be filled with earth and then lined in order to create the various platforms (Fig. 3.4.55–3.4.56). The existing slope would not

3.4.48

3.4.49

3.4.50

3.4.47–3.4.48 Plan and elevation of the Stationspladsen. *ADEPT, LiW Planning, "Måløv Aksen – En oplevelse der skaber sammenhæng," competition proposal, September 2008* **3.4.49** 3D night visualization showing the animation of the square by youth. *ADEPT, LiW Planning, "Måløv Aksen – En oplevelse der skaber sammenhæng," competition proposal, September 2008* **3.4.50** "Traceurs" practicing parkour invest the landscape with life

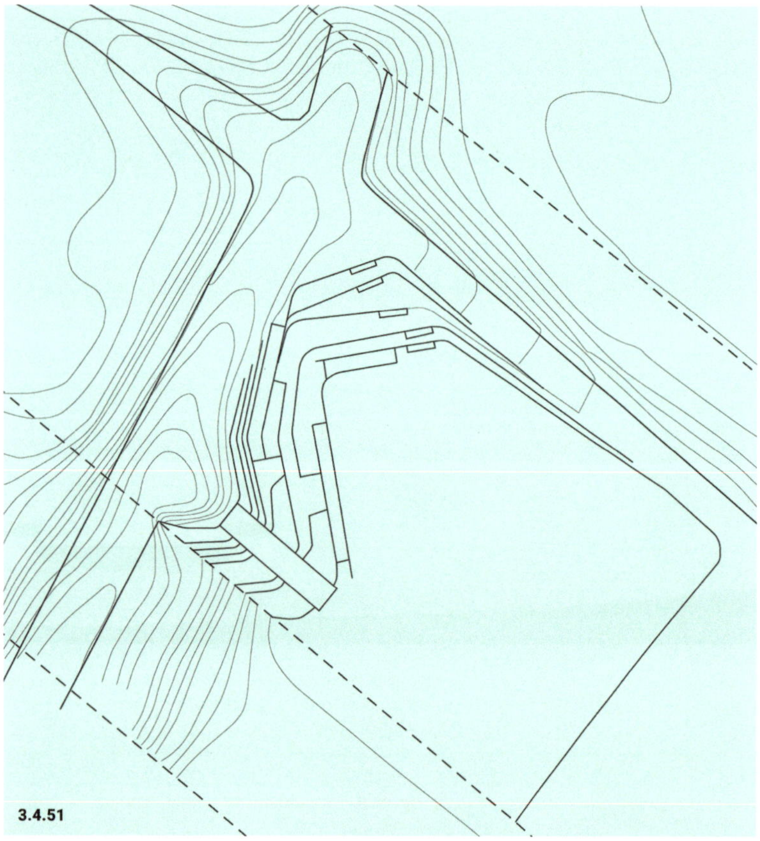

3.4.51

3.4.52

3.4.53

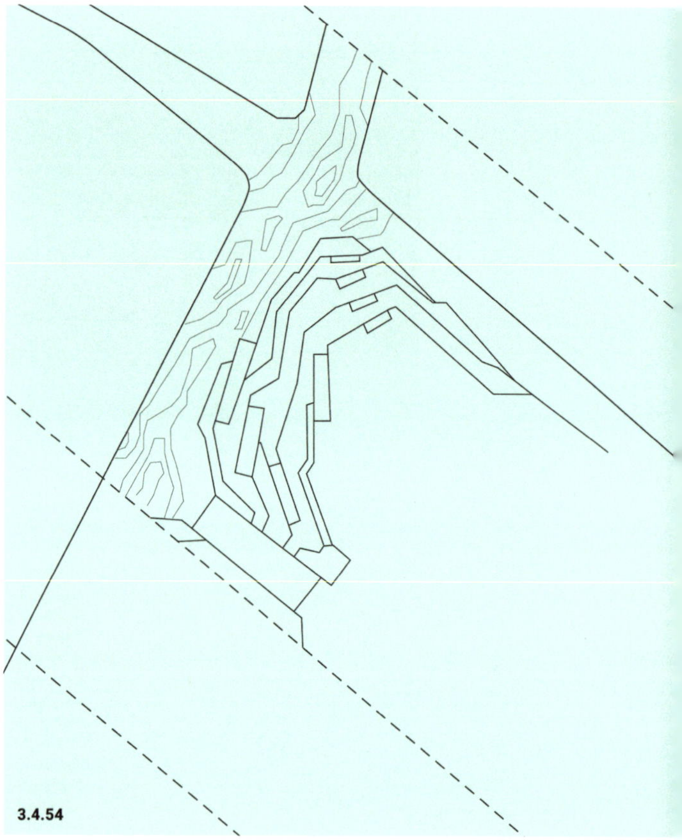

3.4.54

3.4.51–3.4.52 Rounded shapes of the relief at the competition stage. *Redrawn from the competition plan* **3.4.53–3.4.54** Rectilinear forms of the relief as realized resonating with the surface pattern. *Redrawn scheme from aerial photograph of the completed project* **3.4.55–3.4.56** Retaining walls delimiting containers

have been shaped, but rather cleared and then artificially reconstructed. This revealed *modus operandi* amplifies the constructed character of the relief, which takes on an "architectonic" dimension.[38] Thus presented, the *modeling* is more reminiscent of terraced cultivation landscapes than of the glacial deposits to which the designers had referred in the first place

A THEME AS A LOCAL ANCHOR?

This brings us back to the question of the glacial identity defined upstream as the guiding image of the project. It seems legitimate to ask whether, in its spatial translation, this referential field really acts as a local anchor and unifying theme, as the project authors claim in their presentations.

From this local theme, the team seems indeed to handle the pictorial inspirations with a certain freedom, sometimes selecting relatively distant references (Fig. 3.4.45–3.4.46, p. 191). To evoke the glacial watercourse, the designers gather aerial photographs of anastomosing rivers[39] around the world. These images, which are attractive to say the least, do not specifically allude to the melting of ice. In the same vein, the illustration used as a reference for the tunnels does not represent a glacier, but an iceberg. Finally, none of the four photographs presented on the competition submissions appears to be from the surrounding landscape.

Moreover, depending on the needs, the designers refer to different stages of the summoned imaginary glacier: the original state of the glacier is found in the tunnels as ice blocks, the period of ice melt is materialized in the association of the ground with a river bed and, finally, the traces of this geomorphological phenomenon, the moraine deposits, are symbolized by the *modeled* spaces. Only this last reinterpretation could find a formal echo in the surrounding landscape, which would contribute to the local anchoring of the project. Indeed, the only tangible trace that remains today of the glacial past of the place is its particular relief. However, the designers do not seem to have fully studied and revisited certain characteristics of the territory's physical aspect. One can then ask oneself if it is enough that a referential field comes from an interpretation of the site, in order to contextualize the development that is inspired by it. The analysis of the project from this angle reveals, on the contrary, an idea that seems above all to participate in the narration of the project as a communication tool during the design process.

A FRAGMENTED NETWORK OF HETEROGENEOUS SPACES

This freedom of interpretation of the glacial imaginary also results in a juxtaposition of atmospheres, forms, and materialities that seems to exacerbate the differences between the subspaces, rather than unifying them. As an example, the terraced landscape initially imagined by the designers for Krogrunden was finally abandoned in favor of two simple slanted walls, set with orange benches in steps, which underline the natural relief of the terrain. With this singular language, Krogrunden clearly asserts a formal independence from the Stationsplads (Fig. 3.4.57). The light tunnels and the graphic ground coverings add to this diversity of expression on a relatively small area.

ADEPT's associates claim to believe "in strong concepts that are broken down into smaller narratives."[40] Certainly, here, the idea of linking both historically and territorially the development to the glacial past of the site in which it is embedded was powerful. In its abundant spatial translation, however, the concept has lost its force. Is it possible, then, that a theme as a guiding image might not be enough to give coherence to a sequence of spaces if it is not translated into a homogeneous language?

This observation does not in any way detract from the qualities – particularly in terms of use – of each imagined subspace. But in terms of overall coherence, the connection does not appear as a unitary and recognizable public space. One element – not a narrative one this time but a material one – could have contributed to giving coherence to the whole. It is the ground covering, which had been imagined as a "unifying element" by its recognizable pattern. To date, however, only one section of the axis has been paved with the planned pattern, which stops short of the two tunnels (Fig. 3.4.58). This point calls into question the relevance of applying an identity-bearing theme and language to a sequence of spaces that will not be completed in one go.

The issue of overall coherence here is clearly beyond the responsibility of the designers. In such situations, it would be up to the clients to question the exact scope of a commission and the ability to fully implement the project. The partial and uncoordinated realization of the project, which contributes to its fragmented appearance, is compounded by the great freedom of interpretation of the glacial past translated into spaces with an exaggerated distinctive character. These factors combined contribute to the fact that in its constructed reality, the Stationsplads does not read as part of a territory and a network, but as an event in itself.

3.4.57 Krogrunden as built **3.4.58** Sharp edge of the singular pavement

SCULPTING TO ENTERTAIN

A fascination for artistic and geometrical qualities

The analysis of the two projects revealed different motivations for the *modeled* designs. In Måløv, it is a reference to the natural landscape and its glacial past that leads the designers to imagine a station square with an accentuated relief. In Benidorm, the undulating form allows for a play on the land boundary between the urban environment and the beach. Although the narratives legitimizing these formal impulses diverge, in both cases, the *modeling* is affirmed as a way to fluidify the interfaces and to cross an existing difference in elevation.

The analysis of the projects also reveals a certain curiosity on the part of their authors for the sculptural aspect of the imagined *modeled* forms. This formal interest is found in a general way in their production and in their working methods. The ADEPT team seems passionate about the three-dimensional experimentation in models that they develop profusely in their projects. As for OAB, the office claims a fascination for geometry, which would be at the origin of new formal experiences, characteristic of all its work.

These elements also inform us about the working tools favored in the elaboration of *modeled* public spaces. If the development of new softwares could have explained the recent appearance of complex and organic geometries, this link was not clearly confirmed in the analysis of the two examples. The evolution of computer tools has undoubtedly contributed to the shaping of the Benidorm walk and, above all, to enabling its implementation. On the other hand, the initial idea of *modeling* is in no way computer-generated. The sculptural morphology remains the result of a free creative gesture by the authors.

Finally, it should be noted that the authors of the two projects seem to be fond of the sculptural dimension of their *modeled* spaces. They willingly present them according to unusual – even unreal – angles of view allowing appreciation of their artistic quality. Such images contribute to their perception as unique and decontextualized interventions, or in other words, public spaces as objects *per se*.

Modelings as recreational spaces to explore

The understanding of public space in an essentially formal way by these architects and landscape architects must nevertheless be qualified. Indeed, the analyses reveal that this artistic approach does not preclude strong considerations for users and their experience of public spaces. The particularity of the *modeled* public spaces appears to be a strong awareness of city dwellers in their corporeality and in their activities.

Of course, by their relief, these developments inevitably participate in stimulating movement and recreational activities, according to a playful vision of public space. Analysis of the projects also reveals other parameters, in terms of perception and comfort from the user's point of view, which have guided the precise shaping of these reliefs. The choice of bright colors in both projects also contributes to their playful appearance. Their authors are thus conscious of creating recognizable designs, but they consider this singularity as a factor encouraging recreational uses. These *modeled* spaces are above all conceived as spaces to be lived in and explored with enjoyment.

A liberal interpretation of the notion of context

Both examples also have in common the fact that their designers show a certain detachment from the built environment in which they intervene. This assumed position is justified, according to them, by the absence of qualitative built elements on which their proposal could be based. On the contrary, they see their intervention as an opportunity to revitalize sectors that are undervalued or downright neglected. The development of public space is therefore no longer intended to accompany existing values but to act as a motor for change. Consequently, these designers claim a certain freedom of formal and material experimentation.

Despite this uninhibited posture, they consider their development to be highly contextual. The understanding of this term is nevertheless manifold, encompassing rather particular, if not unprecedented, notions. For example, the notion of context is understood in a more cultural perspective at the Poniente promenade, whose playful aesthetic echoes the colorful linens and umbrellas that adorn the beach. The beach area is in fact considered by the architects as a constitutive element of Benidorm, whose economy has been based on its tourist activity since the 1960s. In Måløv, the focus is more on understanding the area's past. A historical study of the geomorphology of the territory led the designers to develop the axis according to the theme of the melting ice. The notion of context was broadened both temporally and spatially, as the development no longer refers to the immediate surroundings but to a wider range.

Universal references

Finally, the analyses reveal the importance of landscape references – whether glacial, rock, river, or seaside – in the projects' narratives. However, when analyzed in detail, these inspirations and their transcription do not reveal themselves to be true elements of local anchors, as the designers would have us believe.

First of all, the imaginaries are inscribed in a contextual narrative, but in practice the reference images used come from more distant environments. In these circumstances, the inspiration seems to emerge more from an intention to seduce through the projects' narratives than from a real search for a relationship with the surrounding landscape elements.

Secondly, it must be noted that the inspirations invoked are very freely interpreted. If the architects and landscape architects claim to draw the forms modeled in natural registers (waves, foam, icebergs, rocks, etc.), their archives and their presentations do not reveal in either case a careful study of these phenomena, a study that would have enabled them to reproduce certain of their physical characteristics. Consequently, nature is considered more as a metaphorical conceptual reference than a truly formal one.

Finally, when transcribing these references into a project, the designers proceed with a certain abstraction and freedom of reinterpretation: smooth, white concrete intensifying the sculptural aspect of the wall supposedly reminiscent of cliffs in Benidorm, irregular polygons symbolizing a river in Måløv. It is thus an abstract image that is implemented in these ultimately very architectonic projects, and not the qualities of a natural landscape that one might try to reproduce. By referring to idealized and widely shared representations of certain landscapes and by reinterpreting them freely, these examples are ultimately expressed in a very universal, formal, and material language.

PASEO MARÍTIMO DE LA PLAYA DE PONIENTE

1 Ayuntamiento de Benidorm, Concejalía de Cultura, *Benidorm, los orígenes de la ciudad vertical*, exhibition catalog, 2006.

2 Anglès, Magda, "Benidorm, Spain: Playa de poniente esplanade," *Topos: The International Review of Landscape Architecture and Urban Design*, n° 72, 2010, pp. 23–25; Julia Macher, "Der paseo de Poniente Benidorm. Architekten, Carlos Ferrater, Xavier Martí Galí (OAB)," *Bauwelt*, n° 101/32, 2010, p. 16.

3 Martorell, Josep, Oriol Bohigas, and David Mackay, "Paseo marítimo Benidorm. Benidorm promenade," *Via Arquitectura*, n° 02, 1997, pp. 68–73. Available online: http://www.via-arquitectura.net/02/02-066.htm [accessed August 25, 2016].

4 Unfortunately it has not been possible to retrieve the official documents (brief, competition entries, jury report) relating to the competition process. The little information we do have comes from Xavier Martí Galí (associate of OAB), Barcelona, interview with the author in French, February 17, 2016.

5 At the time of the competition, the office, established in 1971, carried the name of its founder Carlos Ferrater. It would become OAB in 2005 when he joined forces with his children Borja and Lucía Ferrater and his son-in-law Xavier Martí Galí.

6 Martí Galí, Xavier, interview cited above.

7 *Ibid.*

8 Carlos Ferrater Partnership (OAB), *Synchronizing Geometry, Landscape, Architecture, and Construction*, Barcelona, Actar, 2006, p. 9.

9 Martí Galí, Xavier, interview cited above.

10 This term is used in music to describe a mode of composition based on the recurrence and reorganization of a sequence of notes. Carlos Ferrater Partnership (OAB), *op. cit.*, 2006, p. 96; Carlos Ferrater, Xavier Martí Galí, *Benidorm*, Barcelona, Actar, 2011, p. 28.

11 *Ibid.*

12 Martí Galí, Xavier, interview cited above.

13 See Carlos Ferrater Partnership (OAB), *op. cit.*, 2006, especially the section entitled "The Time of Geometry." This book accompanied the office's retrospective exhibition entitled *Synchonizing Geometry* presented at the Illinois Institute of Technology in Chicago in 2006.

14 Martí Galí, Xavier, interview cited above.

15 Padura, Manel, "Conversation," in Manel Padura and Carlos Ferrater (eds), *Carlos Ferrater: Office of Architecture in Barcelona*, El Masnou (Barcelona), Editorial Manel Padura, 2006, p. 12.

16 "Aménagement littoral, plage du Ponant, Benidorm, Espagne: Carlos Ferrater et Xavier Marti Galí," *Architecture d'aujourd'hui*, n° 363, 2006, p. 105. See also Fig. 3.4.41 and 3.4.42, p. 183.

17 Martí Galí, Xavier, interview cited above.

18 Numerous publications have focused on the motif of paving and this atypical material in its application in a public space. Note that it was to be reused by OAB for the redevelopment of a square in Premià de Mar, near Barcelona (2012–2013).

19 Worthmann, Merten, "Zwischen Sand und Asphalt: Neue Strandpromenade für Benidorm von Studio OAB," *Baumeister*, n° 107(1), 2010, p. 14; "Paseo marítimo, Benidorm (Alicante)/Waterfront, Benidorm (Alicante) Spain," *AV Monografías/AV Monographs*, n° 141–142, 2010, p. 58. Although OAB often refers to Burle Marx's project, according to Xavier Martí Galí, this was not an initial inspiration, but rather a connection made by Josep Maria Montaner that the office would later appropriate. Josep Maria Montaner, "Taxonomía de sistemas formales en la obra de Carlos Ferrater. A Taxonomy of Formal Systems in the Work of Carlos Ferrater," in "Carlos Ferrater. Obra reciente/ Recent Work," *2G*, n° 32, Editorial Gustavo Gili, Barcelona. 2004, p. 17.

20 Martí Galí, Xavier, interview cited above.

21 Montaner, *op. cit.*, 2004, p. 17.

22 Macher, *op. cit.*, 2010, p. 19.

23 Martí Galí, Xavier, interview cited above.

24 *Ibid.*

MÅLØV AKSEN – THE STATIONSPLADS

25 Ballerup Kommune, "Søndergård," n.d., https://ballerup.dk/soendergaard [accessed March 15, 2017].

26 On this topic see: Ballerup Kommune, *Katalog for Byrumskvaliteter i Måløv Aksen*, March 2008 [annex to the competition brief].

27 ADEPT – LiW Planning, Imitio, Søren Jensen consulting engineer and Mikael Sylvest; Arkitekt Kristine Jensens Tegnestue with Arkitektfirmaet Gustin; Schul Landskabsarkitekter, Playground, and Okra Landschapsarchitecten; Thing & Wainø Landskabsarkitekter, Borch & Tuxen, and COWI: plan; 1:1 Landskab, Kant Arkitekter, Eduard Troelsgaard, and Nueva; SLA, Krads Architecture, Sleth Modernism, and Oluf Jørgensen consulting engineer.

28 Ballerup Kommune, *Måløv Aksen. Indbudt projektkonkurrence*, June 2008 [competition brief]. The philanthropic institution Realdania (see note 55, p. 57 and note 22, p.132), which is helping to finance the project, also expects the project to serve as a case study for other similar landlocked situations.

29 ADEPT, LiW Planning, "Måløv Aksen – En oplevelse der skaber sammenhæng," competition proposal, September 2008 [Archives ADEPT], p. 1.

30 Krogh, Martin (partner of ADEPT), Copenhagen, interview with the author, September 21, 2015.

31 ADEPT, LiW Planning, "Måløv Aksen ...," *op. cit.*, 2008, p. 6.

32 *Ibid.*, pp. 6, 11, 12.

33 *Ibid.*, p. 12.

34 This analogy was the origin of the name "Fluid Landscapes" that the architects gave to the realized development. ADEPT, "The Måløv Axis," n.d., http://adept.dk/index.php?id=41#40^2^144 [accessed September 18, 2015].

35 Krogh, Martin, interview cited above.

36 *Ibid.*

37 This term refers to the art of free movement practiced outdoors, especially in urban areas, which has become widespread since the 1990s.

38 Günter Mager distinguishes two forms of topographical treatment in the history of gardens, "architectonic" and "pictorial." The first refers to developments in terraces articulated by stairs, ramps, and embankments, which can be found in Renaissance or classical gardens. The second trend is characterized by a certain dynamics and fluidity of undulating grounds, as in English gardens seeking to dramatize nature. Günter Mader, "Topographie," *Anthos*, n° 1, 2004, pp. 5–6.

39 In fluvial geomorphology, this term designates interwoven rivers, whose different branches separate and join to form a complex weave.

40 "ADEPT," *A + U: Architecture and Urbanism*, n° 10, 2012, p. 95.

NATURE

3.5.1

3.5.2

3.5.1–3.5.2
Wild nature
Certain natural spaces assert themselves by adopting a "wild" appearance in stark contrast to urban language. In a desire to give these heavily vegetated spaces a more bucolic character, the trees are deliberately less controlled, uniform, and pruned. *(1) Forecourt of the Tate Modern, London, Kienast Vogt Partner, 2001; (2) Novo Nordisk Nature Park, Bagsværd, SLA, 2014;*

3.5.3–3.5.5
Mimicry
Another way to naturize open spaces consists in faithfully imitating certain characteristics of natural landscapes using artificial processes or materials. The illusion and mannerism of these projects make them openly recognized as artificial imitations, which take on a metaphorical dimension. *(3) Novartis Campus, Basel, Vogt Landschafts-architekten, 2008; (4) FIFA headquarters, Zurich, Vogt Landschaftsarchitekten, 2006; (5) Plaza de España, Tenerife, Herzog & de Meuron, 2008*

3.5.3

3.5.4

3.5.5

To give a space its unique identity, some developments attempt to reproduce natural environments, such as forests, dunes, mountains, and so on. This trend has been growing for several decades in a variety of forms that underlie equally varied narratives (ecological, sensitive, demagogic, etc.). The inspiration may come from a nearby landscape or a far distant environment that has positive connotations in the collective imagination. In any case, it is a question of the designers creating a piece of nature from scratch in a fundamentally urban setting. Although the strategy has been firmly established in the development of private open spaces, its application to public spaces is more recent.

It is important to point out here that these projects differ from traditional green spaces, parks, and gardens, in that their "landscape" quality is not a given dictated from the outset by the client. The creation of a shard of nature stems from the designers' real desire to imagine these spaces – often squares – as such. Through their strongly evocative dimension, *naturized* projects assert their claim to independence from the surrounding urban fabric, playing on the city/nature duality. This voluntary and initial distancing is probably much more marked than in the other families of projects analyzed here.

SELECTED CASE STUDIES

The Platz der Menschenrechte, by the German landscape architects Valentien + Valentien, is in the newly built Messestadt Riem district on the outskirts of Munich. The project is distinguished by materials and plant species that evoke the wildness of a Mediterranean landscape to which the designers refer. One factor alone distinguishes the square from a real forest: the natural elements are arranged in a geometrical pattern reminiscent of the rational urban fabric of the new part of town in which the square is located.

The second case study is much more assertively artificial, both in terms of form and materials. The Bymilen development, in Copenhagen, combines a sculpted, completely artificial surfacing with a forest whose appearance is deliberately not very controlled. Its topography and lush vegetation distinguish this space from its very mineral and flat surroundings. The Danish design studio SLA, author of the project, has long been developing a passionate narrative on nature in the city. As such, its work could not have been excluded from this limited corpus. It should be noted that the project was carried out for a private owner, but since the space remains entirely accessible to all.

3.5.6 Location of the Platz der Menschenrechte

PLATZ DER MENSCHEN-RECHTE
RIEM, MUNICH 2005

Location Messestadt Riem, Munich, Germany **Client** City of Munich – Represented by MRG Maßnahmeträger München-Riem GmbH **Lead designers** Valentien + Valentien Landschaftsarchitekten und Stadtplaner (Wessling) **Type of commission** Following a competition for the urban development of the area (1993) **Construction** Completed in 2005 **Former status** Space created simultaneously with the new area **Area** 1.36 ha

The Platz der Menschenrechte (Human Rights Square) project, carried out in 2005 by the Bavarian landscape design firm Valentien + Valentien, is part of the development of the new Messestadt Riem district. The construction of this vast urban extension (560 ha – 16,000 inhabitants and housing 13,000 workers) began at the end of the 1990s on the site of the former Munich airport, which had been decommissioned a few years earlier (Fig. 3.5.7–3.5.8).[1]

The young Messestadt was built around a solid structure of public spaces defined beforehand. The area is articulated by the Willy-Brandt-Allee to the north of which the new Munich Trade Fair and Industries Center is found. The southern part is occupied by a residential area and facilities. A perpendicular axis formed by a sequence of public spaces connects the two areas. This axis of reference is made up successively of a large artificial lake that borders the fair to the north, a new subway station, the Willy-Brandt-Platz, and the Platz der Menschenrechte, which will be discussed here. The axis finally opens onto the gigantic Riemer Park, designed by the Parisian office Latitude Nord (200 ha | 1995–2005).[2]

The Platz der Menschenrechte was not the subject of a design competition. It was the result of a long and eventful process in which Valentien + Valentien had been involved from the beginning.[3] As early as 1987, the landscape architects took part in a workshop organized by the City of Munich to define a guiding concept for the future district, thus anticipating the conversion of the airport.[4] One of the major choices resulting from this process was the importance given to green spaces and their complementarity with the built environment, and this was maintained throughout the district's development.

This intention is reflected in the masterplan for the central part of the Messestadt, which Valentien + Valentien were commissioned to develop together with the architects Maya Reiner, Jörg Weber, and Thomas Hammer after a competition in 1993[5] (Fig. 3.5.10). The multidisciplinary team imagined a new district, which Christoph Valentien describes as follows: "The planned residential area [...] is marked by a close interweaving of city and landscape, where sparsely built green spaces will alternate with densely built streets."[6] The built-up part followed an orthogonal grid of streets with small neighborhood squares at the intersections. This network of public spaces, which includes the Platz der Menschenrechte, was intended to be both a driving force and a guarantee for harmonious development over the long term[7] (Fig. 3.5.11).

In 1996, Valentien + Valentien took over the planning of the green spaces, streets, and squares of the district.[8] It is in this context that the landscape architects designed the future Platz der Menschenrechte as we know it today. The Platz der Menschenrechte, which is a square in name only, is a structured forest of pine trees planted in rows on gravel, itself articulated by strips of stone. This crude space, evocative of a distant natural environment, is furnished only with solid oak benches, also arranged according to a parallel logic that seems to dictate the entire layout.

AN URBAN SQUARE AT THE BEGINNING

In the design submitted by the Valentien + Valentien team for the 1993 competition, the area to become the Platz der Menschenrechte is presented as a *Stadtplatz* (city square) (Fig. 3.5.12). This original image seems to be far removed from the landscape, which can be seen *in situ* today. This metamorphosis can be explained by the effects that urban planning in the wider district had on the square over the years, both in its spatial and functional definitions.

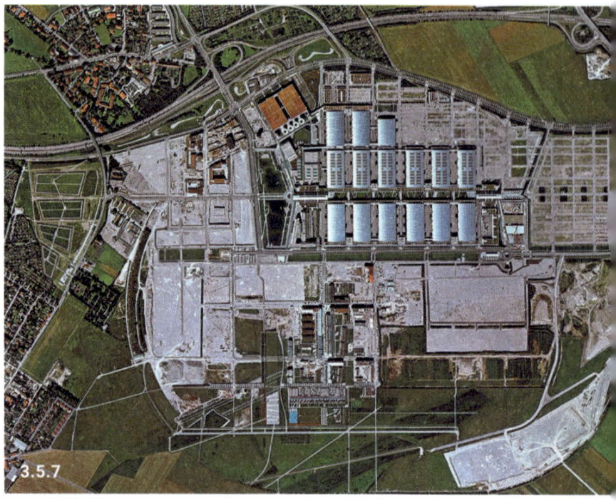

3.5.7

Google Earth | Image © 2021 Geo Content

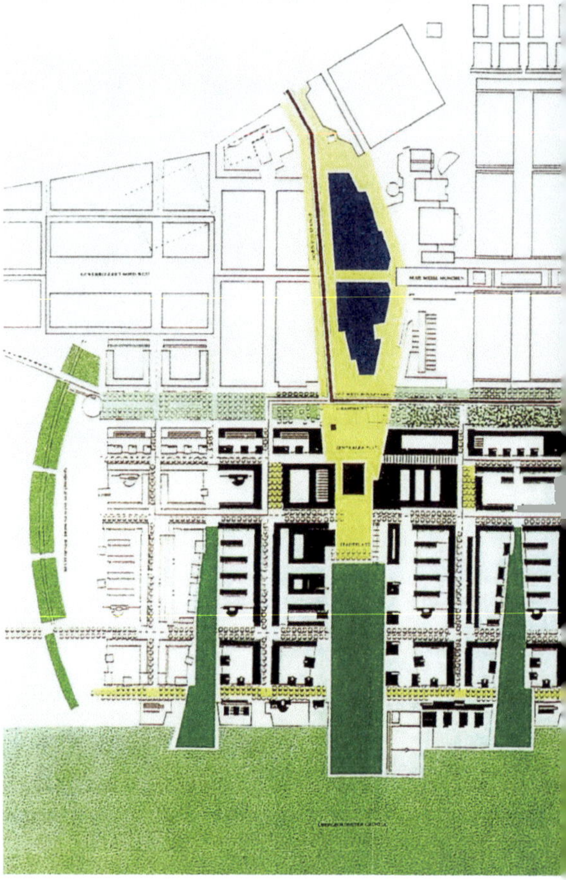

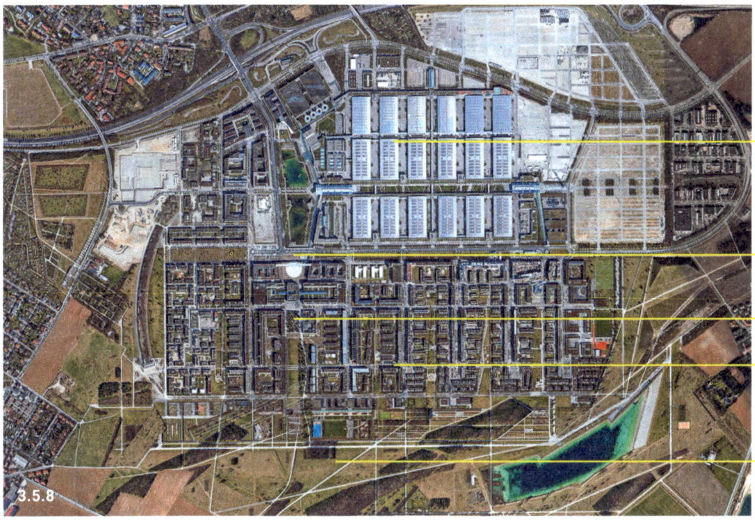

Google Earth | Image © 2021 Maxar Technologies

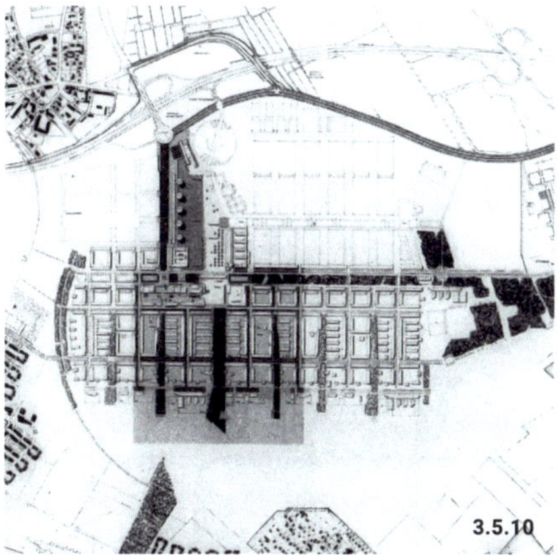

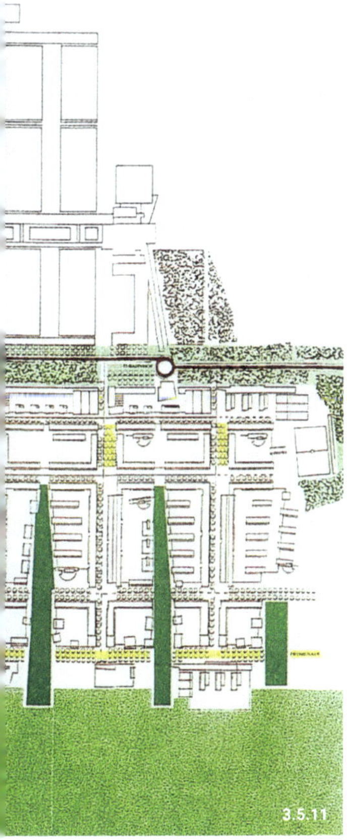

3.5.7–3.5.8 Location of the Platz der Menschenrechte – (7) 2001 and (8) 2020 **3.5.9–3.5.10** Competition for the development of the Messestadt – 1993. *(9) 1st Prize a, Bystrup, Bregenhoj & Partner and Gottfried Hansjakob; (10) 1st Prize b, Maya Reiner + Jörg Weber – Thomas Hammer – Christoph and Donata Valentien* **3.5.11** Strukturplan, Valentien + Valentien, 1998

In a drawing produced in May 1994, the designers still seem to envisage the square as a mineral space, as suggested by an orthogonal grid that distinguishes it from the speckled green spaces to the south (Fig. 3.5.13). A few months later, the public space originally planned was split: a *Messeplatz* (trade fair square), acting as a gateway to the new district, was separated from a *Zentraler Stadtplatz* (central city square) established farther south (Fig. 3.5.14). The functions of the buildings that delimit the new urban square have been defined: a *Stadthaus,*[9] itself adjoining a shopping center and offices, a strip of market stalls, and a religious complex will occupy the three built-up boundaries.

But two major developments radically changed the fate of the Platz der Menschenrechte. The first was programmatic. The arrival of a new investor for the shopping center led to negotiations that resulted in the doubling of the commercial area expected at the beginning.[10] This new deal made it impossible to build small shops around the square in order to animate it. Simultaneously, the *Stadthaus* defined in the 1994 plans disappeared. These decisions led to a general redefinition of the public space frontage: to the north, the shopping mall; to the east, the ecumenical center; and finally, a western frontage of housing, plus a center for the older people.

The second development was that the architecture of some of these buildings became clearer. To increase the profitability of the operation, the new shopping mall was envisaged as a continuous front, pierced by two simple passages linking the Platz der Menschenrechte to the Messeplatz to the north. As for the ecumenical complex bordering the square to the east, it is imagined as a building folded in on itself, with blind walls and whose main entrances do not open onto the square, but onto a small adjacent courtyard.

As a result of these developments, the Valentien team was forced to abandon the originally envisaged animated paved space, lined with shops, cafés, restaurants and public facilities.[11] This new condition of spatial and functional confinement had only one solution in their eyes:

"After we realized that it would be impossible to have public life on this space, that it would be too mineral to make a space going from facade to facade ... it would have been impossible, it is too vast, too hard, too mineral, because there is no life from the church, there is little animation from the center for elderly people and from the housing, or from the commercial center. So we imagined giving this place eine eigene Interpretation, *an interpretation of its own."*[12]

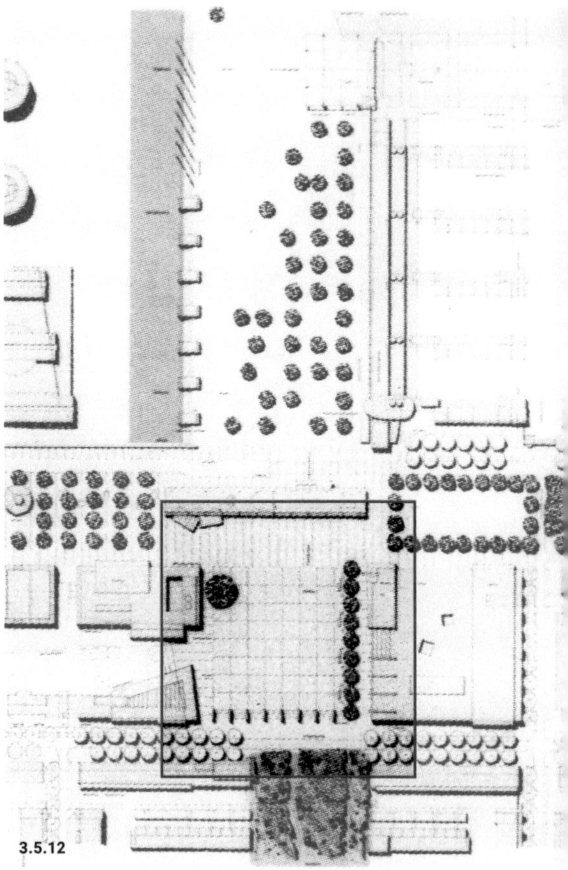

3.5.12

A PINE WOOD

From then on, the square was considered as a space of it own, *ein eigener Raum,*[13] – an object *per se* – for which a new identity had to be found, no longer determined by the buildings, in the formal and functional sense. From this point onward, the sketches drawn up by the landscape architects more closely resemble a green space, following an affirmed landscape logic. The heterogeneity and multitude of variants produced at this stage testify to the fresh start being given to the project.[14]

The exploratory process led the landscape architects to imagine a real shard of nature responding to its internal logic. They resorted to organic forms and attest to a desire to endow the space with a logic other than the rational one that seems to apply to adjacent spaces (Fig. 3.5.15). Other variants delve into the idea of a dual square partially planted with trees: an orthogonal arrangement of trees gives a clear limit to the paved zone occupying the northern boundary of the area. (Fig. 3.5.16).

3.5.13

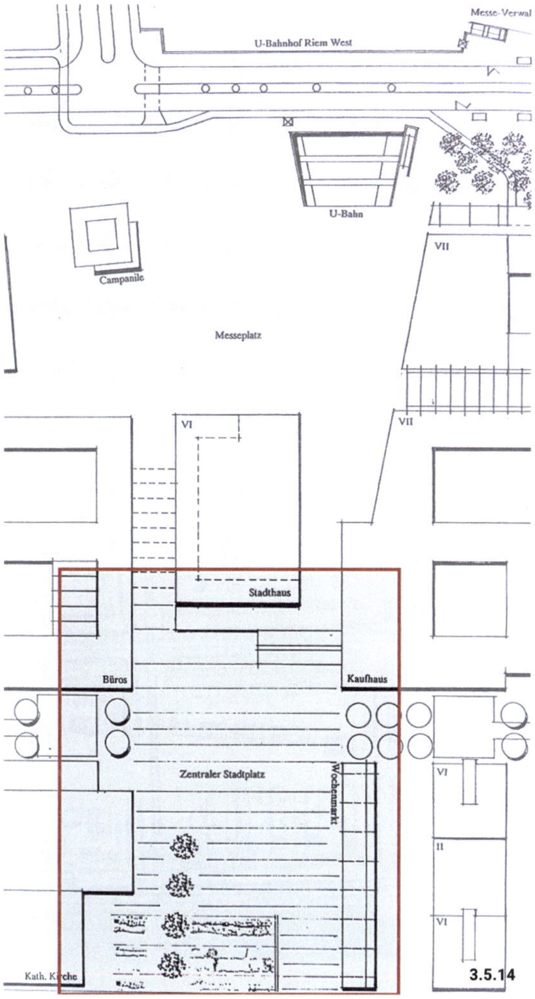

3.5.14

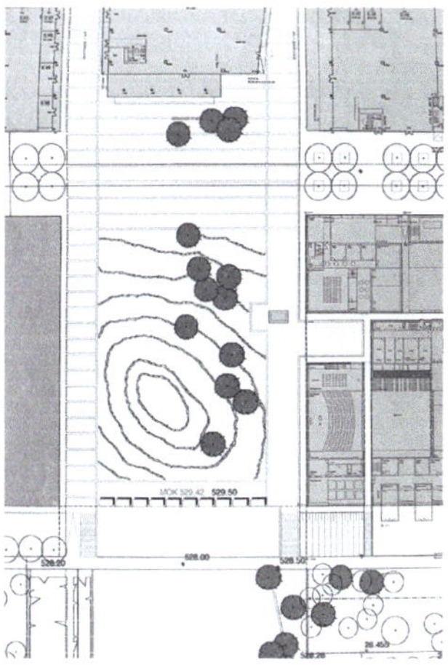

3.5.15

3.5.16

3.5.12 First sketch of the square. *Maya Reiner + Jörg Weber – Thomas Hammer – Christoph and Donata Valentien, competition 1993, Joint 1st Prize* **3.5.13** Sketch of the future district. *Valentien + Valentien, sketch, May 9, 1994* **3.5.14** "Zentraler Stadtplatz." *Valentien + Valentien, August 24, 1994* **3.5.15** The square as a shard of nature. *Valentien + Valentien, sketch, n.d.* **3.5.16** The dual square. *Valentien + Valentien, sketches, September 11, 2001*

These numerous trials (of which a limited selection is presented here) would lead Valentien + Valentien to extend the concept of the wooded area – the word *Baumplatz* appears on some documents – to the entire surface. This idea seems to coincide with the arrival of a rather incongruous reference in the genesis of the project. Deprived of elements on which to articulate their proposal by the lack of high-quality built surroundings, the landscape designers sought to endow the square with a singular identity, a completely arbitrary one if necessary. They found inspiration in a text by Francis Ponge, *Le carnet du bois de pins* (Fig. 3.5.20).[15] This essay presents multitudinous attempts at describing a forest, in the Haute-Loire, near which the French poet stayed during the summer of 1940.[16] The landscape architects, fascinated by this notebook, retain some passages, which they show on the project boards as a "tribute." It should be noted that this literary reference is an exception in the current production of public spaces, where iconographic references seem to be the norm.

From then on, the pine tree became inseparable from the identity of the square, to which it confers, according to Christoph Valentien, a certain unity.[17] The idea of covering the square with an expanse of vegetation first took shape as a homogeneous grid of pine trees planted at regular intervals (Fig. 3.5.17). In other versions, removal of some of the trees allowed the landscape designers to modulate the space (Fig. 3.5.18). In yet more versions, the Cartesian structure was abandoned in favor of a much more random composition (Fig. 3.5.19). The designers also seemed to hesitate about the type of surface covering the area, which was sometimes mineral, sometimes vegetal. This indecision went beyond a simple question of materials and testified to a questioning of the urban square type initially attributed to the space.

SENSITIVE, POETIC IMAGINARY

The transcription of Ponge's text into the project also took on a sensory slant, centered on the notion of effects. In the excerpts selected by Valentien + Valentien, Ponge dwells on the sensations produced by the forest in question:

"One sits, one stretches out at ease [...] There is a reputedly healthy atmosphere, a discreet and tasteful perfume, a vibrant, but soft and pleasant musicality. [...] I definitely must return to the pleasure of the pinewood. Of what is this pleasure made? Mainly of this: the pinewood is a piece of nature, made of trees, all of a clearly defined species; a well-defined area, generally quite deserted, where one finds shelter from sun, from wind, from view [...] It is also a place (this is peculiar to pinewoods) where one moves at ease, lacking undergrowth, lacking branches at man's height, where one can lie on a dry bed, not soft but rather comfortable."[18]

The landscape designers' project, strongly influenced by sensory and bodily considerations, resounds with these statements. For instance, they are very interested in the pines' colors, in the light and its effects; they even make a model to view the effect of sunlight filtering through the branches (Fig. 3.5.21–3.5.22). But the designers do not seem to be satisfied with the purely visual aspect of this man-made pine forest, which mobilizes other senses; the special odor of the pine trees will help to make the place unique.[19] A visitor to the Platz der Menschenrechte would also be surprised by the special, muffled sound of footsteps on the gravel, under the sound-absorbing plant cover. In this, the project echoes the pine wood whose "musicality" and "perfume" Ponge evoked.

3.5.20

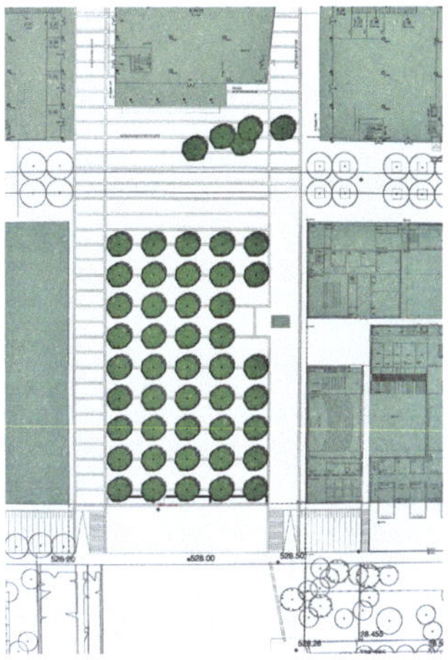

3.5.17

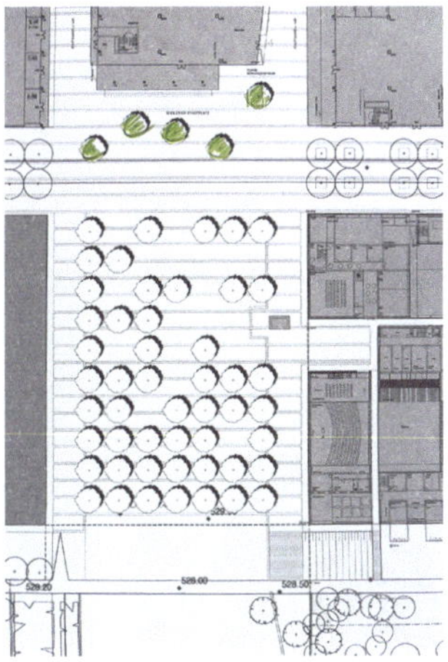

3.5.18

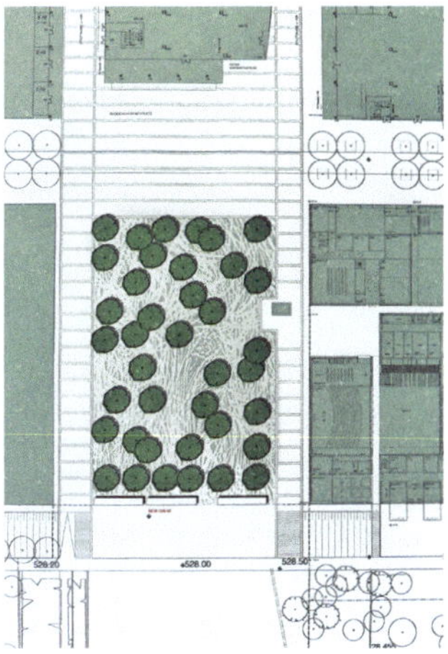

3.5.19

3.5.17 Regularly planted square. *Valentien + Valentien, alternate plan, n.d.* **3.5.18** Modulated regularly arborized square. *Valentien + Valentien, alternate plan, n.d.* **3.5.19** Randomly planted square. *Valentien + Valentien, alternate plan, n.d.* **3.5.20** Francis Ponge, *Das Notizbuch vom Kiefernwald. Reference book* **3.5.21–3.5.22** Study of light effects. *Valentien + Valentien, model photographs, n.d..*

3.5.21

3.5.22

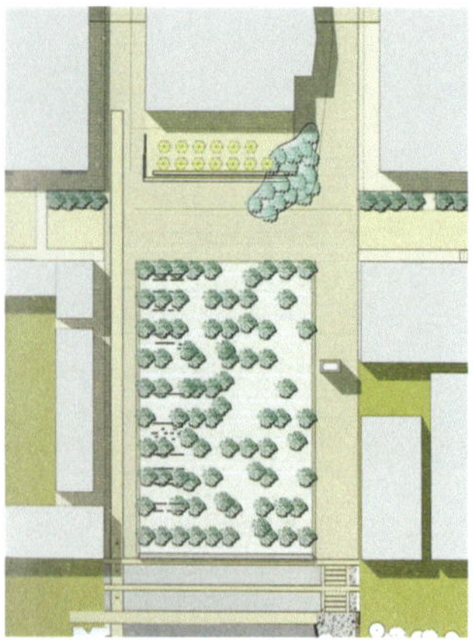

3.5.23

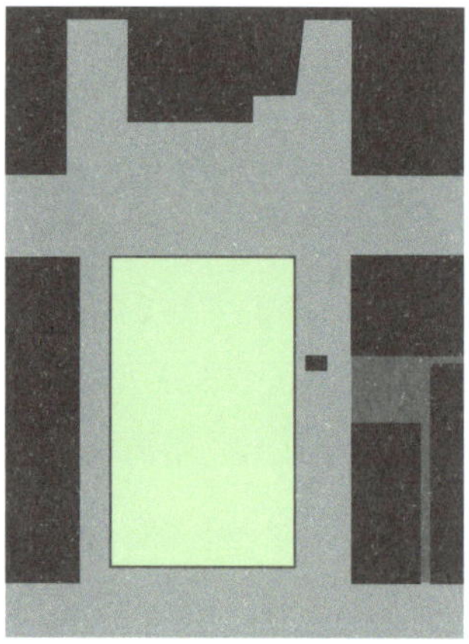

3.5.24

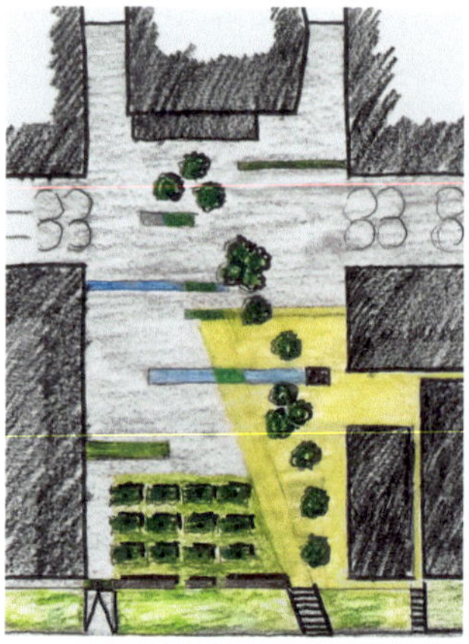

3.5.25

3.5.26

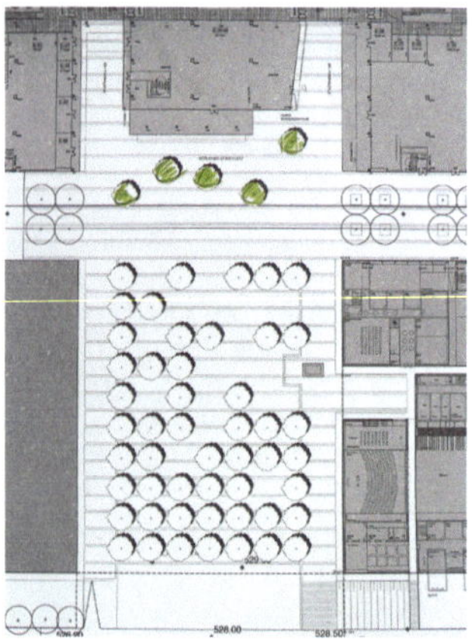

3.5.27

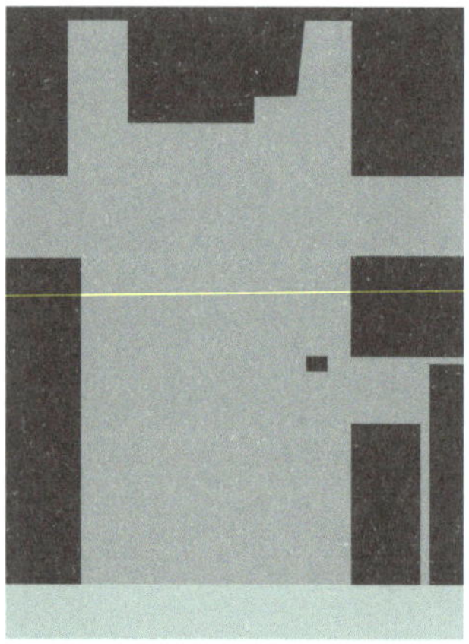

3.5.28

3.5.23–3.5.24 Realized project. *(23) Valentien + Valentien, final plan, n.d.* **3.5.25–3.5.26** A composition integrating the surrounding open spaces. *(25) Valentien + Valentien, sketch, September 14, 2001* **3.5.27–3.5.28** A homogeneous surface. *(27) Valentien + Valentien, variant plan, n.d.* **3.5.29–3.5.30** Willy-Brandt-Platz. *Messestadt Riem, Lützow 7 – Karin Sander, 2004*

The Ponge reference has thus been sensitively treated in the project, but what of the symbolism that the landscape architects associate with it? Although the pine forest described by the poet is located in the Haute-Loire, Ch. Valentien strangely imbues it with a Mediterranean character, more specifically an Italian one. In his opinion, this faraway reference makes sense in the project of the Platz der Menschenrechte.[20] It seems that Italy has a strong resonance within the collective imagination of Munich's citizens, as Bavarians like to spend their holidays there.[21] This project thus offers a new interpretation of the notion of context. It becomes cultural, in that this collective representation of a distant universe, one dear to the local inhabitants, asserts itself as an anchor of the project.

TOWARD A FORMAL SINGULARIZATION OF THE SQUARE

The landscape designers seem to have accepted the idea of a landscape designed as an entity with its own identity and symbolism. This conceptual autonomy will be formalized in the relationship of the square with the built-up surroundings and adjacent public spaces. This can be seen in the treatment of the boundaries, as well as in the framing and partitioning elements added as the project progressed.

Let us first consider the evolution of the ground plan of the Platz der Menschenrechte. The 2005 design is presented as a pure rectangle, delimited by streets and paths running along the foot of the buildings (Fig. 3.5.23). This precise demarcation, modeled on the orthogonal urban fabric, contributes to the perception of the square as a clearly recognizable object. Its gravel surface is not only distinguished from the adjacent spaces by appearance but also by a change in sound and feel. This is in contrast to the approach originally adopted by the landscape designers, who were more interested in continuity of the paving, their earlier sketches displaying the relationship between the square and the adjacent spaces, or even showing it as a homogeneous background, running from facade to facade (Fig. 3.5.25, 3.5.27).

3.5.29

This evolution toward a greater individualization of the square is due to choices made by the landscape designers; but it is also closely linked to the distribution of contracts between the different firms. Thus, the Willy-Brandt-Platz (formerly Messeplatz), designed by the Berlin firm Lützow 7, and the Platz der Menschenrechte, which could have shared a common language in terms of materials and design elements, ended up with very different appearances contingent on the intentions and tastes of their designers (Fig. 3.5.29-3.5.30). This resulted in fragmentation within the network of public spaces.

3.5.30

A formal distancing from the buildings is also clearly expressed in the project. The Platz der Menschenrechte, which was, in the first drafts, intended to be a flat, unified space, will in its final iteration have a slightly *modeled* landscape. In front of the shopping mall to the north, a difference in level was created, emphasized by a long concrete bench, to explicitly demarcate the terrace of a restaurant on the ground floor. This clear materialization of the boundary between public and private domains denotes a desire to keep the commercial complex – which the designers considered less interesting – at a distance.

In the same spirit, the landscape designers planted a group of birch trees to mask the facade of the shopping mall, which was considered too austere.[22] In the square, Valentien + Valentien also used the trees as three-dimensional filters. The pines would be planted more densely to the west, to act as a screen in front of the residential buildings. To the east, a sparser distribution made it possible for the activities of the ecumenical center to spill onto the square. The landscape designers demonstrated, through these adjustments, that they did not entirely reject the built urban fabric that defines the Platz der Menschenrechte.

A HYBRID CHARACTER

In its metamorphosis from mineral urban square to artificial pine forest, the designers are clearly embarrassed by the final character given to this public space. Their hesitations have already been revealed in the analysis of the tree-lined sketches (Fig. 3.5.17–3.5.19). In the built version, a certain ambiguity remains that is perhaps intentional; the landscape designers have used tree species and materials that are not very urban, while the layout does not seem to break away completely from the orthogonal and rational logic of the district.

Variations on the regular or purely random arrangement of the Scots pines finally led to an in-between arrangement. Starting with a grid, the landscape designers proceeded by removing or slightly shifting certain trees (Fig. 3.5.31). This composition allowed them to modulate the space, but also to make the development seem less controlled.

This sought-after uncontrolled character can be seen in the wild-looking Scots pines, which were in fact carefully selected in a nursery: "'Twisted' trees or twin trees [coppiced] were deliberately selected. Thus, the space is not strictly geometric in character, but also playful and joyful."[23] Other elements, this time much more authentic, such as the greenery that grows in the gravel, or the mushrooms that colonize the ground, contribute to the square's wild character. Finally, the square has an intentionally unmanicured appearance, in acceptance of the idea that pine needles and cones are an integral part of the gravel surface (Fig. 3.5.32–3.5.34).

This wild appearance – itself the outcome of more control than it might seem – contrasts with the very rational and urban character of other elements of the development. One is reminded in particular of the general composition that the landscape designers themselves describe as "strict and geometrical" and also "graphic."[24] The pure and clearly delimited rectangle that constitutes the heart of the public space echoes the layout of the adjacent buildings. Its gravel surface is articulated by regular parallel strips of granite slabs. As for the benches, they follow the same linear logic. This formal attitude contrasts with the crude, almost minimalist design found in other parts of the square. The ambivalence between urban and landscape language is also found in the different items of furniture. Lamp-posts and waste bins (probably selected from catalogs) contrast with the solid oak benches that one might find along a forest path.

The development thus seems to play on dichotomies – mineral-vegetational, urban-natural, rational-random, controlled-wild – which is justified, according to some critics, by the square's role as a link between the new district and the wider landscape.[25] In any case, the juxtapositions produce surprising scenes, akin to surrealist collages, where supermarket trolleys, lampposts, rubbish bins, advertising signs, and graffiti seem to have been overlapped on a background of pine forest (Fig. 3.5.35–4.5.36). Perhaps this is the true identity of the Platz der Menschenrechte.

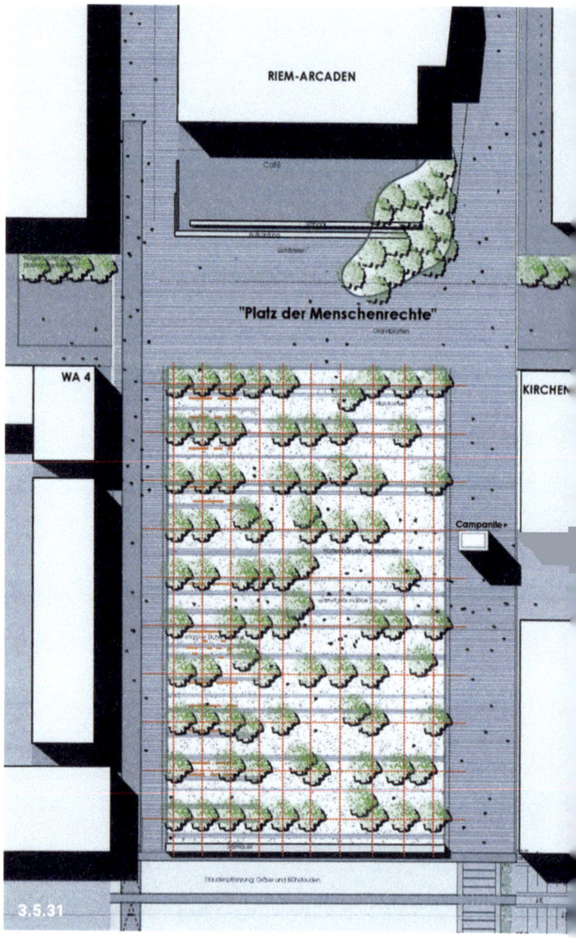

3.5.31

3.5.32

3.5.33

3.5.34

3.5.35

3.5.36

3.5.31 An orthogonal grid as the basis for a random appearance. *Valentien + Valentien, final plan, n.d. – red lines added* **3.5.32–3.5.34** Wild atmosphere **3.5.35–3.5.36** Juxtaposition of atypical signs

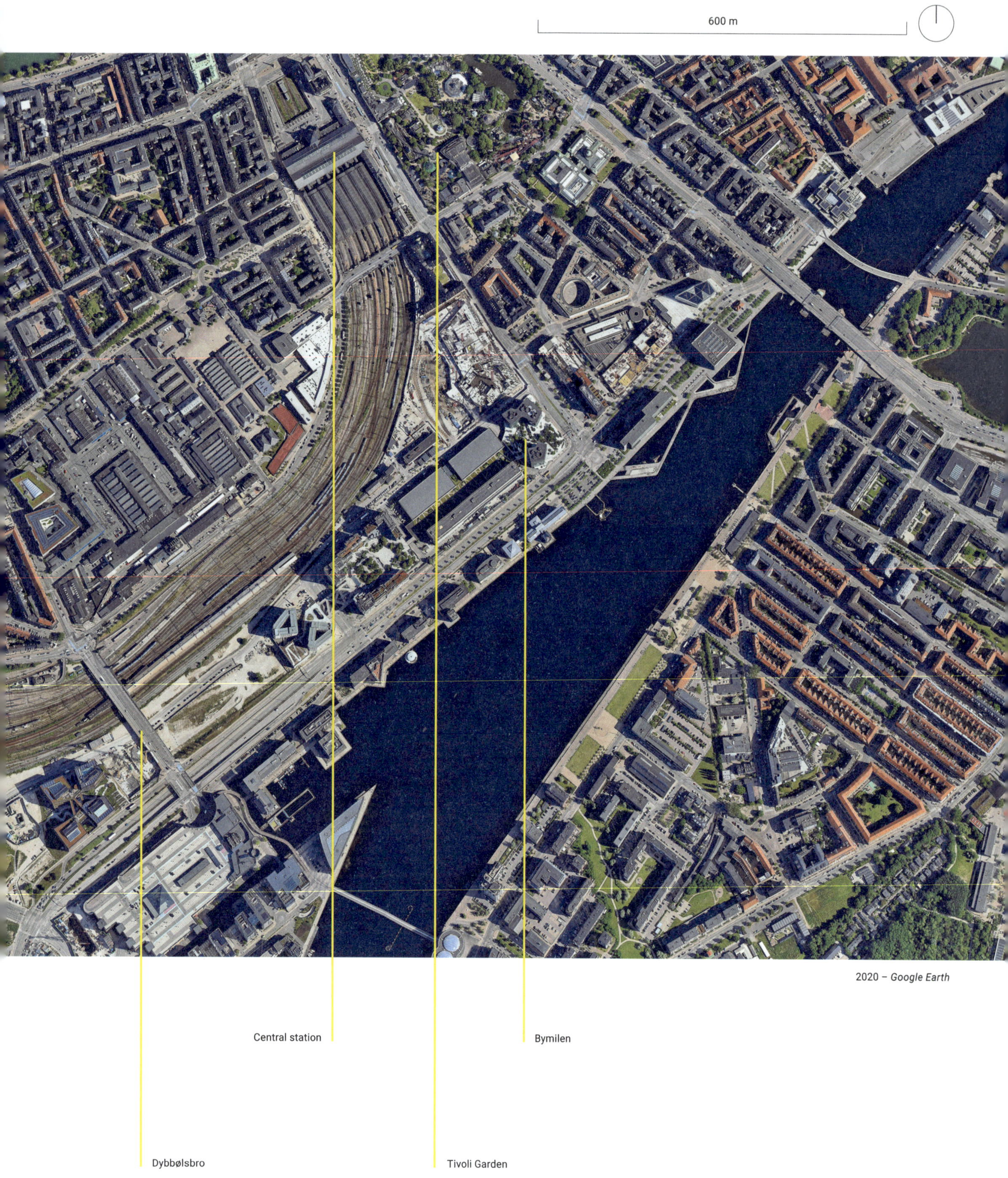

3.5.37 Location of Bymilen

BYMILEN
COPENHAGEN
2007–2010

Location Copenhagen, Denmark **Client** SEB Skandinaviska Enskilda Banken **Lead designers** Landscape: SLA Landskabsarkitekter (Copenhagen) / Buildings: Lundgaard & Tranberg Arkitekter (Copenhagen) **Type of commission** Direct commission (2007–2010) **Construction** 2010–2011 **Former status** Space created ex-nihilo simultaneously with two adjacent buildings **Area** 0.7 ha

The *Bymilen* (urban dune) project is part of the planning of a strategic area in the center of Copenhagen called *Rigsarkivet* (National Archives). This elongated area of nearly 11 ha occupies the site of the former freight station of the national railway company (DSB), which was decommissioned in 1999. It is bounded at the western end by Bernstorffsgade, which leads directly to the central station and the Tivoli amusement park, and at the east by the Dybbølsbro bridge, which connects the Fisketorvet shopping center opened in 2000 in the Vesterbro district. Bordered by the Kalvebod Brygge, a busy road, to the south, and the railroad infrastructure to the north, the area is perceived as an enclave in the monofunctional Kalvebod Brygge quarter (Fig. 3.5.38).

In 2003, it was decided to give it some functional diversity by establishing the National Archives, a hotel, a conference center, administrative services, offices, and housing. Following a parallel study contracts procedure (*parallelopdrag*), the planning of the future district was entrusted to the architects Lundgaard & Tranberg, in association with the landscape designers SLA Landskabsarkitekter.[26]

The concept proposed by the multidisciplinary team comprised locating the future buildings around the perimeter of the narrow area, to free up the center. This would be filled by a structuring and identifying landscape backbone, which the designers called "green infrastructure"[27] (Fig. 3.5.39–3.5.41). Although located on plots of land to be sold to private investors, the green infrastructure had to remain completely accessible to the public; raised 7–8 m above the reference level of the district, it was envisaged as a pedestrian and cyclist link as well as a place of refuge, leisure, and physical exercise.

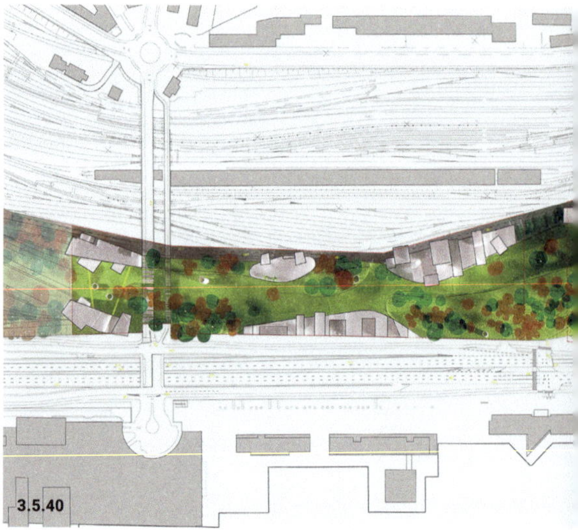
3.5.40

As the masterplan was being finalized, the Swedish bank SEB (Skandinaviska Enskilda Banken) decided to buy the plot at the entrance to the green infrastructure at Bernstorffsgade. It appointed Lundgaard & Tranberg for the construction of two distinct slender office blocks, projected in the local plan (*Lokalplan*) adopted in 2006.[28] The architects then chose to continue collaboration with their associates from SLA, seeking a strong interaction between architecture and open spaces. Together, they imagined a sculpted landscape penetrating the two buildings at ground floor level. This *modeled* surface, under which there would be two floors of parking, was to be covered with an artificial forest comprising a wide variety of tree species rarely seen in an urban setting (Fig. 3.5.43–3.5.45).

The design of the rest of the Rigsarkivet area was entrusted to Kim Utzon and SLA for the Tivoli Congress Center area, and to PLH Arkitekter in association with the landscape architects Schønherr for the design of the central portion hosting the National Archives. The last sub-sector was not to be carried out immediately, so the landscape link was suddenly interrupted, resulting in a dead end.

A DENSE AND SURPRISING FOREST ON SLOPING GROUND

While the brief dictated by SEB for the two buildings were relatively precise, the designers were invited to be very free with the unbuilt part of the plot.[29] The design of this area above all had to convey a positive image of the financial institution, which planned to locate its Danish headquarters in one of the buildings. The project did, however, have to comply with the guidelines set out in the local plan, which emphasizes the role of this future public space as the main access to the landscape backbone.[30]

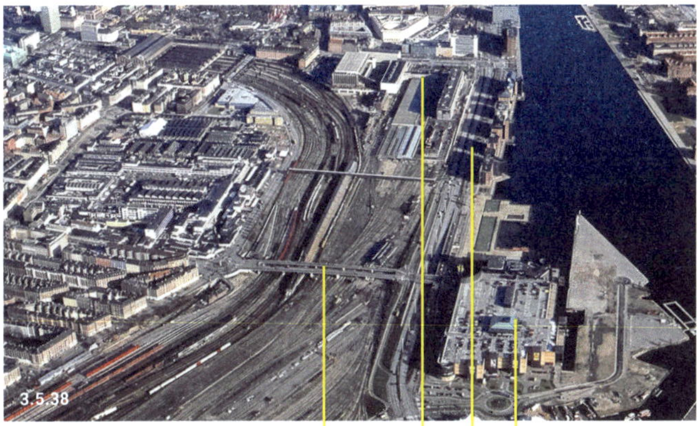

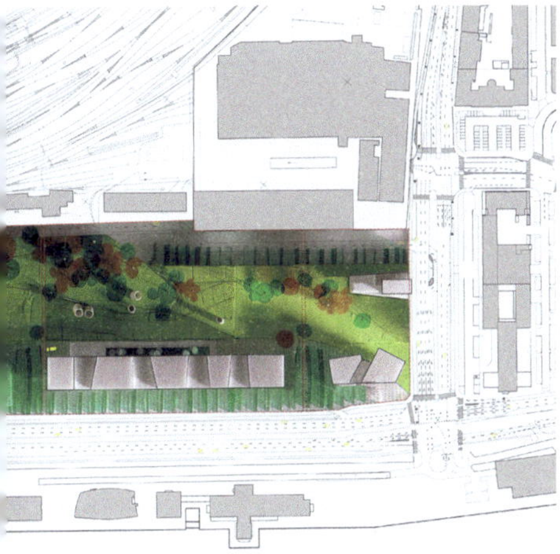

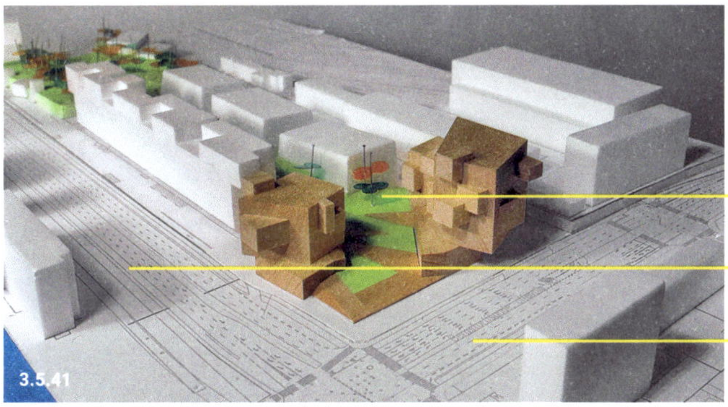

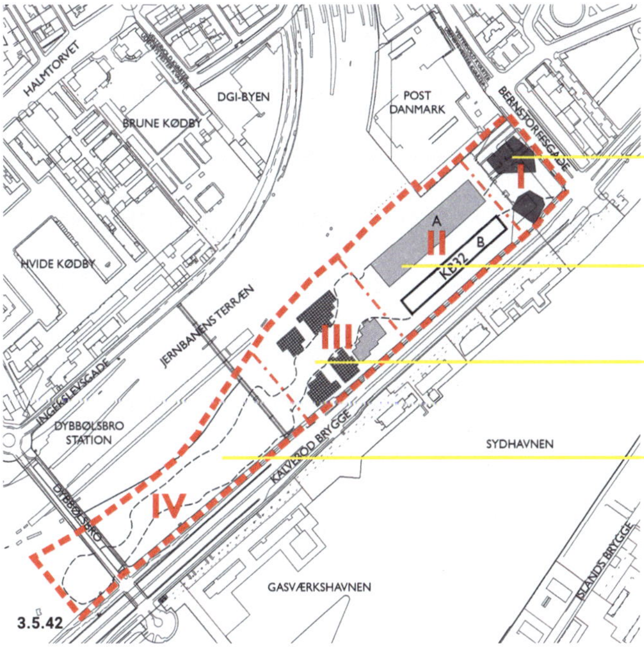

3.5.38 Aerial view of the area **3.5.39–3.5.41** Excerpt from the local plan developed by Lundgaard & Tranberg and SLA **3.5.42** Division into sub-areas. *Københavns Kommune,* Forslag til lokalplan "Rigsarkivet" med kommuneplantillæg, *Copenhagen, 2005*

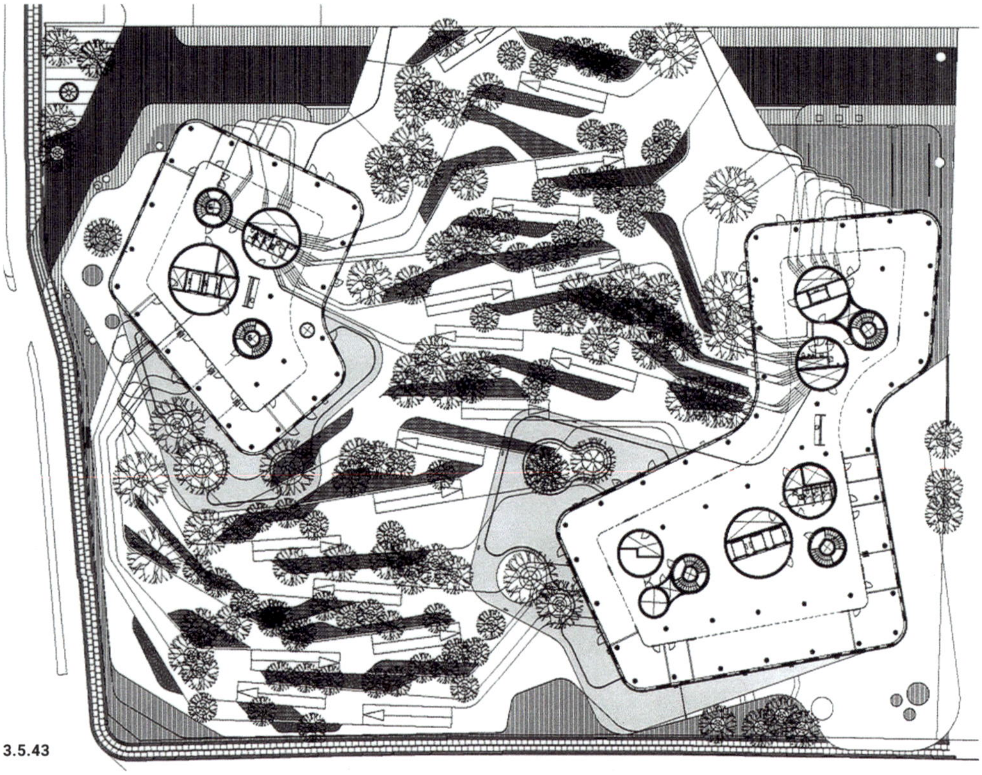

3.5.43

3.5.44

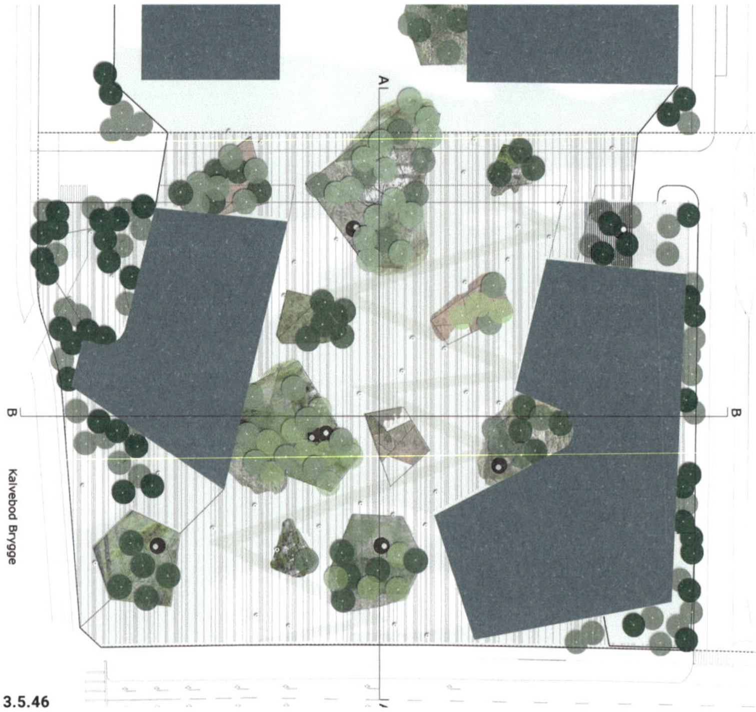

3.5.46

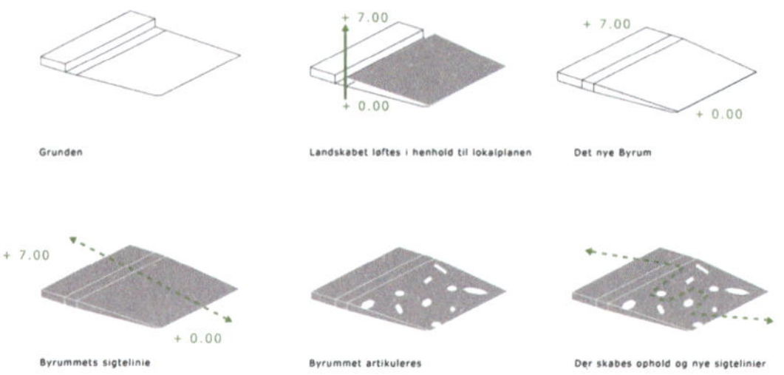

3.5.47

3.5.43–3.5.45 A forest on modeled terrain
3.5.46–3.5.47 Project plan and concetual diagrams at the initial stage
SLA in Lundgaard & Tranberg – SLA, Dispositionsforlag 1, *December 2005*

3.5.45

The very first drafts of the open space produced by Lundgaard & Tranberg and SLA in December 2005 already include the two constituent elements of the future open space, namely a sloping ground covered by a wooded expanse. The challenge for the plot was to connect the street level with the elevated landscape backbone, 7 m higher. The designers proposed to articulate this plan through eleven beds planted with trees, to create "living spaces and new perspectives."[31] A sinuous path winds its way through the sloping terrain between the irregularly shaped and randomly arranged green surfaces (Fig. 3.5.46–3.5.47).

At this early stage of the project, the designers refer to the space as Bernstorffs Plads. However, the development they sketched out had neither the spatial configuration nor the urban characteristics of a square, usually defined by built-up frontages and dominated by a mineral character. Aware of this discrepancy, the authors of the project explain:

"It is not a plaza or a square in the traditional sense. Nor is it a square like those usually seen in ports or other urban areas. These are usually paved, surrounded by cars and sparsely vegetated [...] This is a completely different way of creating urban space. It is precisely a question of creation." [32]

The typological distinction thus made allows the team to officially distance itself from urban language and to justify the "creation" *ex nihilo* of a landscape that draws on inspiration from a natural register. Some of the photographs of models produced at that time already present the space as a forest of wild appearance marked by lush, heterogeneous vegetation (Fig. 3.5.48–3.5.49). The architects and landscape designers seem to be working in opposition to the surroundings, as the caption of one illustration indicates: "Large natural elements like a dense, astonishing forest in the urban center."[33]

ELEMENTS EMBEDDED IN A UNIFYING SURFACE

The next step for Lundgaard & Tranberg and SLA was to interweave the built and open spaces more assertively, according to the principle of strong interaction advocated from the start. A new model produced at the beginning of 2006 seems to point the project in this direction (Fig. 3.5.50). The floors of the buildings are represented as plateaus with rounded corners. These shapes are reflected in the design of the ground, which is made up of contour lines materialized as stepped platforms. Building and landscape now share a common language. The additional step is to make the artificial topography penetrate the buildings, to blur the boundary between outside and inside spaces (Fig. 3.5.51). The contour lines will structure the entire surface of the plot, penetrating the foyers of the buildings in the form of landings and stairs. Through this uniform treatment of the ground, building and landscape become inseparable.

Inspired by a model by Alvar Aalto, the SLA office embarked on artistic experimentations that led them to design a ground formed of undulating lines (Fig. 3.5.52–3.5.56). These sculptural reflections also encouraged the landscape designers to break away from traditional design logic, in the form of contour lines similar to natural topography, and to consider the creation of a "modular surface"[34] composed of inclined triangular planes. The plant masses, that initially structured the plot at random, were to occupy the interstices of this unusual formal system. Geometric figures would also be added as new elements of language: a path through the site composed of identical rectangular ramps and trees arranged randomly in circular pits (Fig. 3.5.57–3.5.60).

The development of this unifying ground, revealed here in all its components, testifies to their research into how to interweave buildings, ground, and vegetation, into a single holistic system. The language thus defined, resulting from artistic considerations completely indifferent to the surrounding context, had already endowed the public space with a unique appearance.

3.5.48

AN ENVIRONMENT TO BE EXPLORED DIFFERENTLY

A large part of the layout's development focuses on the precise design of this unifying ground, involving much give and take between landscape designers and architects, to ensure continuity between open spaces and buildings.[35] For SLA, the shaping of the outside topography was to be guided above all by attention to the movements of users.

SLA tried to imagine different ways of moving in this space, using the inclinations of the ground and the volumes of vegetation to orient possible trajectories. To do this, they favored working with models that allowed them to appreciate the scale of the elements and simulate people's perception[36] (Fig. 3.5.61–3.5.62). The shaping of the terrain would incorporate a mildly sloping ramp, suitable for wheelchairs and pushchairs, but also usable by cyclists. This winding pathway running through the whole site, from one facade to the other, would blend completely with the ground topography.

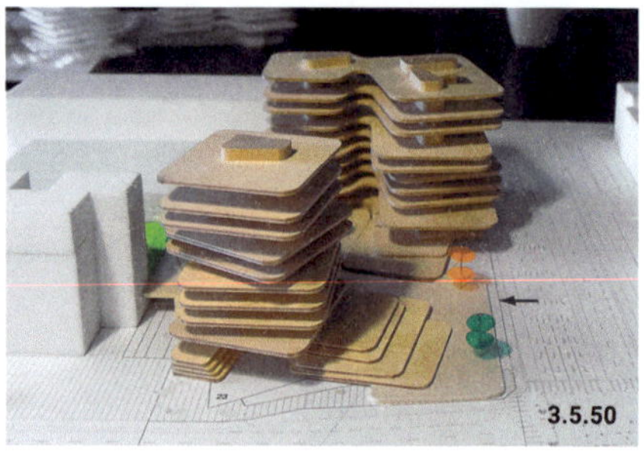

3.5.50

The landscape designers integrated small spaces between the ramps and placed trees at their ends to break up the perspectives. Large intermediate landings composed of triangular surfaces would also allow users to deviate slightly from the main trajectory. Finally, beds planted across the slope would prevent users from crossing the site directly. All these devices were aimed at gently guiding the walkers.

For the designers, it was a question of creating an environment to be explored, which implied a loss of reference points, rather than proposing a place to be understood at first glance. This quest for disorientation corresponded with the concept of "fluid intelligence" developed by SLA:

"Spatial variations in the surface appeal to our fluid intelligence. It is the part of our intelligence that is independent of culture and learning. Spatial variations stimulate our ability to navigate using the information we pick up as we move. This is to be differentiated from the crystallized intelligence we normally use when we are moving around the city. In that case, we already know the structure of the city, with its sidewalks, curbs, and gables. It's the same everywhere and that's why we can move forward completely unconsciously, without paying attention to where we are going and where we are. [...] Bymilen breaks with the traditional spatial structure and organization of the city."[37]

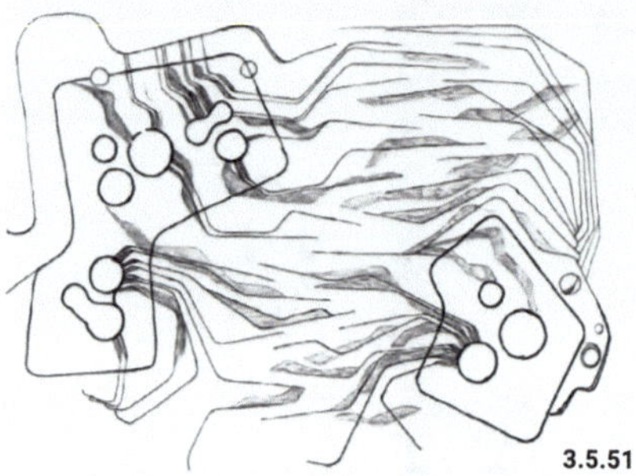

3.5.51

The loss of orientation induced in the project would therefore aim to create a particular experience for its users who would become more aware of their spatial environment and its variations. The originality of a space calling upon fluid intelligence thus runs counter to traditional urban environments, depicted as boring. With this approach, the designers openly assumed a break, in terms of perception, with the immediate environment.

3.5.49

3.5.48–3.5.49 Photographs of models depicting a "wild" forest. *Lundgaard & Tranberg – SLA,* Dispositionsforlag 1, *December 2005* **3.5.50** Common language between buildings and landscape. *Lundgaard & Tranberg – SLA, model, January 2006* **3.5.51** Blurred boundaries between inside and outside that the design process will culminate in. *Lundgaard & Tranberg – SLA, late publication drawing* **3.5.52** Wooden model by Alvar Aalto as a formal reference **3.5.53–3.5.56** Model experiments inspired by Alvar Aalto. *SLA, model photography, May 4–5, 2006*

3.5.52

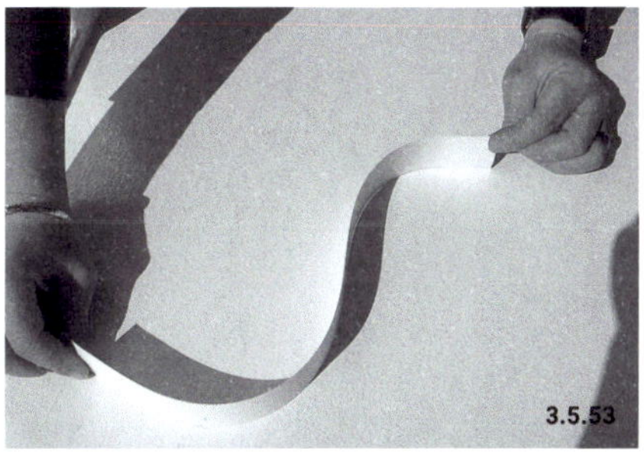

3.5.53

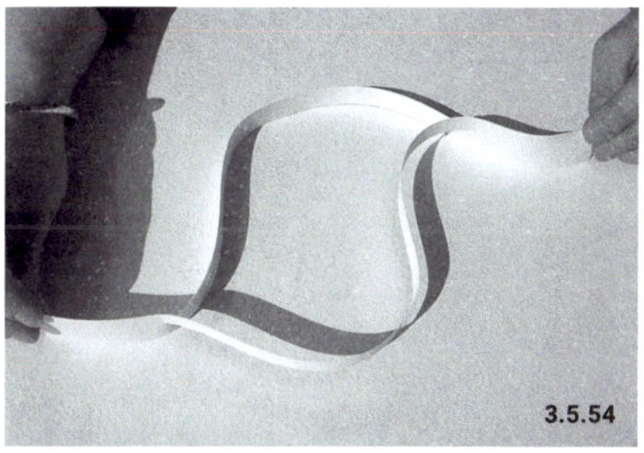

3.5.54

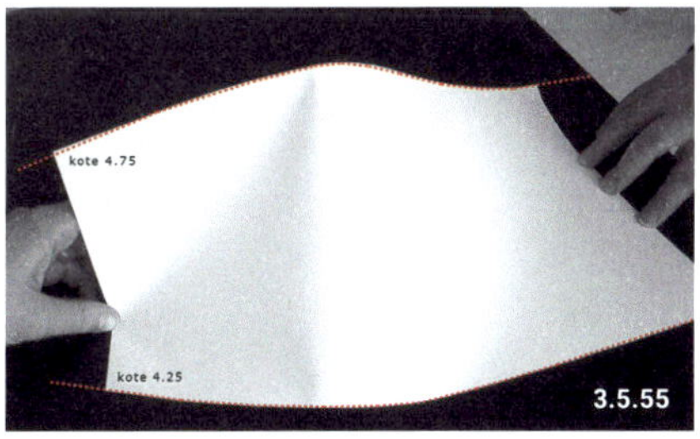

3.5.55

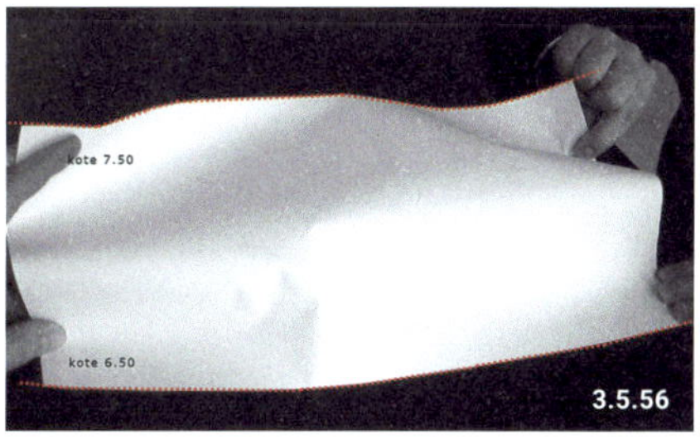

3.5.56

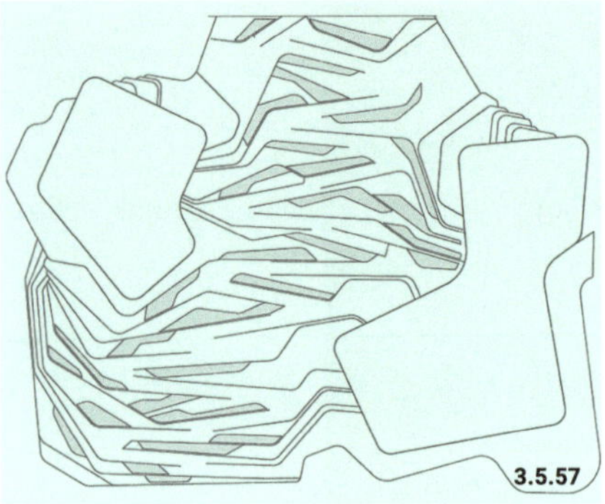
3.5.57

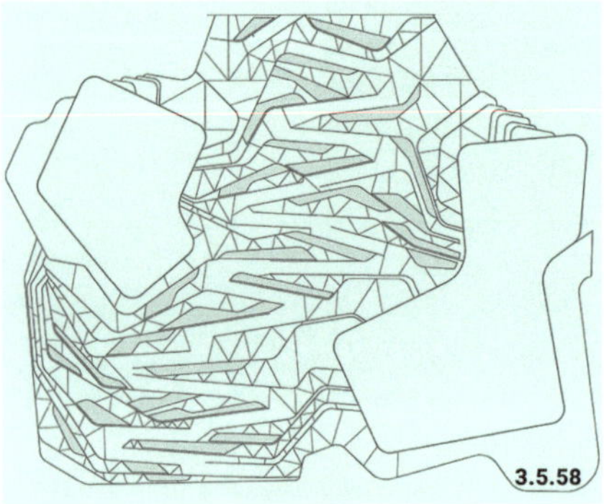
3.5.58

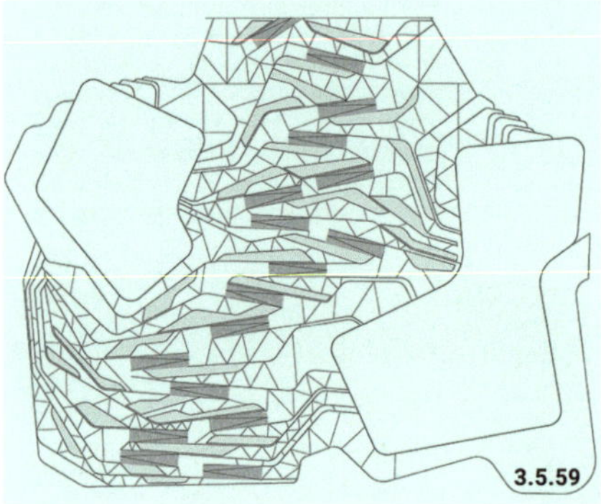
3.5.59

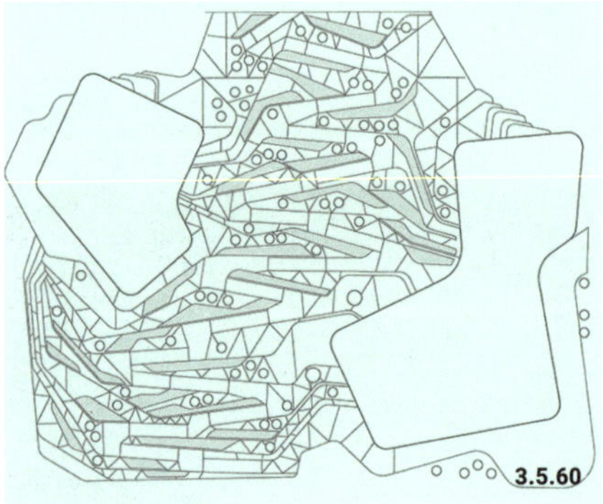
3.5.60

3.5.61

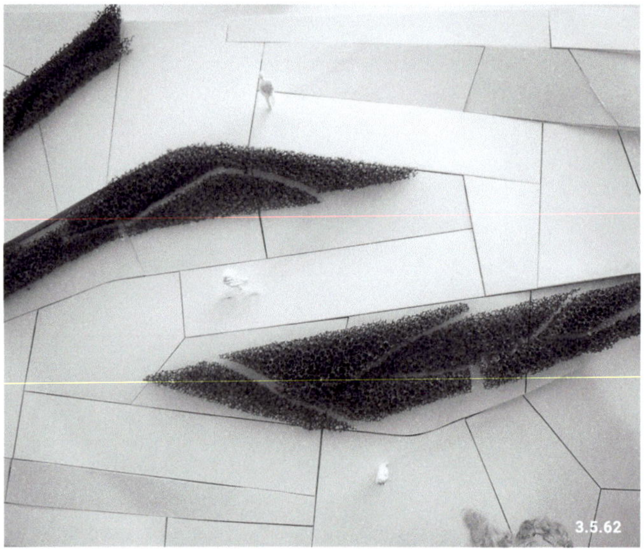
3.5.62

3.5.63

3.5.57–3.5.60 Analysis of design principles and elements. *(57) A system of undulating lines; (58) A "modular system"; (59) Identical rectangular ramps; (60) A free arrangement of the trees. Based on the final design plan (Hovedprojekt)* **3.5.61–3.5.62** Model as a working tool to study user perception. *SLA, model photographs, January 25, 2007* **3.5.63** Reference atmospheres. *SLA et al., reference collage,* Dispositionsforlag 1, *December 2005*

A SENSORY AESTHETIC

The quest for a break with the urban environment also took on a sensory dimension in this project, in a stimulating approach that Stig L. Andersson, founder of the practice, explains: "Yes, I strive for surprises, or even better, wonder. I try to create atmospheres where one experiences wonder, and this can be done by creating differences."[38] If the landscape designer is to be believed, designing a public space could almost be akin to building an enchanting setting.

Early on, SLA collected reference photographs from natural environments to define the development's atmosphere (Fig. 3.5.63). These images display a sensitivity for textures, light, colors, and their combined effects, but also heat and damp. By translating these ambient images into their design, the landscape architects aimed to create a development that would stimulate the physical senses and feelings of users: "Attention is heightened and the senses sharpened. The urban space becomes a universe of sensory experiences," they state in a report presenting the project.[39]

Thus, Bymilen's urban-atypical tree species would be selected for the appearance of their foliage, in some cases evergreen, and the way they glow in the sun, cast shadows on the ground, or rustle in the wind.[40] As for the concrete that makes up Bymilen's ground cover, it was to be "acid washed and coated to give it a beautiful patina and to act as an anti-slip surface, on which water will 'bead'."[41] The interest in materials was primarily for the impressions left on visitors.

The multiple components of the project were carefully chosen for their appearance, but equally for their tactile, odoriferous, sonorous, and refreshing qualities and their interactions with different natural elements (wind, rain, and sun). All of these contribute to a unique experience for city dwellers, one not to be found anywhere else in the capital. The project thus displays another contrast with the immediate environment, this time of a sensory nature (Fig. 3.5.64).

TWO NATURAL IMAGINARIES OF DIFFERING VALUE

The natural sources of inspiration presented so far serve above all to define the desired atmosphere. Two other references – the dune and the forest – also recur in the illustrations and narratives produced by the landscape architects over the years. These two reference environments take on a more metaphorical value in the project's formulation, one that the ambience images did not. The genetic study also reveals that these two references did not play an equivalent role in the design development.

First, it can be seen that they appear at distinct moments in the design process. While forests are already featured in the original reference images presented above and are explicitly mentioned in the first narratives presenting the project,[42] the dune emerges much later, once the project is completed. It nevertheless gives its name to the public space, *Bymilen* meaning "urban dune." Following this new nomenclature, the dune as a reference for the project became surprisingly widespread in the designers' narratives.[43] Images of references previously unseen even appear in late publications (Fig. 3.5.65).

This narrative and post-design nomenclature is confusing, but Ulla Hornsyld, who has managed the project from the beginning, is adamant that "it was not our intention to create a dune in the first place."[44] If that had been the case, the original dune would have undergone a great deal of abstraction to end up with the complex modular concrete surface that we know today. There is every reason to believe that this surface would have been associated a posteriori with a dune, probably to give the bank's headquarters an attractive identity. In terms of reference, there is therefore some distance between the forest, which constitutes an initial inspiration feeding the design process, and the dune, which appears as an evocation subsequent to the project's development.

Another difference is that, while the reference to the dune is rather evocative, SLA seems to have taken a much more mimetic approach to the forest.[45] To amplify its character, the landscape architects chose urban atypical tree species: pines, birches, and beeches. These would be carefully selected in the nursery for their atypical appearance,[46] then arranged at random in the space. Finally, they would not be pruned (as is usually the case with city trees, to enable passage by pedestrians). All these decisions contribute to the public space's wild aspect, one obtained by very elaborate means.[47]

3.5.64

FORMAL SINGULARIZATION OF THE PUBLIC SPACE

The natural imaginaries summoned, and their incorporation in the project, will participate, formally speaking, in singularizing Bymilen from the urban fabric. With its free and luxuriant vegetation, the open space is an exception in the bleak district of Kalvebod Brygge. According to Ulla Hornsyld, the unexpected creation of this shard of nature is justified by a very mineral and low-quality context: "We always start with the context. But here, the context was so urbanized, everything was so man-made. There wasn't really any nature to bring into this area."[48] From this statement comes the idea that the natural and urban environments are inevitably opposed, with the former presenting itself as a beneficial response to the drawbacks of the latter.

In addition to the green character of Bymilen, a formal contrast can also be seen in the clear delineation of the perimeter to which the singular design and its materials apply. At the Bernstorffsgade end, the white concrete breaks with the urban language of the paving stones that cover the paths. The designers were not content with a simple change of surfacing to mark the difference: a slight elevation confirms the desired distancing (Fig. 3.5.68). Similarly, at the other end of the urban forest, the space is clearly demarcated by a change of paving: a strip of dark asphalt, contrasting strongly with the light color of Bymilen, acts as a link with the section laid out by the Schønherr office in front of the archive building (Fig. 3.5.69).

These design choices no longer fit into a dichotomy between city and nature but help to differentiate Bymilen from the other open spaces that border it. This stance of individualization seems all the more surprising here, knowing that the Lundgaard & Tranberg and SLA consortium is at the origin of the idea of creating a landscaped axis intended to give coherence to the district's development. The model presenting the vision for the Rigsarkivet area's development clearly showed the space as a unifying and uniform link at the time, far from the built reality (Fig 3.5.66–3.5.67).

However, for SLA, this succession of places with differentiated characteristics is not problematic.[49] They even claim the creation of singular experiences, positioning themselves as fervent critics of urban uniformity, which they consider "monotonous." They go so far as to urge planners and public authorities to create attractive and differentiated places, capable of attracting city dwellers outdoors.[50] Nevertheless, one may wonder how far this logic of creating unique and spectacular places can be pushed. Isn't a little banality necessary to highlight exceptional places?

3.5.64 Atmospheres of the realized design **3.5.65** Late reference to the dune. *Source: SLA, "Reclaiming Public Space," in Kjeld Kjeldsen et al. (eds),* New Nordic – Architecture & Identity, *exhibition catalog, Humlebæk, Louisiana Museum of Modern Art, 2012, p. 194* **3.5.66** A unified landscape axis. *Lundgaard & Tranberg/ SLA, model photograph, local plan, 2005* **3.5.67** A fragmented network of spaces **3.5.68–3.5.69** A space assuming a clear contrast with the adjacent spaces

The City Bank
Snow bank and sand bank

3.5.65

3.5.66

3.5.67

3.5.68

3.5.69

SHARDS OF NATURE

Artificial nature

The two examples analyzed are presented as real shards of nature created from scratch in very urban environments. It should be emphasized that the designers wanted to transform these public spaces, initially defined as squares, in this way. However, their layouts clearly distance them from the traditional representation of this type of place, as the two urban squares are transformed into real artificial landscapes.

This orientation given to the projects testifies to a radical stance, a Manichean opposition between city (sinister) and nature (idyllic). When the designers of the two open spaces dwell on the surrounding architecture, it is to describe it in pejorative terms. However, the point at which this disapproval appears in the genesis of the project varies from one case to another. It is almost an a priori, general attitude for the landscape architects at SLA. For Valentien + Valentien, however, the will to give the project its own character came late in the process, in reaction to a built context cheapened by real-estate pressure. On the contrary, the firm initially showed a marked interest in the surrounding architecture and its necessary interactions with the public space.

If this rejection of the urban is clear in the designers' narratives, it is not so clear in the reality of the projects. First of all, it should be noted that these schemes have an undeniable relationship with the built environment, as they should be considered above all as built works, rather than landscapes. It is important to note that neither space is built on virgin soil.

This association with the built environment is tightened too by the geometric rules and elements exploited by the designers, intending to bring a certain coherence to the public space. This recourse to geometry also results from its capacity to define a kind of reassuring rationality, on which the deployment of more irregular components can be based. The spontaneous, random, and organic forms of nature used as references undergo an obvious abstraction in the project's development.

The artificiality of the design is also evident in the choice of certain materials and in their use. The concrete modules in Bymilen, for example, are more reminiscent of an urban language than a natural landscape. In this, the Platz der Menschenrechte project is seen as simpler, in that the designers opt for raw natural elements such as gravel and wood. They also assume a certain lack of control over time, accepting that spontaneous plant species – moss, fungi, grasses – will colonize the ground and the furniture.

Finally, it should be noted that neither of the projects' analysis revealed an ecological approach, as might have been expected. The architects and landscape designers clearly seem to endow the natural with virtues other than environmental ones.

A sensory and bodily approach

Indeed, analysis of the projects reveals above all the seductiveness that the designers associate with a demagogic and sensitive approach to a naturized creation. Nature, being readily associated with pleasant sensations, seems above all to be exploited for the positive image it conveys. The late appearance of the dune as a reference for Bymilen, and its widespread appropriation by critics and journalists, reveals the appealing scope of natural references.

But the designers also call upon the natural field of reference to stimulate the senses of the space's target users. An analysis of the projects' development, and the narratives that support them, reveal some interest in a certain sensuality of public spaces. Thus, Valentien + Valentien are interested in the effects of sunlight filtering through the pine branches, but also in the olfactory and auditory arousal that this vegetation will stimulate. Similar concerns can be found in the concept of aesthetics developed by SLA, which seeks to reinstate all five senses at the heart of urban perception.

The study of these developments also reveals an interest in the physicality of future users: in particular, their movements in space are considered. With the concept of *fluid intelligence*, the SLA office seeks to create a landscape that one would walk through differently than an ordinary urban sidewalk. Similar notions of perception and framing of the surroundings are found in the Platz der Menschenrechte, with the plants acting as visual filters. Do these devices, which tend to scenery lining pathways, herald a return to the picturesque in the design of public spaces?

Toward highly individualized public spaces

Through these different strategies, the designers of shards of nature attempt to provoke a feeling of escape from an urban environment for which they admit they have little regard. In the same spirit, they seek to define a unique atmosphere that will stand out in the immediate environment. They take care to depict these dreamlike worlds in models and atmospheric collages designed to delight.

Of course, the landscapes – forest and dune – to which they refer are instrumental in the definition of an identity specific to each space. In both cases, these imaginaries are presented as distant places, whose choice seems somewhat arbitrary. Moreover, the designers appeal to a collective and indeed abstract representation of a pine forest, a Scandinavian forest, or a sandbank.

Transposing these distant and stereotypical worlds seems almost self-evident and requires no further justification in their eyes. In Bymilen it will be a Scandinavian forest, because the bank whose headquarters are being built is Swedish. In Messestadt Riem, the pine forest refers to southern Italy, a region dear to Bavarians. The idea of the picturesque seems to be confirmed in these designs, which seek to project users into specific surroundings.

These seductive imaginaries, and the specific languages that result from them, help to distinguish the spaces from the surrounding urban context. Reinforced by their unique symbolism and equally unusual plants and materials, the distinctive formal registers of these two redesigned areas isolate them within the network of public spaces to which they belong. This individual stance is all the more surprising since the designers of both projects were already involved in the overall planning of the neighborhoods' open spaces. However, the coherence advocated upstream was clearly dropped when the time came to move on to more specific commissions. The choices, tastes, and stances of the various designers resulted in a general fragmentation of the network of public spaces. The notion of a shard of nature then takes on its full meaning, in a conception of open spaces that increasingly seems driven by a principle of fragmentation.

PLATZ DER MENSCHENRECHTE

1 Landeshauptstadt München, *Messestadt Riem. Das Projekt – Planung und Realisierung*, June 2009, p. 2.

2 This extensive green space was also the venue for the 2005 German National Garden Show (Bundesgartenschau), an event that testifies to the impact of the Messestadt's dynamic development.

3 On the development of Messestadt Riem, see Christoph Valentien, "Metamorphose einer Planungskonzeption," *Garten + Landschaft*, No. 12, 1993, pp. 36–43; Christoph Valentien, "Freiraumsystem und gartenkünstlerischer Entwurf," *Der Architekt*, No. 6, 1997, pp. 373–375.

4 Christoph Valentien (partner of Valentien + Valentien), Wessling, interview with the author, June 23, 2015.

5 The multidisciplinary team shared the first prize with the offices of Bystrup, Bregenhoj & Partner and Gottfried Hansjakob, who were ultimately commissioned to plan the northern part of the site and the underground station. Valentien, *op. cit.*, 1993, p. 40.

6 Christoph Valentien, "Neue Messestadt München-Riem/Nouveau 'Messestadt München-Riem'," *Anthos*, no. 37, 1998, pp. 49–50.

7 *Ibid.*, p. 51.

8 *Ibid.*

9 It is not clear whether it is a town hall in the administrative sense of the term. Sometimes the term *Bürgerzentrum* (civic center) appears in the texts of the landscape architects.

10 Valentien, Christoph, interview cited above.

11 Valentien + Valentien, *Platz der Menschenrechte. Messestadt München Riem. Projektbeschreibung*, n.d., [post-project, project presentation report, unpublished document] [Valentien + Valentien Archive], p. 1.

12 Valentien, Christoph, interview cited above.

13 Valentien + Valentien, *Platz der Menschenrechte. Projektbeschreibung*, project description, *op. cit.* n.d., p. 2.

14 If most of the found variants are not dated, the indication of the day of creation of some of them allows us to locate their production around September 2001, which is relatively late.

15 Ponge, Francis, "Le Carnet du bois de pins," in Francis Ponge, *La rage de l'expression*, Paris, Gallimard, Collection, 2011. [1st legal deposit at Gallimard 1976, 1st publication of "Le Carnet du bois de pins," Lausanne, Mermod, 1947], pp. 97–172 [German version consulted by Valentien + Valentien: Francis Ponge, *Das Notizbuch vom Kiefernwald und La Mounine*, Berlin, Suhrkamp, 1995].

16 *Ibid*, p. 157; Albert Camus and Francis Ponge, *Correspondance, 1941–1957*, established edition presented and annotated by Jean-Marie Gleize, Paris, Gallimard, 2013, p. 31.

17 Valentien, Christoph, interview cited above.

18 While Valentien + Valentien were inspired by a German translation of the text, it is the English translation of the original French text that is quoted here, Ponge, *op. cit.* 2011, pp. 99, 105.

19 Valentien, Christoph, interview cited above.

20 In this section dealing with the imaginary and the symbolic, it should be noted that the final name given to the public space, *Platz der Menschenrechte* (Human Rights Square), came about very late and was not the work of the designers.

21 Valentien, Christoph, interview cited above.

22 Valentien + Valentien, *Platz der Menschenrechte.* project description, *op. cit.* n.d., p. 2.

23 *Ibid.*

24 Valentien + Valentien *Platz der Menschenrechte. Messestadt München Riem. Zusammenfassung* (Summary), n.d., [post-project, project presentation report, unpublished document] [Valentien + Valentien Archives], p. 1.

25 "Platz der Menschenrechte," in Lisa Diedrich et al. (eds), *On Site*, Series, Landscape Architecture Europe, Basel/Boston/Berlin, Birkhäuser, 2009. p. 137.

BYMILEN

26 Københavns Kommune, *Lokalplan nr. 403 "Rigsarkivet,"* Copenhagen, January 13, 2006, pp. 3–4.

27 Tranberg, Lene and Stig L. Andersson, "Det grønne flow, The Green Flow," *Arkitektur DK*, n° 6, 2011, p. 6.

28 *Ibid.*

29 Hornsyld, Ulla (SLA project leader), Copenhagen, interview with the author, September 25, 2015.

30 Københavns Kommune, *Lokalplan nr. 403, op. cit.*, 2006, p. 26.

31 SLA, *Dispositionsforlag 1*, report for the client, December 2005 [SLA Archive], "05koncept."

32 *Ibid, "03projektbeskrivelse."* Translation by the author.

33 *Ibid.*

34 SLA, SEB, *SEB nyt byrum. En bjergside på Kalvebod Brygge*, September 8, 2010, project presentation report, p. 1 [SLA Archives, PræsentationSEB08092010.pdf].

35 Hornsyld, Ulla, interview cited above.

36 *Ibid.*

37 Andersson, Stig L., "Sandbanken, vid Banken. Ett Stadsrum i samklang med naturen," *Utemiljö*, n° 5, 2012, p. IV. Translation by the author. See also Stig L. Andersson, "Klimatilpasset Byrum ved SEB i København," *Landskab*, No. 91/7, 2010, p. 158.

38 Vindum, Kjeld, "Stig L. Andersson. Interview," *Arkitektur DK*, n° 6, 2011, p. 10.

39 SLA, SEB, *SEB nyt byrum*, *op. cit.* September 8, 2010, p. 1. Stig. L. Andersson associates this mobilization of the five senses with the notion of aesthetics, see on this subject Stig L. Andersson, *Empowerment of Aesthetics, Catalogue for the Danish Pavilion at the 14th International Architecture Exhibition La Biennale di Venezia 2014*, Skive, Forlaget Wunderbuch, 2014, pp. 9–10. Available online: https://issuu.com/slaarchitects/docs/empowermentofaesthetics-sla [accessed May 5, 2017].

40 Hornsyld, Ulla, interview cited above.

41 SLA, SEB, *op. cit.* September 8, 2010, p. 2.

42 SLA,, *op. cit.* December 2005, *"03projektbeskrivelse."*

43 "Bymilen, København/Copenhagen," in Annemarie Lund (ed.), *Ny Agenda 2. Dansk landskabsarkitektur/New Agenda 2. Danish Landscape Architecture.* 2009–2013, Bogværket, Nykøbing Sjælland, 2014, p. 188; Charlotte Fauve, "Dune danoise. "City Dune" à Copenhague, Danemark," *Ecologik*, n° 35, 2013, p. 42; Rasmus Wærn, "Kommentar. Commentbeskrivelses," *Arkitektur DK*, n° 6, 2011, p. 20. Some texts even go so far as to locate the inspiration precisely in the Jutland region at the northern tip of Denmark. The narrative of the project goes further, stating that the concrete surfacing is a direct reference to a dune because the material chosen is granite sand combined with water and cement. Andersson, *op. cit.*, 2012, p. IV.

44 Hornsyld, Ulla, interview cited above. The archives of the project seem to validate her words: the name of *Bymilen* or reference images showing a dune do not appear in the documents to which we had access.

45 Stig L. Andersson denies that he is imitating nature in this project. However, this denial mainly concerns the dune. Vindum, *op. cit.* 2011, p. 8; Stig L. Andersson, "Klimatilpasset Byrum ved SEB i København," *Landskab*, n° 91/7, 2010, p. 158.

46 Caption of the project presented in the Danish pavilion at the 2014 Venice Architecture Biennale *"Empowerment of Aesthetics."* "In the urban space *The City Dune* (2010), I planted all the trees that the nurseries had discarded: The crooked, the skewed, the freak trees. All those that told a story of their life, their struggle and the conditions that gave them their non-geometrical vertical shapes."

47 It should also be remembered that these trees are planted above a parking lot and require a complex and extensive watering system, making the project not very ecological, as some critics point out. Per Stahlschmidt and Peter Thorsen, "Debat: Procesurbanisme – byøkologi eller varm luft?," *Landskab*, n° 1, 2011, p. 18.

48 Hornsyld, Ulla, interview cited above.

49 *Ibid.* "In the beginning we tried to make a smoother transition from SEB bank to the archives. But in a way we are not that interested in that transition. We don't really aim for smooth ... it is not that we don't care, but if it works in terms of functionality, it is not our intention that they have to look alike or fit together or anything. We like it more that you have different experiences when you walk from space to space."

50 Andersson, Stig L., "Public Open Form and Space" Conference Proceedings *Odprt javni prostor. Public Open Space. Design – Management – Maintenance*, April, 10–11, 2008, Ljubljana, pp. 24–27.

CROSS-EXAMINATION

AN AMBIGUOUS RELATIONSHIP WITH THE MATERIAL CONTEXT

To verify the potential increase in autonomy of public spaces at the beginning of the 21st century, it is first necessary to examine the way in which designers perceive, describe, and treat the material context of the immediate surroundings. Through the various monograph analyses, it has been possible to observe the attention paid to the built area and the adjacent public spaces, both in the design narratives and representations, as well as in the realized projects.

AN ASSERTIVE REJECTION OF THE BUILT CONTEXT IN SOME NARRATIVES

Different readings of the existing context can be clearly distinguished in the narratives. Some designers show a kind of reverence for the buildings surrounding the target public space and perceive their development as a way of enhancing them:

"We have real historical substance, the Halles and the Tour du Molard, so that already gives incredible strength to this space." (Place du Molard, Philippe Béboux)

"This idea of giving a new sensation, a new point of view on the architecture of the late 19th century as an effect of contrast." (Place de la République, Pierre Alain Trévelo)

"We need to bring all these different buildings together on a common ground." (Place Simon-Goulart, Julien Descombes)

But others are decidedly more critical:

"We had the intellectual alibi to propose something quite free, because we were in a totally liberal city, without a guiding principle." (Paseo Marítimo de la Playa de Poniente, Xavier Martí Galí)

"The buildings left no chance of um die Aufgabe zu ubernehmen [literally, "responding to the challenge" of creating a living urban space]. With these facades, in regard to this square, it looks like, an object, another object and yet another object." (Platz der Menschenrechte, Christoph Valentien)

"We didn't care about the buildings [...] There was nothing interesting to continue, so we had to create something of our own." (Superkilen, Martin Rein-Cano)

"We didn't know exactly why the square didn't take shape. There were several ideas: too large, a theatre facade of low quality, whose building fragments the space, but also it has to be said, the general shabbiness of the Antwerp city centre." (Theaterplein, Paola Viganò)

Views on the built surroundings thus differ greatly between designers. Many of them take great care in the study of the characteristics of the surroundings, while others are content with more hasty judgments. The designers interviewed also seem to pay attention to different aspects of the surrounding buildings: Some analyze the buildings primarily as defining the space, others focus more on their activities and their potential for animating the public space. Others describe the architecture itself, detailing its character, the composition of the facade, or the materials of the surrounding buildings.

Generally, the tone adopted regarding the built environment precedes design approaches that can be divided into two types: on the one hand, designers who take into consideration the existing in a perspective of light transformation, and on the other hand, those who take a more critical look and assume the idea of a major change. The former proclaim the discretion of their minimalist interventions (Place de la République, Place du Molard, and Place Simon-Goulart), while the latter claim more radical, spectacular, and autonomous proposals (Superkilen, Paseo Marítimo de la Playa de Poniente, Platz der Menschenrechte, and Theaterplein). In the latter view, because existing surroundings are deemed of low quality, a certain freedom of experimentation and expression is justified.

NON-EXISTENT OR PARTIAL REPRESENTATIONS OF THE EXISTING SURROUNDINGS

In addition to the analysis of narratives, the analysis of representations of the different projects plays a fundamental role in understanding how the designers approach the relationship to the built context. Sketches, drawings, models, or photo-montages, viewed as design tools and also as communication tools, have also been studied from this angle.

Several monographic analyses revealed a tendency to illustrate the development projects in a totally decontextualized manner, giving them an iconic character. Only the perimeter on which the designers intervene – the object – is depicted in the drawings or models produced (Fig. 4.1–4.3). When the context is represented, the built-up volumes are simply drawn as linear contours, sometimes as no more than hatched outlines. This way of doing has the advantage of informing the relationship between built and non-built, thus providing a spatial reading. It also gives indications on the urban fabric and the property structure. In some rarer cases, care is taken to detail the nature of the facade in plan, in particular taking into account the position of the building entrances, and making it possible to focus on closer relationships between interior and exterior spaces (Fig. 4.4–4.5). Situations where the elevation of the facade is represented are exceptional and seem to seek to bring more realism to the illustration without having any conceptual implication on the project's development. Only in a few exceptional cases is care taken in detailing the built environment, so as to provide understanding of the buildings and the public space as an indivisible whole.

It should be noted that several of the projects analyzed revealed a desire to establish a hierarchy between the buildings that delimit the space, by orienting the trajectories and the perception of the space by using design components acting as barriers, visual screens, or framing elements (Platz der Menschenrechte, Place Simon-Goulart, Theaterplein, or MFO-Park). The development thus becomes a mediator of the given state, to which it brings a new understanding.

Despite the distancing from the existing context affirmed in certain projects, the analyses have nevertheless revealed a significant production of physical and digital models. These volumetric representations testify to particular attention being paid to urban morphology, with a view to the continuity of public spaces, as urban voids. Some designers explicitly use the principle of alignment between the built environment and the public space design in order to create harmonious results (MFO-Park, Theaterplein, Platz der Menschenrechte, Place Simon-Goulart). While not all go that far, a large majority of projects reveal an influential morphological link between the development and the existing fabric. As such, their design can be considered attentive to the urban context in the main compositional principles. The same cannot be said, however, of their expression, which is far more indifferent.

INCREASINGLY UNRESPONSIVE FORMS AND MATERIALS

The designers who cast an eye on the materials and architectural details of the immediate surroundings of the development site are much rarer ... and ultimately, it is this aspect of the autonomy of public spaces at the turn of the 21st century that this book reveals.

As an example, let us consider the ground materials of these projects. In this respect, only a few rare cases have revealed choices aimed at creating a dialogue with the surrounding buildings. It is the case for the stone covering of the square in front of the temple bordering the Place Simon-Goulart, the color of which recalls that of the base of the religious building; the concrete slabs of the Place de la République that seek to highlight the minerality of the surrounding Haussmann buildings; or the crushed stone surfacing of the MFO-Park which echoes the color of the yellow bricks of the existing industrial buildings. These relationships between vertical and horizontal surfaces respond to a desire to holistically consider the public space and its facades.

Even rarer are the projects that propose a surface that echoes the grounds of adjacent public spaces, with a view to integrating the site to be developed into a coherent continuum (Fig. 4.6–4.8). Among these exceptions, the Place Simon-Goulart project, for instance, will place a smooth concrete square within more ordinary traditional Geneva patterned paving that covers the entire block. At the Place du Molard, the chosen paving does not correspond directly to the adjacent surfacing, but echoes that of the nearby historical center.

Apart from these few exceptions, the designers of the other cases studied seem to choose atypical materials, often expressly developed for the project in question. The same is true of rules of composition, or certain unusual forms, that stand out from the immediate surroundings. In terms of expression, these projects thus force a strong break with the immediate surroundings, whether it be the buildings or the public spaces that constitute them. They assert themselves as figures. This contrast is then often justified by critical discourse on a given context devoid of intrinsic qualities. The observations in early cross-examination seem to point to a conceptual reversal of the relationship with the existing built surroundings and the adjacent public spaces, which requires explanation.

4.1

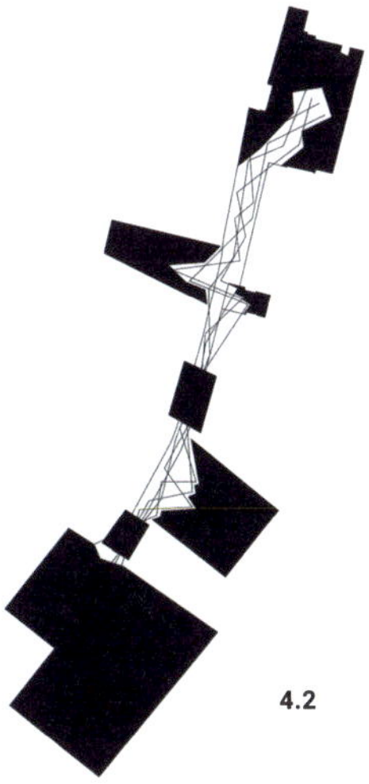

4.2

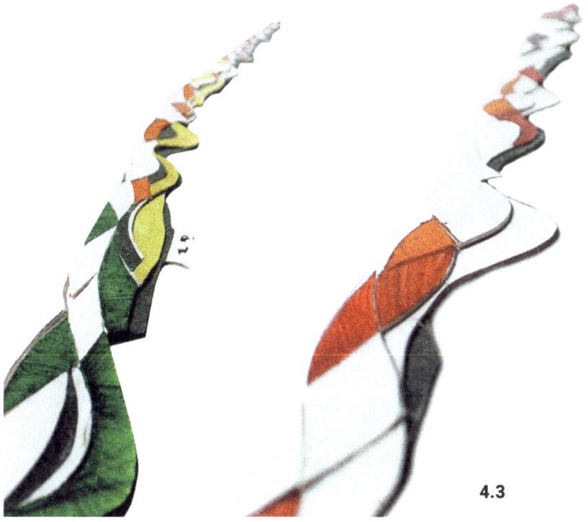

4.3

4.1–4.3
Decontextualized representations. *(1) Superkilen; (2) Måløv; (3) Paseo Maritimo – Playa de Poniente* **4.4–4.5** Detailed facade elements. *Place du Molard*

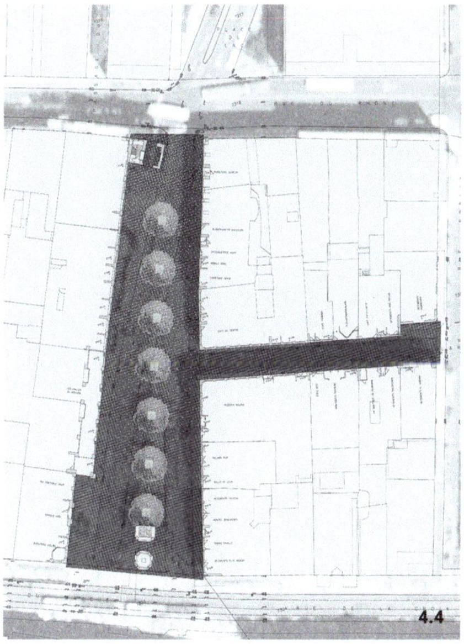

4.4

4.5

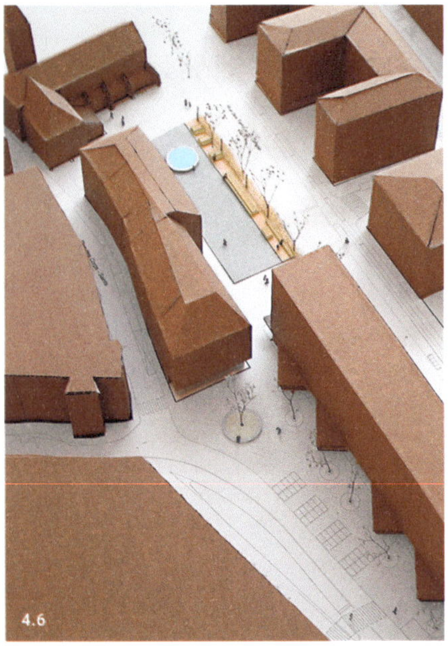

4.6

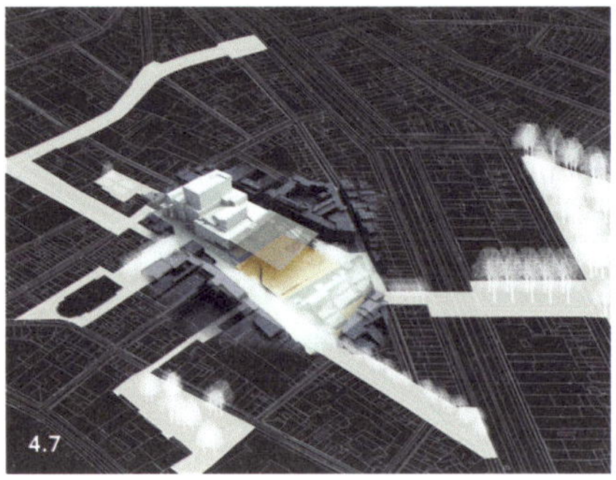

4.7

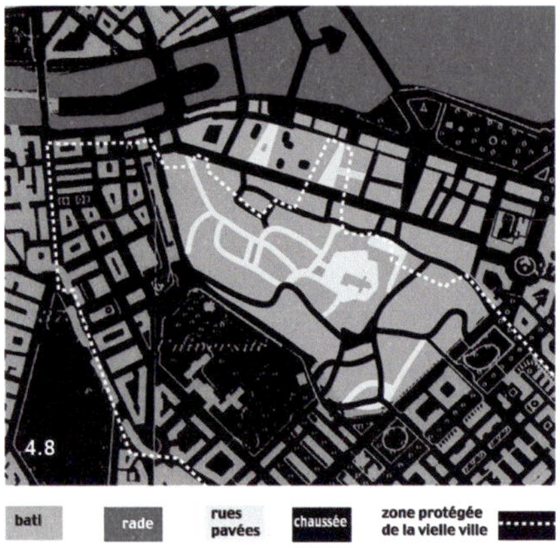

4.8

4.6–4.8 Integration in a material continuity of the network of public spaces. *(6) Place Simon-Goulart; (7) Theaterplein; (8) Place du Molard* **4.9–4.11** Analysis of the large-scale urban context. *(9) Place Simon-Goulart; (10) Place de la République; (11) Theaterplein*

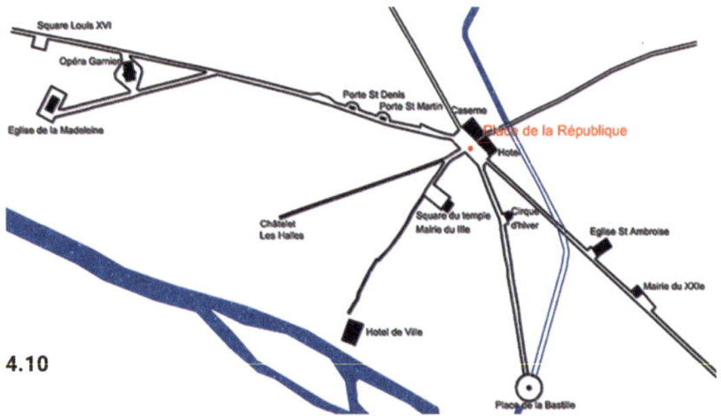

4.10

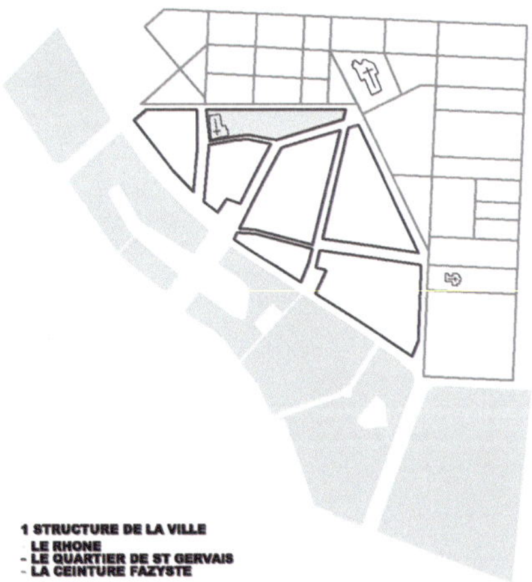

4.9

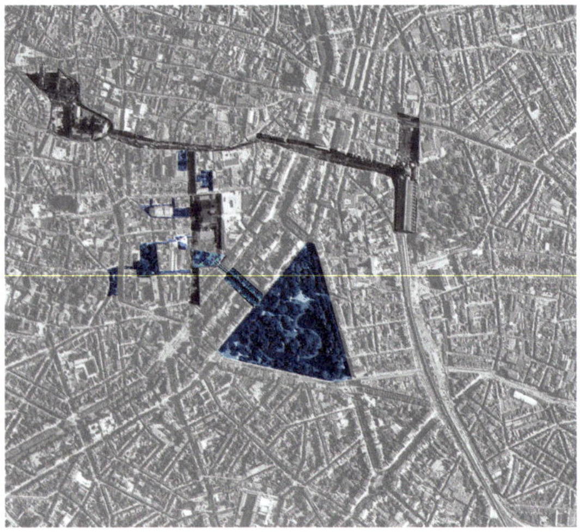

4.11

SALUTARY DESIGNS: BEYOND THE BEAUTIFICATION PROJECT

VARIABLE URBAN CONTEXTS, BUT OFTEN LACKING IN QUALITY

That designers today take such a critical look at the existing material context and formally detach their interventions from it can be explained by the increasing attention that has been paid in recent years to neglected places, sites in need of redevelopment. In fact, voids that are strongly structured by a coherent set of buildings, and that above all need to be redeveloped to respond to current urban uses, are rare (the Place de la République or the Place du Molard are two such).

In the panel of projects analyzed, we find mainly nondescript and inharmonious places, sites bordered by disparate buildings placed there by the vagaries of history, like the Theaterplein or the Place Simon-Goulart. Other heterogeneous contexts are the result of uncontrolled developments under real-estate pressure – such as the Paseo Marítimo de la Playa de Poniente, the Platz der Menschenrechte, or Bymilen – or are simply residual spaces.

Uncertain urban developments, degraded and abandoned places, disparate built environments, absence of clear spatial boundaries, low-quality buildings ... the initial situations of the public spaces analyzed here in depth, show that as of now, the role of public space design goes beyond that of a simple superficial embellishment. It must fix an unsatisfactory given situation or ensure the coherence of hard-to-control future developments. This requires a more profound and ambitious design, a solution that is salutary to the site.

AN AMBITION FOR UNIQUENESS ALREADY PRESENT IN THE BRIEF

If the importance and vitality of a place are no longer guaranteed by high-quality surroundings, it is up to the public space project to remedy this. Spectacular and iconic design is an obvious path to the revival of sites that have been abandoned by the city's inhabitants, and many examples have been successful in this respect (Paseo Marítimo in Benidorm, Superkilen, MFO-Park). On the other hand, high-quality spaces, that are already very popular from the outset, may require less added emphasis from a formal point of view (Place du Molard, Place de la République).

The degree of uniqueness of a project seems to be closely linked to the initial assessment, by the designers and the client, of the site to be developed. Several analyses have shown that the client plays a crucial role in this subjective assessment, by emphasizing expectations regarding the design outcomes. This salutary role sometimes expresses itself plainly in the project brief, which state from the outset a desire to break with the context both through an unusual design, and with assertions of formal and material autonomy. The program of the Superkilen competition goes so far as to declare its ambition for an "attractive," "exceptional," "innovative" public space with "its own character."[1]

In contrast, other clients encourage designers to favor simplicity and economy of means. This is notably the case for the *animated* projects of the Place Simon-Goulart and the Place de la République, as well as of the Place du Molard. Some competition briefs explicitly advocate taking the built environment into consideration in the development's design. Unsurprisingly, the projects that won awards in these competitive procedures were in line with the requirement for restraint and integration into the existing urban context, as expressed by the client at the outset.

In conclusion, the clients – but also the competition juries – play a fundamental role in this assessment of the given built environment. The effects of these initial assessments on the production of spectacular or more discreet designs are clearly measurable.

A REAL FIELD OF EXPERIMENTATION OFFERED TO DESIGNERS

Certain initial negative assessments of the urban context – as insinuated by the clients – will lead to real design freedom for the professionals. More generally, the reclaiming of public spaces has created opportunities to rethink their designs. This new, rapidly developing field is thus very conducive to experimentation.

Under these conditions, designers will tackle the subject with a certain candor and freely develop themes that fascinate them. These fields of experimentation relate as much to formal and material choices, as to questions of construction and implementation. The study of the overall production of each architecture firm, and of the landscape architects, urban designers, and artists concerned also makes it possible to spot predispositions for certain principles of form, materials, or composition.

For instance, the in-depth analyses of the two *modeled* projects revealed, unsurprisingly, a fascination of the design teams for artistic topics, as well as a mastery of complex geometries. Their proposals also take on very photogenic sculptural dimensions, as witnessed through photographs of the completed projects, taken from unusual angles that reveal this aspect for our appreciation. Less obviously at first glance, other designers show an interest in a more elementary geometry, with a view to achieving coherence and formal simplicity in the final project. For instance, some analyses have revealed the presence of a grid to rationalize the composition of the layout (Place du Molard, MFO-Park, Platz der Menschenrechte). The use of elementary geometrical forms is also an appropriate way to generate commonality (Place de la République, Place Simon-Goulart, and Theaterplein) and to avoid unnecessary formal gestures.

The topic of the project as an author's creative gesture appeared repeatedly in the analyses. While some architects and landscape architects seem to accept a degree of subjectivity in their designs, which is controlled down to the smallest detail, others reject overly formalist and arbitrary attitudes. Some designers find a way to avoid this by making the non-controlled or unfinished project a theme. They then entrust certain choices to the workers (Place du Molard), to artists or even to the population (Superkilen, Måløv Aksen). Another way of not completely fixing the final aspect of a development is to accept that the plant species occupying it will grow wild (Platz der Menschenrechte, Bymilen) or that they will evolve over the years (MFO-Park). This uncertainty in the final image of a project – dependent on other actors and on the forces of nature – is a field of investigation in public space design that is typical of our time.

It is also rare for projects to use furniture and lighting elements found in catalogs or in lines of equipment specifically designed for cities. The analyses revealed a real determination to master the design of an entire development down to the smallest detail. The designers set out to develop furniture and construction details that correspond specifically to the public spaces narrative, in terms of expression. This wish to make each project *unique* is also illustrated by the fact that virtually all projects use new and distinctive ground cover materials. These are custom-made to have the effects sought by the designers, particularly in terms of color, texture, and symbolism. The topic of materials is therefore also part of an exploration of new means of expression. These components, developed specifically for each space, nevertheless raise questions regarding terms of daily maintenance, cost, and longer-term management.

Finally, it is noticeable that some professionals deliberately seek to create work constellations that could lead to new formal proposals (within the experimental freedom that characterizes the design of public spaces at the turn of the 21st century). For instance, architects and landscape architects voluntarily call on artists to complete their range of skills (Superkilen and Place du Molard). This artistic contribution is then clearly perceived by a strong pictorial and aesthetic dimension of the developments concerned. Similarly, the intentional collaboration between architects and landscape architects for the MFO-Park reveals a desire to experiment with work methods, which in this case will result in the creation of a novel structure.

To conclude, all of these aesthetic themes and formal and material fields are explored in order to give each space a recognizable identity. This desire to *singularize* each design undoubtedly contributes to an explosion of new public space design languages.

A REDEFINITION OF THE NOTION OF CONTEXT

The previous pages have been an opportunity to reveal, in the majority of the projects studied, a clear distancing from the buildings and from the public spaces directly adjacent to them. Surprisingly, many of the designers insist on this distancing, yet at the same time consider their proposal as fundamentally contextual. This indicates on the one hand that the notion of context still has positive connotations in the eyes of all, but on the other hand, that the understanding of the term largely depends on the protagonists.

A thematic broadening of the elements that define a place is being noticed, with a growing importance in the minds of designers attached to *dynamic material conditions* (such as natural processes and uses) and to *intangible site conditions* (such as memories, atmospheres, and narratives about a place).[2] The monograph analyses also revealed an extension of the scale at which *material* and *immaterial* characteristics are taken into consideration by designers.

A THEMATIC EXPANSION: HISTORICAL, CULTURAL, SOCIOLOGICAL, AND ENVIRONMENTAL CONTEXT

Several analyses of the case studies revealed that particular attention was paid to the history of the site on which the intervention was carried out. This reading of the past sometimes had a direct influence on the project's composition when based on historical traces (Theaterplein); more often it constituted an inspiration for the project themes, according to a more narrative approach (symbolic ornament at Place du Molard, reinterpreted industrial past at MFO-Park). These different examples attest to a new sensitivity to heritage, which is expressed by a strong thematization of the past.

A second intangible dimension of the sites, which appears to be of growing importance in the minds of the designers, is the cultural and sociological one. The local population is thereby considered in terms of profiles, behaviors, social ties, or shared histories. Several designers, in their narratives, take care to analyze in detail the profile of the different users likely to appropriate the space they are developing (Place Simon-Goulart, Place de la République). Elsewhere, there is interest in guaranteeing the continuity of existing uses – institutionalized or informal – such as the weekly market, or the skateboarding that teenagers enjoy at Theaterplein. Finally, it should be noted that some public space designs were preceded by a participatory process, led by the client, encouraging the designers to take into account the wishes of the local population (Place de la République, Måløv Aksen). In the latter case, people practicing the sport of *parkour* were directly involved in shaping the *modeled* public space.

In other instances, this cultural and social understanding of context will have more literal and visible formal implications. In the Place du Molard and Superkilen projects, the diversity of the inhabitants of the neighborhood or the city is used to inspire the development of certain components of the project. In Benidorm, it is the mass seaside tourism of the 1960s–1970s that justifies, in the eyes of the designers, the playful pop aesthetic of the promenade.

Finally, in this impulse of thematic expansion of the notion of context, the site's environmental factors are increasingly being taken into account, to promote the climatic and sensory comfort of future users. Thus, analyses of the sun's path and of prevailing winds according to season dictate the composition of the Place de la République, or the shape of the *modeled* reliefs of the Paseo Marítimo in Benidorm. By integrating these elements, the designers are ready to question strong urban structures, such as the symmetrical Haussmann composition disavowed in Parisian development.

TERRITORIAL ENLARGEMENT: CONTEXT AT THE URBAN AND LANDSCAPE SCALE

Analysis of the projects also revealed a tendency to broaden the context to more than the immediate surroundings of a site. Whether in their narrative or in their graphic imagery, several designers seek to place their proposals in a large-scale network (Fig. 4.9–4.11). This allows them, among other advantages, to define more precisely the status they wish to give the public space to be developed. It also guides certain choices of materials; the block in which the Place Simon-Goulart is sited will be covered with the famous Geneva paving layout, while the colors of the slabs of the Place de la République will echo the Parisian roofs. Elsewhere, this imagery on an urban scale orients the composition of public space more directly. In Antwerp, the designers justify the division of the Theaterplein into square and garden by situating the boundary at the meeting point of two natural networks, respectively mineral and green.

Some designers of public spaces even go so far as to extend the scope of their intervention to a regional scale. This is notably the case with Bymilen, where the aim is to create a Scandinavian forest on a relief reminiscent of the dunes or snowdrifts characteristic of northern Europe. As for the landscape architects Valentien + Valentien, they extend the notion of being part of a territory even further, taking their inspiration from Mediterranean forests located beyond the Alps, which are supposedly visible from the Platz der Menschenrechte in Bavaria.

It is noticeable that these narratives, which are articulated around regional identity, fall under a landscape reading of the territory. This taking account of the surrounding nature, which can also be found in the other *modeled* and *naturized* projects, is indeed an alternative to the more common local focus of a project, which adopts more of a dialogue with the urban fabric. It then finds its place in a dichotomous perspective that pits city against nature, including all the symbols that these two environments evoke. This is the case of the Paseo de la Playa de Poniente in Benidorm, where a relationship with the beach and the sea is favored over one with skyscrapers (Fig. 4.12).

Finally, in the Måløv Aksen project, the designers proceed with a double expansion of the notion of context, both territorial and temporal, focusing on the surrounding landscape elements and their genesis (Fig. 4.13). They use the geomorphological history of the territory thus revealed to develop the theme of melting ice in their project.

CONTEXTUAL READINGS WITH A STRONG NARRATIVE DIMENSION

This broadening of the notion of context, both thematic and territorial, encourages a fresh look at the topic of local anchoring of development projects. Indeed, a certain distancing from the *physical material* framework (i.e., buildings and adjacent public spaces) in favor of new contextual dimensions seems to explain the appearance of novel kinds of public space design. Designers are gradually abandoning an urban language that can be described as traditional in favor of new fields of reference that they consider more seductive. According to their narratives, these novel references are then being self-evidently adopted in a new definition of the characteristics of a place. Taking account of the context in a cultural and social dimension often justifies of itself the drawing of inspiration from the artistic world.

We also note that these new contextual readings feed a more narrative dimension of the public space design project. They involve the reinterpretation of parameters relating to the place, which are in reality hardly visible due to their geographical or temporal remoteness. One thinks, for example, of projects based on historical fabric that has disappeared or on the characteristics of a distant landscape. The intellectual justification of these sources of inspiration is then provided through discourse and representations. However, these references remain enigmatic for a user confronted with the built reality.

In addition, it is noted that a new and expanded definition of local identity legitimizes the appearance of inspiration from further away than the specific qualities found in the immediate site surroundings. Because of distance, designers often end up relying on simplified imagery of the surroundings that inspire them. Indeed, the less precisely the context referred to is identified, the more tempting it is to take as a reference a globally shared image of what these inspiring surroundings would be. These stereotypical reinterpretations partly explain the very *universal* aspect of some of the selected projects.

4.12

4.13

4.14

4.15

4.16

4.12–4.13 Integration of the project in a large-scale landscape context. *(12) Paseo Marítimo – Playa de Poniente; (13) Måløv Aksen* **4.14** Collage of the sought-after atmosphere. *Bymilen* **4.15–4.16** Atmosphere models. *(15) Platz der Menschenrechte; (16) MFO-Park*

PUBLIC SPACES, PURVEYORS OF EXPERIENCES

REFLECTIONS OF THE EXPERIENCE SOCIETY

A third factor, undoubtedly the most important one in explaining the increasing autonomy of public spaces from the context of the immediate built environment, is the growing interest of designers in questions of atmosphere, embodiment, and the feelings of future users, according to an approach that could be described as phenomenological. This evolution in the design of public spaces comes in response to a recent societal shift.[3] The 1970s leisure society would have been supplanted twenty-odd years later by what some researchers define as an experience society. According to Gerhard Schulze, the German sociologist who coined the term, this societal model is rooted in a context of material comfort, in which the meaning of life is defined above all as a search for personal satisfaction through experiences.[4] Experiences are mental processes, consisting of a feeling of personal enrichment – instructive or entertaining – when facing an external situation or stimulus. Because of their subjective dimension, they place the emphasis on the perceptions and feelings of individuals. They differ from leisure activities, which are planned and repetitive, in that they are extraordinary and, in fact, provoke unusual, memorable emotions.[5]

While such experiences are destined to endure in the intangible world of stories and memories, many actually occur in the reality of the physical world. Which brings us back to the topic of public space design. In many ways, these places have always reflected the society in which they were created. Thus, the 1970s leisure society saw the flowering of open spaces specifically intended for recreational activities (parks, playgrounds, sports fields, beaches, riverbanks, footpaths, etc.). But little by little the rigid division between work and leisure has become blurred, and recreational practices, once confined to specific places, have begun to extend to all urban public spaces, even the most commonplace. This evolution explains the growing tendency of designers to adapt their designs to more leisurely urban practices.

The term "experience society" came into widespread use in urban discourse at the beginning of the 21st century, without being truly theorized. Case study analyses have revealed this interest among designers of public spaces.[6] Individual interpretations of what the concept of experience actually is vary greatly, but three views emerge, that can be briefly classified as follows: *physical*, *mental*, and *collective* experiences.

PHYSICAL EXPERIENCE: PERCEPTION, A UNIVERSAL ANGLE OF APPROACH

Analyses have revealed the propensity of a large number of designers to want to attribute *singular* atmospheres to the imagined public space design. This intention generally appears very early in the project process and reference images play a predominant role in the development of such atmospheres. In addition to collages of material sample images taken from specialized magazines or the Internet, photomontages and photographs of models are used to describe the desired sensory qualities (Fig. 4.14–4.16). These media convey the thermal conditions, the sounds, or the smells that one would be likely to experience in the public space in question (Bymilen, Platz der Menschenrechte, MFO-Park).

Other designers will seek a more tactile relationship with the material. The concern then becomes more "bodily" than "sensory," in the sense that the aim is to stimulate city dwellers in their usage of the space with their body as a whole. The ground surface in the center of the Place Simon-Goulart or the Place de la République will be designed to encourage specific uses (rollerblading, dancing, relaxation, etc.) for which the relationship with the ground is essential. The crushed gravel spaces (MFO-Park, Platz der Menschenrechte) deliberately encourage slower and more contemplative ways of moving.

Although curiosity about other senses seems to be growing, visual perception, of the five senses, remains the central preoccupation of the greatest number of designers. For some, this concern is illustrated by the sole aim of guaranteeing a harmonious reading of the whole, through alignments and framed perspectives. Elsewhere, the aim is to offer a more spectacular visual experience, in the sense that its intensity will produce a memorable *effect* on users. For example, the sculptural and pictorial treatment of the Superkilen ground corresponds to a search for optical effects. The use of bright colors in this example, as in the Paseo Marítimo de la Playa de Poniente and Måløv Aksen, also aims to stimulate users physiologically. As noted in the analyses, these processes are reminiscent of the modi operandi of certain artistic movements, such as Op Art or Pop Art, that also promoted the idea of physiological stimuli.

Whether perception is approached from a sensory point of view (and more specifically a visual one) or from a more bodily one, its aim is to create an unusual effect on future users, leaving them with a memorable impression. The public space then moves away from its functional role to become an environment that provides physical, tactile, olfactory, auditory, and visual experiences. These perception-centric concerns generally take precedence over the context of the built environment and the nearby public spaces, which results in a decrease in the local anchoring of projects. Furthermore, the visual effects that designers conjure up to describe an atmosphere – such as the rustling of leaves, the lapping of waves, the sunlight filtering through a leaf – are also *universal* effects. Consequently, the formal and material devices devised to respond to these considerations become easily *transposable* from one project to another.

MENTAL EXPERIENCES: MAKING THEMES OF GENERIC UNIVERSES

The experiences described above are mainly provided by solutions aimed at affording physiological sensations. Another way of approaching the theme of experience is to consider it from a more cerebral perspective, by stimulating the imagination. The aim is to create a curious place that stands out from the surroundings, with the aim of inducing a feeling of escape in the future users of a place. In this quest to create experiences, we again find a narrative approach as detected earlier in the passage dealing with a recent redefinition of the notion of context.

A proven way of provoking a feeling of escape consists in "changing the scenery" by drawing on distant referential fields. In this respect, nature is confirmed as a widespread inspiration, particularly within the *naturized* and *modeled* project groups. Indeed, the natural surroundings appear to be a fertile allegorical source for the making of experiences through their capacity to evoke pleasant emotions in human beings. Moreover, in designers' narratives, there is a common, divisive tendency to oppose nature and the monotonous or rigid surroundings that the city can represent. Nature, like other new and seductive fields to which designers refer, is thus explicitly used to inspire a unique identity and a singular language, which stands out from the site's immediate surroundings. The very principle of escape on which this thematization is based automatically induces an idea of contrast.

A second statement that can be drawn from the sources of natural inspiration revealed in the analyses is that these phenomena or types of landscapes are actually quite generic. The designers do not refer to a clearly identified and located natural space – a place – but to a stereotyped natural form: a sandbank, a wave, a forest, a starry sky, the glint of the sun on water, and so on. They are inspired, as it were, by an abstract model that everyone is capable of bringing to mind in a *universally* shared image, which will be easy to translate into a project (Fig. 4.17–4.18). In some cases, the abundance and diversity of reference images used confirm a tendency to reduce the surroundings that are to serve as models to a stereotypical incarnation. Designers end up reproducing the essential features of these generic surroundings. These stereotypical reinterpretations undoubtedly serve a desire to intensify the experience created, by appealing to the intuition of future users. They have the effect of producing a kind of instantaneity of the emotions provoked, which corresponds to the quest for singular and memorable sensations characteristic of the experience society. Participating more in an intention to seduce through project narratives, they do not prove to be real elements of local anchorage, although some discourses could claim it.

COLLECTIVE EXPERIENCES: BUILDING COMMONALITY

For designers, one last way of approaching the concept of experience is to consider it in terms of social interactions. Urban life is characterized by a multitude of encounters between individuals, which represent many experiences in their daily lives. Naturally, most of these social interactions, whether spontaneous or planned, take place in public space. This pre-eminent relational function of public spaces can become a real design theme for some.

This interest is characterized in particular by the narration of urban scenes in the form of texts and illustrations, detailing a multitude of anecdotes which, assembled, draw a portrait of the social life that will inhabit the public space concerned. These descriptions serve to illustrate the capacity of the development project to accommodate diverse urban practices: spontaneous encounters between individuals, meetings in small groups, planned collective gatherings, cultural events, larger political gatherings, and so on. These narratives, by insisting on the unifying potential of public spaces, seem aimed at illustrating a return to a collective form of urban life, in contrast to the anonymity and solitude often attributed to cities.

In terms of the formalization of this interest, designers have two approaches to the issue. The first is to opt for an abstract vocabulary: general purification of the layout, simple geometric forms, and materials unburdened by any symbolism (Place de la République, Theaterplein). Through their abstract nature, these seemingly minimalist designs take on a *universal* and *transposable* dimension. They nevertheless dialogue easily with the urban context in which they are inserted.

The second way of approaching the social character of public spaces is more narrative (Fig. 4.19–4.20). It is a question of suggesting an idea of conviviality according to a more symbolic and figurative approach. New fields of reference appear, not yet mentioned here, such as the domestic sphere or the village atmosphere, which suggest forms of conviviality that we often fear will disappear in large cities. These universes are found in particular in the lighting and furniture, such as the large

4.17–4.18 Thematization of a generic nature. *(17) Paseo Marítimo – Playa de Poniente; (18) Place du Molard* **4.19–4.20** Public space as a place to meet and experience collective life. *(19) Place Simon-Goulart; (20) Place de la République*

sofa-like benches and long banqueting tables of the Place Simon-Goulart. Calling upon collective imaginary worlds that are delocalized (the house, the village) and stereotyped (the sofa, the banquet), these installations become autonomous from their context and, in fact, *transposable*.

SELF-REFERENCED DEVELOPMENTS

This cross-reading through the prism of the concept of experience allows us to make a number of statements. Firstly, it reveals that public spaces at the turn of the 21st century seem above all to be conceived as spaces to be experienced and explored. Designers are indeed seeking to enhance a bland urban practice by infusing it with sensory, bodily, spiritual, and social experiences, which stimulate the movements, senses, emotions, and imagination of city dwellers. By putting emphasis back on the perception and feelings of individuals, these new developments reflect the experience society in which their creation takes place.

As noted several times, these considerations, which revolve around the concept of experience, clearly take precedence over a search for continuity with the surrounding buildings and public spaces. Designers will often draw their inspiration from new worlds, far removed from the context in which they are working. Nature and art appear to be the dominant sources of inspiration, to which are added the domestic and village spheres.

The need to translate these new referential fields inevitably leads designers to the development of design languages that break with the eminently urban register that has dominated the production of public spaces until now. These linguistic explorations lead to a proliferation of new evocative expressions, to the point that each space now seems to have its own character. These places then become self-referential, putting forth the idea of a double – formal and semantic – autonomy, which confirms our theory of a public space conceived as an object *per se*.

Finally, we note that the designs mentioned readily take on a *transposable* quality, whether because they relate to human perception, which is essentially *universal*, or because they make themes of distant and collective imaginations. The concept of experience as a driving force for design would therefore lead not only to the *autonomy* of public spaces but also to making their design principles *transposable*. We would thus tend, if not contrarily, then at least in complementary fashion, to *singularize* current public spaces and simultaneously *universalize* them.

SINGULARIZE AND UNIVERSALIZE AT THE SAME TIME

One might have imagined that the reclamation of public spaces begun in the 1980s would lead to the definition of a new language specific to this rapidly developing field of design, one better adapted to urban practices and the concerns of the moment. However, from the turn of the century onward, we have seen an explosion of languages reflecting the very varied, if not divergent, interests of designers. This variety oscillates between ordinary and spectacular, minimalist and ostentatious, abstract and narrative, local and global, regulated and random, revealing a great multiplicity of postures, interests, and know-how on the part of designers.

This result speaks for itself: public spaces at the beginning of the 21st century are undeniably heterogeneous in their expression. This rich and stimulating heterogeneity seems essential in any response to the diversity of uses and users that guarantees the urbanity of urban space. However, the excesses of systematic *singularization* raise questions about the risk of ending up with urban spaces that are totally devoid of coherence and identity.

In this context, the scope of each intervention must be fundamental. It is all the more important as the search for innovative and distinctive surface materials seems to have obsessed designers since the 2000s. Through the great emphasis placed on these unique forms of ground cover, public spaces are no longer considered as neutral backgrounds, but become truly identifiable entities. The analyses reveal a tendency for the application of these idiosyncratic ground coverings indiscriminately over all of the available surface. These practices lead to public spaces having a random and indeterminate form, often not matching the spatial definition of the void defined by the surrounding buildings. To ensure overall coherence, the clients of the project, together with the designers, would need to determine with greater precision and acumen the exact extent to be given to a development.

This trend toward *singularization* also raises questions about the more general coherence of the network of public spaces in a district or city. Each new space developed now seems to be the subject of an individual treatment, regardless of its location, role, and initial potential. An abundance of *singular* public spaces seems to proliferate as opportunities arise and not according to an overall vision that would identify the places that should stand out because of their function or their spatial qualities. According to this logic of ad hoc strategies resulting from opportunities, cities may soon appear as assemblages of singular public spaces – isolated and randomly sited art works – in whose signature each designer, client, or mayor in charge would be recognizable. Public spaces would thus compete with iconic buildings, which also seem to be becoming more widespread, producing disparate urban landscapes made up solely of figures.

The analyses conducted in this book have raised yet another paradox, confirming the fear briefly expressed by theorist Jacques Lucan, of "public spaces that, from city to city, tend not to resemble each other within the same city, but paradoxically to resemble each other from one city to another."[7] Of course, a more detailed analysis of each case study revealed some kind of attention to context. But in their expression – and that is the determining factor here – the *universal* character of the projects analyzed is evident. A tendency to *singularize* current developments and, almost contrarily, to *universalize* them simultaneously, seems to be emerging. This phenomenon contributes to making public spaces objects *per se*, by making them both *autonomous* and *transposable*.

This observation calls for the development, in coming years, of more rigorous narratives and a better-informed debate on the topic of the context of public spaces. Clearer and more explicit narratives on a project's contextual dimension should be requested of designers. What interpretations do they make of this concept and in what project elements can we read a desire to fit in with a location? Conversely, which components of the project take on a more *universal* and transposable dimension? A more assertive and better argued position on the topic would have the advantage of ensuring greater coherence between narrative and project reality. It would also quash the frivolity with which figurative or abstract references are still handled today.

IN CONCLUSION

Since this book is focused on design, one could too easily label designers as solely responsible for the various trends revealed here. This would mean neglecting the role of the public authorities and the political world in the evolution of the field over the last twenty years. Although, from the mid-1990s onward, recognition of public spaces as fundamental elements in the construction of cities has become widespread, this recognition has, in fact, too often taken place in the absence of an overall strategic vision. One wonders whether this absence means that public space has lost the fundamental role that it once had. Is it still considered an urgent and crucial issue in the eyes of public authorities? Or is it now only a tool for urban marketing, conveying a positive image through new developments? Public authorities – as guarantors of a reasoned development of cities, but also as the main sponsors of public space design – must take up this subject at a strategic level. It is up to them to define how these places should contribute to guaranteeing the quality of urban life in the long term.

Moreover, it is up to the critics and researchers to provide them with the necessary knowledge and arguments to ensure an informed debate on contemporary production of public spaces. Indeed, theory on the subject is still in its infancy and must catch up with practice as soon as possible. These critical views are fundamental to the provision of a better understanding of current and future developments, and thus contribute to the consolidation of know-how in the field of public space design. We hope that the insights gained from this book will feed the debate and pave the way for further research.

To conclude, the designs of public spaces produced in recent times suggest a return to more restrained expression. This sobriety can, in part, be explained by the end of the era of extreme experimentation that marked the emergence of a new field of design, at the turn of the 21st century. Today, real mastery of public space design can be found throughout the European continent, from the smallest villages to the largest cities. Thanks to several decades of experience, architects, landscape architects, and urban designers now have the tools and methods to design quality, polished, and largely appropriated public spaces. It is now up to them to exploit this know-how and to surround themselves with complementary skills to face the urban, ecological, and social challenges of tomorrow.

1 See note 24, p. 132.

2 This classification is based on a terminology developed by Lisa Diedrich around the concept of "site-specificity" in the transformation of port sites. Lisa Diedrich, *Translating Harbourscapes. Site-Specific Design Approaches in Contemporary European Harbour Transformation*. PhD thesis, Department of Geosciences and Natural Resource Management, University of Copenhagen, Frederiksberg, 2013, see especially pp. 91–92. Carol Burns and Andrea Kahn also make this distinction between tangible and intangible site specificities: Burns and Kahn (eds), *Site Matters. Design Concepts, Histories and Strategies*, New York, Routledge, 2005, p. VIII.

3 Theory initially developed in Sonia Curnier, "Expériences urbaines et espaces publics à Copenhague," *Cahiers de l'Aspan*, n° 2, 2016, pp. 8–13.

4 Schulze, Gerhard, "Erlebnisgesellschaft," in Helmut Reinalter and Peter J. Brenner (eds), *Lexikon der Geisteswissenschaften. Sachbegriffe – Disziplinen – Personen*, Vienna, Böhlau Verlag, 2011, pp. 285–286. See also Gerhard Schulze, *Die Erlebnisgesellschaft: Kultursoziologie der Gegenwart*, Campus Verlag, Frankfurt, 1992.

5 This definition is a synthesis of the multiple interpretations of the term, proposed by Jon Sundbo and Flemming Sørensen (eds), *Handbook on the Experience Economy*, Cheltenham, Edward Elgar Publishing, 2013, p. 4.

6 Several interlocutors spontaneously used the term in their narratives or during the interviews: Superkilen (Martin Rein-Cano), Måløv Aksen (Martin Krogh), Bymilen (Ulla Hornsyld). Others deal with this theme, without using the term. Nevertheless, they have similar intentions to those who consciously conceptualize the experience in their discourse.

7 Lucan, Jacques, *Où va la ville aujourd'hui? Formes urbaines et mixités*, Paris, Editions de la Villette, 2012, p. 182, also see p. 34.

APPENDIX

BIBLIOGRAPHY

A

Adamkiewicz, Eric, "Les pratiques récréatives autonomes urbaines," *Urbanisme*, n° 302, September–October 1998, pp. 44–47.

ADEPT, "The Måløv Axis," n.d., http://adept.dk/index.php?id=41#40^2^144 [accessed September 18, 2015].

ADEPT, LiW Planning, "Måløv Aksen—En oplevelse der skaber sammenhæng," competition boards, September 2008 [Archives Adept]

"ADEPT," A + U: Architecture and Urbanism, n° 10, 2012, pp. 94–115.

Agapé, Sélène, "Place de la République. Paris opte pour le béton," *Techniques et architecture*, n° 47, 2003, pp. 34–35.

Allaman, Martine, "Espaces publics: liberté, identité, continuité," *Diagonal*, n° 112, April 1995, pp. 10–14.

Allaman, Martine, "La griffe du Grand Lyon," *Diagonal*, n° 112, April 1995, pp. 15–18.

"Aménagement littoral, plage du Ponant, Benidorm, Espagne: Carlos Ferrater et Xavier Martí Galí," *L'Architecture d'aujourd'hui*, n° 363, 2006, pp. 104–105.

Amphoux, Pascal and Anne Sauvageot, *La notion d'ambiance. Une mutation de la pensée urbaine et de la pratique architecturale*, Lausanne, IRECDA/EPFL, 1998.

Andersson, Stig L., "Public Open Form and Space," conference proceedings, *Odprt javni prostor. Public Open Space. Design–Management–Maintenance*, April 10–11, 2008, Ljubljana, pp. 24–27.

Andersson, Stig L., "Klimatilpasset Byrum ved SEB i København," *Landskab*, n° 91/7, 2010, pp. 158–161.

Andersson, Stig L., "Sandbanken, vid Banken. Ett Stadsrum i samklang med naturen" *Utemiljö*, n° 5, 2012, pp. IV–V.

Andersson, Stig L., *Empowerment of Aesthetics, Catalogue for the Danish Pavilion at the 14th International Architecture Exhibition la Biennale di Venezia 2014*, Skive, Forlaget Wunderbuch, 2014, pp. 9–10. Available online: https://issuu.com/sla_architects/docs/empowerment_of_aesthetics_-_sla. [accessed May 5, 2017].

Andersson, Sven-Ingvar, "Globale oder regionale Landschaftsarchitektur/Global or Regional Landscape Architecture," *Topos*, n° 50, March 2005, pp. 24–31.

Andersson, Thorbjörn, "Badkultur kring sundet," *Landskap*, n° 7, 2005, pp. 162–167.

Anglès, Magda (ed.), *In Favour of Public Space. Ten Years of the European Prize for Urban Public Space*, Barcelona, Centre de Cultura Contemporania de Barcelona, Actar, 2010.

Anglès, Magda, "Benidorm, Spain: Playa de poniente esplanade," *Topos—The International Review of Landscape Architecture and Urban Design*, n° 72, 2010, pp. 22–27.

Ascher, François, "Loisirs," *Urbanisme*, n° 330, 2003, pp. 70–71.

Atelier Descombes Rampini et al., "Aline," competition boards of the MEP for the development of the Place Simon-Goulart, June 2003 [Archives ADR].

Atelier Descombes Rampini et al, *Note de présentation courte*, descriptive text of project, 27 September 2013 [Archives ADR].

Augustin, Jean-Pierre, "Espaces publics et cultures sportives," *Géocarrefour*, vol. 76, n° 1, 2001, pp. 27–30.

Aymonino, Aldo and Valerio Paolo Mosco, *Contemporary Public Space—Un-Volumetric Architecture*, Milan, Skira, 2006.

Ayuntamiento de Benidorm, Concejalía de Cultura, *Benidorm, los orígenes de la ciudad vertical*, exhibition catalog, 2006.

Azéma, Jean-Louis, "Les espaces publics du Grand Lyon," in Tomas, François (ed.), *Espaces publics, architecture et urbanité de part et d'autre de l'Atlantique*, Saint-Etienne, Université de Saint-Etienne, 2002, pp. 237–249.

B

Bach, Philippe, "Le trottoir à la genevoise, une AOC qui s'ignore," *Le courrier*, August 6, 2011, https://www.lecourrier.ch/le_trottoir_a_la_genevoise_une_aoc_qui_s_ignore?page=2 [accessed August 17, 2017].

Baljon, Lodewijk, *Designing Parks*, Amsterdam, Architectura & Natura Press, 1992.

Ballerup Kommune, Katalog for *Byrumskvaliteter i Måløv Aksen*, March 2008 [annexe of the competition specification].

Ballerup Kommune, *Måløv Aksen. Indbudt projektkonkurrence*, June 2008 [competition specification].

Ballerup Kommune, "Søndergård," n.d., https://ballerup.dk/soendergaard, accessed March 15, 2017.

Barman-Krämer, Gabriela, "Der MFO-Park in Zürich-Oerlikon: ein zukünftiger Parktypus auf dem ehemaligen Industrieareal," *Topiaria helvetica: Jahrbuch*, 2004, pp. 51–55.

Barthes, Roland, "Sémiologie et urbanisme," *L'Architecture d'aujourd'hui*, n° 153, 1970–1971, pp. 11–13.

Bassand, Michel et al., *Vivre et créer l'espace public*, Lausanne, Presses polytechniques et universitaires romandes, 2001.

Béboux, Bender, Collet, Presset, "Chuchotements," competition boards, MEP development of Place du Molard, March 19, 2002 [Archives 2b architectes].

Béboux, Bender, Collet, Presset [BBCP], *Réaménagement de la place du Molard. Annexe au permis de construire*, March 3, 2003 [Archives 2b architectes].

Bender, Stephanie, *Le vide: nouvelles stratégies urbaines*, doctoral thesis n° 4841, Lausanne, Ecole polytechnique fédérale de Lausanne, 2011.

Betin, Christophe, "La construction de l'espace public: le cas de Lyon," *Géocarrefour, revue de géographie de Lyon*, n° 76, 2001.

BIG, Topotek 1, Superflex, "Superkilen, 3 zoner, 3 farver—et globalt kvarter," Superkilen competition boards,, October 5, 2007 [Archives Topotek 1].

BIG, Topotek 1, Superflex, "Superkilen, 3 zoner, 3 farver–et globalt kvarter," Superkilen competition boards, October 5, 2007 [Archives Topotek 1].

BIG, Topotek 1, Superflex, "Superkilen," *Landskab*, n° 93, 2012, pp. 158–161, summary in English, p. 180.

Blanc, Jean-Noël, "Voir l'espace dans l'espace public," *Géocarrefour*, vol. 76, n° 1, 2001, pp. 59–67.

Bloom, Brett, "Superkilen: Park med ekstrem borgerinddragelse!," *Kritik*, n° 207, April 2013, pp. 47–76.

Bohigas, Oriol, "Un programma per Barcellona/A Program for Barcelona," *Casabella*, n° 483, September 1982, pp. 12–23.

Bohigas, Oriol, "Ten Points for an Urban Methodology," in Tim Marshall, *Transforming Barcelona*, London/NewYork, Routledge, 2004, pp. 91–96.

Böhme, Gernot and Jean-Paul Thibaud, *The Aesthetics of Atmospheres*, London/New York, Routledge, 2017.

Boullée, Etienne-Louis, *Architecture. Essai sur l'art*, 1799, edited by Jean-Marie Pérouse de Montclos, Paris, Hermann, 1968.

Bravo Bordas, David, "Theater Square," n.d., http://www.publicspace.org/en/works/f116-theater-square [accessed June 22, 2016].

Breviglieri, Marc, "Une brèche critique dans la 'ville garantie'? Espaces intercalaires et architectures d'usage," in Elena Cogato Lanza, Luca Pattaroni, Micha Piraud and Barbara Tirone (eds), *De la différence urbaine. Le quartier des Grottes/Genève*, Geneva: MétisPresses, 2013, pp. 213–236.

Bridger, Jessica, "Life on the Wedge: in Copenhagen, Superkilen Rolls out a Half-Mile Mash-Up of Global Culture," *Landscape Architecture Magazine*, n° 103, 2013, pp. 86–99.

Buchanan, Peter, "Regenerating Barcelona with Parks and Plazas," *The Architectural Review*, n° 1048, June 1984, pp. 32–45.

Burckhardt+Partner Architekten, Raderschall Landschaftsarchitekten (Arbeitsgemeinschaft), "Parkhaus," competition boards for first round of concept phase of competition for MFO-Park, March 1998 [Archives Raderschallpartner].

Burckhardt+Partner Architekten, Raderschall Landschaftsarchitekten (Arbeitsgemeinschaft), "Parkhaus," competition boards for second round of project phase of competition for MFO-Park, August 1998 [Archives Raderschallpartner].

Burns, Carole and Andrea Kahn (eds), *Site Matters. Design Concepts, Histories and Strategies*, New York, Routledge, 2005.

"Bymilen, København/Copenhagen" in Annemarie Lund (ed.), *Ny Agenda 2. Dansk landskabsarkitektur/New Agenda 2. Danish Landscape Architecture. 2009–13*, Bogværket, Nykøbing Sjælland, 2014, pp. 186–189.

C

Caille, Emmanuel, "Place de la République/berges de Seine. Paris, pour le meilleur et pour le pire," *D'architectures* n° 221, October 2013, pp. 80–87.

Camus, Albert and Francis Ponge, *Correspondances, 1941–1957*, edition presented and annotated by Jean-Marie Gleize, Paris, Gallimard, 2013.

Carlos Ferrater Partnership (OAB), *Synchronizing Geometry: Landscape, Architecture, and Construction*, Barcelona, Actar, 2006.

Chabert, Henry (ed.), *Espaces publics, espaces de vie ... Les réponses lyonnaises*, Lyon, Horvath, 1993.

Charbonneau, Jean-Pierre, "A propos de la place de la République à Paris," *Tous urbains*, n° 0, 2012, pp. 24–27.

Charollais, Isabelle and Bruno Marchand, "De l'opacité à la transparence 1951–1955. La reconstruction des Terreaux-du-Temple à St-Gervais," *Faces*, n° 21, 1991, pp. 40–45.

Chemetoff, Alexandre, "Entretien avec Oriol Bohigas," *AMC–Architecture*, n° 2, October 1983, pp. 44–55.

Chemetoff, Alexandre and Jean-Louis Cohen, "Le droit à la ville. Les espaces publics de Barcelone," *AMC–architecture*, n° 2, October 1983, pp. 42–59.

Choay, Françoise, "Sémiologie et urbanisme," in Françoise Choay et al., *Le Sens de la Ville*, Paris, Editions du Seuil, 1972, pp. 8–10. [Text based on an article published in *L'Architecture d'aujourd'hui*, n° 132, 1967].

Ciuffi, Valentina, "Il parco dei parchi/The Park of Parks," *Abitare*, n° 516, 2011, pp. 50–51, 53–54, 56–59, 61–62, 64–67.

Cohen, Jean-Louis, "La Barcelone de Bohigas: Identité d'une ville," *AMC–architecture*, n° 2, October 1983, pp. 42–45.

Cohen, Jean-Louis, "Learning from Barcelona: vingt ans de projets et leur réception," in Subirós, Pep (ed.), *Ciutat real, ciutat ideal*, Barcelona, Centre de Cultura Contemporània, 1998, pp. 99–108. Available online: http://www.publicspace.org/en/text-library/fra/a002-learning-from-barcelona-vingt-ans-de-projets-urbains-et-leur-reception [accessed November 14, 2017].

Competitionline, "Superkilen—Future Innovate Urban Space in the Outer Nørrebro District. Restricted Competition," February 6, 2007, http://www.competitionline.com/en/results/7445 [accessed March 2, 2016].
Cooper Marcus, Clare and Carolyn Francis (eds), *People Places*, New York, Van Nostrand Reinhold, 1990.
Corboz, André, "Le Territoire comme palimpseste," in André Corboz and Sébastien Marot, *Le Territoire comme palimpseste et autres essais*, Besançon, Les éditions de l'Imprimeur, 2001, pp. 209–229. [Orig. ed. in *Diogène*, n°121, January–March 1983, pp.14–35].
Crunelle, Marc, "La ville à pratiquer," in Jean-Paul Thibaud and Cristiane Rose Duarte (eds), *Ambiances urbaines en partage: pour une écologie sociale de la ville sensible*, Geneva, MétisPresses, 2013, pp. 101–108.
Cullen, Gordon, *Townscape*, London, The Architectural Press, 1961.
Curnier, Sonia, "Programming Play into Public Space?," *Metropolitics*, March 20, 2015. Published online: https://metropolitics.org/Programming-play-into-public-space.html [accessed March 20, 2015].
Curnier, Sonia, "Expériences urbaines et espaces publics à Copenhague," *Cahiers de l'Aspan*, n° 2, 2016, pp. 8–13.
Curnier, Sonia, "Embracing the Ordinary. Behind the Design of Public Spaces," in Bruno Marchand, Julien Descombes and Marco Rampini (eds), *Common Grounds. Atelier Descombes Rampini 2000–2015*, Basel, Birkhäuser, 2017, pp. 189–195. [French version, *Lieux Communs*, Gollion, Infolio 2017].

D

Dahhan, Bernard, *Victor Vasarely ou la connaissance d'un art moléculaire*, Paris, Editions Denoël/Gonthier, 1979.
Darrieus, Margaux, "TVK: Place de la République, Paris 3e," *Moniteur Architecture AMC*, n° 226, 2013, pp. 56–59.
David, Brigitte, "Le Plan Lumière. Lyon vit aussi la nuit," *AMC—architecture*, n° 44, September 1993, p. 39.
De Biasi, Pierre-Marc, "L'approche génétique de l'architecture," *Genesis*, special issue, "Architecture," n° 14, 2000, pp. 13–66.
De Jong, Erik, "Vistas of the Imagination," *'scape*, n° 1, 2008, p. 46.
De Solà-Morales, Manuel, "The Impossible Project of Public Space," in Magda Anglès (ed.), *In Favour of Public Space. Ten Years of the European Prize for Urban Public Space*, Barcelona, Centre de Cultura Contemporania de Barcelona, Actar, 2010, pp. 24–32.
Dezeuze, Anna, "The 1960s: A Decade of Out-of-Bounds," in Amelia Jones (ed.), *A Companion to Contemporary Art since 1945*, Oxford, Blackwell Publishing, 2006, pp. 38–59.
Diedrich, Lisa, *Translating Harbourscapes. Site-specific Design Approaches in Contemporary European Harbour Transformation*, doctoral thesis, Department of Geosciences and Natural Resource Management, University of Copenhagen, Frederiksberg, 2013.
Diedrich, Lisa et al. (ed.), *Fieldwork*, Series, Landscape Architecture Europe, Basel/Boston/Berlin, Birkhäuser, 2006.
Diedrich, Lisa et al. (ed.), *On Site*, Series, Landscape Architecture Europe, Basel/Boston/Berlin, Birkhäuser, 2009.
Diedrich, Lisa et al. (ed.), *In Touch*, Series, Landscape Architecture Europe, Basel/Boston/Berlin, Birkhäuser, 2012.
Diedrich, Lisa et al. (ed.), *On the Move*, Series, Landscape Architecture Europe, Wageningen, Blauwdruk, 2015.
"Dossier: Acupuncture," *'scape*, n° 1, 2011, pp. 18–43.
"Dossier: Loisirs urbains," *Urbanisme*, n° 319, July–August 2001, pp. 52–87.

E

"Europa—Der Stand der Dinge/Europe— The State of the Things," *Topos: The International Review of Landscape Architecture and Urban Design*, n° 27, 1999.

F

Farrando Sicilia, Jordi, "Vom Wandel der Formen und Konzepte/The Changes in Forms and Concepts," *Topos: The International Review of Landscape Architecture and Urban Design*, n° 29, 1999, pp. 74–81.
Fauve, Charlotte, "Dune danoise. "City Dune" à Copenhague, Danemark," *Ecologik*, n° 35, 2013, p. 42.
Fernández Per, Aurora and Javier Arpa, *The Public Chance: New Urban Landscapes*, Vitoria-Gasteiz, a+t architecture publishers, In Common Series, 2008.
Ferrater, Carlos and Xavier Martí Galí, *Benidorm*, Barcelona, Actar, 2011.
Fleury, Antoine, *Les espaces publics dans les politiques métropolitaines. Réflexions au croisement de trois expériences: de Paris aux quartiers centraux de Berlin et Istanbul*, doctoral thesis, Paris, Université de Paris 1 Panthéon-Sorbonne, UFR de géographie, 2008 [version of February 29].
Foret, Catherine, "La création d'un service 'espace public' au sein de la communauté urbaine de Lyon (1990): une initiative pionnière en France," *millénaire3*, le Centre de Ressources Prospectives du Grand Lyon, May 2008, http://www.millenaire3.com/ressources/la-creation-d-un-service-espace-public-au-sein-de-la-communaute-urbaine-de-lyon-1990-une-initiative-pionniere-en-france [accessed October 10, 2017].
Foret, Catherine, "Un nouveau mobilier urbain pour l'agglomération lyonnaise (1991)," *millénaire3*, le Centre de Ressources Prospectives du Grand Lyon, May 2008, http://www.millenaire3.com/ressources/un-nouveau-mobilier-urbain-pour-l-agglomeration-lyonnaise-1991, [accessed October 10, 2017].
Fromonot, Françoise, "Surface de réparation," *Criticat*, 14, 2014, pp. 45–61.

G

Gao, Arthur, *Public Square Landscapes*, Hong Kong, Design Media Publishing Ltd, 2011.
Gartenbau- und Landwirtschaftsamt der Stadt Zürich, *MFO-PARK/Zentrum Zürich Nord. Zweistufiger Konzept- und Projektwettbewerb. Wettbewerbsprogramm*, November 25, 1997 [competition programme].
Gaventa, Sarah, *New Public Spaces*, London, Mitchell Beazley, 2006.
Gehl Institute, "Twelve Quality Criteria," n.d., available online: https://gehlinstitute.org/tool/quality-criteria/ [accessed January 11, 2017].
Gehl, Jan, *Life Between Buildings: Using Public Space*, New York, Van Nostrand Reinhold, 1987, reprinted by Island Press, 2011. [Orig. ed. *Livet mellem husene—udeaktiviteter og udemilljøer*, Arkitektens Forlag, 1971].
Gehl, Jan, *Cities for People*, Washington D.C., Island Press, 2010.
Gehl, Jan and Stig L. Andersson, *Bedre byrum*, Copenhagen, Foreningen Realdanmark, 2002.
Gehl, Jan and Lars Gemzøe, *New City Spaces, Strategies and Projects*, Copenhagen, The Danish Architectural Press, 2001.
Gehl, Jan and Birgitte Svarre, *How To Study Public Life*, Washington D.C., Island Press, 2013.
Genestier, Philippe, "Ville culturelle et espace touristique: sur quelques logiques et réification à l'œuvre dans l'économie post-industrielle," in Luc Doumenc et al., *L'espace public dans la ville méditerranéenne. Actes du colloque de Montpellier, 14–15–16 mars 1996*, Montpellier, Editions de l'Espérou, 1997, pp. 43–56.
Grosjean, Michèle and Jean-Paul Thibaud (eds), *L'espace urbain en méthodes*, Marseille, Editions Parenthèses, 2001.
Guillaume, Paul, *La Psychologie de la forme*, Paris, Flammarion, 1937.

H

Hajer, Marteen and Arnold Reijndorp, *In Search of New Public Domain*, Rotterdam, Nai Publishers, 2002.
Hallain, Marc, *Vasarely*, Paris, Fernand Hazan, 1974.
Hochbaudepartement der Stadt Zürich, "Neu-Oerlikon/Bahnhof Oerlikon," n.d., https://www.stadt-zuerich.ch/hbd/de/index/entwicklungsgebiete/neu-oerlikon.html [accessed May 16, 2016].
Houzelle, Béatrice, "Entre Saône et Rhône … Les aménagements de la Presqu'Île," *Techniques et architecture*, n° 419, May 1995, pp. 34–38.
Huber, Werner, "Platz da!," *Hochparterre*, n° 10, 2013, p. 73.
Huet, Bernard, "Une génétique urbaine," *Urbanisme*, n° 303, 1998, pp. 56–59.
Huet, Bernard, "Les enjeux de la critique," in Agnès Deboulet, Rainier Hoddé, and André Sauvage, *La critique architecturale. Questions-frontières-desseins*, Paris, Editions de la Villette, 2008, pp. 76–86. [Orig. ed., *Le visiteur*, n° 1, fall 1995].
Høyer, Steen, "Scenografisk landskab/Scenographic Landscape," *Architektur DK*, n° 1, 2002, pp. 4–11.

I

Ibelings, Hans, *Designing for the Public*, Amsterdam, Sun Architecture Publishers/Flemish Government architect, 2009.
"Industriegebiet und Bahnhofareal Zürich-Oerlikon, Überarbeitung," *Schweizer Ingenieur und Architekt*, Wettbewerbe, n° 48, 1992, pp. 918–922.
"In Common, Collective Spaces," a+t, n° 25–27, 2005–2006.

J

Jacobs, Jane, *Déclin et survie des grandes villes américaines*, Marseille, Parenthèses, 2012. [Orig. ed. *The Death and Life of Great American Cities*, New York, Random House, 1961].

K

Klanten, Robert et al. (ed.), *Going Public, Public Architecture, Urbanism and Interventions. The Creative Revival of Public Space*, Berlin, Gestalten Verlag, 2012.
Københavns Kommune, *Lokalplan nr. 403 "Rigsarkivet,"* Copenhagen, January 13, 2006.
Koolhaas, Rem, "Singapore Songlines: Thirty Years of Tabula Rasa," in O.M.A., Rem Koolhaas, and Bruce Mau, *S,M,L,XL*, New York, The Monacelli Press, 1995, pp. 1,008–1,087.
Kottas, Dimitris, *Urban Spaces: Squares and Plazas*, Barcelona, Links International, 2007.
Krauel, Jacobo, *New Urban Spaces*, Barcelona, Links International, 2006.
Krauel, Jacobo, *Urban Spaces: Design and Innovation*, Barcelona, Links International, 2013.
Kuben, *Superkilen—Det urban liv. Konkurenceprogram*, n.d. [competition brief].

L

Lacaton & Vassal, "Place Léon Aucoc, Bordeaux," n.d., http://lacatonvassal.com/index.php?idp=37 [accessed March 16, 2016].
Landeshauptstadt München, *Messestadt Riem. Das Projekt—Planung und Realisierung*, June 2009.
Le vocabulaire des espaces publics, *les références du Grand Lyon*, Lyon, Communauté urbaine de Lyon, Service Espace Public, 1994.

Lenler, Jens and Torben Benner, "Borgere på Nørrebro: Det blev som Realdania ville," *Politiken.dk, Kultur*, July 14, 2010, https://politiken.dk/ibyen/byliv/art5620901/Borgere-på-Nørrebro-Det-blev-som-Realdania-ville en ligne [accessed October 20, 2015].

Loderer, Benedikt, "Die Heimliche Hauptstadt," *Hochparterre*, n°10, 2001, pp. 14–21.

Loderer, Benedikt, "Neueste Masche: Kein Gewebe," *Beilage zu Hochparterre*, n° 6–7, 2005, pp. 10–11.

Lopez Silvestre, Federico, "Técnicas de representación y proyectos de intervención: breve historia de une relación cuestionada. Representation Techniques and Intervention Projects: A Short History of a Questioned Relationship," *paisea*, n° 014, 2010, pp. 11–17.

Lucan, Jacques, "Entretien avec Henry Chabert. Reconquérir les espaces publics," *AMC—architecture*, n° 44, September 1993, pp. 32–33.

Lucan, Jacques, "Les espaces publics du Grand Lyon," *AMC—architecture*, n° 44, September 1993, pp. 28–42.

Lucan, Jacques, "L'irrésistible ascension des paysagistes," *AMC— architecture*, n° 44, September 1993, p. 41.

Lucan, Jacques, "Généalogie du poché®," *Matières*, n° 7, 2004, Lausanne, Presses polytechniques et universitaires romandes, pp. 41–54.

Lucan, Jacques, *Où va la ville aujourd'hui? Formes urbaines et mixités*, Paris, Editions de la Villette, 2012.

Lucan, Jacques, *Précisions sur un état présent de l'architecture*, Lausanne, Presses polytechniques et universitaires romandes, 2015.

Ludwig, Karl H. C., "Die Inszenierung des öffentlichen Freiraums/La mise en scène de l'espace libre public," *Anthos*, n° 3, 2000, pp. 4–9.

Lussault, Michel, "Espace public II," in Jacques Lévy and Michel Lussault (eds), *Dictionnaire de la géographie et de l'espace des sociétés*, Paris, Belin, 2003, pp. 339–340.

Lussault, Michel and Jacques Lévy, "Espace public I," in Jacques Lévy and Michel Lussault (eds), *Dictionnaire de la géographie et de l'espace des sociétés*, Paris, Belin, 2003, pp. 333–339.

Lynch, Kevin, *L'image de la cité*, Paris, Dunod, 1971. [Orig. ed. *The Image of the City*, Cambridge, The MIT Press, 1960].

M

Macher, Julia, "Der paseo de Poniente Benidorm. Architekten, Carlos Ferrater, Xavier Martí Galí (OAB)," *Bauwelt*, n° 101/32, 2010, pp. 14–21.

Madden, Kathy and Andy Wiley-Schwartz, *How to Turn a Place Around: A Handbook for Creating Successful Public Spaces*, New York, Project for Public Spaces, 2000.

Mader, Günter, "Topographie," *Anthos*, n° 1, 2004, pp. 4–9.

Maeder, Thierry, "An Approach through Milieu," in Bruno Marchand, Julien Descombes and Marco Rampini (eds), *Common Grounds. Atelier Descombes Rampini 2000–2015*, Basel, Birkhaüser, 2017, pp. 197–200. [French version, *Lieux Communs*, Gollion, Infolio 2017].

Mairie de Paris, *Aménagement de la place de la République. Le programme d'aménagement*, Paris, June 9, 2009.

Mairie de Paris, Direction de l'Urbanisme, *République, histoire d'une place*, Paris, n.d. [annex to competition brief].

Mairie de Paris, *Bilan de la concertation sur le projet d'aménagement de la Place de la République du 15 décembre 2008 au 15 mars 2009*, Paris, document n.d. [annex to competition brief].

Mairie de Paris, Atelier Parisien d'urbanisme (APUR), *Concertation. Projet d'aménagement de la place de la République. Diagnostic. Pistes de réflexion pour le programme du concours*, n.d. [annex to competition brief].

Mairie de Paris, *2010 DVD 112 Signature du marché de maîtrise d'œuvre pour l'aménagement de la place de la République à Paris, (3e), (10e), et (11e) avec le groupement TREVELO ET VIGER-KOHLER (mandataire), Martha Schwartz Partners, AREAL, ATEC, AIK Yann Kersalé*, n.d.

Mangin, David, "Les trottoirs de Barcelone," *L'Architecture d'aujourd'hui*, n° 260, December 1988, pp. 2–5.

Marchand, Bruno, "Preface," in Bruno Marchand, Julien Descombes and Marco Rampini (eds), *Common Grounds. Atelier Descombes Rampini 2000–2015*, Basel, Birkhäuser, 2017, pp. 19–24. [French version, *Lieux Communs*, Gollion, Infolio 2017].

Marchand, Bruno, Julien Descombes, and Marco Rampini (eds), *Common Grounds. Atelier Descombes Rampini 2000–2015*, Basel, Birkhäuser, 2017. [French version, *Lieux Communs*, Gollion, Infolio 2017].

Marot, Sébastien, "L'alternative du paysage," *Le Visiteur*, n° 1, 1995, pp. 54–80.

Marshall, Tim, *Transforming Barcelona*, London/NewYork, Routledge, 2004.

Marti Casanovas, Miquel, "Barcelone (1979–2004). Monumentalité et renouveau de la voie publique," *Urbanisme*, n° 346, January–February 2008, pp. 56–58.

Martorell, Josep, Oriol Bohigas, and David Mackay, "Paseo Marítimo de Benidorm. Benidorm Promenade," *Via Arquitectura*, n° 02, 1997, pp. 68–73. Available online: http://www.via-arquitectura.net/02/02-066.htm [accessed August 25, 2016].

Masboungi, Ariella, "Un urbanisme des ambiances," in Alain Bourdin and Ariella Masboungi, *Un urbanisme des modes de vie*, Paris, Le Moniteur, 2004, pp. 67–85.

Miles, Malcolm, *Cities and Cultures*, London/New York, Routledge, 2007.

(Mollie-) Stefulesco Caroline, "De quelques impostures," in introduction of Seron-Pierre, Catherine, "Détails. L'arbre dans la ville," *AMC – architecture*, n° 162, June–July 2006, pp. 112–113.

Montaner, Josep Maria, "Taxonomia de sistemas formales en la obra de Carlos Ferrater. A Taxonomy of Formal Systems in the Work of Carlos Ferrater," in "Carlos Ferrater. Obra reciente/Recent Work," *2G*, n° 32, Editorial Gustavo Gili, Barcelone. 2004, pp. 4–19.

Montaner, Josep Maria, "Matière et technique de la critique," in Agnès Deboulet, Rainier Hoddé, and André Sauvage, *La critique architecturale. Questions-frontières-desseins*, Paris, Editions de la Villette, 2008, pp. 123–136. [Orig. ed. *Arquitectura y crítica*, Barcelona, Editorial Gustavo Gili, 1999].

P

Padura, Manel, "Conversation" in Manel Padura and Carlos Ferrater (eds), *Carlos Ferrater. Office of Architecture in Barcelona*, El Masnou (Barcelona), Editorial Manel Padura, 2006, pp. 10–19.

Paquot, Thierry, "Editorial. Espace(s) public(s)," *Urbanisme*, n° 346, January–February 2006, pp. 41–42.

Paquot, Thierry, *L'espace public*, Paris, La Découverte, coll. Repères, 2009.

"Paseo Marítimo, Benidorm (Alicante)/ Waterfront, Benidorm (Alicante) Spain," *AV Monografías/AV Monographs*, n° 141–142, 2010, pp. 52–59.

Pattaroni, Luca, "The Urban Art of Possibility," in Bruno Marchand, Julien Descombes and Marco Rampini (eds), *Common Grounds*, Basel, Birkhäuser, 2017, pp. 113–124. [French version, *Lieux Communs*, Gollion, Infolio 2017].

"Piazza del teatro ad Anversa, Belgio/ Theater square, Antwerp, Belgium," *Industria Delle Costruzioni*, n° 46/428, 2012, pp. 22–27.

Plan Urbain, *Espaces publics*, Paris, Ministère de l'Equipement et du Logement-DAU-DRI, 1988.

"Platz der Menschenrechte," in Lisa Diedrich et al. (ed.), *On Site*, Series, Landscape Architecture Europe, Basel/Boston/Berlin, Birkhäuser, 2009. p. 137.

Ponge, Francis, "Le Carnet du bois de pins" in Francis Ponge, *La rage de l'expression*, Paris, Gallimard, Collection, 2011. [1st legal deposit at Gallimard 1976, 1st publication of "Le Carnet du bois de pins," Lausanne, Mermod, 1947], pp. 97–172. German version consulted by Valentien + Valentien: Francis Ponge, *Das Notizbuch vom Kiefernwald und La Mounine*, Berlin, Suhrkamp, 1995.

Project for Public Spaces Inc., *How to Turn a Place Around: A Handbook for Creating Successful Public Spaces*, New York, Project for Public Spaces Inc., 2000.

Q

Quatremère de Quincy, Antoine Chrysostome, "Caractère," in *Dictionnaire historique d'architecture: comprenant dans son plan les notions historiques, descriptives, archéologiques ... de cet art.*, Paris, A. Le Clère et Cie, 1832, vol. 1, pp. 302–308. Available online: http://gallica.bnf.fr/ark:/12148/bpt-6k1045594m/f316.item.zoom [accessed October 18, 2017].

R

Rauterberg, Hanno, "Der Aufbruch hält an/Reconquering Barcelona," *Topos: The International Review of Landscape Architecture and Urban Design*, n° 29, 1999, pp. 6–11.

Reeh, Henrik, "Der Superkeil von Kopenhagen," *StadtBauwelt*, n° 193, 2012, pp. 60–67.

"Rem, Do You Know What This Is?," *Hunch, the Berlage Institute Report*, n° 3, 2001, pp. 32–33.

Riesto, Svava and Jan Støvring, "Stories under your Feet: Renovation of Købmagergade in Copenhagen," *Topos: The International Review of Landscape Architecture and Urban Design*, n° 89, 2014, pp. 42–49.

Ripoli, David, "Pavé, caillou, ciment: histoire matérielle du revêtement de sol à Genève," *k+a, Art+architecture en Suisse*, n° 3, 2012, pp. 30–36.

Roth, Ueli, "Neuer Stadtteil Zentrum Zürich Nord," *Topos: The International Review of Landscape Architecture and Urban Design*, n° 3, 2002, pp. 31–35.

Rowe Colin and Fred Koetter, *Collage City*, Gollion, Infolio, 2002. [Orig. ed., *Collage City*, MIT, Cambridge, 1978].

S

Sabbah, Catherine, "Espaces publics. L'invention d'une politique," *Techniques et architecture*, n° 419, May 1995, pp. 46–48.

Schäfer, Robert, "Der Park der Wunder—Superkilen," *Garten + Landschaft*, n° 122, 2012, pp. 15–19.

Schulze, Gerhard, *Die Erlebnisgesellschaft: Kultursoziologie der Gegenwart*, Campus Verlag, Frankfurt, 1992.

Schulze, Gerhard, "Erlebnisgesellschaft," in Helmut Reinalter and Peter J. Brenner (eds), *Lexikon der Geisteswissenschaften. Sachbegriffe— Disziplinen—Personen*, Vienna, Böhlau Verlag, 2011, pp. 285–286.

Secchi, Bernardo, "Progetto di suolo," *Casabella*, n° 520, 1986, pp. 19–23.

Simon, Axel, "Das grüne Park-Haus," *Garten + Landschaft*, n° 112, 2002, pp. 31–33.

Sitte, Camillo, *L'art de bâtir les villes. L'urbanisme selon ses fondements artistiques*, Paris, Seuil, Points Essais, 1996. [Orig. ed. *Der Städtebau nach seinen künstlerischen Grandsätzen*, 1889].

SLA, *Dipositionsforlag1*, report for client, December 2005 [Archives SLA].

SLA, SEB, "SEB nyt byrum. En bjergside på Kalvebod Brygge," September 8, 2010 [project presentation report, *Præsentation_SEB_08092010.pdf*, Archives SLA].
Stahlschmidt, Per and Peter Thorsen, "Debat: Processurbanisme—byøkologi eller varm luft?," *Landskab*, n° 1, 2011, pp. 18–19.
Steigmeier, Andreas, "Asea Brown Boveri (ABB)," in *Dictionnaire historique de la Suisse (DHS)*, vol. 1, Hauterive, Attinger, 2002, pp. 534–535.
Steiner, Barbara (ed.), *Superkilen. A Project by BIG, Topotek 1, Superflex*, Stockholm/Oslo, Arvinius + Orfeus Publishing, 2013.
Steiner, Barbara (ed.), *Creative Infidelities: On the Landscape Architecture of Topotek 1*, Berlin, Jovis Verlag, 2016.
Stevens, Quentin, *The Ludic City: Exploring the Potential of Public Spaces*, London, Routledge, 2007.
"Strategy Public, Landscape Urbanism Strategies," *a+t*, n° 35–36, 2011.
"Strategy Space, Landscape Urbanism Strategies," *a+t*, n° 37, 2011.
"Strategy and Tactics in Public Space," *a+t*, n° 38, 2011.
Studio 04 Bernardo Secchi and Paola Viganò, Dirk Jaspaert, "Spazio s-misurato," album accompanying Open Oproep competition boards, n.d. [date estimated December 2004], [non-paginated]. [Archives Studio Associato Secchi-Viganò].
Sundbo, Jon and Flemming Sørensen (eds), *Handbook on the Experience Economy*, Cheltenham, Edward Elgar Publishing, 2013.

T
Thibaud, Jean-Paul and Cristiane Rose Duarte (eds), *Ambiances urbaines en partage. Pour une écologie sociale de la ville sensible*, Geneva, MétisPresses, 2013.
Tomas, François (ed.), *Espaces publics, architecture et urbanité de part et d'autre de l'Atlantique*, Saint-Etienne, Université de Saint-Etienne, 2002.
Toussaint, Jean-Yves and Monique Zimmermann, *User, observer, programmer et fabriquer l'espace public*, Lausanne, Presses polytechniques et universitaires romandes, 2001.
Tranberg, Lene and Stig L. Andersson "Det grønne flow, The green flow," *Arkitektur DK*, n° 6, 2011, pp. 6–7.
Trévelo & Viger-Kohler et al., "Aménagement de la Place de la République à Paris 3ème, 10ème et 11ème arrondissements," architectural, technical and financial presentation notice, n.d. [November 2009], competition boards [Archives TVK].
Trévelo & Viger-Kohler, *Dossier de presse—Place de la République*, June 2013 [several versions of the press kit were published in 2013], [Archives TVK].

V
Vago Pierre, "La critique architecturale—entre carcan et utilité," in Agnès Deboulet, Rainier Hoddé, and André Sauvage, *La critique architecturale. Questions-frontières-desseins*, Paris, Editions de la Villette, 2008, pp. 28–36. [Orig. ed., *L'Architecture d'aujourd'hui*, n° 117, 1964–1965].
Valentien + Valentien, *Platz der Menschenrechte. Messestadt München Riem. Zusammenfassung*, n.d. [Archives Valentien + Valentien].
Valentien + Valentien, *Platz der Menschenrechte. Messestadt München Riem. Projektbeschreibung*, n.d. [Archives Valentien + Valentien].
Valentien, Christoph, "Metamorphose einer Planungskonzeption," *Garten+ Landschaft*, n° 12, 1993, pp. 36–43.
Valentien, Christoph, "Freiraumsystem und gartenkünstlerischer Entwurf," *Der Architekt*, n° 6, 1997, pp. 373–375.
Valentien, Christoph, "Neue Messestadt München-Riem/Nouveau 'Messestadt München-Riem'," *Anthos*, n° 37, 1998, pp. 48–51.
Valle, Pietro, "Riding a Fake Cow on a Movable Landscape, Heading to the Beach," in Thilo Folkerts (ed.), *Topotek 1 Rosemarie Trockel: Eine Landschaftsskulptur für München*, Basel/Boston/Berlin, Birkhäuser, 2011, pp. 93–104.
Van Toorn, Roemer, "The Ultimate Value of Beinahe Nichts," in *The Specific and the Singular: Architecture in Flanders*, Antwerp, Flemish Architecture Institute, 2010, pp. 118–125.
Van Uffelen, Chris, *Urban Spaces, Plazas, Squares & Streetscapes*, Salenstein, Braun, 2012. [French translation, *Architecture et espaces urbains*, Paris, Citadelles & Mazenod, 2013].
Vanderburgh, David and Carlo Menon, "The Finger and the Moon: Belgian Competitions in Their Representational Context," in Jean-Pierre Chupin, Carmela Cucuzzella, and Bechara Helal, *Architecture Competitions and the Production of Culture, Quality and Knowledge. An International Inquiry*, Montreal, Potential Architecture Books, 2015, pp. 36–53.
Vidal Pla, Miquel, "Spanien: Weiterarbeiten am Modell Barcelona/Spain: Developing the Barcelona Model," *Topos: The International Review of Landscape Architecture and Urban Design*, n° 27, 1999, pp. 41–49.
Vienne, Véronique, "In Paris, a Celebrated Place for Protest Gets a Quietly Radical Facelift," *Metropolis Magazine*, October 7, 2014, http://www.metropolismag.com/ideas/paris-place-protest-gets-quietly-radical-facelift/ [accessed April 29, 2015, the title was then "Place for Protest"].
Viganò, Paola, "I territori dell' urbanistica/The Territories of Urbanism," *Lotus International*, n° 150, 2012, pp. 106–113.
Ville de Genève, Mandat d'étude parallèle, *Réaménagement de la place du Molard*. regulations and brief, February 2002.
Ville de Genève, Connaissance du site: *la Place du Molard, parcours historique*, January 2002 [annex to competition brief MEP].
Ville de Genève, Mandats d'étude *parallèles pour le réaménagement de la place du Molard. Rapport du groupe d'experts*, expert group report, March 26, 2002
Ville de Genève, Département municipal de l'aménagement des constructions et de la voirie, *Mandat d'études parallèles. Réaménagement des places Longemalle, Pré-l'Evêque, Simon-Goulart. Règlement et cahier des charges*, regulations and brief, Geneva, n.d.
Ville de Genève, Département municipal de l'aménagement des constructions et de la voirie, *Mandat d'études parallèles. Réaménagement des places Longemalle, Pré-l'Evêque, Simon-Goulart. Rapport du groupe d'expert*, expert group report, Geneva, June 24, 2003.
Vindum, Kjeld, "Stig L. Andersson. Interview," *Arkitektur DK*, n° 6, 2011, pp. 8–11.
Vlaams Bouwmeester, "De Open Oproep," n.d., http://www.vlaamsbouwmeester.be/nl/instrumenten/open-oproep/info [accessed June 20, 2016].
Vlaams Bouwmeester, *Heraanleg van het Theaterplein en omgeving te Antwerpen* n.d., Available online: https://www.vlaamsbouwmeester.be/sites/default/files/open_call_project_files_not_started/55dfcf5ed48445359d6089fc78595fdf.pdf [accessed June 20, 2016].

W
Wærn, Rasmus, "Kommentar. Comments," *Arkitektur DK*, n° 6, 2011, pp. 20–23.
Waterman, Tim, "At Liberty: A Piece of Paris has been Recivilized for Walking (or Skating, or Scootering, or Protesting)," *Landscape Architecture Magazine*, n° 104, 2014, pp. 112–127.
Weil, Marcos, "Aménagement des places publiques à Genève," *Interface*, n° 18, 2013, pp. 8–14.
Whyte, Wlilliam H., *The Social Life of Small Urban Spaces*, Washington D.C., The Conservation Foundation, 1980.
Wollheim, Ralf, "Vereinte Nationen," *DB—Deutsche Bauzeitung*, n° 10, 2013, pp. 14–15.
Worthmann, Merten, "Zwischen Sand und Asphalt: Neue Strandpromenade für Benidorm von Studio OAB," *Baumeister*, n° 107(1), 2010, pp. 14–15.

DOCUMENTATION BY PROJECT

PLACE SIMON-GOULART | GENEVA | 2003–2013

Official documents

Ville de Genève, Département municipal de l'aménagement des constructions et de la voirie, *Mandat d'études parallèles. Réaménagement des places Longemalle, Pré-l'Evêque, Simon-Goulart. Règlement et cahier des charges.* Geneva, n.d.

Ville de Genève, Département municipal de l'aménagement des constructions et de la voirie, *Mandat d'études parallèles. Réaménagement des places Longemalle, Pré-l'Evêque, Simon-Goulart. Rapport du groupe d'expert*, Geneva, June 24, 2003.

Ville de Genève, *Aménagement espace public. Place Simon-Goulart*, documentary triptych, Geneva, June 2013.

Archives and interviews

Consultation: all preserved digital archives, premises of Atelier Descombes Rampini, Geneva, March 17–25, 2015.

ADR et al., "Aline," MEP competition boards for the development of the Place Simon-Goulart, June 2003 [Archives Atelier Descombes Rampini].

ADR et al, *Note de présentation courte*, descriptive text of the project, September 27, 2013 [Archives Atelier Descombes Rampini].

Guided tour in the presence of Gregory Bussien and Julien Descombes during the open days organized by the SIA (Swiss society of engineers and architects), May 9, 2014.

Bussien, Gregory (project architect at l'Atelier Descombes Rampini), Geneva, interview with the author in French, March 24, 2015.

Descombes, Julien and Marco Rampini (associates of the Atelier Descombes Rampini), Lausanne, interview with the author in French, July 14, 2016.

Books, chapters, and articles consulted

"Genève: Place de quartier/Quartierplatz," *Hochparterre*, thematic book Flâneur d'or, December 2014, p. 20.

Huber, Werner, "Platz da!," *Hochparterre*, n° 10, 2013, p. 73.

"Place Simon-Goulart" in Bruno Marchand, Julien Descombes and Marco Rampini (eds), *Common Grounds. Atelier Descombes Rampini 2000–2015*, Basel, Birkhäuser, 2017, pp. 220–221. [French version, *Lieux Communs*, Gollion, Infolio 2017].

Background and related topics

Bach, Philippe, "Le trottoir à la genevoise, une AOC qui s'ignore," *Le courrier*, August 6, 2011, https://www.lecourrier.ch/le_trottoir_a_la_genevoise_une_aoc_qui_s_ignore?page=2 [accessed August 17, 2017].

"Place!," *Interface*, n° 18, 2013.

Charollais, Isabelle and Bruno Marchand, "De l'opacité à la transparence. 1951–1955. La reconstruction des Terreaux-du-Temple à St-Gervais," *Faces*, n° 21, 1991, pp. 40–45.

Ripoli, David, "Pavé, caillou, ciment. Histoire matérielle du revêtement de sol à Genève," *k+a, Art+architecture en Suisse*, n° 3, 2012, pp. 30–36.

Söderström, Ola, Béatrice Manzoni, and Suzanne Oguey, "Lendemains d'échecs. Conduite de projets et aménagements d'espaces publics à Genève," *Disp*, n° 145, 2001, pp. 19–28.

Weil, Marcos, "Aménagement des places publiques à Genève," *Interface*, n° 18, 2013, pp. 8–14.

Marchand, Bruno, "Preface," in Bruno Marchand, Julien Descombes and Marco Rampini (eds), *Common Grounds. Atelier Descombes Rampini 2000–2015*, Basel, Birkhäuser, 2017, pp. 19–24. [French version, *Lieux Communs*, Gollion, Infolio 2017].

Pattaroni, Luca, "The Urban Art of Possibility," in Bruno Marchand, Julien Descombes and Marco Rampini (eds), *Common Grounds. Atelier Descombes Rampini 2000–2015*, Basel, Birkhäuser, 2017, pp. 113–124. [French version, *Lieux Communs*, Gollion, Infolio 2017].

"Simon-Goulart," *Interface*, n° 18, 2013, p. 23.

"Trois places à Genève. Mandat d'études parallèles," *Anthos*, n° 42, 2003, pp. 61–63

Van Der Poel, Cedric, "Un nouveau Square pour St-Gervais," *Tracés*, n° 18, 2013, pp. 20–21.

PLACE DE LA RÉPUBLIQUE | PARIS | 2009–2013

Official documents

Mairie de Paris, Direction de l'Urbanisme, *République, histoire d'une place*, Paris, n.d. [annex to the competition brief].

Mairie de Paris, Atelier Parisien d'urbanisme (APUR), *Concertation. Projet d'aménagement de la Place de la République. Diagnostic. Pistes de réflexion pour le programme du concours*, n.d. [annex to the competition brief].

Mairie de Paris, *Bilan de la concertation sur le projet d'aménagement de la Place de la République du 15 December 2008 au 15 mars 2009*, Paris, document n.d. [annex to the competition brief].

Mairie de Paris, *2010 DVD 112 Signature du marché de maîtrise d'œuvre pour l'aménagement de la place de la République à Paris, (3e), (10e), et (11e) avec le groupement Trevelo & Viger-Kohler (mandataire), Martha Schwartz Partners, AREAL, ATEC, AIK Yann Kersalé*, n.d.

Mairie de Paris, *Aménagement de la Place de la République. Le programme d'aménagement*, Paris, June 9, 2009.

Mairie de Paris, *Fiche simulations trafic – Pl. Répu*, 09.06.2009 [annex to the competition brief].

Archives and interviews

Consultation of the archives: models and all digital documents in the presence of Vincent Hertenberger, TVK agency premises, Paris, July 22, 2015.

Trévelo & Viger-Kohler et al., "Aménagement de la Place de la République à Paris 3ème, 10ème et 11ème arrondissements," architectural, technical and financial presentation notice, n.d. [November 2009], competition boards [Archives TVK].

Trévelo & Viger-Kohler et al., "Aménagement de la Place de la République à Paris 3ème, 10ème et 11ème arrondissements," competition boards, November 12, 2009 [Archives TVK].

Trévelo & Viger-Kohler et al., *Aménagement de la Place de la République à Paris 3ème, 10ème et 11ème arrondissements*, November 17, 2011 [Archives TVK].

Trévelo & Viger-Kohler, *Dossier de presse—Place de la République*, June 2013, [several versions of the press kit were published in 2013], [Archives TVK].

"Place de la République," http://republique.tvk.fr [accessed July 20, 2017].

Hertenberger, Vincent (project leader at Trévelo & Viger-Kohler), Paris, interview with the author in French, July 22, 2015.

Trevelo, Pierre Alain (partner of Trévelo & Viger-Kohler), Paris, interview with the author in French, July 22, 2015.

Books, chapters, and articles consulted

Agape, Sélène, "Place de la République. Paris opte pour le béton," *Techniques et architecture*, n° 47, 2003, pp. 34–35.

Albert, Marie-Douce, "TVK, enfants du Périphérique, rénovateurs de la République," *Le moniteur*, published June 13, 2013, https://www.lemoniteur.fr/article/tvk-enfants-du-peripherique-renovateurs-de-la-republique-21484846 [accessed online April 30, 2015].

Baus, Ursula, "Politikwechsel. Neugestaltung der 'Place de la République' in Paris," *DB—Deutsche Bauzeitung*, n° 4, 2014, pp. 18–25.

Bouchouchi, Corinne, "Delanoë enfonce le clou. La République se libère des autos," *L'obs*, January 18, 2012, http://tempsreel.nouvelobs.com/regions/paris-ile-de-france/20120112.REG0008/delanoe-enfonce-le-cloula-republique-se-libere-des-autos.html [accessed online July 15, 2017].

Caille, Emmanuel, "Place de la République/berges de Seine. Paris, pour le meilleur et pour le pire," *D'architectures* n° 221, October 2013, pp. 80–87.

Catsaros, Christophe, "La nouvelle Place de la République par l'agence TVK," *Tracés*, n° 139, 2013, pp. 20–21.

Charbonneau, Jean-Pierre, "A propos de la Place de la République à Paris," *Tous urbains*, n° 0, 2012, pp. 24–27.

Darrieus, Margaux, "TVK: Place de la République, Paris 3e," *Moniteur Architecture AMC*, n° 226, 2013, pp. 56–59.

"Edito. La Place de la République," *Urbanisme*, n° 395, 2015.

Fromonot, Françoise, "Surface de réparation," *Criticat*, 14, 2014, pp. 45–61.

Mayou, Géraldine, "La République pacifiée," *Traits urbains*, n° 62, 2013, pp. 64–66.

Rechi, Loïc, "Nouvelle tentative d'épuisement d'un lieu parisien," *Snatch*, n° 19, 2013, pp. 36–43.

Trévelo & Viger-Kohler Architectes Urbanistes, *Take 01, Building Paris*, Paris, TVK, 2014.

Vienne, Véronique, "In Paris, a Celebrated Place for Protest Gets a Quietly Radical Facelift," *Metropolis Magazine*, October 7, 2014, http://www.metropolismag.com/ideas/paris-place-protest-gets-quietly-radical-facelift/ [accessed on April 29, 2015, the title at the time was "Place for Protest"].

Vincendon, Sibylle, "L'architecte de la Place de la République: 'Cette place a tout de suite joué un rôle de symbole'," *Libération, Société*, January 14, 2015, http://www.liberation.fr/societe/2015/01/14/l-architecte-de-la-place-de-la-republique-cette-place-a-tout-de-suite-joue-un-role-de-symbole_1180623 [accessed online April 30, 2015].

Waterman, Tim, "At Liberty: A Piece of Paris has Been Recivilized for Walking (or Skating, or Scootering, or Protesting)," *Landscape Architecture Magazine*, n° 104, 2014, pp. 112–127.

Background and related topics

Martin, Lise, "Embouteillage de candidats à République," online blog, *Le Nouvel Observateur*, Paris, March 3, 2008. http://municipales2008.blogs.nouvelobs.com/archive/2008/03/03/embouteillage-de-candidats-a-republique.html [accessed November 3, 2015].

PLACE DU MOLARD | GENEVA | 2002–2004

Official documents

Ville de Genève, *Mandat d'étude parallèle, Réaménagement de la place du Molard. Règlement et cahier des charges*, February 2002.

Ville de Genève, *Connaissance du site: la Place du Molard, parcours historique*, January 2002 [annex to the MEP brief].

Ville de Genève, *Mandats d'étude parallèles pour le réaménagement de la place du*

Molard. Rapport du groupe d'experts, March 26, 2002
Ville de Genève, *Aménagement. Espace public. Place du Molard*, documentary triptych, Geneva, May 2009.

Archives and interviews

Consultation: all preserved paper and digital archives, premises of 2b architectes, Lausanne, July 14 and 16, 2015.
Groupe Béboux, Bender, Collet, Presset, "Chuchotements," competition boards, MEP development of Place du Molard, March 19, 2002 [Archives 2b architectes].
BBCP [Groupe Béboux, Bender, Collet, Presset], *Réaménagement de la place du Molard. Annexe au permis de construire*, March 3, 2003 [Archives 2b architectes].
Beboux, Philippe (partner of 2b architectes), Lausanne, interview with the author in French, June 29, 2015.
Bender, Stephanie (partner of 2b architectes), Lausanne, informal discussion with the author, July 15, 2015.

Background and related topics

Bender, Stephanie, *Le vide: Nouvelles stratégies urbaines*, doctoral thesis n° 4841, Lausanne, Ecole polytechnique fédérale de Lausanne, 2011.

Books, chapters, and articles consulted

"Place du Molard, Ginebra, Suiza," *Paisea*, n° 009, June 2009, pp. 28–31.
"Molard," *Interface*, n° 18, 2013, p. 22.
Dewarrat, Jean-Pierre, "Vom Geist des Ortes zum Geist von Genf/De l'esprit du lieu à l'esprit de Genève," *Anthos*, n° 47, January 2008, pp. 28–29.
Mavrocordatos, Alexandra, "Eclairage des villes: essayons d'y voir clair," *24 heures Immobilier*, week November 26 to December 2, 2014, p. 8.
Veillon, Emilie, "2b architectes: Architektur schafft Einklang zwischen strategischem Denken und kontextuellem Bewusstsein/ Une architecture contextuelle et stratégique," *Viso*, n° 2, 2008, pp. 70–79.
Wirz, Heinz (ed.), "2b–stratégies urbaines concrètes," *De aedibus*, n° 43, Lucerne, Quart Verlag, pp. 34–39.

SUPERKILEN | COPENHAGEN | 2007–2012

Official documents

Kuben, *Superkilen–Det urban liv. Konkurenceprogram*, n.d. [competition brief].

Archives and interviews

Archive consultation: selection of BIG digital documents consulted in the presence of Marie Lançon, BIG premises, Copenhagen, September 29, 2015; Topotek 1 digital documents, consulted in the presence of Vinzenz Adldinger, Topotek 1 premises, Berlin, February 11, 2016.
BIG, Superkilen, Superflex, "Superkilen, 3 zoner, 3 farver–et globalt kvarter," competition boards, October 5, 2007 [Archives Topotek 1].
BIG, Superkilen, Superflex, "Superkilen, 3 zoner, 3 farver–et globalt kvarter," competition submission album, October 5, 2007 [Archives Topotek 1].
Gyldholm Møller, Nanna (project leader at BIG), written interview, October 22, 2015.
Rein-Cano, Martin (partner of Topotek 1), Berlin, interview with the author, February 11, 2016.

Books, chapters, and articles consulted

Benner, Torben, "Nørrebro skal have palmer og springvand," *Politiken.dk, Kultur*, May 20, 2009, https://politiken.dk/kultur/art5589874/Nørrebro-skal-have-palmer-og-springvand online, [accessed October 20, 2015].
"BIG, Topotek 1, Superflex. Superkilen. Copenhagen (Denmark) 2011," *a + t*, n° 38, 2011, pp. 58–65.
BIG, Topotek 1 et Superflex, "Superkilen," *Landskab*, n° 93, 2012, pp. 158–161, English summary, p. 180.
"BIG + Topotek 1 + Superflex. Superkilen. Copenhagen, Denmark," in Jacobo Krauel, *Urban Spaces: Design and Innovation*, Barcelona, Links International, 2013, pp. 54–63.
Bloom, Brett, "Superkilen: Park med ekstrem borgerinddragelse!," *Kritik*, n° 207, April 2013, pp. 47–76.
Bridger, Jessica, "Culture Riot: Copenhagen's Superkilen," *Topos: The International Review of Landscape Architecture and Urban Design*, n° 78, 2012, pp. 41–46.
Bridger, Jessica, "Life on the Wedge: In Copenhagen, Superkilen Rolls Out a Half-Mile Mash-Up of Global Culture," *Landscape Architecture Magazine*, n° 103, 2013, pp. 86–99.
Bridger, Jessica, "Superkilen," *Anthos*, n° 2, 2013, pp. 10–14.
Ciuffi, Valentina, "Il parco dei parchi/ The Park of Parks," *Abitare*, n° 516, 2011, pp. 50–51, 53–54, 56–59, 61–62, 64–67.
Competitionline, "Superkilen–Future Innovate Urban Space in the Outer Nørrebro District. Restricted Competition," February 6, 2007, http://www.competitionline.com/en/results/7445 [accessed March 2, 2016].
Curnier, Sonia, "Expériences urbaines et espaces publics à Copenhague," *Les Cahiers de l'Aspan*, n° 2, 2016, pp. 8–13.
Curnier, Sonia, "Superkilen, Supercherie. Représentation dans les médias spécialisés," *e-publicspace.net*, 2014.
Darrieus, Margaux (ed.) "Aires de jeux," *AMC–Le moniteur architecture*, n° 225, 2013, p. 81.
Georgeva, Krasimira, "Caso studio/Cas d'étude/Case Study. Superflex, Topotek 1, BIG. Superkilen Urban Park. Cultural Diversity Shaping the Urban Space," *Arca International*, n° 117, 2013, pp.14–23.
Hertlein, Vera, "Superkilen in Kopenhagen-Nørrebro," *Bauwelt*, n° 41, 2008, pp. 10–11.
Laugesen, Gerd, "Nørrebro/NV = nørrebro/ copenhagen NV northwest," *Arkitektur DK*, n° 56, 2012, pp. 14–41.
Lenler, Jens and Torben Benner, "Borgere på Nørrebro: Det blev som Realdania ville," *Politiken.dk, Kultur*, July 14, 2010, https://politiken.dk/ibyen/byliv/art5620901/Borgere-på-Nørrebro-Det-blev-som-Realdania-ville [accessed October 20, 2015].
Lenler, Jens and Torben Benner, "Embedsmand benægter telefonsamtale," *Politiken.dk, Kultur*, July 17, 2010, https://politiken.dk/kultur/arkitektur/art5590031/Embedsmand-benægter-telefonsamtale [accessed October 20, 2015].
Marwaha, Parvinder, "BIG Finds Common Ground through Uncommon Objects," *Mark: Another Architecture*, n° 42, 2013, pp. 42–43.
"Parque urbano Superkilen Copenhague (Dinamarca)/Superkilen Urban Park, Copenhagen (Denmark), 2007–2012," *AV Monografías/AV Monographs*, n° 162, 2013, pp. 54–59.
"Projektwettbewerb Superkilen, Kopenhagen," *Anthos*, n° 1, 2009, p. 59.
Reeh, Henrik, "Der Superkeil von Kopenhagen," *Stadt Bauwelt*, n° 193, 2012, pp. 60–67.
Reggiani, Elvira, "Riqualificazione di un'area ferroviaria dismessa, Nørrebro/ Superkilen urban revitalization, Nørrebro," *Industria Delle Costruzioni*, n° 47, 2013, pp. 92–97.
Schäfer, Robert, "Der park der Wunder–Superkilen," *Garten + Landschaft*, n° 122, 2012, pp. 15–19.
Schafranek, Henrik and Christina Møller, "Superkilen. Nørrebro," *Arkitektur DK*, n° 56, 2012, pp. 32–35.
Steiner, Barbara (ed.), *Superkilen. A Project by BIG, Topotek 1, Superflex*, Stockholm/ Oslo, Arvinius + Orfeus Publishing, 2013.
"Superkilen. The Super Wedge Copenhagen," *Arkitektur DK*, n° 6, 2009, pp. 48–51.
"Superkilen," in Yukio Futagawa, *BIG, Bjarke Ingels Group, Recent Project*, Tokyo, A.D.A. Edita, 2013, pp. 30–35.
"Superkilen. Topotek 1," in Chris Van Uffelen, *Pedestrian Zones: Car Free Urban Spaces*, Salenstein, Braun Publishers, 2015, pp. 114–117.
Topotek 1, "Superkilen, Kopenhagen, Dänemark/Superkilen, Copenhagen, Denmark," in Bund von Deutscher Landschaftsarchitekten, *Zeiträume–Time Scales: Zeitgenössische deutsche Landschaftsarchitektur Contemporary/German Landscape Architecture*, Basel/Boston/ Berlin, Birkhäuser, 2013, pp. 72–73.
Wollheim, Ralf, "Vereinte Nationen," *DB–Deutsche Bauzeitung*, n° 10, 2013, pp. 14–15.

Background and related topics

Brorman Jensen, Boris, "Towards a Critical Pragmatism," *Arkitektur DK*, n° 6, 2009, pp. 2–7.
"Fake Realities. Martin Rein-Cano and Lorenz Dexler in Conversation with Thilo Folkerts," in Thilo Folkerts (ed.), *Topotek 1. Eine Landschaftsskulptur für München/A Landscape Sculpture for Munich*, Basel/Boston/Berlin, Birkhäuser, 2010, pp. 9–35.
Kaasa, Adam and Ricky Burdett, "Color and the City," in Gareth Doherty (ed.), "Urbanism of Color," *New Geographies*, special issue, n° 3, 2010, Cambridge, Harvard University Press, pp. 54–63.
"Kile" in Andreas Blinkenberg and Poul Høybye, *Dictionnaire Danois-Français. Dansk Fransk Ordbog*, Copenhagen, Nyt Nordisk Forlag, Arnold Busck, vol. 1, 1975, p. 827.

About Op Art

Bridget Riley: Flashback. London, Hayward Publishing, 2009.
Dahhan, Bernard, *Victor Vasarely ou la connaissance d'un art moléculaire*, Paris, Editions Denoël/Gonthier, 1979.
Doherty, Gareth (ed.), "Urbanism of Color," *New Geographies*, special issue, n° 3, 2010, Cambridge, Harvard University Press.
Dezeuze, Anna, "The 1960s: A Decade of Out-of-Bounds," in Amelia Jones (ed.) *A Companion to Contemporary Art since 1945*, Oxford, Blackwell Publishing, 2006, pp. 38–59.
Hallain, Marc, *Vasarely*, Paris, Fernand Hazan, 1974.
Moorhouse, Paul (ed.), *Bridget Riley*, London, Tate Publishing, 2003.
Musée d'Art moderne de la Ville de Paris, *Bridget Riley: Retrospective*, Paris, Paris Musées, 2008.
Schröder, Klaus Albrecht, "Utopie de la géomètrie/Utopia of Geometry," in Musée Olympique Lausanne, *Victor Vasarely. 50 ans de création/50 Years of Creation*, exhibition catalog, Lausanne, International Olympic Committee, 1995, pp. 14–21.

MFO-PARK | ZURICH | 1998–2002

Official documents

Gartenbau- und Landwirtschaftsamt der Stadt Zürich, *MFO-PARK/Zentrum Zürich Nord. Zweistufiger Konzept-und Projektwettbewerb. Wettbewerbsprogramm*, November 25, 1997 [competition program].

Archives and interviews

Archive consultation: all paper documents kept, Raderschallpartner premises, Meilen, August 16, 2015 and December 17, 2015; selected digital documents transmitted by e-mail, January 16, 2016.
Burckhardt+Partner Architekten, Raderschall Landschaftsarchitekten (Arbeitsgemeinschaft), "Parkhaus,"

competition boards for the first round—concept phase—of the competition for the development of MFO-Park, March 1998 [Archives Raderschallpartner].
Burckhardt+Partner Architekten, Raderschall Landschaftsarchitekten (Arbeitsgemeinschaft), "Parkhaus," competition boards for the second round—project phase—of the competition for the development of MFO-Park, August 1998 [Archives Raderschallpartner].
Aubort Raderschall, Sibylle (partner at Raderschallpartner), Meilen, interview with the author, August 26, 2015.
Aubort Raderschall, Sibylle and Roland Raderschall (partners at Raderschallpartner), Meilen, informal discussion with the author, December 17, 2015.

Books, chapters, and articles consulted

Aberle, Waltraud, "Das 'Park-Haus' nach dem Vorbild einer 'Treillage'," *Der Gartenbau*, n° 23, 2002, pp. 16–17.
Adam, Hubertus, "Intervention erwünscht: Parks in Zürich neu-oerlikon," *DB—Deutsche Bauzeitung*, n° 141, 2007, pp. 22–47.
Andersson, Thorbjörn, "A Critical View of Landscape Architecture," *Topos: The International Review of Landscape Architecture and Urban Design*, n° 49, 2004, pp.22–32.
Architekturforum Zürich, Grün Stadt Zürich, "Zürcher Gartenlust, Neue Parkanlagen für Zürich," exhibition catalog, Zurich, Architekturforum Zürich (August 27–October 27, 2003).
Barman-Krämer, Gabriela, "Der MFO-Park in Zürich-Oerlikon: ein zukünftiger Parktypus auf dem ehemaligen Industrieareal," *Topiaria helvetica: Jahrbuch*, 2004, pp. 51–55.
"Burckhardt+Partner Architects, MFO-Park," in Virginia McLeod, *Detail in Contemporary Landscape Architecture*, London, Laurence King Publishing, 2012, pp. 26–29.
"Eine Riesen-Pergola: Das Rankgerüst des MFO-parks in Zürich," *Garten + Landschaft*, n° 12, 2002, p. 48.
Glanzmann, Jutta, "Die Pflanzenhalle. Der Neue Park in Zürich Nord," *tec 21*, n° 46, 2002, p. 7–10.
Holl, Christian, "Im Massstab: Zwei neue Parks im Zentrum Zürich Nord," *DB—Deutsche Bauzeitung*, n° 137, 2003, pp. 47–53.
Hönig, Roderick and Claudia Moll, "Die Entdeckung neuer Räume," *Hochparterre*, n° 4, 2009, pp. 20–28.
Kingsbury, Noel, "Supporting Role," *Garden Illustrated*, n° 118, 2006, pp. 58–63.
"Landscape—ein modulares Möbelsystem. Fünf Möbeltypen—eine Designsprache von Burri," *Garten + Landschaft*, n° 12, 2010, pp. 40–41.
Lerch, Gabi and André Schmid, "Und noch viel mehr/Et bien plus encore," *Anthos*, n° 1, 2003, pp. 4–9.
Lootsma, Bart, "Angehäufte Entfremdung. Neu-Oerlikon in Zürichs Norden," *werk, bauen + wohnen*, n° 9, 2006, pp. 34–41.
Meret, Ernst, "Seil um Seil," *Hochparterre*, n° 10, 2006, pp. 30–33.
"MFO-park in Zürich," *Architektur + Wettbewerbe*, n° 200, 2004, pp. 26–29.
"MFO-park, Zürich 2002," *a+t*, n° 26, 2005, pp. 102–105.
"MFO-park, Zurich, Switzerland," *Topos: The International Review of Landscape Architecture and Urban Design*, n° 60, 2007, pp. 116–117.
"Parc MFO à Oerlikon, Zürich, Suisse. Burckhardt+Partner et Raderschall," *L'Architecture d'aujourd'hui*, n° 363, 2006, pp. 70–71.
"Park in Zürich," *Detail*, n° 44, 2004, pp. 664–669.
Raderschall, Roland and Christoph Wieser, "MFO-park, Zürich: Arkitekt, raderschall landschaftsarchitekten," *Arkitektur: The Swedish Review of Architecture*, n° 102, 2002, pp. 40–47.
Roth, Steffen, "Urbane Landschaftsarchitektur in Zürich," *Garten + Landschaft*, n° 11, 2004, pp. 18–21.
Roth, Ueli, "Neuer Stadtteil Zentrum Zürich Nord," *Topos: The International Review of Landscape Architecture and Urban Design*, n° 3, 2002, pp. 31–35.
Schindler, Anne, "Unter Lianen," *Hochparterre*, n° 10, 2002, p. 62.
Simon, Axel, "Zürich fegt, blüht und baut," *Garten + Landschaft*, n° 11, 2001, pp. 22–24.
Simon Axel, "Das grüne Park-Haus," *Garten + Landschaft*, n° 112, 2002, pp. 31–33.
Van Der Plas, Hein, "Von Bank zu Bank/D'un banc à l'autre," *Anthos*, n° 2, 2005, pp. 8–13.
Weilacher, Udo, "Green Fur on a Steel Skeleton. MFO-Park in Zurich," in Udo Weilacher, *Gardens: Profiles of Contemporary European Landscape Architecture*, Basel/Berlin/New York, Birkhäuser, 2004, pp. 137–141.
Weilacher, Udo, "Grüner Pelz auf Stahlskelett," *NZZ Folio, Gärten*, March 2003, pp. 62–63.
Wieser, Christoph, "Von Parks und Plätzen im Zentrum Zürich Nord," *werk, bauen + wohnen*, n° 5, 2003, pp. 18–29.
Wullschleger, Peter, Hayal Oezkan, and Lucas Handschin, "Landscape Architecture in Zurich. A Historical Timeline," *Topos: The International Review of Landscape Architecture and Urban Design*, n° 73, 2010, pp. 1–15 [supplement for 48th IFLA World Congress, Zurich, 2011].

Background and related topics

Colonna, Francesco, *Hypnerotomachie, ou Discours du songe de Poliphile, déduisant comme amour le combat à l'occasion de Polia*, trans from Italian to French by Jean Martin and Jacques Gohorry, Paris, Payot, 1926. [Orig. ed. in Italian, *Hypnerotomachia Poliphili*, 1499].
Foster, Norman, "Sainsbury Centre for the Visual Arts. East Anglia, Norwich, G.B.," *L'Architecture*, n° 213, 1981, pp. 72–74.
"Industriegebiet und Bahnhofareal Zürich-Oerlikon, Überarbeitung," *Schweizer Ingenieur und Architekt*, Wettbewerbe, n° 48, 1992, pp. 918–922
Joedicke, Jürgen, "Technologie und Architektur: Sainsbury Centre for the Visual Arts, University of East Anglia, Norwich," *Bauen + Wohnen*, n° 33, 1979, pp. 287–294.
Loderer, Benedikt, "Skelett oder Gewebe," *Hochparterre*, n° 12, 1992, p. 57.
Loderer, Benedikt, "Zentrum Zürich Nord," *Hochparterre*, n° 11, 1994, p. 31.
Loderer, Benedikt, "Die Heimliche Hauptstadt," *Hochparterre*, n° 10, 2001, pp. 14–21.
Loderer, Benedikt, "Wohnanteil, Parkplätze, Freiraum," *Hochparterre*, n° 3, 2004, pp. 12–13.
Loderer, Benedikt, "Neueste Masche: Kein Gewebe," *Beilage zu Hochparterre*, n° 6–7, 2005, pp. 10–11.
Roth, Ueli, "Neuer Stadtteil Zentrum Zürich Nord," *Topos: The International Review of Landscape Architecture and Urban Design*, n° 3, 2002, pp. 31–35.
Steigmeier, Andreas, "Asea Brown Boveri (ABB)," in *Dictionnaire historique de la Suisse (DHS)*, vol. 1, Hauterive, Attinger, 2002, pp. 534–535.
Von Salis, Peter C., "Maschinenfabrik Oerlikon (MFO)," in *Dictionnaire historique de la Suisse (DHS)*, vol. 8, Hauterive, Attinger, 2009, p. 312.

THEATERPLEIN | ANTWERP | 2004–2008

Official documents

Vlaams Bouwmeester, *Heraanleg van het Theaterplein en omgeving te Antwerpen*, n.d. Available online: https://www.vlaamsbouwmeester.be/sites/default/files/open_call_project_files_not_started/55dfcf5ed48445359d6089fc78595fdf.pdf [accessed June 20, 2016].

Archives and interviews

Consultation of the archives: selection of preserved paper and digital documents, Studio Paola Viganò premises, February 25, 2016.
Studio 04 Bernardo Secchi and Paola Viganò, Dirk Jaspaert, "Spazio s-misurato," album accompanying Open Oproep submission, n.d. [date estimated December 2004], [non-paginated]. [Archives Studio Associato Secchi-Viganò].
Studio 04 Bernardo Secchi et Paola Viganò, Dirk Jaspaert, "Spazio s-misurato," oral presentation for Open Oproep, n.d. [estimated December 2004], [Archives Studio Associato Secchi-Viganò].
Studio Associato Bernardo Secchi Paola Viganò, "Theaterplein, Antwerp—International competition," n.d., http://www.secchi-vigano.eu/atS04/at%20S04_theaterplein.html [accessed June 29, 2015].
Viganò, Paola (associate of Studio Associato Secchi-Viganò/Studio Paola Viganò), Lausanne, interview with the author, July 1, 2015.

Books, chapters, and articles consulted

Bravo Bordas, David, "Theater Square," n.d., http://www.publicspace.org/en/works/f116-theater-square [accessed June 22, 2016].
Leloutre, Géry and Hubert Lionnez, "Rationalité minimum: interview of Bernardo Secchi and Paola Viganò," *A+*, n° 197, 2005, pp. 40–41.
"Piazza del teatro ad Anversa, Belgio/Theater square, Antwerp, Belgium," *Industria Delle Costruzioni*, n° 46/428, 2012, pp. 22–27.
"Studio Associato Secchi-Viganò: Theater square, Antwerp (Belgium), 2008," *A + t*, n° 37, 2011, pp. 100–107.
Vanderburgh, David and Carlo Menon, "The Finger and the Moon: Belgian Competitions in Their Representational Context," in Chupin, Jean-Pierre, Carmela Cucuzzella, Bechara Helal, *Architecture Competitions and the Production of Culture, Quality and Knowledge. An International Inquiry*, Montreal, Potential Architecture Books, 2015, pp. 36–53.
Van Toorn, Roemer, "The Ultimate Value of Beinahe Nichts," in *The Specific and the Singular: Architecture in Flanders*, Antwerp, Flemish Architecture Institute, 2010, pp. 118–125.

Background and related topics

Ibelings, Hans, *Designing for the Public*, Amsterdam, Sun Architecture Publishers/Flemish Government architect, 2009.
Secchi, Bernardo, "Progetto di suolo," *Casabella*, n° 520, 1986, pp. 19–23.
Studio Associato Bernardo Secchi Paola Viganò, "Along the Dijle in Mechelen," n.d., http://www.secchi-vigano.eu/atS00/at%20S00_dijle-lamot%20(mechelen).html [accessed June 28, 2015].
Viganò, Paola, *La città elementare*, Skira, Milan, 1999.
Viganò, Paola, "I territori dell' urbanistica/The Territories of Urbanism," *Lotus International*, n° 150, 2012, pp. 106–113.
Vlaams Bouwmeester, "De Open Oproep," n.d., http://www.vlaamsbouwmeester.be/nl/instrumenten/open-oproep/info [accessed June 20, 2016].

PASEO MARÍTIMO DE LA PLAYA DE PONIENTE | BENIDORM | 2002–2009

Official documents

Unavailable

Archives and interviews

Consultation of the archives: impossible (digital archives lost). Refer to the books published by the OAB office and the monograph on the project detailed below.

Martí Galí, Xavier (associate at OAB), Barcelona, interview with the author in French, February 17, 2016.

Carlos Ferrater Partnership (OAB), *Synchronizing Geometry. Landscape, Architecture and Construction,* Barcelona, Actar, 2006.

Padura, Manel and Carlos Ferrater (eds), *Carlos Ferrater. Office of Architecture Barcelona*, El Masnou (Barcelona), Editorial Manel Padura, 2006.

OAB, *Office of Architecture in Barcelona. Carlos Ferrater & Partners*, Barcelona, Actar, 2010.

Martí Galí, Xavier, "Benidorm West Beach Promenade," in OAB, *Office of Architecture in Barcelona. Carlos Ferrater & Partners*, Barcelona, Actar, 2010, pp. 200–229.

Ferrater, Carlos and Xavier Martí Galí, *Benidorm*, Barcelona, Actar, 2011.

Books, chapters, and articles consulted

"Aménagement littoral, plage du Ponant, Benidorm, Espagne: Carlos Ferrater et Xavier Martí Galí," *L'Architecture d'aujourd'hui*, n° 363, 2006, pp. 104–105.

Anglès, Magda, "Benidorm, Spain: Playa de poniente esplanade," *Topos: The International Review of Landscape Architecture and Urban Design*, n° 72, 2010, pp. 22–27.

"Carlos Ferrater and Xavier Martí Galí/ OAB. Seafront of Benidorm," *A + U: Architecture and Urbanism*, n° 5, 2011, pp. 108–113.

"Carlos Ferrater and Xavier Martí Galí/OAB. Seafront of Benidorm," *A + U: Architecture and Urbanism*, n° 1, 2014, pp. 86–89.

"Carlos Ferrater. Obra reciente/Recent Work," *2G*, n° 32, Editorial Gustavo Gili, Barcelona. 2004.

"Carlos Ferrater: Paseo Marítimo de la Playa de Poniente, Benidorm, España, 2003," *Lotus International*, n° 125, 2005, pp. 88–91.

Lentz, Linda, "Making Waves/Beachfront, Benidorm" *Architectural Record*, n° 198/7, 2013, pp. 54–55.

"Lungomare di Benidorm, Spagna/ Benidorm West Beach Promenade, Spain," *Industria Delle Costruzioni*, n° 47/430, 2013, pp. 28–37.

Macher, Julia, "Der paseo de Poniente Benidorm. Architekten, Carlos Ferrater, Xavier Martí Galí (OAB)," *Bauwelt*, n° 101/32, 2010, pp. 14–21.

Montaner, Josep Maria, "Taxonomia de sistemas formales en la obra de Carlos Ferrater. A Taxonomy of Formal Systems in the Work of Carlos Ferrater," in "Carlos Ferrater. Obra reciente/Recent Work," *2G*, n° 32, Editorial Gustavo Gili, Barcelona. 2004, pp. 4–19.

"OAB. Poniente Beach Promenade, Benidorm, Spain, 2009," *a + t*, n° 35–36, 2010, pp. 200–211.

"OAB—Carlos Ferrater & Martí Galí. Requalification du front de mer, Benidorm, Espagne/Reinvention of the Seafront, Benidorm, Spain," *AMC—Le moniteur architecture*, special issue, "Terre cuite," 2013, pp. 120–123.

Padura, Manel, "Conversation" in Manel Padura and Carlos Ferrater (eds), *Carlos Ferrater. Office of Architecture Barcelona*, El Masnou (Barcelona), Editorial Manel Padura, 2006, pp. 10–19.

"Paseo Marítimo, Benidorm (Alicante)/ Waterfront, Benidorm (Alicante) Spain," *AV Monografías/AV Monographs*, n° 141–142, 2010, pp. 52–59.

"Paseo Marítimo de Benidorm, Alicante/ Waterfront of Benidorm, Alicante. OAB/ Ferrater & Martí Galí," *Arquitectura Viva*, special issue, "Ceramica," 2010, pp. 16–21.

Worthmann, Merten, "Zwischen Sand und Asphalt: Neue Strandpromenade für Benidorm von studio OAB," *Baumeister*, n° 107(1), 2010, pp. 14–15.

Background and related topics

Ayuntamiento de Benidorm, Concejalía de Cultura, *Benidorm, los orígenes de la ciudad vertical*, exhibition catalog, 2006.

Martorell, Josep, Oriol Bohigas, and David Mackay, "Paseo Marítimo de Benidorm. Benidorm Promenade," *Via Arquitectura*, n° 02, 1997, pp. 68–73. Available online: http://www.via-arquitectura.net/02/02-066.htm [accessed August 25, 2016].

MÅLØV AKSEN – THE STATIONSPLADS | MÅLØV | 2008–2010

Official documents

Ballerup Kommune, *Katalog for Byrumskvaliteter i Måløv Aksen*, March 2008 [annex to the competition brief].

Ballerup Kommune, *Måløv Aksen. Indbudt projektkonkurrence*, June 2008. [Competition brief].

Ballerup Kommune, *Måløv Aksen. Indbudt projektkonkurrence. Dommerkomiteens Betænkning*, October 2008. [Jury report], available online http://www.arkitektforeningen.dk/sites/arkitektforeningen.dk/files/DB_maaloevakse_0.pdf [accessed September 11, 2015]

Archives and interviews

Consultation of the archives: impossible (digital archives misplaced). Competition submission and presentation material sent by email on October 23, 2015.

ADEPT, LiW Planning, "Måløv Aksen—En oplevelse der skaber sammenhæng," competition illustration boards, September 2008 [Archives ADEPT]

ADEPT, LiW Planning, "Måløv Aksen—En oplevelse der skaber sammenhæng," competition brochure, September 2008 [Archives ADEPT]

Hjort, Annegrite and Martin Laursen, "Måløv Aksen—nu med graffiti. Den Trygge Kommune, 10. oktober 2013," presentation media, October 2013 [Archives ADEPT].

ADEPT, "The Måløv Axis," n.d., http://adept.dk/index.php?id=41#40^2^144 [accessed September 18, 2015].

Krogh, Martin (partner at ADEPT), Copenhagen, interview with the author, September 21, 2015.

LiW Planning, "Krohaven," n.d., http://www.liwplanning.dk/eng/#/krohaven [accessed March 23, 2017].

LiW Planning, "Måløv Aksen," n.d., http://www.liwplanning.dk/#/url_maaloevaksen [accessed September 18, 2015 and March 23, 2017].

Books, chapters, and articles consulted

"ADEPT," *A + U: Architecture and Urbanism*, n° 10, 2012, pp. 94–115.

"ADEPT Præsentation af tegnestuen og dens arbejder/Presentation and Selected Works," *Arkitektur DK*, n° 1, 2012, pp. 12–21.

"ADEPT. Måløv Axis," in Jacobo Krauel, *Urban Spaces, Design and Innovation*, Barcelona, Links International, 2013, pp. 184–189.

Akademisk Arkitektforening, "Et tiltrængt løft til Måløv," May 11, 2012, https://www.arkitektforeningen.dk [accessed September 8, 2015].

Bustler editors, "Danish Landscape Award 2010 Goes to Måløv Axis," www.bustler.net, October 4, 2010, http://bustler.net/news/1786/danish-landscape-award-2010-goes-to-m-229-l-248-v-axis [accessed September 11, 2015].

Curnier, Sonia, "Expériences urbaines et espaces publics à Copenhague," *Les Cahiers de l'Aspan*, n° 2, 2016, pp. 8–13.

"Eje Måløv/Måløv Axis. Ballerup, Denmark," *Paisea*, n° 029, 2014, pp. 60–62.

Fischer, Jacob, "Landskabsprisen 2010," *Landskab*, n° 7/91, 2010, p. 153, summary in English, p. 176.

"Måløv Aksen | Måløv," in Ministeriet for By, Bolig og Landdistrikter, *66 Nyere byrum, Et inspiraonskatalog*, 2012, pp. 64–65, 149, 151.

Westergaard, Lisbeth, "Måløv aksen—fra et ingenmandsland til et allemandsland," *Landskab*, n° 7/91, 2010, pp. 154–157, summary in English, p. 176.

Background and related topics

Ballerup Kommune, "Søndergård," n.d., https://ballerup.dk/soendergaard [accessed March 15, 2017].

Le Maire Wandall, Barbara and Karen Margrethe Krogh, "Dialog eller arkitektur ? ... eller begge dele?," *Landskab*, n° 7, 2008, pp. 150–155, summary in English, p. 172.

Mader, Günter, "Topographie," *Anthos*, n° 1, 2004, pp. 4–9.

PLATZ DER MENSCHENRECHTE | RIEM – MUNICH | – 2005

Official documents

Landeshauptstadt München, *Messestadt Riem. Das Projekt—Planung und Realisierung*, June 2009.

Landeshauptstadt München, *Messestadt Riem. Das Projekt—Vom Flugfeld zum neuen Stadtteil—eine Zwischenbilanz*, n.d.

Archives and interviews

Archive consultation: selection of paper documents, Valentien + Valentien premises, Wessling, June 23, 2015.

Valentien + Valentien, *Platz der Menschenrechte. Messestadt München Riem. Zusammenfassung*, n.d. [Archives Valentien + Valentien].

Valentien + Valentien, *Platz der Menschenrechte. Messestadt München Riem. Projektbeschreibung*, n.d. [Archives Valentien + Valentien].

Valentien + Valentien, *Planungsphase III Entwurf vom 16.11.2002/Bürgerbeteiligung*, November 2002 [work report, unpublished] [Archives Valentien + Valentien].

Valentien + Valentien, *Platz der Menschenrechte., Messestadt München Riem*, n.d. [post-realisation], [project presentation report, unpublished document] [Archives Valentien + Valentien].

Valentien, Christoph (partner of Valentien + Valentien), Wessling, interview with the author, June 23, 2015.

Books, chapters, and articles consulted

Herwig, Olivier, "Die Mitte der Peripherie Riem, Munich," *Garten + Landschaft*, n° 115/6, 2005, pp. 19–22.

Loschwitz, Gesa, "Platz der Menschenrechte," *Garten + Landschaft*, n° 5, 2005, pp. 18–20.

"Menschenrechte Platz. Munich. Alemania. Valentien + Valentien," *Paisea*, n° 009, 2009, pp. 56–59.

"Platz der Menschenrechte," in Lisa Diedrich et al. (eds), *On Site*, Series, Landscape Architecture Europe, Basel/ Boston/Berlin, Birkhäuser, 2009. p. 137.

Background and related topics

Camus, Albert and Francis Ponge, *Correspondances, 1941–1957*, edition presented and annotated by Jean-Marie Gleize Paris, Gallimard, 2013.

Diedrich, Lisa, "Stadtentwicklung mittels public-private-partnerships in München: Privatwirtschaft und Kommune: die Karten neu mischen," *werk, bauen + wohnen*, n° 87, 2000, pp. 20–23.

Ponge, Francis, "Le Carnet du bois de pins" in Francis Ponge, *La rage de l'expression,* Paris, Gallimard, Collection, 2011. [first legal deposit, Gallimard 1976, first publication of "Le Carnet du bois de pins," Lausanne, Mermod, 1947], pp. 97–172. German version consulted by Valentien + Valentien: Francis Ponge, *Das Notizbuch vom Kiefernwald und La Mounine,* Berlin, Suhrkamp, 1995.

Valentien, Christoph, "Metamorphose einer Planungskonzeption," *Garten+Landschaft*, n° 12, 1993, pp. 36–43.
Valentien, Christoph, "Freiraumsystem und gartenkünstlerischer Entwurf," *Der Architekt*, n° 6, 1997, pp. 373–375.
Valentien, Christoph, "Neue Messestadt München-Riem/Nouveau 'Messestadt München-Riem'," *Anthos*, n° 37, 1998, pp. 48–51.

BYMILEN | COPENHAGEN | 2007–2010

Official documents

Københavns Kommune, *Lokalplan nr. 403 "Rigsarkivet,"* Copenhagen, January 13, 2006.

Archives and interviews

Archive consultation: preserved set of digital documents, SLA premises, Copenhagen, September 25, 2015.
SLA, *Dipositionsforlag1*, report of the presentation for the client, December 2005.
SLA, *Præsentation_SEB_08092010*, report of the presentation for the client, September 8, 2010.
SEB, SLA, "SEB nyt byrum. En bjergside på Kalvebod Brygge," 2010 [report of the project presentation, *Præsentation_SEB_08092010.pdf*, Archives SLA].
Visit of the project with Morten Leicht Jeppsen from SLA on a guided tour entitled "Why We Love Trees" during the RISING Architecture Week, Copenhagen, September 16, 2015.
Hornsyld, Ulla (project leader SLA Landskabsarkitekter), Copenhagen, interview with the author, September 25, 2015.

Books, chapters, and articles consulted

Andersson, Stig L., "Klimatilpasset Byrum ved SEB i København," *Landskab*, n° 91/7, 2010, pp. 158–161.
Andersson, Stig L., "Processurbanisme—Byen som økosystem," *Landskab*, n° 1, 2011, pp. 15–17.
Andersson, Stig L., "Både vision och method. Processurbanismen om staden som aktivt ecosystem," *Utemiljö*, n° 5, 2012, pp. II–III.
Andersson, Stig L., "Debat: Efter Naturen," *Landskab*, n° 4, 2012, pp. 125–126.
Andersson, Stig L., "In Search of Lost Nature," *Healthscape*, n° 1, 2012, pp. 110–127.
Andersson, Stig L., "Sandbanken, vid Banken. Ett Stadsrum i samklang med naturen," *Utemiljö*, n° 5, 2012, pp. IV–V.
Bomsdorf, Clemens, "Verbindende flora: Aussenraum der SEB-bank," *DB - Deutsche Bauzeitung*, n° 146/3, 2012, pp. 38–43.
"Bymilen, København/Copenhagen" in Annemarie Lund (ed.), *Ny Agenda 2. Dansk landskabsarkitektur/New Agenda 2. Danish Landscape Architecture. 2009–13*, Bogværket, Nykøbing Sjælland, 2014, pp. 186–189.
Colazza, Laura, "Sede centrale della SEB Bank. SEB Bank Headquarters," *Industria Delle Costruzioni*, n° 47/431, 2013, pp. 74–77.
Fauve, Charlotte, "Dune danoise. 'City Dune'" à Copenhague, Danemark," *Ecologik*, n° 35, 2013, p. 42.
Hauxner, Malene, "Supergraphik und Superlogik. Supergraphics and superlogic," *Topos: The International Review of Landscape Architecture and Urban Design*, n° 40, September 2002, pp. 79–85.
Olsen, Asger, "Debat: The Flower Power Man," *Landskab*, n° 1, 2011, p. 21.
"SEB Banken/Bymilen. Offentlighed omkring kontorhuset," in Ministeriet for By, Bolig og Landdistrikter, *66 Nyere byrum, Et inspiraonskatalog*, 2012, pp. 96–97, p. 151.
"SLA—Stig L. Andersson. The City Dune," in Jacobo Krauel, *Urban Spaces, Design and Innovation*, Barcelona, Links International, 2013, pp. 290–299.
Stahlschmidt, Per and Peter Thorsen, "Debat: Processurbanisme—byøkologi eller varm luft?," *Landskab*, n° 1, 2011, pp. 18–19.
Thorsen, Peter, "Debat: Landskab og den faglige debat," *Landskab*, n° 1, 2011, p. 20.
Toftsø Nyholm, Line and Kjeld Vindum, "SLA Bymilen Bypark/Urban Park," *Arkitektur DK*, n° 6, 2011, pp. 12–19.
Vindum, Kjeld, "Stig L. Andersson. Interview," *Arkitektur DK*, n° 6, 2011, pp. 8–11.
Wærn, Rasmus, "Kommentar. Comments," *Arkitektur DK*, n° 6, 2011, pp. 20–23.

Background and related topics

Andersson, Stig L., "Eine Wolke ist wie ein zerknülltes Blatt Papier. A Cloud is Just Another Sheet of Crumpled Paper," *Topos: The International Review of Landscape Architecture and Urban Design*, n° 40, September 2002, pp. 86–93.
Andersson, Stig L., "Public Open Form and Space," conference report, *Odprt javni prostor. Public Open Space. Design—Management—Maintenance*, April, 10–11, 2008, Ljubljana, pp. 24–27.
Andersson, Stig L., *Empowerment of Aesthetics, Catalogue for the Danish Pavilion at the 14th International Architecture Exhibition La Biennale di Venezia 2014*, Skive, Forlaget Wunderbuch, 2014, pp. 9–10. Available online: https://issuu.com/sla_architects/docs/empowerment_of_aesthetics_-_sla [accessed May 5, 2017].
Natur Vårds Verket, "Naturum," n.d., http://www.naturvardsverket.se/Naturum [accessed May 3, 2017].
"Projekte aus dem Büro SLA. Projects by SLA Landscape Architects," *Topos: The International Review of Landscape Architecture and Urban Design*, n° 40, September 2002, pp. 94–106.
Strømberg, Ulla, "Arkitekturbiennalen Venedig 2014. Arkitektur, tak, men ingen Arkitekter!," *Landskab*, n° 5, 2014, pp. 132–142.
Tranberg, Lene and Stig L. Andersson, "Det grønne flow, The Green Flow," *Arkitektur DK*, n° 6, 2011, pp. 6–7.
Vindum, Kjeld, "Lene Tranberg. Interview," *Arkitektur DK*, n° 6, 2011, pp. 24–27.

IMAGE CREDITS

The author wishes to express her sincere gratitude to all those who assisted her in the compilation of this iconography, by providing images, granting permission to reproduce their archive documents, or supplying other information.

Cover illustration Jenna Gesse based on the plan of Superkilen's black square, Copenhagen, Denmark. Original drawing by Topotek 1 / BIG

Icons (p. 13–15 / p. 65 / p. 101 / p. 135 / p. 169 / p. 205) Sonia Curnier based on a figure by Gehl Architects

3.2.14 / 3.2.16 /3.2.52 / 3.2.54 / 3.2.56 / 3.2.58 / 3.3.1 / 3.3.11–3.3.12 / 3.3.26–3.3.28 / 3.3.45–3.3.47 / 3.3.51–3.3.53 / 3.3.55 / 3.3.57 / 3.3.59 / 3.4.7 / 3.4.14 / 3.4.16–3.4.19 / 3.4.24–3.4.29 / 3.4.33 / 3.4.35 / 3.4.51/ 3.4.54 / 3.4.57–3.4.58 / 3.5.5 / 3.5.24 / 3.5.26 / 3.5.28–3.5.30 / 3.5.32–3.5.36 / 3.5.57–3.5.60 / 3.5.68–3.5.69 Sonia Curnier

1.1 Collage Sonia Curnier – Photos Jan Gehl, Lars Gemzøe, source: GEHL Jan, GEMZØE Lars, *New City Spaces, Strategies and Projects*, Copenhague, The Danish Architectural Press, 2001
1.2 Collage Sonia Curnier – Photos (from top left to bottom right): Valentien + Valentien, photo Christoph Valentien; KBP.EU (Karres en Brands – WERK – Sangberg Architects), photo Ty Stange; photo Sonia Curnier; BIG – Topotek1 – Superflex, photo Iwan Baan; Atelier Descombes Rampini; ADEPT – LiW Planning; 2b / S.Bender-Ph. Béboux – S.Collet – CA.Presset – Ch. Robert-Tissot; Studio Associato Bernardo Secchi Paola Viganò, photo © Teresa Cos; © SLA; OAB, photo Alejo Bagué; photo Sonia Curnier; BIG – Topotek1 – Superflex, photo Iwan Baan; J. Mayer H. architects, photo Fernando Alda; TVK architectes urbanistes, Clément Guillaume; Paredes Pino; PPAG – photo © Roland Krauss

0.1 / 2.25 / 3.2.2 LLP – Front Design, photo Tor Lindstrand
0.2 / 3.4.5 JDS Architects – Urban Agency Sloth Møller, photo © Julien Lanoo
0.3 / 2.34 Gehl Architects
0.4 / 2.17–2.18 / 3.1.22 / 3.2.11 / 3.2.34 Ville de Genève, photo Alain Granchamp
0.5 / 3.3.48 / 3.3.60 / 3.3.62 Studio Associato Bernardo Secchi Paola Viganò, photo © Teresa Cos
1.3 Plan du place des Terreaux, Lyon, 1991–1994, Christian Drevet Architecte © 2022; ProLitteris, Zurich – Daniel Buren © DB / 2022, ProLitteris, Zurich
1.4 / 3.2.27–3.2.28 KBP.EU. (Karres en Brands – WERK – Sangberg Architects)
2.1–2.7 Photos Alexandre Chemetoff, Jean-Louis Cohen, Carmen Fiol Costa. Source: *AMC-architecture* n°2, October 1983, pp. 42–59
2.8–2.9 Photos Jan Gehl, Lars Gemzøe
2.10–2.16 Photos © Gérard Dufresne
2.19 / 3.5.1 Vogt Landschaftsarchitekten
2.20 / 3.2.1 Topotek 1, photo © Hanns Joosten
2.21 Latitude Nord, photo Wolfgang Mülke, München
2.22 Photo David van der Mark, https://commons.wikimedia.org/wiki/File:Westerpark_zomer.jpg, CC BY_SA 2.0
2.23 © photo haut-relief
2.24 In Situ / Jalbert – Tardivon, photo Karolina Samborska
2.26 OMGEVING, photo Pol De Wilde
2.27 / 3.1.1 Buro Lubbers
2.28 / 3.2.5 / 3.4.4 1:1 Landskab
2.29 Carve NL, photo Marleen Beek, Amsterdam
2.30 Rainer Schmidt, photo Müller-Naumann
2.31 Photo © Roland Fischer, Zürich (Switzerland) / Wikimedia Commons / CC-BY-SA-3.0 Unported
2.32 Atelier Descombes Rampini, photo Martin Stollenwerk
2.33 Lolà Domènech, arqt, photo Adrià Goula
3.1.2 Miralles Tagliabue EMBT, photo Alex Gaultier
3.1.3 PPAG architects, photo © PPAG architects
3.1.4 / 3.1.9–3.1.21 / 3.1.23–3.1.27 / 4.6 / 4.9 / 4.19 Atelier Descombes Rampini
3.1.5 Stutz Grafik + Design – Stauffenegger + Partner – Lee Mundwiler, photo Ruedi Walti, Basel
3.1.6 photo Joël Deltreil
3.1.7 / 3.1.28 / 3.2.7 / 3.2.35 / 3.3.38 / 3.4.6 / 3.4.36 / 3.5.6 / 3.5.37 Google Earth
3.1.8 / 3.2.23 Ville de Genève
3.1.29 État de la place du Château-d'Eau en 1811, à partir des plans Verniquet (1793–1799) et Jacoubet (1836), plan de synthèse © DU-SDER, Ville de Paris, Direction de l'Urbanisme
3.1.30 État de la place du Château-d'Eau en 1867, à partir du plan Place du Château-d'Eau, 1879, AP, VO11 3032, plan de synthèse © DU-SDER, Ville de Paris, Direction de l'Urbanisme
3.1.31 État de la place de la République en 1884, à partir du plan d'ensemble, signé Bouvard, 22 février 1881, AP, VM 93.1, plan de synthèse © DU-SDER, Ville de Paris, Direction de l'Urbanisme
3.1.32–3.1.33 Bernard Millot / Ville de Paris
3.1.34 / 3.1.36 / 3.1.38–3.1.40 / 3.1.43–3.1.49 / 3.1.51 / 4.10 TVK architectes urbanistes
3.1.35 / 3.1.42 TVK architectes urbanistes – myluckypixel, photo Air-images
3.1.37 TVK architectes urbanistes – ATEC
3.1.41 TVK architectes urbanistes – Transsolar
3.1.50 TVK architectes urbanistes, photo Clément Guillaume
3.1.52–3.1.57 / 4.20 TVK architectes urbanistes – Martin Etienne
3.2.3 OMGEVING
3.2.4 Hannes Thalmann for Carlos Martinez Architekten
3.2.6 KBP.EU (Karres en Brands – WERK – Sangberg Architects), photo Ty Stange
3.2.8–3.2.10 / 3.2.12–3.2.13 / 3.2.15 / 3.2.17–3.2.22 / 3.2.24–3.2.26 / 3.2.29–3.2.33 / 4.4–4.5 / 4.8 / 4.18 2b / S. Bender-Ph. Béboux – S. Collet – CA. Presset – Ch. Robert-Tissot
3.2.36–3.2.39 / 3.2.45–3.2.46 / 3.2.49 / 3.2.51 / 3.2.53 / 3.2.55 / 3.2.59 / 3.2.62 / 3.2.67 / 4.1 BIG – Topotek 1 – Superflex
3.2.40–3.2.44 / 3.2.47–3.2.48 / 3.2.50 / 3.2.57 / 3.2.60 BIG – Topotek 1
3.2.61 © Bridget Riley 2022. All rights reserved. Photo Tate
3.2.63 Manipur -Neg, Victor Vasarely, 1957 © 2022, ProLitteris, Zurich
3.2.64 Cheyt-J, Victor Vasarely, 1970 © 2022, ProLitteris, Zurich
3.2.65 BIG – Topotek 1 – Superflex, photo Iwan Baan
3.2.66 Alphabet VR, Victor Vasarely, 1960 © 2022, ProLitteris, Zurich
3.3.2 Foster + Partners, photo Nigel Young
3.3.3 AWP office for territorial reconfiguration – Atelier Oslo, photo Bosheng Gan
3.3.4 J. Mayer H. & Partner Architekten, photo Fernando Alda
3.3.5 Paredes Pino
3.3.6 / 3.5.8 Google Earth – 2010 | Image © 2021 Maxar Technologies
3.3.7 / 3.3.13–3.3.15/ 3.3.20–3.3.21 / 3.3.29–3.3.30 / 3.3.35–3.3.37 / 4.16 Planergemeinschaft MFO-Park (Burckhardt + Partner – Raderschall Landschafts-architekten)
3.3.8–3.3.10 Richtlinien ZZN: Silva Ruoss, Cary Siress and Karen Schrader. Project development, models, and photos: Büro ur Ueli Roth
3.3.16–3.3.18 Roland Raderschall
3.3.19 Heinz Moser
3.3.23–3.3.25 Foster + Partners, photos Alan Howard
3.3.31–3.3.32 Frédéric Dedelley with Planergemeinschaft MFO-Park (Burckhardt + Partner – Raderschall Landschafts-architekten)
3.3.33 F. Colonna, *Hypnerotomachia Poliphili*, Venice, Aldus Manutius, 1499, n.p., Bibliothèque Nationale de France
3.3.34 Kunstmuseum Solothurn, Depositum des Kunstvereins Solothurn. Source: *Von Anker bis Zünd, Die Kunst im jungen Bundesstaat 1848–1900*, Zurich, Kunsthaus Zürich, 1998 / public domain
3.3.39–3.3.44 / 3.3.49–3.3.50 / 3.3.54 / 3.3.56 / 3.3.58 / 3.3.61 / 3.3.63 / 4.7 / 4.11 Studio Associato Bernardo Secchi Paola Viganò, Dirk Jaspaert
3.4.1 / 3.5.3–3.5.4 Christian Vogt
3.4.2 Photo Thibaud Giddey
3.4.3 Snøhetta, photo © Jens Passoth
3.4.8 / 3.4.34 OAB, photo Alejo Bagué
3.4.9–3.4.10 / 3.4.12 / 3.4.15 / 3.4.20–3.4.23 / 3.4.30 / 4.3 / 4.12 / 4.17 OAB
3.4.11/ 3.4.13 Xavier Martí Galí – OAB
3.4.31–3.4.32 OAB – Actar
3.4.37 Ballerup Kommune
3.4.38–3.4.44 / 3.4.47–3.4.50 / 3.4.52–3.4.53 / 3.4.55–3.4.56 / 4.2 / 4.13 ADEPT Arkitekter – LiW Planning
3.4.45 Wiebe de Jager
3.5.2 / 3.5.44–3.5.45 © SLA
3.5.7 Google Earth | Image © 2021 Geo Content
3.5.9 Gottfried Hansjakob, Bystrup, Bregenhoj & Partner
3.5.10 / 3.5.12 Maya Rainer + Jörg Weber, Thomas Hammer, Valentien + Valentien Landschaftsarchitekten und Stadtplaner
3.5.11 / 3.5.13–3.5.19 / 3.5.21–3.5.23 / 3.5.25 / 3.5.27 / 3.5.31 / 4.15 Valentien + Valentien Landschaftsarchitekten und Stadtplaner
3.5.20 Suhrkamp Insel Verlag
3.5.38 Københavns Kommune / City of Copenhagen, photo JW Luftfoto (Luftfoto Danmark)
3.5.39–3.5.41 / 3.5.43 / 3.5.48–3.5.51 / 3.5.66 Lundgaard & Tranberg – SLA
3.5.42 Københavns Kommune / City of Copenhagen
3.5.46–3.5.47 / 3.5.53–3.5.56 / 3.5.61–3.5.64 / 4.14 SLA
3.5.52 Photo: Petrelius, Artek Collection/ Alvar Aalto Foundation / Alvar Aalto Museum
3.5.65 SLA. Source: SLA "Reclaiming Public Space", in KJELDSEN Kjeld et al. (ed.), *New Nordic – Architecture & Identity*, Exhibition catalogue, Humlebæk, Louisiana Museum of Modern Art, 2012, p. 194
3.5.67 Luftfoto Danmark

GLOSSARY

Many terms that appear in this research are used by urban professionals in a commonly accepted way without any formal definition. Some of these terms are derived from the architectural and landscape lexica. Their meaning can be slightly changed through this transposition, if their definition has not been updated or adapted to the field of public spaces. So, in order to avoid any confusion, here is a definition of these terms as understood and used in this book.

ATMOSPHERE The impression that a space or design makes on an observer through its appearance.

CHARACTER The capacity of a space or a design to intentionally produce impressions in an observer—with the intention of conveying or symbolizing something—by its appearance and by the associations that the latter provokes (monumentality, banality, conviviality, etc.).

CONTEXT All the tangible and intangible elements that define a space.

CONTEXTUAL That weaves links with the tangible and intangible elements that are characteristic of a place.

COMPOSITION The organizing of the constituent elements of a public space in accordance with principles or rules (syntax).

DESIGN The process of creating or intellectually developing a project guided by intentions and decisions.

EXPRESSION The ability of a space or design to mean something.

FIELD OF REFERENCE Imaginary or real environment serving as inspiration and/or reference for designers (natural, industrial, harbor, seaside, or urban landscape; art, play, domestic sphere, etc.).

LANGUAGE A set of formal and material elements that make up the design of a public space (vocabulary) and the rules (composition) that organize them. By extension, a language can be figurative or non-figurative.

MATERIAL URBAN CONTEXT The environs of a public space, including both buildings and adjacent public spaces.

MATERIALITY The tangible elements of a public space, defined by its composition, shape and size, but also by its characteristic materials and their textures, its equipment, furniture, plants, colors, and light.

MATERIALIZATION Operation of transposing the project from intellectual elaboration to built reality.

OPEN SPACE A generic term for any outdoor space, landscaped or not, public or private.

REFERENCE A term of broad scope that includes the idea of source of inspiration as a model for design (see definition). Also used in the sense of evocation, to describe an object or environment to which a project refers a posteriori, in particular by a certain formal analogy that one would become aware of after the fact.
A conceptual reference is a reduction of the original model to a theoretical schema, whereas a formal reference is considered in its immediate appearance, its prima facie aspect. A reference can be explicit, in the sense that it is instantly understood, or more suggestive, requiring some interpretation.

REGISTER All the formal and material elements that make up a public space (words, signs). These elements can be figurative, in the sense that they symbolize something or evoke a field of reference. Conversely, a non-figurative, or abstract, register does not refer to an object or an identifiable field.

SOURCE OF INSPIRATION A model that inspires the development of a project or one of its components. Inspiration directly precedes or feeds into the design, according to the term source of inspiration (see reference definition).

URBAN PUBLIC SPACE An open space, which is part of the urban fabric and connected to a wider network of open spaces, that is freely accessible to all, and designed, built, and fitted out to accommodate activities whether necessary or just for leisure.

AUTHOR'S BIOGRAPHY

SONIA CURNIER, born in 1985 in Lausanne, Switzerland, holds a master's degree in Architecture, a minor in Urban Planning and Territorial Development, and a doctorate in Sciences of the City from the Swiss Federal Institute of Technology in Lausanne (EPFL). Her doctoral dissertation (2018) "L'espace public comme objet *per se?* Une analyse critique de la conception contemporaine," (Public space as an object per se? A critical analysis of contemporary design) earned her several academic awards and is at the origin of this book. Between 2019 and 2022, she was a visiting researcher at KTH (Royal Institute of Technology – Stockholm) and then a postdoctoral researcher at SLU (Swedish University of Agricultural Sciences – Alnarp/Malmö), where she studied transdisciplinary collaborations in public space design. She is currently a postdoctoral researcher at the Urban Sociology Laboratory of EPFL. Since 2015, she has had an independent practice as a consultant, critic, and curator, specializing in urban issues, with a focus on public spaces.

TRANSLATION Richard Palmer
COPY EDITING Julia Dawson
PROJECT MANAGEMENT Alexander Felix, Nora Kempkens
PRODUCTION Anja Haering, Amelie Solbrig
LAYOUT, COVER DESIGN AND TYPESETTING Jenna Gesse

PAPER Magno Natural, 120 g/m²
LITHOGRAPHY LVD Gesellschaft für Datenverarbeitung mbH, Berlin
PRINTING Grafisches Centrum Cuno GmbH & Co. KG, Calbe

Library of Congress Control Number: 2022944666

BIBLIOGRAPHIC INFORMATION PUBLISHED BY THE GERMAN NATIONAL LIBRARY The German National Library lists this publication in the Deutsche Nationalbibliografie; detailed bibliographic data are available on the Internet at http://dnb.dnb.de.

ISBN 978-3-0356-2094-8
E-ISBN (PDF) 978-3-0356-2100-6
FRENCH PRINT-ISBN 978-3-0356- 2095-5
DOI https://doi.org/10.1515/9783035621006

Published with the support of the Office de l'Urbanisme – Département du Territoire – Canton de Genève and Jean-Claude Girard Architecte. The open access publication of this book has been published with the support of the Swiss National Science Foundation.

REPUBLIQUE ET CANTON DE GENEVE
POST TENEBRAS LUX
JEAN CLAUDE GIRARD ARCHITECTE
Swiss National Science Foundation

published by Birkhäuser Verlag GmbH, Basel
P.O. Box 44, 4009 Basel, Switzerland
Part of Walter de Gruyter GmbH, Berlin/Boston

The book is published with open access at www.degruyter.com.

9 8 7 6 5 4 3 2 1 www.birkhauser.com